Principles and Techniques of Appraisal Review

Compiled and Edited by

THE NATIONAL ASSOCIATION OF

REVIEW APPRAISERS &

MORTGAGE UNDERWRITERS

Published by

Todd Publishing, Inc., 8383 East Evans Road, Scottsdale, Arizona 85260

Published in the United States of America By
Todd Publishing, Scottsdale, Arizona, 85260
First Printing, 1987
Second Printing, 1988
Third Printing, 1989
Fourth Printing, 1992
Fifth Printing, 1995

Library of Congress Catalog Card Number: 86-051460

International Standard Book Number: 0-935988-27-0

Preface

"Principles and Techniques of Appraisal Review" is a response to the need for a collection of information specifically designed for the review appraiser and mortgage underwriter. Recent Federal and State laws and regulations governing the lending and real estate industries have placed a great emphasis on the importance of appraisal review. It is now recognized as one of the most important factors in the loan process.

The National Association of Review Appraisers and Mortgage Underwriters has provided information and education for the professional Reviewer and Underwriter since 1974. It is the largest organization of its kind, with over 7,500 members. NARA/MU has developed materials and information that have become a standard in the industry. Thousands of lending institutions recognize NARA/MU and our members as the leaders in the field of appraisal quality control.

Professionals in the field who would like to learn more about NARA/MU and the many benefits of belonging to the Association should call, fax or write for information.

National Association of Review Appraisers
& Mortgage Underwriters
8383 East Evans Road
Scottsdale, Arizona 85260 USA

(602) 998-3000 / Fax (602) 998-8022

Robert G. Johnson, Executive Director

Acknowledgments

The National Association of Review Appraisers and Mortgage Underwriters would like to express our sincere thanks and appreciation to the following authors for sharing their knowledge and experience with the appraisal review and mortgage underwriting industry.

Robert Whelan, CRA, RMU
Fred A. Ergenbright, CRA
E. I Tarin, CRA
Greer Allen, CRA
Jeffrey D. Baize, CRA
Joyce Brown Riske, CRA
Walter S. Hanni, CRA
Suzanne Mellen
Julius A. Gilliam, CRA
Bruce J. Coin, CRA
Rowland F. Sweet, CRA
Otto Tronowsky
Harry Joachim

Marc A. Louargaud
Stephen P. Bye
Fayette "Bud" Arnold, CRA
Marion E. Everhart, CRA
Richard D. May, CRA, RMU
James H. Schmidt, CRA
Sue Ann Dickey
James Oakham
Samuel L. "Les" King, CRA
Tom McKenzie, Ph.D., CRA
Shannon P. Pratt, CRA
James Smith

Introduction

Real estate appraisals have been reviewed by someone ever since the first appraisal was made, owing to the fact that the appraisals have been made in almost all cases for someone other than the appraiser himself, to make a decision to buy, sell, encumber, dispose of, tax, litigate, manage, or for some other real estate related reason. Because real estate is the major source of wealth in nearly every economy, the accuracy and validity of the appraisal is of the utmost importance, thus the need for competent qualified reviewers.

The employer, client, or person the appraisal is prepared for or whomever has reason to peruse the report is a reviewer, in effect, and as such must be convinced, beyond any reasonable doubt, as to the reasonableness and adequacy of the conclusions of the appraiser. The layman perusing the report, who does not have the necessary professional education and background does not usually have the technical ability to make that important decision.

Over the past half century or so, this branch of the appraisal profession has grown in stature and the need for it has increased in equal degree to the increase in growth and technical ability of the appraisal profession itself. While much has been written on the principles and techniques of appraising - there have been many books and monographs written on its various categories and phases, including innumerable articles in the various trade journals - research and investigations of bibliographies reveal a few articles and no formal publication, as such, on appraisal review.

Reviewing is a vital process and adjunct to the appraisal process. The establishment in 1975 of the National Association of Review Appraisers & Mortgage Underwriters has, as a major objective, sought to rectify this situation in this highly specialized field. The rapid growth it has experienced is an obvious indication that this specialized field of review appraising is an area that was long overdue in being represented on an individual professional basis. The association recognizes all the existing appraisal organizations and it is not the intent to duplicate, but rather to complement and augment their services to the real estate profession as a whole.

The National Association of Review Appraisers & Mortgage Underwriters, in response to the obvious need and to satisfy its dedicated objectives, has conducted professional developmental seminars on appraisal review across the United States and in international areas since 1976. These educational seminars have been the forerunners for the official publication which was introduced in 1978 - the "N.A.R.A./M.U. Appraisal Review and Mortgage Underwriting Journal".

The absence of any formal publication on appraisal review has instigated the publication of this text. Its aim is to present a coordinated practical study of reviewing that can be used as an authoritative source of information on modern appraisal review.

There has often been a great deal of misconception or lack of understanding as to what the reviewing appraiser's real role or function is - not only by the client and others, but also even by reviewers themselves. It is believed that this book will clarify some of these misconceptions as well as point out the importance and objectives of the National Association of Review Appraisers & Mortgage Underwriters.

Walter S. Hanni, CRA
Past President
National Association of Review Appraisers
and Mortgage Underwriters

Contents

Part I - Principles & Techniques

Chapter

Part II - Review Appraisal Guidelines and Examples

Part III - Appraisal Review

PART I

Principles and Techniques

CHAPTER ONE

WHAT IS APPRAISAL REVIEW

The professional review appraiser has an important function and duty to his employer and is essential in the overall appraisal process. His responsibilities include:

a) Clarifying and correcting appraisal deficiencies
b) Reviewing and analyzing documentation contained in the report
c) Verifying the appraiser's final fair market value estimate
d) Verifying whether the appraisal satisfies his client's "purpose of appraisal" and contract instructions
e) Making sure the report follows the standard professionally acceptable appraising format and methods of analysis and conclusions with a justified valuation
f) Providing professional, technical assistance to his employer or client

It is exceedingly difficult, especially for the layman, to distinguish between a good and bad appraisal, or between a good appraisal and a fraudulent one. The costs associated with appraisal review are minimal when compared to the potential loss from not having this critical step in quality control. Federal and State regulators and agencies have recognized the need for appraisal review and now require it to some degree in almost every transaction involving an appraisal.

The National Association of Review Appraisers and Mortgage Underwriters has had a strong influence on the training and education (since 1975) of the review appraising industry. The designation CRA - Certified Review Appraiser, is widely recognized throughout the lending and real estate industries as a sign of competence and professional achievement. The future growth of the appraisal review industry is excellent. Government agencies such as the RTC (Resolution Trust Corporation), OTS (Office of Thrift Supervision) and VA (Veterans Administration as well as Banks/ Savings & Loans are requiring the establishment of a quality control program which includes appraisal review. This has increased the need for the valued opinion of a professional review appraiser to methodically review and verify the appraiser's estimate of market value.

The best appraisal reviewers will be those who are able to identify and properly analyze those factors that make any particular appraisal unique, as well as those factors common to most appraisals. The review appraiser should not adhere exclusively to the formats discussed within this text. Rather, it is the intention of the author to show the appraisal reviewer that he or she should approach each appraisal report aware of the uniqueness of each individual real estate project and the importance of identifying the subtle factors affecting value.

There are some times when the reviewer must be able to "read between the Lines" of the written report. The reviewing of appraisals is actually, in many respects more difficult than the preparation of the appraisal report itself. It is essential that the review appraiser have a keen, logical and analytical mind capable of assimilating all the facts presented. When making that important decision he must ensure that the conclusions reached have been sufficiently documented.

When conducting an appraisal, the appraiser can sometimes exclude certain relevant factors that may affect the value estimate. Therefore, it is important that the review appraiser is cognizant of these overlooked factors if he or she is to provide the appropriate recommendation. This text contains a discussion of a number of important factors that the reviewer should bear in mind when analyzing appraisal reports. It isn't necessary that an individual must be an appraiser in order to be a competent review appraiser, although having that experience can help. Many institutions have training programs and methods that allow non-appraisers to become appraisal reviewers. The following are some types of experience that are useful to a reviewer:

a) It is logical that the trained experienced appraisers are well prepared persons when it comes to understanding the duties and responsibilities of a reviewer.

b) Review appraising has become a highly specialized field within the appraisal profession. Not only must the reviewer be versed in appraisal education and experience aspects, but desirably, they should have a background in administrative work.

c) They must be able to work competently and productively with clients, other fee or staff appraisers, as well as other management personnel.

Valuation Estimates

The review appraiser should bear in mind that there are several different types of value estimates in the appraisal industry, but that, as of the date of the appraisal, the most important value estimate is the market value "as is." Market value "as is" is defined as the estimated market value of the property as it physically and legally exists without any hypothetical assumptions and limiting conditions and should be effective as of the date of the inspection. The review appraiser must be sure that the appraiser has indicated the proper effective date and has taken into consideration any existing leases that may affect the value. For new construction projects, it is recommended that the appraiser provide an estimate of the prospective future value of the property based upon completion of the improvements, as well as the value "as is." Therefore, it is necessary that the appraiser forecast the date of completion and estimate the value as of that date. In addition, the appraiser should be required to include the prospective future value of the property upon reaching stabilized occupancy. The effective date should be forecasted, and the estimated market value should be based upon the forecasted trends influencing value as of that moment in time. In the case where the loan matures before the effective date stabilized occupancy would occur for the subject property, the lending institution should require the appraiser to estimate the prospective future value as of the date the loan matures rather than the date occupancy is expected to stabilize. The review appraiser must be sure that any assumptions used by the appraiser regarding absorption are well documented to ensure that the value provided is a realistic estimation. The review appraiser must consider what competing projects are under construction, announced and funded, etc., to see what true competitive inventory will need to be absorbed, not just current vacancy inventory. Some lending institutions, at times, require an appraiser to provide the downside value of the subject property upon reaching stabilized occupancy. The review appraiser must realize that this is not a liquidation value or distressed sale value, but rather a value that is based upon the assumption that the improvements achieve a lower rent and higher expenses than are forecasted.

Another important consideration in the estimation of value is the normal marketing period for this type of property The market value definition specifically states that it is assumed that the property has been exposed to the marketplace for a reasonable period of time. The appraiser must determine a reasonable estimate of the normal marketing period for the type of property appraised. For example, if the appraiser indicates that the normal marketing time for a specific piece of property is two years, our estimation does not reflect the market value of the property "as is," unless the value is derived by discounting the future sale price in two years to present, at an appropriate discount rate. This is important for the review appraiser to understand because the length of the period in which a piece of property is marketed can have a significant impact on the final value. The appraiser must also take into account any creative financing or sales concessions when analyzing the sale contract for the subject property, previous sales of the subject property, the comparable land sales and the comparable improved sales. In real estate appraisal, the market value definition indicates a value in terms of U.S. dollars without the effect of special or creative financing. The appraiser should make the necessary adjustments in consideration of the market's reaction to the financing.

History

The sales history of the subject property can be a source of very useful information. Transactions occurring within the last five years are essential to estimates of value "as is" and should be thoroughly researched and documented. The appraiser should consider any current agreements of sale, options or listings of the subject property, as well as any special financing or other factors which would have had an impact on the sale price. The reviewer must check any adjustments made by the appraiser, based on the subject's history, to ensure that all relevant information was incorporated. Some characteristics of the subject property's historical transactions that should be considered by the appraiser include the original assembly of the property, acquisition prices, construction costs, capital additions or modernization expenditures, financial data, date of transfer, and nature of the relationship of the parties involved, i.e., was the transaction considered arms-length. These historical factors are important to the review appraisal, because it is helpful to know how the market has perceived the subject property in the past. If there has been a substantial increase in value, the manager will want to ensure that the increase is documented and supported by the analysis.

Regional and City Data

It is insufficient for an appraiser to include demographics and economic data without considering the four basic factors that influence value: physical, sociological, economic and environmental. The reviewer should be confident that any demographic or economic data included in the appraisal is relevant to the subject property but should realize that this data alone does not provide the information necessary to properly account for regional and city factors effecting the value of the subject property. The reviewer should require the appraiser to discuss any rational conclusion regarding the probable future for property values within the geographical area.

The Neighborhood

The immediate neighborhood in which the subject property is located is naturally of great interest to the reviewer. Familiarity with the neighborhood will help the reviewer to assess the direction, life cycle and trends in the neighborhood including price levels, income levels, rent and vacancy levels. As with the demographic and economic data discussed above, any neighborhood information incorporated into the appraisal should directly relate to the subject property.

Zoning

Does the property currently conform to the existing zoning regulations? The reviewer must ensure that the appraiser has considered this question since zoning regulations have a direct bearing on the property value "as is." For example, if the borrower is requesting a change in zoning, the value of the property for collateral purposes must be based upon the existing zoning regulations until a change in zoning has been approved.

If the property does not conform to the current zoning regulations, the appraisal reviewer should consider the effect that a zoning change will have on the value of the subject property. The reviewer must be confident that the appraiser has obtained the legal, architectural or engineering information that may be necessary to properly analyze the zoning regulations.

Real Estate Taxes and Assessment Data

The tax burden or projected tax burden can have a negative or positive impact on the value of the real estate. Therefore, the reviewer must be sure that the real estate taxes are carefully calculated, especially since in certain jurisdictions real estate is reassessed upon sale. A miscalculation of the taxes could be a source of potential embarrassment for the reviewer and appraiser upon reassessment of the real estate. Furthermore, it is equally important that the reviewer be confident that the appraiser has properly considered and analyzed the effects of any special abatements, tax incentives or special assessments. These extraordinary factors may have a significant impact on the value estimation of the subject property. The influence on value should be separated from the overall value.

Property Description

The marketability and acceptability of the subject property are important factors because if the owner wants to sell the property in the future, he or she will want to know if the proposed improvements meet the needs, desires and the standards of the typical buyer for that type of property in that specific market area. The site description and the description of the improvements must be sufficient to assist the reviewer in determining the acceptability of the site and the improvements in the marketplace based upon the existing use or the proposed use of the subject property. The reviewer must ensure that the appraiser has drawn a conclusion about the acceptability and marketability of the site and the existing or proposed improvements.

Highest and Best Use Section

The review appraiser should ensure that the report includes the proper definition of the highest and best use, as well as a statement which indicates the highest and best use of the property "as if vacant" and "as if improved." The appraiser should discuss whether or not the existing or proposed use of the subject property is physically possible, legally permissible, financially feasible, and maximally productive. The review appraiser must be able to ascertain from the appraisal report whether or not these criteria have been satisfied. If the criteria are not fully satisfied, the reviewer should require the appraiser to indicate how the proposed improvements differ from the ideal and to comment on the marketability of the proposed improvements. The reviewer should also be certain that improvements represent the highest and best use of the property if the land residual technique is used to estimate value.

Site value

The reviewer should check that the site value is based upon existing zoning regulations and comparable sales if available. In certain areas it may be extremely difficult to obtain comparable land sale information, in which case value may be estimated using an alternative method. The history of the comparable sales should be considered especially when ownership has changed frequently during a brief period or when prices have been increasing or decreasing at a rapid rate. It is the responsibility of the reviewer to ensure that the appraiser has made the proper adjustments based upon a careful analysis of market information. These adjustments for items such as financing, conditions of sale, date of sale, location and physical factors should be based upon the absolute dollar adjustment as well as the net adjustment to indicate if in fact the comparable are truly similar to the subject. Comparable properties offered for sale or expired listings should also be included if there is insufficient comparable land sale information. This would provide the reviewer with additional information for analyzing the property by setting the upper limits of value.

Cost approach

The cost approach bases the value on the costs required to

replace or reproduce the subject property, taking depreciation and age into consideration. If the appraiser has utilized a cost service to estimate the replacement or reproduction cost new of the improvements, the review appraiser should be familiar with the source material. The reviewer can compare this information to the data submitted by a developer on a proposed construction, rehabilitation, or conversion project.

Properly applied, the indicated value by the cost approach will provide a realistic indication of value. But the reviewer must pay special attention to estimates of depreciation since these are often extremely difficult to support. The review appraiser should be satisfied that the appraiser has clearly explained, justified and supported depreciation estimates, as well as discussed all factors that have an influence on accrued depreciation.

Sales Comparison Approach

In the sales comparison approach, value is based on comparison to similar transactions. The reviewer should require a minimum of three comparable sales. If only one or two sales have occurred, the appraiser may include them for informational purposes but should not base any estimation of value on this limited and insufficient data. Sales in similar communities can be considered and may provide useful information in analyzing the subject property. A reviewer should prefer a few well-substantiated comparable sales to many unreliable sales.

The review appraiser should ensure that the appraiser has discussed the history of comparable sales. This is important, because the reviewer should be aware if a comparable property has been sold and resold several times during a brief period or if prices of comparable properties have been increasing or decreasing at a rate atypical for the local real estate market; these are both important factors because they provide insight into market perceptions of this type of property. The reviewer should also carefully analyze any sales to syndications used as comparable since these often incorporate other factors, such as the cost of formation of the partnership and sponsor fees, that may skew the indication of value. The direct sales comparison approach can provide a realistic indication of value if all factors are considered and properly analyzed. The reviewer should ensure that each comparable sale is well documented and that the appraiser has made all the appropriate adjustments.

Income Approach

The income approach bases value on the future earnings the subject property is expected to generate. When reviewing an analysis based on the income approach, the appraisal reviewer must ensure that the appraiser has properly treated certain essential factors. For one, the manager must be certain that the appraiser has not ignored existing leases in forecasting the future cash flow. The reviewer should be satisfied that income projections are well documented and supported, and that the rationale for projected tenant rollovers, vacancies, absorption and any assumptions are reasonable. If the income or part of the income is directly related to non-real estate items, such as intangibles, furniture, fixtures and equipment, this should be clearly stated, explained and justified. It is important that the reviewer require this of the appraiser, since these factors can have a substantial influence on the value of a project and the yields that are anticipated by investors are directly related to the credit strengths of the tenancy and the anticipated cash flow. The reviewer must also ensure that proper attention has been given to expenses (including omittance and allowances), capital expenditures, the holding period, growth rates, discount rates, reversionary value, selling expenses, tenant improvement costs, and leasing commissions. Net income or gross income multipliers may be used to support direct capitalization or the discounted cash flow analyses but are not acceptable by themselves in providing an indication of value by the income approach. The lending institution should provide guidelines to the review appraiser concerning mortgage terms and debt service coverage ratios . Based upon these criteria provided by management, the reviewer can check the accuracy of the value estimated upon stabilization of occupancy.

Reconciliation

The review appraiser should read the reconciliation and final estimate of value carefully to verify the quantity and quality of the data examined in each approach. The appraiser should have discussed the advantages and disadvantages of each approach, as well as the appropriateness of each approach to the property that has been appraised. As a final consideration, the reviewer should be certain that the appraisal did not rely solely on one approach, all methodologies have been applied properly, and any wide discrepancies have been properly explained.

Environmental Hazard

It is the appraisal reviewer's responsibility to ensure that the appraiser has included in the appraisal report the uses of the surrounding property. If there is even the slightest concern, the reviewer should obtain an environmental assessment on each property; however, the review appraiser may not be qualified to interpret this report. It should be interpreted by a qualified professional, such as a member of the Environmental Assessment Association, who submits his findings to the reviewer. This is very important to consider at the time of the appraisal because future law suits could prove irreparably damaging to the lending institution.

In adjusting for environmental hazards that may exist on the property, the reviewer must understand that cleaning up or curing the environmental hazard may not restore the property to its former market value. Certain factors that may contribute to the loss in value include potentially lower rent levels, higher operating expenses, and higher risks of ownership. In addition, there is generally a stigma associated with environmental hazards. This results in the value being somewhat lower than comparable properties unaffected by environmental hazards.

SPECIAL FACTORS IN SPECIFIC APPRAISAL ASSIGNMENTS

The review appraiser must realize that different types of property have different factors driving the underlying value. For example, the underlying value of a recreational facility will be affected by factors different from those affecting industrial property. The valuation of different types of property often requires that the appraiser not only consider factors common to all types of properly but also that identify and emphasize the factors relevant to a specific type of property. Some specific cases are discussed below.

Golf Courses

Obtaining relevant regional and local data is normally helpful in most appraisals, but in the appraisal of golf courses, this type of data is particularly important. The review appraiser must ensure that the appraiser has obtained the necessary information for the industry, and other factors that may influence the growth of the community.

Typically 20,000 to 30,000 people in a region are necessary to support every 18-hole course. Although this is a reliable criterion, the reviewer should require the appraiser to conduct extensive research regarding demand for a golf course in the region since population per course should not be the only factor considered in the analysis. Given proper conditions, i.e., more leisure time, more disposable income, and heightened popularity of the game, as few as 10,000 people in a region, or even 2,500 in a resort or retirement community with enough avid golfers, can support an 18-hole course. There are a number of factors affecting demand that should be considered. For instance, data on the composition of the community is essential. The appraisal reviewer should also consider per capita income for the region. The reviewer should be assured that the income of potential golfers will be sufficient to cover the yearly membership fees of private clubs or daily fees of public courses. He or she will also want to know whether the consumers have a significant amount of free time or work many overtime hours, which can be inferred from employment patterns in the area. The appraisal reviewer should also require the appraiser to analyze and discuss the regional climate and weather patterns, paying particular attention to the characteristics, i.e. direction and velocity of the wind and the frequency of storms, that create hazardous conditions for golfers. The reviewer must not jump to the conclusion that courses in warmer climates will be more profitable than those in colder climates. The playing season may be longer in warmer climates, but expenses continue at high levels even during the off season. Whereas during the off season in colder climates, expenses are minimized.

A golf course attracts players through a combination of intangibles, such as the serenity offered by the scenery, and tangibles such as the challenge of the course. This is why it is imperative that an appraiser is able to accurately assess the quality of a course. The reviewer should require the appraiser to seek and discuss the opinions of the golfers who play the course, since they are one of the best sources of information regarding the tangible and intangible qualities of a golf course. The reviewer should require the appraiser to research the supply of private and public courses in the area and relate this to the demand. This is important because simply meeting the population-per course criterion does not imply equilibrium of supply and demand. Golfers may not play a particular course for a number of reasons including poor management inadequate maintenance, or a design that is so uninteresting that it discourages repeat play. The appraisal reviewer should keep in mind that avid golfers would rather play a good course that is far away than a bad course that is close by. A special consideration for the reviewer is the appraiser's determination of highest and best use. In many appraisals the existing use of the subject property is the highest and best use. But this is not necessarily the case with golf courses, which are not regularly sold or exchanged in the marketplace and are not zoned like other properties. Consequently, the reviewer should require the appraiser consider the golf course land on both its existing use (unless the function of the appraisal is to determine an alternate use) and its probable alternate use. The reviewer must also be sure that the appraiser has applied the same basis of use for the land and for the improvements.

Shopping Centers

The success of the shopping center is directly related to several factors, mainly tenant mix, location, and personal disposable income in the primary market area. The reviewer must ensure that the appraiser has analyzed the primary market area, considering demographic factors and economic factors associated with the residents who would be utilizing the shopping facility. The appraiser must also consider several other factors in analyzing a shopping center, which include the leasing company, strategy, management, percentage rent clauses and the physical characteristics of the improvements. The reviewer must be confident that the appraiser has adequately considered these factors, since the resulting projection of the gross income is based upon all these factors, and it can be extremely difficult to forecast the potential gross income in a new facility. The reviewer should carefully consider the discount rate used by the appraiser when analyzing the average rent. Since there is a greater degree of risk associated with this type of payment, a higher discount rate might be have to be applied. Access to Dollars and Cents of Shopping Centers, published by the Urban Land Institute, will provide the reviewer with additional information to assist him in analyzing the income and expenses of the proposed shopping center. The reviewer should verify the reasonability of operating expense estimates and tax comparables used (if tax estimates could not be obtained from the Department of Assessment).

Some additional factors that the reviewer must be certain the appraiser has properly treated include expense pass-throughs or recaptures, parking requirements, and pads and surplus land (which should be valued based upon its existing utilization). It is important that the proper adjustments have been made for these factors, since many lending institutions do not like to lend on land that is not yet fully developed.

Apartment houses

If an institution is considering lending on a new apartment construction project in excess of 50 units, the reviewer should require a marketability study. A marketability study, generally, analyzes the present and future demand for a specific use, taking into consideration for each type of unit designed, the rents that can be achieved in the current market, estimates of the quantity that can be absorbed into the market (including the size of the space, the number of rooms, bedrooms, baths and amenities that should be included by the developer), and any special factors that may be required to market the project. Based upon a marketability study, a feasibility study, which would indicate the potential economic profitability of the proposed project, could also be useful to the reviewer. This would include an analysis of population and employment trends, market conditions such as, vacancy and absorption rates, and several other factors which would assist the reviewer in assessing the quality of a potential loan. In the site description, the appraisal reviewer must be convinced that the appraiser has adequately considered the availability and costs of utilities, any nearby hazards or nuisances, parking, and the design and appeal of the improvements. This last factor is particularly important, since in certain market areas a mid-rise building would provide higher potential income than a high-rise; whereas in other areas the high-rise may provide greater income because the units on the higher floors may have a view which would result in a premium rent. The reviewer must be certain that the appraiser has properly identified those factors which would influence the income to the property. The highest and best use analysis is also important for the reviewer to consider. For example, the highest and best use of the property as improved may be for conversion to a condominium or cooperative form of ownership. If this is the highest and best use, then the reviewer must ensure that the appraiser has taken this into consideration in estimating the market value of the property. The value of a specific property that could be converted is generally higher than a traditional apartment complex.

In the income approach, the reviewer should ask a number of questions. Has the appraiser considered the potential income from other sources such as laundry facilities, parking, and commercial rental income, as well as the associated extra charges for air conditioning units, submetered electricity and other items? Is the income forecasted by the appraiser competitive with comparable facilities? Has the appraiser properly considered the value contributed by amenities such as recreational facilities, including tennis courts and swimming pools? Has the appraiser considered the potential for rent control or rent stabilization laws, which can have a drastic impact on achievable potential rent increase, when forecasting the potential gross income? Have expenses been properly allocated on either a square foot basis or on the units typical in that specific market area?

In analyzing the discounted cash flow analysis, the reviewer should be sure that the appraiser has taken into consideration the initial costs to lease the project which are generally higher and would be phased out over a period of time based upon the absorption forecasted. The reviewer should be aware that there will be fluctuations in income and expenses that must be properly allocated. In the cost approach, the reviewer must make sure that the appraiser has estimated the site value based upon the existing zoning regulations. If the site were vacant, in many instances, an apartment project could not be constructed on the property. The appraiser must allocate the value of the site between the property, as if vacant, and the permitted use by the municipal authority. The preferred method of analysis is to base the estimated site value on the price paid per unit or price per square foot. The price per acre is generally not applicable in most areas.

Office buildings

Many of the factors considered in the marketability and feasibility studies required in the appraisal of apartment houses will also be relevant in the appraisal of office buildings. But, of course, there are some factors, discussed below, which should be emphasized by the reviewer in his or her analysis of an appraisal report for office buildings.

There are two types of office buildings that a lender might need appraised: an owner-occupied office building, or a multi-tenanted building . This is an important distinction because the reviewer must determine if there are other users for an owner-occupied office building, which are often built to exact specifications for the particular user, in the event of default. The reviewer must be sure that the appraiser has estimated the market value to the typical buyer or user, not the "value in use," by excluding the contributory value of special building features that may be included in an owner occupied office building. The reviewer should make sure that the appraiser has considered and discussed the influence on value of any covenants and restrictions, any required off-site improvements, and any donation of the subject property required to obtain the necessary approvals to construct the office building. It is also important for the review appraiser to determine whether or not the utilities are sufficient for any proposed improvements. In reviewing the description of the improvements, the reviewer must understand the methodology used by the appraiser to determine the building area. Terminology and definitions vary across the country, and, as a result, the reviewer should ensure that the appraiser has properly defined the area described and has considered the loss factor or the building efficiency ratio in comparison to comparable buildings in that particular market area. The appraiser should address any functional deficiencies that may be apparent from reviewing the plans and specifications or inspecting the existing building. The reviewer should require the appraiser to discuss any problems in the design and layout.

When analyzing the cost approach, the reviewer should be certain that the appraiser has estimated the reproduction, or replacement cost new, based on comparable buildings using national and local market data where available. The construction costs should be compared to the proposed budget submitted by the developer. It is also important that the appraiser has properly accounted for indirect costs, such as tenant improvement costs and leasing commissions and made the proper adjustments. The reviewer must also consider functional and external obsolescence, which is often overlooked, since even new buildings may fall victim to such factors. The sales comparison approach can provide the reviewer with an indication of the range in value for the subject property. But many times, large adjustments are required, which reduces the reliability of this approach. It is important that the reviewer evaluate the adjustments made by the appraiser and be satisfied with their accuracy. Generally, the income approach is the most reliable approach for multi-tenanted buildings. The reviewer should be sure that expense pass-throughs have been properly calculated and supported by market evidence. In certain instances, all operating expenses may be passed through to the tenant. In other cases, only a portion of the expenses is passed through to the tenant. The reviewer should ensure that the pass-throughs are estimated considering the projected vacancy factor.

Industrial Buildings

There are many types of industrial properties, including warehouse distribution facilities, manufacturing plants, research and development parks, owner-occupied buildings and multi- tenanted buildings. Naturally, when appraising an industrial property, the appraiser should include an industrial market overview that which addresses proposed construction, rental rates, vacancy factors, major users, the supply of land, land prices and demand. The reviewer will also want to pay special attention to the neighborhood section of the appraisal report, since location is particularly important to this type of property. Some of the factors that must be considered include proximity to highways and markets, the labor supply, availability of suitable land, availability of rail service, air service, and raw materials, state and local tax structure, proximity to related industries, and the cost of labor. In analyzing the building, the reviewer should make sure that the appraiser has considered floor loads, bay sizes, clear ceiling height, electrical service, HVAC, percentage of office space, dock types and sizes, and elevators and lifts. The review appraiser should assess whether or not the industrial building is suitable for multiple uses, which would improve marketability, and be sure that the appraiser has not included specific improvements for owner-occupied buildings that have limited market appeal.

Proposed Projects

Rehabilitation and new construction projects are the most difficult to appraise and to review, because the estimates of value are based upon historical information used to forecast income, absorption, rent or price levels, operating expenses and other items occurring two or three years from the date the appraisal is actually made. The reviewer must assess the risks with the proposed project, based upon the information that has been provided in the appraisal report. This is a tricky task, because the risks vary throughout the stages of construction and the property value changes over this period of time, as well. The greatest risk is on land loans prior to development, but as the project nears completion, the risks of estimating value are generally reduced. In the lender's view, the greatest risk is at the point of completion, because at that time they will have advanced the highest capital outlay. The reviewer should make sure that the estimate of value provided by the appraiser is calculated at this point in time. This would be the prospective value upon completion and would represent the property's potential liquidation value. It is important that the reviewer check that the appraiser has made the proper adjustments at this point for holding costs, leasing commissions, tenant improvements and other items. In the direct sales comparison approach, the best comparable sales usually involved real estate owned by banks. However, this data can be difficult to obtain. If preferred comparable sales are not available, the reviewer should make sure that the appraiser has adjusted the comparables for occupancy, developer's profit, carrying costs, marketing cost, and all income and expenses expected during the absorption period.

SUMMARY

The topics discussed above should be taken into consideration by the appraisal reviewer but are by no means all inclusive. Every appraisal is unique and should be treated as such.

CHAPTER TWO

QUALIFICATIONS FOR A REVIEW APPRAISER

Appraisal reviewing is not a new sphere. It is only in the last ten years that it has received the professional recognition that it deserves. During that time, some attempt has been made to establish uniformity in the requirements, functions, processes and methods of appraisal reviewing as well as expanding the education and knowledge of those "saddled" with this chore. The National Association of Review Appraisers and Mortgage Underwriters has been in the forefront in "projecting" this highly specialized field. One of its major objectives is the education and improvement of those entrusted with this important endeavor. The review appraiser has a separate "niche" in the overall decision making process. Many of the appraisal reports need to or must be reviewed. The appraisal review is one of the necessary "checks and balances" required to assure the decision makers and the public that the valuation arrived at is well substantiated and justified in all respects. In addition, ensure that the individual performing the reviewing function is qualified and working under ethical and established controls.

Qualifications for a Review Appraiser

The review function requires a highly experienced individual capable of mature judgment and cannot be properly accomplished by amateurs, auditors, or trainees. There are some times when he must be able to "read between the lines" of the written report and others where he may be faced with making that "Solomon's Decision". The reviewing of appraisals is actually, in many respects, more difficult than the preparation of the appraisal report itself. It

23

is essential that the review appraiser not only be a good Appraiser, but must have a *keen, logical* and *analytical mind,* capable of assimilating all the facts presented. When making that important decision he must ensure that the conclusions reached have been sufficiently documented and justified to indicate just and reasonable compensation.

1. Experience Requirements. It is logical that the trained and experienced appraisers are the best prepared persons available to understand the duties and responsibilities of such a job. What kind of person is qualified to do this type of work? In other words, what qualifications must one have to "re-examine", resurvey and decide if an appraisal is adequate or to decide if improvement is needed?

2. Review appraising has become a highly specialized field within the appraisal profession. Not only must the reviewer be well qualified in all appraisal education and experience aspects, but desirably, he should have background and administrative experience in his particular aspect of employment.

3. He must also be able to work *competently* and *productively* with fee and staff appraisers, as well as other management personnel in the organization in which he is associated.

With this in mind—What experience and competence should the reviewing appraiser have to perform a competent professional job?

Technical and Educational Requirements

1. Formal Educational Requirements

In the past thirty years or so, degrees from a University have become of ultimate importance. Many organizations, institutions and licensing agencies are now requiring, at minimum, a Bachelor's degree in the major field of real estate. Many organizations look for a Master's degree in the particular field of endeavor. The necessity of degrees can be questioned; however, it is certainly a "starter" and should not be discounted in any way as contributing to a reviewers qualifications—it is an enhancement.

2. Technical Educational Requirements

Of probably greater importance than formal education, since this is a technically oriented profession, is the technical education which the reviewer has acquired in the area of valuation and reviewing. Those in review appraising should have acquired some technical valuation education including:

1. Basic Course on Appraisal Principles and Practices
2. Advanced Course - Capitalization Theory and Techniques
3. Valuation Analysis and Report Writing
   Also depending upon the specific category of Valuation he is involved in, the following courses are applicable:
1. Residential Value
2. Advanced Capitalization and Theory
3. Rural Valuation
4. Real Estate Investment and Analysis
5. Industrial Valuation
6. Litigation Valuation
7. With respect to the specific specialty of review appraising, the following technical education:
8. Educational programs conducted by N.A.R.A./M.U. and their formal publications.
9. Specialized courses on review and evaluation of apparatus.

Valuation experience

The function and procedures of competent review appraising cannot be adequately learned in the absence of previous appraisal experience and formal technical appraisal education.

Ideally, there should be some experience in the field as an appraiser, producing appraisal reports, preferably as a staff appraiser or fee appraiser on a full time basis.

Five years is a generally accepted term, but this can possibly be argued with since one can learn theory and practice possibly in less than that time. However, to experience the many problems which one may encounter in any type of valuation and the accepted solutions to solving these problems, a time period of five years is quite probably a reasonable "trainee" time period as a prerequisite to becoming a review appraiser.

Specialized Experience

Valuation has become highly specialized for the purposes for which the appraisals are made. As to the purposes we have:
1. Acquisition
2. Disposition
3. Financial of various forms—including mortgage lending
4. Litigation for various reasons—including condemnation
5. Insurance purposes
6. Accounting purposes
7. Tax purposes
8. And many other specialized purposes

On the other hand, we have numerous types of properties upon which valuations are required including:

1. Single family residences
2. Multi-family residence—high rise apartments, condominiums
3. Office buildings
4. Industrial properties
5. Easements and various rights of way
6. Specialized type properties
7. Timber Properties
8. Mineral Properties
9. Recreational Properties
10. And many others, including various separate interests in the "bundle of rights"

The reviewing appraiser should have specialized experience in the particular *purpose* and *type* of property which it is his responsibility to review—he should be extremely knowledgeable and this includes knowledge of the policies and procedures of the particular organization in which he is associated or for which he is doing work. Without such qualifications, the review appraiser may defeat the primary purpose of his function.

Court Experience

With respect to court experience or acquisition under eminent domain proceedings—if the reviewer is involved in this type acquisition he should certainly be experienced as an expert witness and be familiar with the specific laws involved.

Managerial and Administrative Requirements

The review appraiser is usually not only a technician in appraisal procedures and practices, but also is a member of the management/administrative "team" who are responsible for the "decision making" process. He therefore must have other qualifications of an administrative nature among which are the following:

1. *Knowledgeable of policies and procedures.* Complete knowledge of the policies, procedures, requirements of the organization he is working for, whether it be on a staff or fee basis.
2. *Knowledgeable of projects being reviewed.* Complete knowledge of the particular projects he is involved in reviewing, real estate-wise, engineering-wise, legal-wise and otherwise.
3. *Work competently and productively with others.* Have the ability to work competently and productively with fee and staff appraisers as well as other management personnel in which he is associated.
4. *Convincing Negotiator.* Must have the ability to be a convincing arbitrator and negotiator in the course of reviewing valuations in order that just and sound decisions are made.

5. He must be able to establish and perform the personnel management function of appraisal staffs and establish and oversee sound contractual procedures in the case of contracting for appraisal services and administration of these contracts.

Characteristics of the Reviewer

1. Integrity. The reviewing appraiser must be respected in the honesty and judgment of his conclusion—you must be able to rely upon and respect his recommendations without question.

2. Intelligence. One of the prime factors is that the Reviewer has the capacity, the intellect, the discernment; the long foresighted discerning ability to come up with the reviewing valuation conclusion, which will be the right one and that will *not* detrimentally affect the objective for which he was hired.

3. Intuition. This valuation being an inexact science, the reviewer must have some intuition or as you might say ESP—that there may be something wrong with this valuation conclusion and maybe he should look into it further. Intuition is closely aligned to judgment, if not almost the same thing. Some people have it and some don't. Those that don't will never be good reviewing appraisers.

4. Instruction. One must have had some instruction in his endeavor in order to adequately perform his services. The objectives of the N.A.R.A./M.U. is attempting to do just that. However, the reviewer or prospective reviewer must realize that he must accept that instruction which is available and he must accept it as such.

5. Inquisitiveness. Probably one of the greatest attributes of an appraiser or reviewer is that he is inquisitive. This means that he is seeking information upon which to base a justified conclusion. He, in effect, is an "analyst" and is not merely accepting "someone's" conclusion, but insists that whatever this conclusion may be, it has been substantially justified and that he is not merely satisfied with an opinion.

6. *Informative.* The reviewing appraiser must be informative. He must be very conversant with and adhere to the professional appraisal principles and standards of the particular type and purpose of valuation he is considering. In other words, he is not an amateur, and he must be capable of informing the decision makers of these concepts in a manner which will be understandable to them.

7. *Image.* The reviewing appraiser, in his daily work, must be able to project what the real concept of the reviewing appraiser is and the necessity of his existence in the valuation process. He is accorded by his clients or employer, the appraisers he reviews, and the reviewing profession.

8. *Invaluable.* He must be able to prove he is invaluable to the profession and be able to prove that he is needed and a recognized professional. He must be associated and recognized by a professional organization and thus accepted as such in the field—in this case by the National Association of Review Appraisers and Mortgage Underwriters.

Reviewing Professionalism

Professionalism as we knew it in the past, or as it generally originated in our society was only applied to a few vocations—law, medicine, and the ministry. Within more recent times there have been numerous vocational groups which have sought to achieve or have theoretically achieved the distinction of professional status. These include the appraisal or valuation profession in its various related capacities. There are also many who claim to be professionals who do not really know the real meaning of the term, what the ingredients are or what obligations are incurred by being a true professional. It is in comparatively recent times that the valuation practitioners have professed professionalism.

1. Definition of Professionalism

There have been many different definitions of professionalism as defined in the various dictionaries and also expounded by any profound intellectuals through the years. A learned profession may be defined as an organized exclusive group in a specific vocation or occupation requiring purely intellectual or manual skills. Especially those of which are controlled by the expertise of the practitioners, selling service, guidance or other specialized skills to persons who are not such experts and whose function is to perform such services at his level best, at all times, and with integrity and respect. It is also one who is trained by education and experience to perform these functions better than the unskilled for whom he is performing these services, and also whose prime duty is to raise the standards of his group by specialized educational endeavors to improve performance and service to the public which he serves, as well as to admit only those with such established skills to his group who conform to established ethical standards and conduct. He is one who holds a particular distinction.

In realty, it is the general public who require his service, who make the determination of whether or not he who claims to be is truly professional. In other words, his standing and performance in the public's eyes will give him this distinction. The economic and social trends of our modern times, with the greater emphasis upon scientific knowledge, greater occupational training, higher motivation, and the insistence of society in general for superior performance, has been the motivating influence forcing the numerous vocations. Including that of valuation to aspire to become true professionals.

2. Criterion: Ingredients of a Professional

Appraisers and those in the vocation of valuation, must be

cognizant of the ingredients upon which professionalism is based and adhere to their precepts, which are the following:

a. *An organized assemblage of education doctrine.* The current valuation processes and practices utilized were basically established some 50 years ago and many groups, individuals, and both private and governmental entities have made the contributions through the ensuing years by means of articles, monographs, bulletins, books, courses, seminars, regulations, etc. This is to establish and upgrade the vocation to the level it has today attained. Many disciplines make up the field of valuation. An appraiser, as such, must be knowledgeable of many interrelated disciplines or fields which make up valuation, as such. These include, but are not limited to, mathematics, engineering, economics, law, social sciences, agriculture, construction, ecology, psychology, accounting, etc. Valuation, as such, has acquired much of its concepts and teachings from other fields of endeavor which have been developed into a well defined and separate functional entity peculiar to this particular occupation. Also, within particular professions, there are commonly developed specialties or vocations wherein their own educational doctrine and concepts have been developed into standardized procedures such as review appraising. The specific or sub-vocations are not fixed or unchangeable in their concepts. They must be in a constant state of renewal with a fresh supply of factual data and upgrading by means of seminars, conferences, educational tours, etc.— for today's needs and tomorrow's realities.

b. *Standards of technical proficiency and ethical conduct.* The requirement or attainment of certain standards of ability and practical experience before one can attain membership or acceptance. Admitting only the skilled, competent and ethically motivated. All professional groups, as such, must have ethical codes of conduct usually established by their organized groups, which require those accepted practitioners to perform competently, honestly and within certain prescribed areas of conduct in offering his services and expertise to the users and the public in general. He must present a truly professional image.

c. *Established and Designated Organizations.* Technical groups, which are aspiring to attain professionalism are usually organized into associations, institutes or societies. As such, they are more responsive to the demands and requirements of their specific fields of endeavor and to the public interest than are unorganized and isolated individuals and also to be more concerned with achievement to meet social requirements. It in effect "knits" them together in common goals and is a "protective" influence as well.

d. *Publicly recognized.* A profession, as such, must be of vital importance in the vocation recognized by the public especially in the highly specialized, complex and sophisticated world in which we live. With time and distance being so short, and countries of the world being only a matter of hours apart, modern means of transportation, having so much mutually in common as well as relying more and more upon each other for our existence and mutual protection, such should be international recognition. Any profession must also perform a public service to some degree or another for such recognition. The general consensus of others in the field is that the National Association of Review Appraisers and Mortgage Underwriters meets this criteria. It has been said "when one uses his knowledge and expertise acquired in his vocation to help improve the performance of others, he is serving his vocation as a professional". This is one of the major roles of a review appraiser in his reviewing function. Also, one of the major objectives of N.A.R.A./M.U. the *"bringing together"* and dissemination of *"reviewing expertise"* and education of others who are performing or are aspiring to this chosen vocation.

Ethics of the Review Appraiser

Any profession, to be recognized as such, must have professional ethics. This gives the organization some prestige and, *more important,* acceptance by the public clientele as being reliable qualified professionals. The ethics or regulations, whatever they may be, must be meaningful and enforced to some degree or another. The professional appraisal organizations are equally applicable to the review appraiser as such:

1. When performing a review assignment he must perform his professional services without advocacy for his clients or employer's interests or the accommodation of his own interests.
2. He must have no present or intended future interest in the property he is reviewing.
3. He must not violate the *confidential nature* of the reports he is reviewing.
4. *His fee* should in no way be related to the valuation of the property he is reviewing, or the *appraiser's fee* for preparing the report. In other words, a *percentage fee.*
5. In rendering such professional services, he must *perform competently* at all times.
6. Shall not review any appraisal and recommend a valuation in which he also acts as *principal-negotiator.*
7. It is unethical to *persuade or coerce* an appraiser to write, state or imply a value estimate which is contrary to his *professional* opinion.
8. It is unethical to review a fee appraisal if his employment is contingent upon the appraiser supporting a *predetermined* conclusion—this may be difficult for the reviewer to be aware of.

Code of Professional Ethics

The purpose of this code is to establish clear and ethical guidelines for the professional review appraiser and mortgage underwriter.

1. Members of the National Association of Review Appraisers and Mortgage Underwriters must conduct themselves in a professional manner at all times.

2. A member should always strive to maintain and improve professional standards in Appraisal Review and Mortgage Underwriting practices and be willing to assist the National Association of Review Appraisers and Mortgage Underwriters to that end.

3. A member should help to maintain a public awareness that the profession is treating all parties fairly and equally.

4. A member should recognize his or her responsibilities to the public, the profession, all parties having an interest in the case under consideration and his or her employer.

5. A member should have access to all pertinent facts relating to a case before arriving at a decision as to market value or the acceptability of a given loan package.

6. A member should never accept less than a proper appraisal report or loan submission package.

7. A member should be unwilling to assign a market value or arrive at a conclusion until all problems relating to the case have been resolved.

8. A member should attempt to reconcile all substantive discrepancies in reviewing appraisal reports and/or loan packages.

9. A member should report any conflicts of interest which may be involved in a case.

10. A member should be aware of all state and federal laws which may apply to the case he or she is considering.

11. A member should maintain his or her professional competence in the Appraisal Review and Mortgage Underwriting profession through continuous educational study.

12. Members should give independent, honest and objective opinions relating to appraisal reports and other information contained in any given underwriting package.

13. Members should not **falsify or purposely misinterpret** the facts on an appraisal report or in an underwriting package.

Integrity

Another important factor and one of the most essential ingredients which the reviewing appraiser must have is integrity. This is defined in Webster's, i.e. as "moral soundness", "honesty", "uprightness".

If the appraiser is recognized as having these important characteristics, his reviewing work and decisions will be accepted with the least amount of question and he will be professionally accepted. Integrity, honesty and morality, as such, go hand in hand in the course of reviewing. It is also a highly essential element if he is ever called upon as an expert witness.

It is also an essential element for the reviewer in order to live up to the Code of Professional Ethics which he has agreed to prescribe to and uphold.

The reviewer alone must live with his conscience and he must examine himself and the work he produces in this respect. There can be no substitute for this important factor in reviewing.

Certification by Review Appraiser

This certifies to the authenticity of the report, states his position in the valuation "spectrum" and amplifies his professional integrity and validity of his review. This is as important for the review appraiser as any other profession. Being a professional, the reviewer should be willing to certify his findings. This certification should cover certain points:

1. That he has no interest in the property—present, past or future.
2. That his compensation is not contingent upon the valuation conclusions he has reached.
3. That it is based upon the information furnished to him for review.

4. That it has been made in accordance with the professional organization of his designation.

Certification

I certify that I have no undisclosed interest in the subject property covered herein, present, past or contemplated. That my employment and compensation are not contingent upon the valuation as estimated by the appraiser nor the conclusions and recommendations which I have made. That the appraisal report complies with acceptable appraisal standards as established by the nationally recognized professional appraisal organization. This review has also been made in compliance with the Code of Professional Ethics of the National Association of Review Appraisers and Mortgage Underwriters of which I am a member.

The recommendations that I have made, as set forth above, are the result of careful review and analysis I have made, and represents my considered professional opinion of the appraisal made.

_____

Reviewing Appraiser

Summary

The review function requires a well experienced and highly qualified individual with professional characteristics and administrative ability in this specialized field. He must be highly ethical with proven sound integrity and be one who can truly be called a professional.

CHAPTER THREE

DUTIES AND FUNCTIONS OF THE REVIEW APPRAISER

Introduction

The duty and function of the review appraiser has been an extremely important one in the profession of appraising. It is an area that has taken on added importance as the appraisal profession has advanced through the years from the days of "windshield appraising" to the modern sophisticated approaches to value used today. Thus, the reviewer has an important place in the overall valuation picture. Appraisals have been reviewed ever since appraisals have been originated, by someone in some form or another. However, until more recent times, these reviews were accomplished by individuals who were not experienced as appraisers, with no consideration being given to the "appraisal process". The past procedures were inadequate to meet the administrators' or clients' requirements and to protect the expenditure or guarantee of funds no matter what the purpose of the appraisal may have been. Governmental institutions followed by financial institutions have been in the forefront which has changed this past situation. From this has evolved the present highly functionalized duties and responsibilities of the review appraiser as will be discussed herein.

Duties and Functions of the Review Appraiser

Why are Appraisal Reviewers Necessary?

To start with, why are appraisal reviewers used, or why is it necessary to review appraisals, assuming they are made by competent, qualified appraisers, probably designated by one of the professional organizations. This, on the surface, appears to be an "unnecessary function". Then why is the review appraiser necessary or required? There are some very good reasons why.

To Justify the Expenditure of Funds

The administrator of the organization, whether it be a public body who is responsible to the "taxpayers", or the private body with responsibility to the stockholders, or whomsoever has a responsibility to conserve funds and justify, without any reasonable doubt, any expenditure or loan guarantee as to value received. The review procedure, in effect, is the additional "hedge" or "buffer". In other words, it was appraised by a professional and reviewed by a professional for added "safety".

Correction of Errors, and Omissions

We must also keep in mind that appraisers, both fee and staff, are human like all of us; subject to mathematical error, misunderstanding of the assignment, rendering an estimate of value based upon a wrong premise, unclear rationale or many other faults. The reviewer is absolutely necessary to clarify and correct these deficiencies. In other words, as the "technical intermediary", to secure a report from the appraiser that fully convinces the decision making offices of the validity of the estimate.

Mandatory Requirement

Some organizations or agencies have a mandatory requirement that all or certain categories of appraisals be reviewed and approved by a professional reviewer—in other words, regulatory requirements.

Bolster Appraisers Conclusions

There is also a well-grounded theory that two professional conclusions are better than one. In effect, the second professional, the reviewer, could be considered almost a "joist appraiser". He has corroborated the appraiser's conclusion and thus adds additional weight thereto.

Technical Check for Administrators

The administrator may also not have any direct control over the appraiser. He has need for the services and advice of the knowledgeable and technically reliable people under his control and who are conversant with his own organization's requirements— in other words, the appraisal may have been furnished from a second or third source over which he had no control in the hiring of or the specifications for performance.

As a Check on Quality Performance

He may also perform another function, in larger appraisal organizations, as a "training vehicle" or check on "quality performance" of staff appraisers and/or fee appraisers regularly hired. This could also be true in small private organization.

Failure of Appraiser to do Thorough Job

Failure on the part of the prime appraiser to do a thorough job is probably one of the major reasons for the need of the review appraiser. The written work is often times ambiguous. The appraiser has sometimes, without realizing it, failed to include in his written narrative report the thinking or "rationale" which led him to a particular conclusion or estimate. It thus may leave many unanswered questions in the mind of his client or the reviewer. Many mistakes made in appraisals go-back to failure to recognize and theoretically perform the old "kindergarten" appraisal process. Also, the sufficiency and quality of data presented by the Appraiser is of ultimate importance.

Not ALL Are Competent and Qualified

Let's also admit that there are good review appraisers and poor review appraisers. The fact that poor ones do exist does not obviate the necessity for, nor the importance of, the review appraiser.

Another Important Function—Knowledge of Prospective Review

If the appraiser knows, beforehand, that his appraisal is going to be professionally reviewed, he just might be more careful in the production of his finished product than if it were being reviewed by someone who is not fully knowledgeable of appraisal techniques and procedures. This has often made the difference between submission of an unsatisfactory report and an approvable report.

Compatibility of the Administrative Function and the Review Function

In effect, the review appraiser is the organizational representative who gives technical organization approval regarding appraisal and valuation matters; his position is specialized and necessary. It implicates the specialized appraisal techniques, the rendering of sound judgment, and the making of unbiased decisions. While the reviewing appraiser is a representation of the management organization, he must also, to a high degree, be "autonomous", not in any way subject to "directed" reviews or decisions to meet the particular desires of management—let us say to make a "project fly". However, this also does not mean that the reviewer must be "inflexible". As a part of the management organization, in the course of and as part of the review function, conferences with management echelons concerned with a project are often desirable and essential. He should be fully oriented as to the requirements, problems and objectives of the organization, as well as the particular project itself economics, engineering and other matters.

The appraisal is one of the "cogs" in the overall wheel—the review appraiser functions as the valuation interpreter and advisor to management in this respect. The most important observation one can make concerning the review appraisal function is:

"The appraisal review is the last defense between the valuation opinion and consummation of the acquisition or whatever the purpose may be."

Reviewer's Function to Approve, Not Disapprove

It is not the reviewer's function to disapprove, as such, but more to attempt to secure an approvable, and justified valuation, within a measurable degree of value probability, of the property in question and which solves the intended purpose of the appraisal requirement.

Summary

The Review Appraiser has an important function and duty to his employer and is an essential element in the overall valuation procedure, and his duties and functions are:
1. Responsibility to assure just compensation
2. Clarify and correct appraisal deficiencies
3. Perform mandatory reviewing requirements
4. Corroborate and bolster appraiser's conclusions
5. Perform professional technical assistance to his employer
6. Appraisal quality and performance evaluation—function as a training vehicle
7. Secure proper performance from the appraiser in accordance

with the appraisal contract and instructions
8. Professionally monitoring of the Appraiser
9. Documentation of the review performed
10. Gives final organization approval regarding appraisal and valuation matters
11. Operate in an autonomous position not subject to directed reviews
12. Must confer with management on valuation matters and be fully oriented as to the requirements, problems and objectives of the organization he represents
13. Reviewer's function to secure an approvable and justified valuation

Appraisal review is the last defense before acceptance of the final valuation.

CHAPTER FOUR

REQUIREMENTS AND METHODS OF THE REVIEWING APPRAISER

Introduction

The reviewing of appraisals in their various forms and types has been a regulatory requirement of most Federal Agencies, many other public agencies and other corporate and financial organizations for many years. In the distant past, this function was performed by individuals who were not professionally or technically qualified. Whether or not the appraisal met contractual requirements, accepted appraisal principles and practices, completed substantiation and justification of conclusions reached, professional competency and ethical procedures of the appraiser, the resolution of divergencies between two appraisals and other technical matters were completely overlooked or not considered as being consequential. This was a result of the reviewer's incompetence to make such professional determinations, and is still done in some instances today.

Through the years, especially in the last 25 years, appraisal reviewing has developed into a highly technical sub-art of the appraisal profession with experienced, professional appraisers performing this function. The National Association of Review Appraisers and Mortgage Underwriters was established to organize and assist those in this important function and their mission as reviewing appraisers.

The reviewing appraiser has certain responsibilities to himself, as a professional in his field of endeavor; to his employer from whom he receives his compensation; to the appraiser, whose work he is reviewing; and, to the public in general, who may be ultimately paying the "bill" for the services rendered.

There are also certain requirements which the Reviewer is obligated to do. Also, there are certain established methods or procedures through which the reviewing process is accomplished. These and other functions will be discussed in this chapter. From practice and experience there are certain methods of reviewing procedures which have been developed by those experienced in the "field", and which are recommended to be followed in "most" situations of appraisal reviewing.

There have been many requirements or regulations to be followed in the course of review appraising, as well as forms used in the procedure. These will vary with every organization and the appraisal purpose involved. While we cannot refer to all of the many varied requirements or forms used, we will attempt to give you some insight or reference to some of these areas on appraisal reviewing.

There are certain factors or conditional requirements prior to the actual preparation of the required appraisal, which the reviewer should have some control over in order to not only perform his responsibilities, but also to assist the performance of his function and to secure the objective of his principal—which is to secure an approvable appraisal report.

There are certain accepted processes or procedures, which have been developed through the recent years of appraisal reviewing, which are generally accepted in the reviewing profession. These are general concepts as such. However, they are the ones which we in the profession have used in the past to be most effective and indicative in our professional capability. There are also those procedures which are generally accepted in our professional field as being sound, and meeting our objective as reviewing appraisers.

PART I

Responsibilities

and Requirements of

the Reviewing Appraiser

When we speak of responsibilities and requirements of the reviewing appraiser, we are actually speaking of several or numerous different functions.

Scope

The review appraiser, in effect, is the person responsible for appraisal quality control and the decisions upon which his employer relies for his valuation decisions or whatever his purpose may be. This quality control, as such, is not solely dependent upon the actual review of the final product—it goes back before the production of the appraisal itself. There are certain important factors which are conducive to producing the "product" which we require and which will facilitate our review.

Selection of the Appraiser

A good system of selecting the best qualified appraiser for the particular type of property is in the various geographical areas covered by the appraiser. Qualifying the appraiser, as such, as to his ability to perform the assignment, is a subject within itself, which will not be discussed herein.

Appraisal Contract Specifications

Appraisal contract specifications and instruction, which are not only all encompassing, but which are clearly set forth and are understandable to the appraiser as to the appraisal requirements are of extreme importance. The reviewing appraiser should have a part not only in preparing these specifications, but in administering them with the Appraiser and with the organization he represents. An example of such a comprehensive contract specification is shown in Exhibit 1 (Page xxx). Skimpy or brief specifications, are of no value. When contracting for appraisals, many of the misunderstandings or shortcomings in appraisal reports are directly the result of inadequate specifications and instructions to the appraiser as to what the principle wants.

Exhibit 1

Specifications and Instructions for Preparation of Appraisal Reports

1. Format

The report shall be bound in book fashion, in the left margin in a durable cover with a typewritten or printed label on the face thereof, identifying the appraised property, the project number and name of the Local Authority. The paper used shall be good grade bond (the heavier, the better in order to withstand repeated usage), of size 8 1/2" by 11". All pages shall be numbered consecutively from the beginning of the report to the end, including maps, plans, photographs and exhibits, and each important heading and subheading shall be shown in the Table of Contents.

2. Outline

a. In order to facilitate professional review, easy reading, proper grouping and uniformity, the text shall be divided into three parts: Part l; Part II, A and B; Part III. The report shall contain brief tabulations (schedules) of computative, comparable, and/or supporting data with brief explanations thereof, and with references to fuller records or more extensive computations of discussions which are included as exhibits in Part III.

b. The outline, instructions and description of contents below specifies the general pattern for appraisal reports using accepted appraisal principles and practices, and represents as a minimum the essentials which should be included. Any other data, information, approaches, etc., among other things which may be considered necessary or essential, should be included in the report. This outline may vary, dependent upon the type of property under appraisal and/or different parcels involved. Additional data may be recited with respect to the property or properties involved, as considered necessary, in an appropriate place within this outline. Any items omitted as being not applicable (such as information or valuation of improvements on vacant land) should be shown in the report with the statement "Not Applicable", and the justification or reason for its omission.

3. Instructions and Description of Contents

Part I - Introduction

1. Title Page

This shall include:
a. Project Number
b. Location of Property (Name and Street Address or other location identification)
c. Date of the Report
d. For Whom Prepared
e. Name of Appraiser

2. Letter of Transmittal

The purpose of this is to transmit the report. It shall be addressed to the individual or Local Authority who requested the services, and should contain:
a. Location of Property Appraised
b. Statement of Interest being Appraised and Purpose of the Appraisal

c. Statement that a Valuation Investigation and Analysis was made, give the name of the individuals making such investigation and the dates thereof

d. Total Valuation Estimate

e. Date as of which the Valuation Estimate Applies

f. Signature of Appraiser (Seal if applicable)

3. Table of Contents

This shall be arranged in accordance with the topical headings and subheadings with corresponding page numbers.

4. Photograph of Area

A large size photograph of the location and/or general area shall include: preferably, an aerial photograph, if such is available, with the specific property outlined thereon.

5. Statement of Limiting Conditions

This shall include statements as to the following contingent and limiting conditions:

a. That the title is marketable. (There can be no "market value" of property that is not marketable.)

b. That no responsibility is answered by the appraiser for legal matters, especially those affecting title to the property. (This may be qualified if legal advice has been and included in the report concerning certain matters.)

c. That the legal description furnished him is correct.

d. That certain opinions, estimates or other data furnished him by others (and were properly identified) are correct.

e. Any other limiting conditions or assumptions (completely spelled out).

6. Summary

This summary of important conclusions is, in fact, a resume

of the essential highlights of the report and its purpose is to offer an immediate and convenient reference, in brief, which shall include the following:

a. Parcel Number
b. Owner's Name
c. Highest and Best Use
d. Type of property
e. Present Zoning
f. Type of Improvements (if vacant, so indicate)
g. Parcel Area (Square Feet)
h. Breakdown of Valuation of each Parcel

Certificate of Value may also be included in Letter of Transmittal if so desired.

(1) Land
(2) Indicated value per S.F. or acre as applicable
(3) Improvements
(4) Severance or other damages
(5) Total Value
(6) Salvage Value of Improvements

The above may be in tabulation or chart form on folding sheets if necessary.

7. References

List sources of data incorporated in the report; that is, records, documents, persons consulted and technical specialists utilized.

Part II - Analysis and Conclusions

This section comprises the analysis, valuation estimates and conclusions of the appraiser and is divided into two parts: Part A, General Data, which is applicable to all the properties included in the appraisal, and Part B, which comprises the data and valuation information applicable to the property in particular. Where more than one parcel is involved, the information shall be included for each parcel separately as the parcel appraisal. Where certain items may be applicable to all parcels, it should be set out separately ahead of the parcel appraisals and so indicated as being applicable to all parcels involved.

Part A. General Data - (Applicable to all properties in project area)

8. Purpose of the Appraisal

This should detail the purpose for which the appraisal is made and define each of the values required.

9. Legal Description

There should be recited here, a description by subdivision name, square or block and lot number, metes and bounds or such other description as will properly identify the property appraised. The legal description may be an exhibit in Part III; if so, state here, especially for long descriptions. Where there are a number of parcels involved, the description of each parcel should be included in Part B under each individual parcel valuation data.

10. City and Area Data

Detailed information relative to the social, economic and political background of the city and area or region should be included in this section of the report and discussed to the extent that it affects the value of the property being appraised. (Major employment in the area, employment centers and relation of the same to property being appraised.)

11. Neighborhood Data

Under this item there shall be included a detailed discussion of all data, mostly social and economic, as they pertain to the neighborhood in which the appraised property is located. Among other factors which should be included, the following should be discussed.

a. Life State of Neighborhood
b. Population Trend
c. Percent of Home Ownerships
d. Vocations, Wage Levels and Rent Levels
e. Conformity of Development
f. Vacancy in Residential and Commercial Units
g. Prestige and/or Pride of Ownership
h. Restriction and Zoning
i. New Construction Activity
j. Percent of Vacant Land
k. Encroachment- Changing Use
1. Availability of Housing

The above factors will all be discussed in detail and the Appraiser's opinion as to their effect upon the market value of the appraised property.

12. Utilities

Under this item detailed information shall be given on the availability, source and adequacy to serve the property on all utilities. Location and distance from the property on all utilities should be indicated. Where a particular utility, such as sewers, is not available to the site, it should be so indicated. The availability and effect upon the valuation of the property should be fully discussed.

a. Water
b. Gas
c. Electricity
d. Sanitary Sewer
e. Storm Sewer
f. Other (Specify such as steam for heat)

13. Street Improvements

Under this item, access, or lack thereof, to the property should be fully discussed. A brief description of the character and type of street improvements bounding the site as well as in the surrounding area should be included as well as the street or road net to major thoroughfare in the area. Where streets are not improved or not in at all, it should be so stated.

14. Transportation

The availability and distance to the nearest local public transportation should be stated. The type, cost, adequacy and frequency of schedules should be indicated. Information as to other transportation generally serving the city and area should also be indicated.

15. Amenities

The location, distance from the appraised property and adequacy of miscellaneous facilities should be discussed in detail, including their relationship and effect upon market value of the property.
a. Schools
b. Markets and Stores
c. Churches
d. Parks
e. Playgrounds
f. Public Libraries
g. Other Community Facilities (Specify)

16. Favorable and Unfavorable Factors

Under this item, the various factors which are favorable to the property should be enumerated and discussed. Any hazards or nuisances which affect the property, such as obnoxious facilities, smoke, smell, noise, traffic, etc., should be thoroughly discussed, indicating their location and relationship to the property as well as its effect upon market value.

17. Real Estate Market Conditions

Market activity and level of the current real estate market conditions including supply and demand factors affecting the area as well as the specific type of property and future indicated trends shall be discussed in detail and the extent to which they affect the value of the property being appraised.

Part B. Property Data and Valuation

This section shall comprise the parcel appraisal valuation portion of the report with the data being applicable to the specific property or properties being appraised. The information and data concerning each parcel will be set out separately and be so identified by parcel number, "tabbed" for easy reference. Detailed narrative discussion of each item should be included.

18. Property Data

A narrative description of the land, all improvements, and other factors shall be included.

a. *Ownership* - Name and address of owners of record

b. *Area*—This item shall include the shape, dimensions and land area in both square feet and acreage as well as comparative effects of size or shape from a market value standpoint. A plat of the parcel should be included in this section

c. *Size*—Under this item, a narrative discussion should include type of soil and soil bearing capacity, topography, grading or fill requirements, drainage, easements, rights-of-way, canals, streams, and any other characteristics which affect the parcel's value should be included.

d. *Improvements*—Describe each structure and each utility or outside improvement, structural and construction details, number and type of units, age and size of buildings, condition along with a discussion of functionality in utility and analysis of layout. A plat of the building should be included.

e. *Equipment*—Under this item, include a narrative descriptive analysis of the mechanical equipment installed in each structure including lighting, heating, air conditioning, water supply, plumbing, fire protection, power, stoves, refrigerators, blowers, ventilation. This discussion should include the type and purpose of the equipment, physical condition adequacy or inadequacy, obsolescence, etc.

f. *Assessed Value and Annual Tax Load*—Include the current assessment of land and improvements separately and dollar amount of real estate taxes and tax rate. In this discussion, the appraiser should reflect his opinion as to the effect of this tax burden upon the marketability of the property. Special assessments should be separately set out and discussed. The appraiser should determine if the site area or any portion thereof is subject to special assessments. The nature of same and the total amount yet due on each parcel should be so indicated. Inasmuch as special assessments are to be paid in full by the seller at the time of closing, the valuation of parcels involved with assessments should be made as though the properties were free and clear of all assessments and the appraiser should so indicate in his report. The appraiser is therefore cautioned that comparable sales used should be carefully analyzed for such assessments and adjusted accordingly on a comparative basis with the subject property.

g. *Zoning*—Indicate the existing zoning for subject property or properties including a definition and restrictions of such zoning, including height limitations, parking requirements, etc. It should also be indicated if the property is presently operating at a variance to the existing zoning. The appraiser should discuss the effect of such zoning related to the highest and best use upon the marketability of the property being appraised and whether or not any prospective change in zoning is indicated or probable.

h. *Property History*—The history of the property's use, mainly in recent years, should be discussed. The date acquired by the present owner, price paid and whether such was considered a "market sale" the time of acquisition. Where the appraiser's current estimate of market value is substantially at variance with the price paid by the present owner, the reason and justification for such a difference should be fully discussed and the adjustments which were made to bring this previous sale up to present date. The attitude of the owner towards sale of the property as well as the possibility or probability of condemnation shall also be included herein.

i. *Photographs of Property or Parcel—A* photograph or photographs of different views at least 3" x 5" in size shall be included for each parcel at the beginning of the parcel valuation of each parcel.

19. Analysis of Highest and Best Use

This section should contain a narrative discussion of the appraiser's conclusions concerning the highest and best use and reasons therefore. If the property is presently developed to its highest and best use, it should be so stated and, if not, the Appraiser should indicate his opinion as to what the use should be and for which there is a market, along with his justifications and reasoning. This should also be related to the existing and/or prospective zoning of the property.

20. Land Value

This should include the appraiser's opinion of the value of the land, supported and justified fully by sales and offerings of comparable, or most nearly comparable lands having like optimum uses. Differences shall be carefully analyzed and weighed for location, size, shape, date of sale, zoning, utility and any other pertinent factors, each being clearly stated and explained as to the various adjustments made and how it indicates the value of the land being appraised. This must be fully justified and substantiated.

21. Estimate of Value by Summation Approach

This is the appraiser's estimate of the market value of the property as indicated by cost in the form of computative data, arranged in the following sequence, stating sources and justification of costs or prices used and for each type of depreciation.
a. Estimated cost of all improvements and equipment new in today's market.
b. Estimated accrued depreciation of all kinds.
c. The subtraction of b from a above.
d. The addition of the Land Value, Item 19 to c above.

The use of flat percentage figures (age method) for estimating depreciation is not considered acceptable without full substantiation and justification for any percentage used. The breakdown methods of observed depreciation should be used wherein application of the following factors of depreciation are fully treated and substantiated:
a. Estimate of Rehabilitation Cost
b. Estimate of General Deterioration
c. Estimate of Curable Functional Obsolescence
d. Estimate of Incurable functional Obsolescence
e. Estimate of Economic Obsolescence—justified by market data

The land value portion of this approach should be justified upon the basis of section 19. Where this approach is not applicable, the Appraiser should so indicate with the reasons therefore.

22. Estimate of Value as Indicated by Income Approach

a. This is the appraiser's estimate of the property's value based upon an analysis of the present worth of the future potential benefits of the property measured by the net income which a fully informed person is warranted in assuming the property will produce during its remaining useful life, which is then capitalized at a justified rate to reflect its current value from a prudent investment standpoint (particularly in the case of income or investment real estate). This approach is arranged in the form of computative data to show the following, along with whatever else may be considered pertinent, and to include factual data and justification to support each figure and factor used.

(1) Estimated Gross Income—Derived from rental analysis of unit rates being paid for similar competitive accommodations

(2) Vacancy and Credit Losses—From experience records and the market

(3) Effective Gross Income

(4) Operating expenses, itemized under three subheads to show:
   (a) Operating Costs
   (b) Reserves for Replacements
   (c) Fixed Charges (Taxes, Insurance, etc.)

(5) Net Income (3 less 4)

(6) Capitalization of Net Income shall be at the rate prevailing for this type property and location. It shall reflect current market conditions and trends, interest rates, return that will attract equity capital, reliability of constant stream and all other factors which may influence the rates applicable to the particular property. The capitalization rate and technique used shall be justified by narrative explanation supported by sources of rates and factors used.

b. Where properties are vacant and unimproved and are suitable under their optimum use for income development, the "residual approach" to value must be fully explored and set out in his report. Under this approach technique, by the development of a hypothetical improvement upon the site, the computative analysis and capitalization will result in a "residual" value to the land. This approach, if used, and the computation used shall be fully justified and substantiated in all respects.

c. Where vacant land has a potential use developed for subdivision purposes, the appraiser must also include the "Development Method", which technique reflects the value of the land if it were subdivided and sold, subtracting all development costs, profit, etc., resulting in a residual value to the land in its present unimproved condition. Under this approach, all development costs used, income from the sale of finished lots, profit and other items must be fully substantiated and justified as well as the proper interest and discount for the time element involved. A sketch plat of the proposed subdivision will also be included in this section. In connection with this approach, it is often necessary that the appraiser secure the services of technical engineering specialists to develop a proposed plan of development and engineering cost estimate. In such cases, the engineer's report should be referred to in this section of the appraisal and a copy of his report included in Section III, Addendum.

Where any form of the Income Approach is not utilized, the Appraiser should so indicate with the reasons therefore.

23. Estimate of Value as Indicated by Comparative Method (Market Approach)

This shall recite the appraiser's opinion of the property's value as substantiated by records of sales and offerings of comparable properties. All recent sales should be listed and reflected in this valuation or omission explained. Differences shall be weighed for location, size, shape, date of sale, zoning, utility and such other factors as may be pertinent shall be clearly stated and explained in relation to its comparability and reflection of the value of the subject property. Where there are no directly comparable or recent sales of properties, it may be necessary for the appraiser to utilize older sales, less comparable properties or go farther afield to secure an adequate number of sales to justify value and thus more extensive adjustments are necessary. A statement that there are not recent comparable sales in the area will not be acceptable.

24. Correlation and Interpretation of Estimate and Conclusion of Value

Under this item, the appraiser shall include a narrative discussion wherein he has interpreted all the foregoing valuation estimates as well as all other pertinent factors affecting value, with his reasons why one or more of the conclusions of value reached is not indicative of the market value of the property. The scope of this final correlation is dependent upon the purpose of the appraisal and the complexity of the appraisal problem as well as the adequacy or inadequacy of pertinent data as well as the processing procedures and reasonableness thereof, which have been carried out. This will be thoroughly discussed in order that his reasoning and conclusions are beyond question. The unit basis of value for land (square feet, acre, lot, etc.) and the buildings (square feet) should be included for the convenience of the reviewer in relating the value of the subject land and improvements to historical transactions.

25. Salvage Value of Improvements

The appraiser shall include the salvage value for removal off site for each of the structures on each parcel separately in the parcel valuation. This is required in the event the owners elect to retain the improvements. This amount will be deducted from the market value of the property. In the event the improvements on a parcel have a minus value and are a detriment to the highest and best use of the property, their removal or demolition cost should be estimated and deducted from the market value of the parcel.

26. Severance Damage

If any of the properties are partial takings of an ownership, severance damage must be fully described and discussed. If it is the appraiser's opinion that there is none, it should be so stated with the reasons therefore. The method of estimation and the valuation therefore must be fully discussed and supported by justifiable evidence or persuasive argument.

27. Plottage or Assemblage Value

Where a project site is comprised of a number of smaller parcels and it is indicated in the market that after acquisition of these smaller parcels by the Local Authority, the combined assemblage of smaller parcels will have greater per square foot value than the smaller parcels, before assemblage, the Appraiser should so indicate and include a detailed discussion of this factor with his estimate supported by market data sales clearly justifying this plottage value.

28. Certification of Appraiser

If the appraiser so desires, this certification may be included in the letter of transmittal; however, as a minimum, it shall include the following statements:

a. That the appraiser has no undisclosed interest in the property, or contemplated interest

b. That the appraiser's employment and his compensation are not contingent upon the valuation found

c. That he has personally and thoroughly inspected the property

d. That according to the best of his knowledge, everything contained in the report is true and that no important facts have been withheld or overlooked

e. That the appraisal has been made in accordance with the standards of practice or code of ethics of the professional group or association in which he may hold membership

f. That the values required of the described property are a certain number of dollars as of a certain date

g. Signature of the appraiser

PART III - Addenda

Under this section shall be included all exhibits, charts, plats, plans, graphs, maps, photographs, reports, documents, specifications, detailed estimates, etc., which may be referred to in his report or are used to further substantiate his findings or are considered pertinent thereto. All exhibits must be presented in a neat, attractive and convenient manner. All charts, maps, graphs, etc., must be prepared in a professional and workmanlike manner.

29. Vicinage Map

An adequate sized city or area map, the scale of which will readily identify the site location and other important facilities, as required or necessary. The site area should be shown in red in the map legend.

30. Comparative Data Map

The site area should be shown in red and all sales numbered and shown in yellow. If feasible, this map may be combined with the Vicinage Map.

31. Detail of Comparative Data

A sales analysis sheet shall be included for each sale and will include, among other things that may be necessary, the following:
a. Photograph of the Property
b. Grantor
c. Grantee
d. Date of Sale
e. Type of Transfer
f. Amount of Internal Revenue Stamp
g. Source of Information

h. Verified Sales Price
i. By Whom Verified
j. Breakdown of Sales Price
    (1) Amount to Land
    (2) Amount to Improvements
k. Terms of Sale
1. Improvements at Time of Sale
m. Use of Property
n. Zoning
o. Description—Location of Property
p. Assessment Data
q. Remarks—Including Comparison Adjustments

32. Plot Plans

33. Floor Plans

34. Other Pertinent Exhibits

Charts, Graphs, Historical Income and Expense Data, Detailed Estimates, Abstracts of Leases, etc.

35. Special Reports—

Prepared by Technical Specialists hired by the Appraiser in connection with the Appraisal.

36. Qualifications of Contract Appraiser

The appraisal shall include a statement of his diversified qualifications as evidence that he is qualified to make such an appraisal. This should include facts about his education, technical training, type and years of experience, trade and

All Plats and Plans may be bound as facing pages opposite the description, tabulation or discussions they concern, professional organizations of which he is a member, courts in which he has appeared as an expert witness, individuals and organizations for whom he has made appraisals and important and similar assignments.

General

1. Parcel

The term parcel, as used herein, means any tract or contiguous tracts of land the apparent title to which is held by the same person or persons, regardless of whether such tract or tracts consist of platted lots or are otherwise normally divided. The appraiser shall collaborate with the Local Authority in numbering each parcel in order that such numbering will be the same as those used in the Project Surveys, Title Reports, and other land documentation.

2. Review of Reports

It should be understood by the appraiser that the appraisal reports are subject to careful, professional review. Therefore, they must be fully detailed, narrative type reports with all items and factors clearly set forth, and fully substantiated and Justified in every respect and in such a manner that there will be no doubt in the reviewer's mind as to his conclusions. All deficiencies or items which, in the reviewer's opinion, require further substantiation or justification must be performed by the appraiser in the form of a supplemental report at the appraiser's own expense in accordance with the appraisal contract.

Responsibility to the Appraiser

Effective and expeditious contract approval, review and approval of the appraisal, including payment of the fee is imperative. Any delays in these aspects can result in reviewing problems as well as cause dissension between the parties involved. It is also important that any definitive instructions for special considerations and conditions be made known to the appraiser prior to entering into any contract for appraisal.

It is also imperative that the principle requiring the appraisal furnish the appraiser with everything he has and knows about the property, and gives the appraiser what he needs to know in order to do the job which is expected of him. Don't hold back any data on the property—let him decide on how important it is to reach a decision of market value. There have been numerous occasions where information was withheld from the appraiser, which could have made a difference on the conclusions reached, on the assumption that "let him find it out on his own, this is what we are hiring him for". This is a very erroneous attitude, since many times such information may not be readily obtainable by the appraiser and could make some material difference in his conclusion were it known to him. The reviewing process should insure that staff review appraisers thoroughly document inquiries made of appraisers regarding items of major importance to evaluating the adequacy of the report.

On the other hand? Give the appraiser the latitude to present his best "professional work" without restricting him to "rules and regulations" which may restrict him from presenting his professional opinion—as he sees it. Allow the appraiser to have at least some degree of flexibility, and to use his initiative unless it violates the purpose and objective upon which the appraisal is being made. *The reviewer must always remember that he is dealing with a professional who also has certain rights to express his professional conclusions.*

Professional Counseling

Another important factor in the process of review appraising is that *the review appraiser be available for professional counsel to the contract appraiser, whereby questions which are answered prior to, or during the course of preparation of n appraisal may be resolved or clarified*—rather than after the fact. Close corroboration between the parties involved is extremely important in expediting the overall valuation procedure and approval of the appraisal. If agreement can be reached on questionable matters, approaches or other factors of an appraisal in advance of the review, it will reduce any questions which may be raised during the course of the reviewing process and also make the reviewer's job less of a problem.

Review Appraiser, Not the Negotiator

The reviewing appraiser should confine himself to the task of *reviewing the appraisal itself and not becoming directly involved* in the negotiation settlement. He should be an unbiased party in the overall transaction, merely giving his opinion as the validity of the market value as appraised. This does not mean that he should ignore any other appraisals presented by the parties involved. In the event an appraisal is presented by the party opposing his principle, this should be considered along with the appraisal he has already reviewed and should be reviewed and given the same credence as a second appraisal. However, he must always maintain his position, and function as the "advisor" on valuation methods to the negotiators rather than the advocating participant. This does not mean, however, that the reviewer cannot operate in a quasi-advisory capacity in the course of negotiations, and he should do so. *It was never intended that the review appraiser should have any kind of veto power over negotiations or condemnation settlements.* This is a matter which should be resolved by the negotiation and legal elements, rather than the reviewer.

One important "rule" that should always be remembered that the reviewer is not the appraiser. It is not anticipated, nor part of his purgative, that he will substitute his judgement for that of the appraiser unless the judgment of the appraiser is irrefutably erroneous and the reviewer can adequately justify this conclusion. This is a "weakness" of many "inexperienced" review appraisers. They attempt to do the appraisal and substitute their judgment, rather than strictly perform a review of the appraisal that has been made. They often attempt to substitute a value coinciding with their preconceived conclusions, rather than reviewing that which the appraiser has arrived at in an "unbiased" professional manner. *The reviewer is the "interpreter," not the "performer."*

Reviewer as Expert Witness

The use of the reviewing appraiser as an expert witness is not recommended because frequently they are subject to the accusation of being "advocates" for their principle. Also, they did not actually make the appraisal and cannot testify as though they had made the appraisal. However, they can be called upon and may testify as to their "opinion" of the appraiser's conclusions if they have made a detailed analysis and field review of the appraiser's report—if they are called upon to do so. They can't testify to the value as though they were the appraiser, unless they have actually made a "full scale" appraisal themselves. They are then the appraiser, not the reviewer.

Practical Reviewing

Sometimes reviewing incompetence takes the form of the "theorist" who is lost in appraisal philosophy, or the "technician" who is incapable of essential analysis and mature judgment which is required to make that "weighted" decision as a professional reviewing appraiser. The Reviewer has to be "practical" and "realistic" in all respects. I theory and philosophy are important— but they must be kept in their place and not go "overboard". We must always respect and keep in mind the competence and ability of those whose appraisals we are reviewing; usually they are well experienced, competent, and not amateurs.

Assumption of Appraiser's Honesty

Another assumption that we must make in reviewing is that

the appraiser is "honest" and that what he states is "true" and not *"fake information"* or data, *unless we know it to be otherwise. We must* give the appraiser the *"benefit of the doubt"*.

Substitution of Judgment

Appraising being an inexact science, one of the most important elements in appraising is *"sole judgment"*—this is used by the appraiser throughout the appraisal process, as such. What is this so called judgment—judgment is a mental act in the operation of the mind which involves *"comparison"* and *"discrimination"* by which knowledge of values and relations are mentally formulated. It is the power of arriving at a wise decision which involves discernment as well as discretion. Judgment being such an important element in appraising, then how is this governed in the course of appraisal reviewing? An important rule which must be remembered in the course of appraisal reviewing is that the review appraiser must not attempt to substitute his judgment for that of the appraiser unless he can Justify that the appraiser's judgment, in connection with some particular factor of the report is obviously unsound. You also have to, *to a reasonable extent,* accept the appraiser's judgment unless you can prove otherwise. Appraisers often state "my considered judgment is" or "based on my observations". What do these mean? Judgment occurs for a reason—what are the reasons he used? What are the observations he made? Are they stated in his report? Are they factual? Are they sound? Are they conclusive? Has he convinced you?

Reviewer Documentation

It is extremely important that, in the course of the reviewing process, the staff reviewing appraisers thoroughly document their actions during the course of their review. This will facilitate any inquiries which may subsequently be made in respect to the appraiser's conclusion concerning any items of major importance to evaluating the adequacy and validity of the report. For a reviewing appraiser to not document his findings, on at least any major appraisal, is not considered to be professionally acceptable or ethical.

PART II

Appraisal Reviewing Methods and Process Used In Reviewing

Scope

There are normally two major methods through which the appraisal review function is usually accomplished and some variations thereof.

The First Method - Individual Review

The "one shot method", whereby the appraisal is delivered to the principle and is reviewed in its entirety by a single reviewer or process and does not proceed beyond that point. The reviewer may or may not be remote from the property or the appraiser. However, under this method no further review is made other than in the instance of a multiple or joint review which may actually take other factors into consideration, in addition to the actual value of the property itself, or other considerations.

This method of review is usually made by smaller or local organizations and many financial institutions. The individual reviewer performing this function usually has full approval or disapproval authority.

The Second Method—The Echelon Or Sometimes Called The Cumulative Process Or Method

The "shot gun method", involves more than one professional opinion or review. Under this method the appraisal report is reviewed in whole or in part at several different levels or echelons. The final review is usually made by a reviewer who is remote from the property or project and the appraiser. His is the type of review which is often performed by larger organizations, many governmental agencies, and larger organizations with field offices, regional offices and central offices. In many instances, each echelon has to perform a review of some sort and make their own determinations and recommendations. Under this method, one or the other of the echelons may be delegated the major reviewing authority and the others merely corroborate or disagree with the conclusions. The basis for major approval authority is sometimes based upon the 'dollar amount" of the property or the "size of the project". Other echelons not having major approval authority may only make a "cursory" or concurrence type of appraisal review.

Multiple Person Reviews

In some instances, the review at a particular echelon may be done by more than one individual. Where there are large appraisal work loads, an initial review may be made by a "technician" who merely checks clerical, mathematical, or possibly a check list of essential contractual items covered. This is normally followed by a more detailed technical review by a professional reviewer. In this procedure, the individual who finally signs the reviewing statement and recommendation is the "responsible reviewer'. He should verify and corroborate any determinations made by others which he has relied upon to formulate his opinion conclusions.

Two Step Method

The review process can also be accomplished in more than "one step" or by one reviewer. This is often done in many agencies whereby they have a "Senior Reviewing Appraiser" who reviews all staff and/or contract appraisals and who prepares a detailed review and analysis of all reports which is later reviewed and approved by a "Chief' reviewing Appraiser in the same element of the organization. This is done to further assure or "fireproof" the conclusions.

Citizen Review

There is another type of appraisal review, which is an extension of the normal "echelon" review procedure which was previously outlined to some degree. Any appraisals which are provided to Federal Agencies on any projects are subject to "Freedom of Information Act" (5 U.S. Code 522) which has made most information in Federal government files accessible to any interested citizen. There are a few statutory exceptions to this general policy. One of these exceptions is for "trade secrets" and also for personal or financial information obtained from a person and which may be classified as privileged or confidential. The various agencies of our Federal government have interpreted this regulation in somewhat different degrees as is usually the case. An appraisal may be obtained for review, only if it is a completed acquisition action. If it is still under litigation, it is not available. Another restriction, you must know the particular document you are requesting. The point is that this is an additional review element that an appraiser and reviewer may be selected to and he should be prepared to protect or "fireproof" himself accordingly. Where an individual appraiser prepares an appraisal for a federal acquisition or disposition, he should probably consider asking the agency to include an amendment to its standard appraisal contract committing the agency to confidentiality of the appraisal should so include this in his limiting assumptions and conditions of his appraisal; however, a contract provision, as such, is not an absolute protection against disclosure if such is included it may require the individual to file suit to secure the appraisal. This in no way is meant to be a "legal" interpretation of this act, or protection for the appraiser. It is recommended that you contact your legal counsel for advice on this matter and secure a "clause" in your contract which will protect you.

The point is that appraisals are open to the possibility of another review by individuals who are not professionally competent or qualified to review an appraisal and as such can "misinterpret", "take out of context" or in some other way discredit the appraisal or the review made, which is usually their primary objective to see their "cause".

Congressional or Committee Reviews

An additional type of review which Chief Appraiser of Federal Agencies in Washington are subjected to is the review made by Congressional Committee Staff Personnel. Most acquisition and disposition projects, of federally owned properties, require committee approval, of the various congressional committees involved, in order to secure funds or approval. The site reports, appraisals made and reviews thereof are often required to be submitted to these various committees. The individuals reviewing these projects are not usually well qualified or experienced professionally and as such may take issue to something rather minor which would not influence the valuation conclusion, to discredit the value, one way or another. While any such objective analysis should be gratefully accepted, one must be prepared to refute if it is unwarranted. It is also recommended that any chief reviewing appraisers should be somewhat careful in their detailed reviewing analysis. Since, as we all know, almost every appraisal may have some "shortcomings" or something we may take issue with to some degree. When these things are mentioned, even though they may not be of such consequence to materially change the valuation conclusion, they can *"open the door"* to make a *"material case"* to refute the valuation conclusion reached and create additional, unnecessary problems.

Recordation of Review Made

The review record should be in writing of some form and should always be signed by the reviewer authorized to do so, and in many cases it is concurred by someone in higher authority of other management or organizational elements. This is dependent upon

Exhibit 2. U.S. Department of Interior—Reviewer's Appraisal Analysis—U.S.D.1—Bureau of Land Management Form Type Review—9300-11 (with approval to use)

UNITED STATES DEPARTMENT OF THE INTERIOR BUREAU OF LAND MANAGEMENT	Serial Number	Type of Case
REVIEWER'S APPRAISAL ANALYSIS	Name of Applicant	

Appraiser	Legal Description

CONTRACT			
Fee $		Time Allowed	
Number		Date	Type of Property
DATE			
Appraisal	REVIEW		
	Field	Office	Size / Appraised Value $

INSTRUCTIONS: Items 1 through 44 are provided as an aid in answering major questions (H). Explain all negative answers (J).
Comment fully on inadequacies and recommendations.
A – Adequate – meets Departmental Standards.
I – Inadequate – does not meet Departmental Standards. Revisions or clarification necessary.
Check (✔) appropriate box. If not applicable, place (0) in box "A".

ITEM	A	I	ITEM	A	I
A. FORM AND PRESENTATION			C. COST APPROACH (CON.)		
1. Conformance to Departmental Standards (inclusion and sequence of all significant items)			26. Land value		
			a. adequate sales and offerings		
2. Purpose—definition of value			b. date and condition of each sale or offering		
3. Legal description			c. sales verification		
4. Certification—standard clauses, signature, and date			d. adjustments to current market		
5. Owner given opportunity to accompany appraiser			e. similarities and differences with subject property—explained, weighted, justified		
6. Maps showing subject and comparables, plats, and photos			f. logical conclusion based on fact		
			27. Land value added ☐ yes ☐ no		
7. Statement of limiting conditions			28. Summation value		
8. Rights being appraised					
9. Area, neighborhood data			D. INCOME APPROACH		
10. Property description, condition, and adaptable use			29. Gross annual rent by comparison		
11. Taxes, assessments, and rates			30. Vacancy and credit loss		
12. Highest and best use			31. Expenses and fixed charges		
a. for land			32. Net annual income from rent		
b. for total property			a. attributable to whole property		
13. Approaches to be used			b. attributable to improvement		
			c. attributable to land		
B. MARKET APPROACH			33. Method of capitalization		
14. Adequate sales and offerings			34. Capitalization rate—justified		
15. Last sale of subject property analyzed			35. Value		
16. Date and condition of each sale or offering					
17. Sales verification			E. CORRELATION AND VALUE		
18. Adjustment to current market			36. Correlation of estimates		
19. Similarities and differences with subject property—explained, weighted, justified			37. Approach that is controlling		
20. Contributing value of minerals, timber, etc.			38. Value conclusion		
21. Value indicated and justified based on fact			F. FAIR RENTAL		
			39. Logical relationship to comparables		
C. COST APPROACH			40. Differences factually justified		
22. Cost estimates			41. Does estimate reflect contemplated lease provisions? ☐ yes ☐ no		
23. Depreciation—physical					
24. Depreciation—functional			G. EMINENT DOMAIN		
25. Depreciation—economical			42. Plats submitted showing relation of partial take to whole property		
			43. Damages and/or benefits justified and properly measured		
			44. Damages separately stated		

ITEM	YES	NO	ITEM	YES	NO
H. OVERALL EFFECTIVENESS			H. OVERALL EFFECTIVENESS (CON.)		
45. Is the appraisal problem clearly stated?			51. Do you recommend the report:		
46. Is the property accurately delineated and described?			a. as a basis for contemplated action?		
47. Is the best and most profitable use of the property stated, and used for basis of value?			b. without further clarification?		
			I. APPLICABLE TO FEE APPRAISERS ONLY		
48. Is supporting data accurate?			52. Do you recommend the report for fee payment?		
49. Is conclusion logically and factually related to supporting data?			53. Does the appraiser's panel rating seem appropriate?		
50. Are all essential items included?			54. Would you recommend this appraiser for other similar assignments?		

J. REVIEWER'S COMMENTS *(Use Additional Sheets if Necessary)*

Exhibit 3. General Services Administration Form GSA 1305

REVIEWER'S APPRAISAL ANALYSIS (For use by Staff Appraiser in Reviewing Appraisal Reports)			PURPOSE OF APPRAISAL ☐ IN-LEASE ☐ ACQUISITION ☐ TRANSFER ☐ OUT-LEASE ☐ DISPOSAL
APPRAISER		FEE $	TYPE OF PROPERTY
CONTRACT NO.	CONTRACT DATE	TIME ALLOWED	NAME AND ADDRESS OF PROPERTY
EFFECTIVE DATE OF REPORT	DATE REVIEWED		
REVIEWER			APPRAISED VALUE $ ‖ CASE NO.

INSTRUCTIONS

Items 1 through 45 are provided as an aid in answering Major Questions in Part VII.
Explain all negative answers on reverse (Part VIII). Comment fully on inadequacies and recommendations.

E - Excellent - Meets or exceeds specifications.
A - Adequate - Meets minimum needs. Clarification may be desirable.
I - Inadequate - Does not meet needs. Revision or clarification necessary.

ITEM	E	A	I	ITEM	E	A	I
I. FORM AND PRESENTATION				**E. MARKET APPROACH**			
1. CONFORMANCE TO GSA SPECIFICATIONS (As to format, inclusion and sequence of all significant items)				30. LIST OF SALES AND OFFERINGS			
2. AREA, CITY, NEIGHBORHOOD DATA				31. SAME LIST ADJUSTED TO CURRENT MARKET			
3. LEGAL DESCRIPTION INCLUDED? ☐ YES ☐ NO				32. SPECIAL CONDITIONS TO EACH SALE			
4. PROPERTY DESCRIPTION, CONDITION, AND ADAPTABLE USE				33. RELATION OF SALE OR OFFERING TO SUBJECT PROPERTY - SIMILARITIES AND DIFFERENCES WEIGHTED			
5. INSURANCE AND TAX LOAD: PLANS, PHOTOS AND MAPS				34. VALUE INDICATED AND JUSTIFICATION			
6. CERTIFICATION - STANDARD CLAUSES, SIGNATURE AND DATE				35. DESCRIPTION AND CONDITION			
II. DELINEATION OF ASSIGN.				36. ANALYSIS OF UTILITY			
7. PURPOSE, INCLUDING DEFINITION OF VALUE				37. VALUE FOR IN-PLACE USE (If applicable)			
8. HIGHEST AND BEST USE - FOR LAND - FOR TOTAL PROPERTY				38. VALUE FOR OFF-SITE USE " "			
9. STATEMENT OF LIMITING CONDITIONS				39. FAIR RENTAL ESTIMATE " "			
A. LAND VALUE BY COMPARISON				40. LOGICAL RELATIONSHIP TO COMPARABLES .			
10. ADEQUATE LISTINGS				41. BASED ON INTEREST PLUS CAPITAL RECAPTURE (If applicable)			
11. DATE AND CONDITIONS OF EACH SALE				42. DOES ESTIMATE REFLECT CONTEMPLATED LEASE PROVISIONS? ☐ YES ☐ NO			
12. SAME LIST ADJUSTED TO CURRENT MARKET				43. CORRELATION OF ESTIMATES			
13. SIMILARITIES AND DIFFERENCES WITH SUBJECT PROPERTY				44. THE APPROACH THAT IS CONTROLLING: ___			
14. LOGICAL CONCLUSION				45. VALUE CONCLUSION			
15. MAP SHOWING COMPARABLES					YES	NO	
B. LAND RESIDUAL TECHNIQUE (If used)				46. IS THE APPRAISAL PROBLEM CLEARLY STATED?			
16. LOGICAL CONCLUSION				47. IS THE PROPERTY ACCURATELY DELINEATED AND DESCRIBED?			
C. COST APPROACH				48. IS THE BEST AND MOST PROFITABLE USE OF THE PROPERTY STATED, AND USED FOR BASIS OF VALUE?			
17. COST ESTIMATES				49. IS SUPPORTING DATA ACCURATE?			
18. DEPRECIATION - PHYSICAL				50. IS CONCLUSION LOGICALLY RELATED TO SUPPORTING DATA?			
19. DEPRECIATION - FUNCTIONAL				51. ARE ALL ESSENTIAL ITEMS INCLUDED?			
20. DEPRECIATION - ECONOMIC				IS THE REPORT RECOMMENDED:			
21. LAND VALUE ADDED? ☐ YES ☐ NO				52. AS A BASIS FOR CONTEMPLATED ACTION?			
22. SUMMATION VALUE				53. WITHOUT FURTHER CLARIFICATION?			
D. INCOME APPROACH				54. FOR FEE PAYMENT?			
23. GROSS ANNUAL RENT BY COMPARISON				AS EVIDENCED BY THIS REPORT:			
24. VACANCY AND CREDIT LOSS				55. DOES THE APPRAISER'S PANEL RATING SEEM APPROPRIATE?			
25. EXPENSE AND FIXED CHARGES INCLUDING RESERVES FOR REPLACEMENT				56. WOULD YOU RECOMMEND THIS APPRAISER FOR OTHER SIMILAR ASSIGNMENTS?			
26. NET ANNUAL INCOME FROM RENT							
27. METHOD OF CAPITALIZATION							
28. CAPITALIZATION RATE - JUSTIFIED							
29. VALUE							

Side labels (left column): **I. FORM AND PRESENTATION**, **II. DELINEATION OF ASSIGN.**, **III. ANALYSIS AND TECHNIQUE**
Side labels (right column): **III. ANALYSIS AND TECHNIQUE (Con.)**, **IV. MACHINERY AND EQUIPMENT**, **V. FAIR RENTAL**, **VI. CORRELATION AND VALUE**, **VII. OVERALL EFFECTIVENESS**

VIII. REVIEWER'S COMMENTS

the policy requirements and procedures of the organization and does not detract from or reduce the initial reviewer's primary responsibility to perform his function as a reviewer.

Review Record:

The review record may be in any of the following forms:

Signature of Concurrence Type

This is the type which is often used on the form type of appraisals. This merely states that you have reviewed the subject report and it is approved or disapproved—or even merely the word approved. In the case where such an appraisal is not approved, there may or may not be justification for its disapproval. It may be left unsigned and a second appraisal obtained, or it may be disapproved with a justifying statement. However, for the record, if the appraisal is not approvable, some statement and justification for the action taken should be made in writing and placed in the records of the organization.

Check Sheet or Form Type Review

This is sometimes called the "positive" type review-detailing and recording by a "check sheet" or other type of form all the actions or steps taken in the course of the review. This form may be quite elaborate or short, depending upon the circumstances and the type of appraisal being reviewed. This form can also be used as a "quality control guide", depending upon the 'ability" and "quality" of appraisals prepared by both staff and fee appraisers in other words, a "training vehicle". In connection with this type of review, see the following examples of appraisal review Forms on pages xxx.

Exception Type Review

This type of review is a short form narrative review and records only exceptions taken by reviewers, recording these exceptions and the actions taken regarding them and agreement for approval or disapproval. The reasoning taken is usually in a short memorandum of no more than one page or so. This type of review is more than a mere approval or disapproval or occurrence type review, but is less than a detailed narrative, formal type review.

Combination Form Type Review

This combines the check sheet type review, with the exception type review. The advantage of this type over the strictly check sheet type of review is that it gives the reviewer an opportunity for further elaboration upon the deficiencies found, action taken, and concluding recommendations. Also, an actual field review can be incorporated in this type of review which can be made in any form applicable to the particular situation.

An example of this type form is as follows (see Exhibits 4 and 5).

Detailed Formal Type Narrative Review

This is a fully detailed narrative type of review which covers the major factors in an appraisal, indicating what the appraiser covered, the adequacy or inadequacy of his justification and substantiation of each item, and the reviewer's acceptance or rejection of each item. It also recites the steps which were taken to rectify any deficiencies, or omissions and the results of these items, thus giving any subsequent reviewers or management a concise analysis of the important factors which affect the valuation as well as the purpose and needs upon which the appraisal was premised. These factors include economics, highest and best use, various approaches used, sales data and analysis, and the numer-

Exhibit 4

RESIDENTIAL APPRAISAL REVIEW FORM

Lending Institution _____
Lender's Address _____
Name of Borrower _____
Property Address _____
Loan Number _____
Appraised Value $ _____ Date _____
Lender's Appraiser _____ Phone _____
Appraiser's Address _____
Review Appraiser _____ Phone _____
Reviewer's Address _____

FORMAT AND PRESENTATION	LENDER SECTION

	YES	NO	N/A		YES	NO	N/A
1. Is the Appraisal format in conformance with company appraisal requirements?	□	□	□	2. Is the lender section of the report complete and accurate?	□	□	□

NEIGHBORHOOD SECTION

3. Does the neighborhood section provide the reviewer an adequate understanding with respect to locational factors, growth rate and economic trends, property values, housing supply, marketing time, land use, price ranges, convenience to employment and amenities, adequacy of utilities and recreational facilities, property compatibility, appearance of properties, detrimental conditions and marketability?
4. Does the appraisal report enable the reviewer to spot healthy growth patterns or trends that may indicate a deteriorating neighborhood with limited market appeal?

5. Are comments in the neighborhood section relevant and do they give insight into those conditions which positively or negatively affect the appraised properties value and marketability?
6. Have all fair and poor ratings in the neighborhood section been explained?
7. If marketing time is over six months, has the appraiser commented on the reasons for slow market conditions in the subject area?
8. If the market is slow, has the appraiser indicated whether or not this has resulted in a decline in values?
9. Is the neighborhood section of the report completed and accurate?

Reviewer's Comments _____

SITE SECTION

10. Has the appraiser commented on unfavorable site factors?
11. Does the appraiser indicate whether or not the subject property meets all the criteria for a desirable lot in the area?
12. Has the appraiser addressed and commented on problems relating to poor drainage, flood conditions, adverse easements, encroachments or other detrimental factors?

13. Does the appraiser indicate the subject's zoning and whether or not the subject conforms with present zoning requirements?
14. Has the appraiser accurately indicated the dimensions and size of the subject lot?
15. Does the appraisal report reveal whether or not site improvements and services to the site are adequate and acceptable in the market place?
16. Is the site section of the appraisal report complete and accurate?

Reviewer's Comments _____

IMPROVEMENTS SECTION

17. If the subject property is a condominium, are the project improvements and project rating sections complete and accurate?
18. Did the appraiser comment on physical and functional inadequacies and indicate whether or not repairs and modernization are needed?
19. Has the appraiser explained fair or poor improvement ratings?
20. Does the appraiser indicate whether or not factors receiving poor or fair ratings, adversely affect the property's marketability?
21. Have factor's relating to age, condition, quality or construction, finish and equipment, as well as size and utility been properly handled?
22. Has the appraiser given serious attention to structural problems?
23. Did the appraiser comment on unusual layouts, peculiar floor plans, inadequate equipment and amenities?
24. Has the appraiser indicated whether or not factors relating to unusual layouts, peculiar floor plans, in-

adequate equipment and amenities, limit the value and market appeal of the subject?
25. If there is evidence of dampness, termites or settlement, did the appraiser comment on these factors?
26. Has the appraiser provided the reviewer with a clear and accurate understanding of the physical and functioning attributes of the subject property?
27. Is the property rating section accurate as well as consistent with other data contained in the report?
28. Has the appraiser presented information on construction features in a manner that gives an accurate and adequate view of the subject property?
29. Has information relating to the improvement been well handled?
30. In the reviewer's opinion, is the descriptive section of the appraisal report (page one) acceptable?
31. Has appraiser required all needed repairs?
32. Is the improvement section of the report complete and accurate?

Reviewer's Comments _____

COST SECTION

33. Are the appraiser's measurements for gross living area correct?
34. Has the appraiser commented on functional and economic obsolescence?
35. In estimating reproduction costs, has the appraiser used cost figures that are appropriate for the local market?
36. Do figures for physical, functional and economic de-

preciation appear reasonable in light of the subject's age, condition, state of modernization, size, utility, and location?
37. Is the estimate of land value appropriate?
38. Are the appraiser's mathematical calculations accurate?
39. Is the budget analysis section accurate and complete (if condo)?
40. Is the cost section complete and accurate?

Reviewer's Comments _____

Review Form No. 2002
Revised 1/88

MARKET ANALYSIS SECTION

	YES	NO	N/A			YES	NO	N/A
41. Has the appraiser selected his or her comparables from the subject neighborhood?	☐	☐	☐	56. Does the appraiser's final value conclusion relate for the adjusted comparables?		☐	☐	☐
42. If not, has the appraiser explained why comparables were selected from a different neighborhood?	☐	☐	☐	57. Has the appraiser selected good market data and handled it well?		☐	☐	☐
43. In your opinion, are the comparables really similar with respect to location, site, design and style, quality and amenities, as well as size and utility? If no, Comp. # _____ needs to be replaced.	☐	☐	☐	58. Has the appraiser commented on the subject's marketability?		☐	☐	☐
				59. Does the appraiser's marketability information appear to be accurate?		☐	☐	☐
44. Are all of the comparables recent sales of similar properties from the subject neighborhood?	☐	☐	☐	60. Has the appraiser avoided the appearance of backing into any or all of the approaches to value?		☐	☐	☐
45. If the comparables are over three months old, has the appraiser explained why he or she failed to use recent sales?	☐	☐	☐	61. Is there clarity with respect to the appraiser's reasoning?		☐	☐	☐
46. Are room counts and square foot areas of the subject and comparables and similar?	☐	☐	☐	62. Can you read the appraisal report, step by step, and arrive at the same conclusion of value as the appraiser?		☐	☐	☐
47. Do the sale prices of the comparables correlate and indicate comparability?	☐	☐	☐	63. Does the appraiser appear to be an individual offering an independent and impartial third party opinion of value rather than an advocate?		☐	☐	☐
48. Do the prices per square foot of the comparables correlate and indicate comparability?	☐	☐	☐	64. Are all the required photographs attached and do they adequately show the subject and surrounding properties?		☐	☐	☐
49. Has the appraiser bracketed his or her sales data (before making adjustments)?	☐	☐	☐	65. Is other needed illustrative material attached and properly completed?		☐	☐	☐
50. Do time adjustments, for date of sale, appear reasonable in light of market trends and current market conditions?	☐	☐	☐	66. If the appraiser is using computer generated data, are the facts and comments in the report accurate and applicable to the subject and comparable properties?		☐	☐	☐
51. Has the appraiser avoided numerous adjustments?	☐	☐	☐	67. Does it appear that the appraiser has clearly thought through this process rather than using a computer as a substitute?		☐	☐	☐
52. Has the appraiser adjusted all three comparables in a reasonable and consistent manner?	☐	☐	☐	68. Has the appraiser identified which comparable(s) are the most relevant?		☐	☐	☐
53. Are total gross adjustments exceeding 25% of the comparable's sales price and individual line adjustments exceeding 10% of the comparable's sales price adequately explained and justified?	☐	☐	☐	69. Is the market analysis section complete and accurate?		☐	☐	☐
54. Are the appraiser's mathematical calculations accurate?	☐	☐	☐					
55. Is there a convincing value range with respect to the three adjusted comparables— In brief, are the adjusted value conclusions reasonably similar?	☐	☐	☐					

Reviewer's Comments _____

_____

_____

_____

INCOME APPROACH SECTION

	YES	NO	N/A			YES	NO	N/A
70. Has the income approach been completed?	☐	☐	☐	72. Is supporting data valid and correctly analysed?		☐	☐	☐
71. Has supporting data been submitted?	☐	☐	☐					

Reviewer's Comments _____

_____

_____

RECONCILIATION SECTION

	YES	NO	N/A			YES	NO	N/A
73. In your opinion, has the appraiser proven his or her case?	☐	☐	☐	76. Is it clear which approach to value was given the most weight in the final estimate of value?		☐	☐	☐
74. Do you concur with the value conclusion of the appraiser, based upon data contained within the report?	☐	☐	☐	77. Is the final estimate of value weighted by the most appropriate approach to value?		☐	☐	☐
75. Are the appraiser's comments and final reconciliation of value adequate and does the appraisal give insight into the value and marketability of the subject property?	☐	☐	☐	78. Is the appraiser's value conclusion reasonable?		☐	☐	☐
				79. Has the appraiser signed the report and typed his or her name under the signature?		☐	☐	☐
				80. Is there a phone number on the report and/or cover letter which would enable the reviewer to contact the appraiser and clarify a questionable appraisal report?		☐	☐	☐

Reviewer's Comments _____

_____

_____

_____

REVIEWER'S SUMMARY

Appraisal report was: Good ☐ Fair ☐ Poor ☐

Recommendation:

☐ Accept as is   ☐ Accept when revised-See items # _____

☐ Have another appraisal perpared by someone else   ☐ Other

Comments: _____

_____

_____

_____

_____

Field Review was made   ☐ YES   ☐ NO

Sales price $ _____   Appraisers Value $ _____   Reviewers Recommendation $ _____

Reviewer's Signature _____   Title _____   Date of Review _____

Reviewer's Signature _____   Title _____   Date of Review _____

See Attached ☐

Exhibit 5

RESIDENTIAL APPRAISAL REVIEW NARRATIVE FORM

Lending Institution _____

Lender's Address _____

Name of Borrower _____

Property Address _____

Loan Number _____

Appraised Value $ _____ Date _____

Lender's Appraiser _____ Phone _____

Appraiser's Address _____

Review Appraiser _____ Phone _____

Reviewer's Address _____

REVIEW ANALYSIS

1. Does the appraisal report present a consistent and convincing anaylsis? _____

2. Are there serious omissions, false information, faulty reasoning or the possibility of calculated deception? _____

3. Comment on the report's quality, completeness, consistency and accuracy. _____

4. Do you agree with the appraiser's value conclusion? Comment on the adequacy of the appraiser's value analysis as well as the soundness of the value conclusion? _____

5. If there is a difference between your opinion and that of the appraiser, what is the reason for the difference? _____

6. Does it appear that the subject property has been over appraised? Comment on your opinion of value and the appraiser's opinion of value: _____

7. How would you rate the appraisal report with respect to overall quality (poor, fair, good, very good, excellent)? _____

REVIEWER'S SUMMARY

Recommendation:

☐ Accept as is

☐ Have another appraisal prepared by someone else

☐ Accept when revised-See items # _____

☐ Other

Comments: _____

Field Review was made ☐ YES ☐ NO

Sales price $_____ Appraisers Value $_____ Reviewers Recommendation $ _____

Reviewer's Signature_____ Title_____ Date of Review_____

Reviewer's Signature_____ Title_____ Date of Review_____

See Attached ☐

Review Form No. 2004
Revised 1/88

ous other factors which are covered under the basic appraisal process as well as the particular characteristics of the project being appraised and the particular requirements of the organization for which the appraisal is being prepared.

An example of an outline for this type of review is shown in Exhibit 6, "Outline For Detailed Review and Analysis".

Exhibit 6

OUTLINE: FOR DETAILED REVIEW AND ANALYSIS
SUBJECT: Appraisal Review and Analysis
TO:

In compliance with your request and in accordance with my authority, I have carefully reviewed the attached appraisal report which covers Subject report as of was prepared by

_____.

I have reviewed the subject report from the standpoint of meeting established specifications and requirements, as well as conforming to acceptable professional appraisal practices and techniques; scope of the appraisal investigation; factual data considered; reasoning and logic of the appraisal process and reasonableness of the valuation conclusion of _____.

    I. FORM AND PRESENTATION:

    I. DELINEATION OF ASSIGNMENT:

    III. ANALYSIS TECHNIQUES AND DATA UTILIZED: *A. Factual Data Considered B. Factual Errors or Omissions: C. Reasoning and Logic of Appraisal Process Utilized: D. Reconciliation and Reasonableness of Conclusion Reached: E. Adequacy of Report:*

    IV. APPRAISER'S QUALIFICATIONS:

    V. FIELD REVIEW:

    VI. APPRAISER DISCUSSION (Conference):

    VII. SITE REPORT VALUATION:

    VIII. OFFER TO SELL:

    IX. REVIEWER'S CONCLUSIONS AND RECOMMENDATIONS:

    X. CONTRACT DATA:

1. Contract number:
2. Date of Contract:
3. Time Element:
4. Date Received:
5. Appraisal Fee:
   BY_____
   CONCURRED_____

Some actual examples of detailed narrative appraisal reviews—approvals—disapprovals are shown under Chapter Five 'Reviewer's Final Decision Or Recommendation".

This type of review is the ultimate type of review, and is only made on full detailed narrative appraisal reports, or substantial properties for important acquisition or disposal purposes and on those which may involve controversial, litigation or eminent domain proceedings.

Minimum Review Requirements

At a minimum, the review process should include an initial review for appraisal content and technique and where considered essential or feasible, a field review of the subject property including relevant market and economic data. During either of these steps, the reviewer may request supplemental data for clarification, further substantiation or corrections from the appraiser, which is then made a part of the original report and must be included as part of the field review. Where a field review is made, it is advisable, if possible, to have the appraiser accompany the reviewer—much more can be accomplished and questions resolved on the spot rather than "second hand". Telephone discussions between the reviewer and the appraiser are also advisable for clarification and should be followed by supplemental data from the appraiser. The appraisal review is normally not completed until all supplemental data has been obtained and reviewed. In some cases, a review can be completed subject to receiving the requested data which has previously been agreed upon and corroborated between the parties.

Other Data Utilized By The Reviewer

There is considerable data which the reviewer may have in his own "data plant" in the organization files, other reliable sources, previous planning reports on subject site or vicinage sites, his own knowledge and experience in the area which can be beneficially used by the reviewer in the course of his review. This is important, especially if there is any question about any of the factors or decisions reached in the appraiser's report and can also be used to "bolster" the appraiser's conclusions or estimates or vice-versa—if the appraisal is weak.

It is perfectly permissible to use whatever information he may have to further substantiate or refute any conclusions reached, providing that he can fully substantiate and justify his opinions with factual data.

When A Second Appraisal Is Obtained

The procedure normally used when it is necessary to secure a second appraisal is to separately review the second appraisal, independently as was done on the first appraisal) in its entirety and then prepare a separate or consolidated joint reviewing statement of both appraisals. The result of this is an overall reviewing conclusion and recommendation including discussions with each appraiser and a field review of each appraisal, plus a field review conclusion. An example of such a two appraisal review is shown in Chapter Twelve, Exhibit 3.

Field Review Requirements

Any major appraisal, especially if there is any question involved, should be field reviewed. There are many in the professional reviewing field that maintain that all appraisal reports must be reviewed —let us say that this would be "ideal", however, the ideal is not always possible. There are several rules or "criteria" which apply to this theory or principle.

1. *If you have a small review or appraisal* work load and a small geographical area of coverage—not involving a lot of travel time—such may be entirely feasible and should be done in every case.

2. *Volume, time and expertise* are important factors. However, these should not eliminate the requirements for review where such is considered required or essential.

3. *Necessity is another factor* why to field review an appraisal which is approvable in all respects, just for the trip.

4. *Cost is another factor*—It costs additional funds and time to review an appraisal. This can be an important factor where there is a "high volume" of reviews being performed. It may be impossible to review every appraisal and only "spot" review particular ones or those which appear to be "out of line" or as a "performance" check.

5. *Realistic*—To, let's say, field review every V.A. or similar appraisal would not be practical—spot checks and field reviews—yes for a reason—yes.

6. *Depending upon policy* may be that all appraisals involving large monetary amounts or over certain limits must be or should be field reviewed. Even though the valuations appear to be realistic, it is suggested that all multiple-ownership projects and large monetary acquisitions "automatically" be field reviewed.

7. *Selective basis*—The best "general" basis for field review from the reviewer's personal standpoint is the selective basis. Those which the reviewer, from his review, feels that a field review is necessary or essential to satisfy his conclusions or those that are required for some special reason or another; or certain conditions are known in advance which will create problems such as serious negotiating problems, controversial prob-

lems involving highest and best use, transitional use, improvement value, etc., should be field reviewed to make a determination in the reviewer's mind as to the validity and justification of the appraiser's conclusion.

Securing Supplemental Data From The Appraiser

Occasionally, there are instances where an appraiser is uncooperative and refuses to furnish supplemental data, however, most appraisers are very cooperative and accept any reviewing comments or suggestions concerning their reports.

True—we may not have always agreed with the appraisers, as to their explanations or justification submitted in supplement, that it really answered the questions which were raised. However, they performed satisfactorily—perhaps to the best of their ability and within their professional peroggative.

Many factors in appraising are "judgment factors" and must be accepted to a "reasonable degree" by the reviewer. Although all factors must be justified and substantiated to the "fullest degree possible" by factual data. However, we must still accept the fact that appraising is not an exact science—and therefore cannot be reviewed as such.

Rule of Thumb Checks

Rule of thumb checks are of extreme importance to the review appraiser. While these are not infallible? If the appraiser varies widely from them, they can raise a signal to the reviewer. As an example where "motels" of a certain size category are selling for "let's say" five times their income and the appraiser concludes a value which "let's say" is ten times—then maybe we should investigate his conclusion more closely unless the appraiser has adequately indicated and substantiated the wide divergence in his report.

Echelon Reviewer's Securing of Additional Data

In the case of the echelon reviewing system, the reviewer at a higher echelon who takes exception to a report should go directly to the appraiser for additional data and not back to the previous reviewer. Once a review is completed at a particular echelon, that is completed staff action. However, an information copy of any disagreements should be sent to the lower echelon.

Summary

In summarization of this chapter, the following important points were discussed.

1. Reviewing has been a regulatory requirement by most Federal Agencies, many other public and private agencies for many years.
2. Over the past 25 years or so, appraisal reviewing has developed into a highly technical sub-art of the appraisal profession, being performed by experienced reviewing professionals.
3. There are certain requirements to which the reviewer has obligations.
4. There are certain established methods or procedures under which the review process is performed.
5. There have been many requirements or regulations to be followed in review appraising, as well as varied forms or types used in reviewing.
6. The objective is to secure an approvable appraisal report.
7. Selection of the most competent qualified appraiser to do the job is an initial step.
8. Detailed appraisal contract specifications and instruction to the appraiser are of major importance.
9. Professional counseling to the appraiser, prior to and during

the course of preparation of the appraisal, is of the utmost importance.

10. The review appraiser should never act as the negotiator, except on an "advisory" basis.
11. The reviewer must always remember that he is not the Appraiser—rather, he is the "interpreter, not the performer".
12. The reviewer does not "normally" act as an expert witness.
13. The reviewer must always be practical and realistic. 14. The reviewing appraiser should always document his findings in some form.
15. The appraisal review is normally functioned under one of the following methods:
   a. Single review
   b. Echelon review
   c. Multiple person review (variation of a)
   d. Two-step method (variation of b)
   e. Citizen Review
   f. Congressional or Committee Reviews
16. Recordation of the review may be in any of the following forms:
   a. Signature of concurrence type
   b. Check sheet or form type review
   c. Exception type
   d. Combination form type review
   e. Detailed narrative type review
17. Other data available may be utilized by the reviewer in the course of his review.
18. Where a second appraisal is obtained, the second should be individually reviewed and then a "joint' review and recommendation of both made.
19. Field review is not always considered essential or required. There is certain criteria which governs this theory or principle.
20. Securing supplemental data from the appraiser or settlement of questionable items can usually be obtained.

21. Appraising is not an exact science and therefore cannot be reviewed as such.
22. Rule of thumb checks are often useful to the appraiser.
23. An "upper echelon" reviewer should not go back to the previous reviewer but rather go back to the appraiser himself for additional data.

CHAPTER FIVE

THE REVIEWER'S FINAL DECISION AND RECOMMENDATION

Introduction

In the course of a formal review of any appraisal, the final step in the reviewing process is the reviewer's final decision and recommendation, and his formal written report thereon; or other indication of his determination as a result of his review. This determination may take several different forms or types; from that of merely a determination of approval or disapproval with the signature of the reviewer, to that of the formal detailed narrative written review, or some form in between these two. This depends, to a great extent, upon the type of appraisal being reviewed and the organizational policy, requirements and regulations. However, generally these final decisions will all fall into certain classifications, which will be discussed herein.

Classification of Reviewing Decisions or Recommendations

Approved or Approval Recommended

In this instance, the appraisal was found, by the reviewer, to be acceptable in all respects; meeting contractual requirements, fully substantiated and justified of all factors and conclusions, as well as meeting sound professional appraisal principles and practices. "Approval Recommended" is the term used where higher authority or other echelons of an organization may be the final approval authority. This may also be applicable in the case where a reviewing appraiser is working on a fee or contractual basis for a principal, and he is authorized, under his contract, to only make recommendations to his principal. An example of a detailed narrative approval is shown in Chapter 9 Guidelines and Examples addenda exhibit I.

Qualified Approval or Recommendation

In this instance, the appraisal report is not approved in its entirety; in other words, a qualified complete approval. This may be applicable in a case of an appraisal comprising numerous parcels in the acquisition may not be approved; however, certain parcels are approved, and certain parcels disapproved for justifiable reasons. Another instance may be that, in the reviewers judgment, the appraisal is approved as an upper limit of value or a lower limit of value, which is a judgment determination that the appraiser has justified his valuation—to a reasonable degree, but there is some reasonable doubt in the Reviewer's mind as to fully substantiating and justifying his conclusions. Under economic circumstances, certain properties do not have a "value", but can only be valued on a "range of value" basis. In support of this theory, appraising is not an exact science. Therefore, in some cases we can only resort to a "range" as being the closest proximity we can estimate.

Non-Approval At This Time

In this instance, an appraisal report is highly questionable on being indicative of true fair market value for one of many reasons from the standpoint of the review and analysis by the reviewer.

In this event, the reviewer can disapprove the appraisal "at this time", subject to:

a. Securing additional justification and substantiation from the appraiser to support his conclusions.

b. Conditionally—subject to securing a second appraisal with a joint review of the two appraisals being made after the second appraisal is obtained.

c. Supplementing his review with information the reviewer has obtained from either his own sources and/or field review which tends to indicate a different conclusion than that the appraiser has arrived at.

The conclusion on this classification can be resolved by:

a. Additional supplemental data from the appraiser to adequately substantiate his conclusion.

b. Securing a second appraisal—in which event the final conclusion rests upon a joint review of both appraisal reports.

A qualified valuation from the reviewer is based upon his determinations of the revised value he has estimated. In this case, he actually becomes the appraiser and must be prepared to defend any changes he has made in the appraiser's valuation conclusion, and be prepared to testify as the appraiser, if litigation is involved.

Acceptable for Fee Only

Any appraisal may be acceptable as having met the contractual requirements; however, the conclusions may not have met the reviewing appraiser's and/or organizational requirements as to what they expected. Although the appraiser may have produced a product which was to the best of his ability, it may not have met his principal's full expectations. While he may have done a job which was to the best of his professional ability, there may have been some areas which could be questioned, which is the reviewer's or principal's prerogative. If he has met his contractual requirements, he is entitled to his fee, no matter whether or not he has made an appraisal which is absolutely in agreement with what the reviewer would have done or would have liked. He must be paid his fee, if he has met his contractual agreement.

Disapproval with Recommendations

An appraisal may be disapproved for any justifiable reason, by the reviewer; however, these reasons must be justified and substantiated by the reviewer beyond any reasonable doubt, and must be based upon unquestionable facts which the appraiser has not adequately justified and substantiated or where the reviewer has information or factual data which will refute the appraiser's conclusions. In no way must the reviewer disapprove any appraisal based solely upon his unsupported opinion or "seat of the pants" judgment. These recommendations on disapproval may include the following:

a. That a second contract or additional fee appraisal he obtained from an independent, unbiased appraiser on the same project property.

b. That a staff appraisal be obtained in addition to whatever has previously been done.

c. That the reviewer prepare his own appraisal, in which case he becomes the appraiser rather than the reviewer. Also, he is no longer in the position of reviewing his appraisal or valuation.

An example of this type of disapproval is shown in Chapter 10 Guidelines and Examples, Addenda Exhibit 2.

Disapproval Without Recommendations

In this instance, the appraisal report is recommended for disapproval in all respects. It has not met contractual requirements and therefore should not be accepted. Also, if not having met contractual requirements, the recommendation should be made that any fee not be paid. This classification is very rare, and should not be initiated unless the appraiser has not unequivocally met his contractual requirements, and refuses to do so after the opportunity to rectify his deficiencies has been offered to him. Whatever the reviewer may find wrong with an appraisal, in his opinion, the appraiser should be offered the opportunity to correct it or refute the reviewer's contention and questions. In no event should an appraisal be disapproved without offering the appraiser an opportunity to correct or refute the reviewer's determination. Also, the reviewer must substantiate and justify his conclusion.

Disapproval with Reviewer's Adjustments

In this instance, the reviewer generally agrees with the appraiser's findings to a limited extent. However, based upon his field review or other data available to him, he is not in full agreement with the appraiser, and adjusts the appraiser's conclusions according to his own justifiable factual data and judgment, which he must justify and substantiate and adequately explain. In this case, the reviewer, as such, becomes, to a great degree, the appraiser, since he has changed the Appraiser's conclusions. Therefore, the reviewer must be in the position to defend his conclusions and, in the event of litigation, he must be willing to testify to his findings.

Alterations of Appraisal

It is a cardinal rule that in no event may a reviewer ever alter, in any way, an appraisal made by another, without his permission—this permission should usually be in writing. In the case of minor changes, such as corrections of typographical errors, or other obvious errors, it is within the reviewer's discretion to correct these, provided he has checked with the appraiser and his determination is correct; however, he should always check with the appraiser and secure verification for all such corrections. He should also note that it has been approved by the appraiser.

Two Appraisal Reviews

In the course of the review of two independent appraisals on the same property, a major problem may often develop when two appraisers, who are considered to be professionally qualified, arrive at widely differentiated opinions of value. From the reviewer's approach, the initial step is to attempt to determine what is the major problem or difference of opinion. If it appears to be factual basis of difference, both appraisers should be consulted for confirmation of the factual data submitted, in each report, and consider reanalysis of possible changes which may have resulted since their conclusion. Judgment differences, between any two appraisers, are not usually reconcilable by reanalysis. Differences may result from different interpretations of the purpose or other concepts upon which the property is being appraised. When such differences of opinion or judgment, the reviewer is faced with a "Solomon's Decision". He must make a decision as to which appraiser has best justified and substantiated his conclusions. In all respects, and which most reasonably evaluates the property under consideration. At this point, he must also make an evaluation of each appraiser, as to their experience, capabilities on appraising such properties, and other professional factors. After his review and analysis, and determination of where the differences are, he should consult with each of the appraisers, separately or jointly, and attempt to reconcile these differences and/or make his own determination as to which is most correct or what procedure should be followed at this point. Additional information and data may be required from each appraiser to justify his conclusion. In the event the differences cannot be reconciled, the reviewer must make a decision as to whether or not an additional appraisal is required, or make his own decision as to what his conclusion of value should be and must adequately justify and substantiate his conclusions. It has been normally accepted that a differential ten percent (10%) between any two appraisals is reasonable; however, that can vary somewhat, depending upon the type of property, market conditions, and the purpose of the appraisal. An "absolute" ten percent (10%) is not, "concrete"?—It can vary one way or another from this figure.

Consolidated or Joint Reviewing Statement

Where two appraisals are obtained on a project or property, it is a recommended procedure to independently review each appraisal and prepare a report on each. Then, prepare a consolidated or joint review appraisal statement, which purpose is to reconcile the differences between the two and arrive at the reviewer's conclusion of a justifiable valuation based upon the two appraisals, field review and whatever additional information is available to the reviewer. The final conclusion or recommendation of the reviewer may or may not be one or the other conclusion of each appraiser. However, whatever conclusion the reviewer arrives at, he must fully explain, substantiate and justify his conclusion. When one appraiser has more adequately substantiated his conclusions, the reviewer will naturally tend to reach a conclusion or recommendation in the area of this valuation. However, when both have reasonably justified their conclusions, the reviewer may tend to arrive at a conclusion somewhere between the two. Whatever decision he arrives at must be fully substantiated and justified. An example of a consolidated reviewing statement of two appraisals is shown in Chapter 11 Guidelines and Examples, Addenda Exhibit 3.

Reported Different From The Appraiser By The Reviewer

In some instances, the reviewer's decision or valuation conclusion may differ from that as estimated by the appraiser. In this event, the reviewer, in effect then becomes the appraiser and not the reviewing appraiser. There may be some exceptional cases where a valuation is made up of say two or more separate elements compensable items—value for governmental use vs.. value for highest and best use. The reviewer may approve one and not the other. However, whenever the reviewer approves a valuation, substantially different from that concluded by the appraiser, he must be able to substantiate and justify his conclusion in all respects. Also, in the event of litigation, he must be prepared to testify to his conclusions.

Reviewer Not Only Dependent Upon Appraisal

In the course of his review, the reviewer is not solely dependent upon the information contained in the appraisal report for his conclusion. Other information, which may be available to him from his "data plant", as well as his own experience and knowledge of values in the area, and of the property in question, should be utilized. This information should be set forth and substantiated in his review to justify his conclusions, especially if his conclusion of value differs from that of the appraiser.

Disqualification of Reviewer

It has been said by some that a reviewer should disqualify himself from reviewing an appraisal of a type with which he has had limited or no experience. The reviewer should mainly restrict himself to reviewing appraisals of properties that he is most familiar with and experienced in. This criteria will be applicable only if he is entirely without knowledge of the methods and procedures of appraising such a property. He may not have appraised such a property himself, but he may have versed himself (secured the necessary knowledge or consulted or associated himself with an expert in the field) to be adequately qualified to make such a determination. He therefore cannot be considered as being without knowledge and be disqualified from such a review.

Furnishing The Appraiser Copies Of The Appraisal Review

This question has been raised to the association on several occasions, *on the premise* that the appraiser has the right *to know* if his appraisal has been approved or disapproved. Also, some insist that it should be the *"objective"* to *"educate"* the appraiser if his appraisal is disapproved for any reason.

National Association of Review Appraisers and Mortgage Underwriters is *in complete disagreement* with those that advocate such procedures for the following reasons:

1. Providing the appraiser has been paid for the performance of his services, it is "really" none of his or her business, whether or not the appraisal has been approved or disapproved nor should he be really that concerned.

2. Under accepted reviewing procedures, the appraiser has been advised of any questions or deficiencies and been offered the opportunity to supplement or further explain his report and in this respect he has done his job to the best of his ability—whether or not you, as the reviewer, accept it or not. The furnishing to him of a copy of the review will not add any to the conclusion at this point.

3. An appraisal review *is "confidential" in nature,* between the reviewer and his principal *"only",* and must be kept as such. Furnish the appraiser a copy of the review, after the fact of completion, would violate this trust.

4. The appraiser was hired as a competent professional, *as such,* and he has already been paid for his supposed educational and professional competence. It is not the *purpose or objective* of an appraisal review, *except in cases* where it is actually used as a *"training vehicle"* or *"performance check"* to educate an appraiser in his profession—there are "sources" from which he can secure this education, if necessary, and it is up to him to do so, not up to the organization that hires him, as a qualified appraiser for a fee.

5. There could possibly be some "legal *implications"* in furnishing the results of a *"Review"* especially a disapproval.

The current trend is to sue anyone and everyone for whatever he might say, especially if it might be implied to be "derogatory" or "impinge" upon his professional *capability* or standing, or upset him whatsoever. You are better off to let him *"sleep in his own bed"* and not unduly disturb him.

Summary

The end result, the total accomplishment, the completed work of the review appraiser, then should be a report in which he has outlined his explanation of the steps the appraiser did or did not do, or the work that he failed to perform or did incorrectly, or the conclusion which the reviewer has arrived at independently. The report should set forth an explanation by the reviewer, of why it is considered wrong and the effect this erroneous determination would have upon the conclusion reached by the appraiser. The decision which the reviewer decided to adopt will vary with the circumstances of each case, and it calls for excellent seasoned judgment by the reviewer. At the final stage, the review appraiser should sit back and look at the appraisal, as a whole, to see if a sound, justified, logical result has been arrived at. This is the last major step where the reviewer reviews the appraisal in its totality, as against all information, his findings on the field review and supplemental data. At this point, the reviewer must make a final decision as to the acceptability of the final appraisal product, and whether or not the appraiser has complied with the contract terms, specifications and instructions, as well as accepted appraisal principles and practices. In some cases, the Reviewer must make what is commonly called a "Solomon's Decision". A "nit picker," or an individual who becomes "lost" in methodology and theory (while these factors have their importance) will never make a good Reviewer. It takes a fully qualified individual who can comprehend reported data, interpret and understand its relationship to the appraised property, and who can reverify and double check its validity, to be a good reviewing appraiser and be classified as a "C.R.A." (Certified Review Appraiser). Appraising is classified as an "inexact science" and therefore must be reviewed as such by the reviewer. The reviewer's objective is to secure an approvable appraisal and not merely to act as a "disapprover" as such.

CHAPTER SIX

APPRAISAL REVIEWING ADMINISTRATION

With respect to fees for appraisal reviewing services, *"How much can I, or should 1 charge for an appraisal review?"* There are no schedules of standardized fees, as such and under today's rapid escalation in inflation, it is a difficult question.

Controversial in Nature

Fees are a rather "controversial" subject and also a very *"individual" subject.* When we say *controversial*—we mean there is really no *"standard" fee, as such,* and fees will vary from one part of our country to another. Also, some consider their professional services worth $100 per day, some $100 per hour.

Individual Nature

Each individual works in a different manner—some have a large staff, fancy office, several secretaries, etc. In other words, they have a large overhead. Some work as a *"Lone Ranger"*, perhaps his office is in his home, no full time secretary—low overhead. Also, fees will vary in different parts of our country. Therefore, probably no set pattern of fees could ever be set forth; however as a "professional", he should *be fairly compensated* for his ability, and *efforts* and *the expenses entailed.* Basically, any such fee should be based upon the following factors:

1. The individuals *time* to perform the Job.
2. *Professional qualifications* of the individual performing the services. *3. Experience* of the individual as a *Reviewing Ap-*

praiser, as well as *specialized type of experience". 4. Actual expenses involved,* other than the individual's time, typing, overhead, travel, and all other interrelated expenses which may be involved in the course of the review.

Qualifications

Another factor which probably should be considered, is that any Reviewing Appraiser, as such, should be at least equally, or better qualified, than the Appraisers he is reviewing. In other words, from this standpoint, he should be able to command at least equal or possibly a somewhat higher fee *(per day or per hour)* than the Appraiser preparing the report, which he is reviewing.

Field Review

Where a field review, in addition to an office review, is required, *or considered essential,* the time should be increased accordingly, depending upon where the property and the appraiser are located, plus travel time and expenses, and all other additional expenses hotels, meals, rental cars, etc., necessary to perform the required review.

Time Involved

As to time involved, this is also a rather open and individual question. We all work at a *different pace,* and some of us are more exacting than others; however, on an *"average"* detailed narrative appraisal, without any complications, figure at 1 1/2 to 2 days time.

This would be on a fairly "simple" property. A complicated property or purpose could go up to a week or more. This would not include any *field review.* Field review is normally figured in addition to the office review. Complicated, large appraisals could require much more time than "simple" form appraisals, as well as the fact that field reviews could be rather extensive, time consuming and costly. Reviewing of two divergent appraisals, which is complicated, would also increase the time and cost materially.

Estimate of Reviewing Cost or Fees

When a reviewing assignment is offered to a reviewer, he should make an estimate of time and costs, in order to give the client a figure for which he will perform the services. This should be completed in advance of accepting any assignment. There are some cases where there may be a "flat fee" for reviewing particular properties or the reviewer is doing *"continuing contract work"* with a principal who merely approves his "billing" under prearrangements. However, for his own benefit, every Review Appraiser should make a *pre-estimate of costs and fees* to be charged, for his own records. This will also assist him in what he should charge on similar jobs in the future. In other words, keep a record of every job you have done—what you originally estimated the cost to be—what the actual costs were, how much time you spent on it, and how much you made for yourself. This will give you a "criteria" *or basis* upon which to charge for similar jobs.

Form For Estimating Reviewing Costs

A "form" or outline to estimate the cost can be of great assistance in connection with a reviewing assignment. This can be altered, depending upon the particular conditions and the requirements of the assignment. However, it is a "basis" upon which you can work. Reference is made to Exhibit A "Appraisal Review Cost Estimate".

Proposal for Reviewing Services

Many organizations, especially governmental bodies, are required by regulation *to secure proposals* from two or more prospective reviewing appraisers for a particular assignment, from which they will choose the reviewing appraiser to prepare the review. The proposal made by the reviewer, is usually required to be in writing, indicating the *fee to* perform their services, the *time* element of completion, and possibly other factors, including the *qualifications of the reviewer.* Often times, the organization will call prospective reviewers in advance of a formal request for a proposal to find out their *availability interest* in making a written proposal.

In making any proposal, there are certain elements or factors which the reviewer should be cognizant of, before he submits a written proposal.

1. Type of appraisal to be reviewed - detailed narrative, short form, or other type
2. Number of appraisals or parcels involved
3. Type of property involved
4. Location of property and appraiser
5. Whether or not a field review is required
6. Type and extent of review required—detailed formal narrative type review or something lesser.
7. Time element allowed for completion - it is unconscionable to take assignment if your current work load is such that you could not complete the assignment in the allotted time period.
8. Who is to pay the fee, and when? The Attorney? His Client? The Organization requesting? Or someone else? How long will I have to wait for my money? Upon delivery? When the case is settled? When the project is approved? Or what?

These are all questions which the reviewer should have answered to his satisfaction prior to making any proposal. Unless you are knowledgeable on the appraisal requirements of the principal requiring the review, it may be advantageous to go to the principal's office, take a quick perusal of the appraisal and *discuss* their specifications for the review, prior *to submitting any* . This will greatly assist the reviewer in setting his fee and deciding if he wants the assignment, or is in a position to perform it at that time. Proposals are *not always accepted* upon the basis of the *lowest fee*. Many organizations will base their acceptance on the following criteria:

1. *Amount* of fee
2. Qualifications of the appraiser or reviewer
3. *Time element* in which the reviewer can perform the assignment

In explanation of this, you may have submitted the lowest fee, however, one of the other reviewing appraisers may be considered to be better *qualified* for the particular assignment, or *your time element may be too long* to meet their *"deadline"*, and the assignment would then be given to one of the other prospective reviewers and can be justified by them, irrespective of your lower fee.

EXHIBIT A

(Prepared by the reviewer)
ESTIMATE OF THE APPRAISAL REVIEWING COST

Project:
Location of Property and Address:
Reviewed For:
Number of Parcels or Reports:
No. Improved _____ No. Unimproved_____
Type of Property Involved:_____
Special Reviewing Problems:_____
_____
Other Factors to be Considered:_____
_____
_____

Field Review Required: Yes   No

ESTIMATED REVIEWING COSTS

1. Office Review
   Reviewer _____days @ $_____ per day = $_____
2. Stenographic Work
   _____days @ $_____ per day = $_____
3. Supplies & Miscellaneous: Overhead and Other Costs
                                                 $_____

4. Field Review
   Reviewer _____days @ $_____ per day = $_____
   Estimated Travel- Cost:
   Per Diem (Hotels, Meals, Etc.)
   _____days @ $_____ per day = $_____
   Estimated Miscellaneous Costs: $_____
   Total Estimated Cost: $_____

APPRAISAL REVIEW CONTRACTING AND ADMINISTRATION

Introduction

This discussion is devoted to the professional contract reviewer, who is doing work on a fee basis for a principal, or those who *desire to secure the services* of a reviewing appraiser on a fee basis, and wish to form some type of written agreement with him.

The review appraiser and employer should have some type of agreement, *preferably in writing,* for the protection of each, as well as to setting forth and clarification of instructions as to what is required and expected of each. Such an agreement or contract, *in ,* will limit any *disagreements "after the fact"* and at least give better "legal" *protection* to the parties involved.

Where an individual is involved in a large assignment, or in one in which he wishes to be as adequately protected as possible, it is *recommended that you consult your legal counsel* for the preparation of such a contract or agreement.

Appraisal Reviewing Administration

Types of Agreements and Contracts:

1. Oral Type Agreement

This type of agreement is merely what it says it is. An agreement to perform a reviewing assignment may be conducted orally over the telephone or through a personal visit on an informal basis. Only memorandum notes are made by the parties as to what type of review is required, the time element or performance, and the fee and other important factors. This is often done in small communities on smaller reviewing assignments *where the parties are well known to each other,* have sincere trust in each other, and the principal securing the services *is familiar and satisfied with the reviewers competency and the fees he charges.* In some instances, a fee may not even be mentioned, or a standard fee is charged based upon previous agreements. This type of agreement is normally not later reduced to a written agreement - *the agreement is reached by a mere "handshake" only.* This type of an agreement is also often used where an individual review appraiser has continuously been doing all, or most, of a clients reviewing, from time to time, over a long period of time, and *both have mutually agreed as to the requirements* and *standards* of the review required and *the fees involved.* They may be rather routine types of reviews. This is not the recommended type of agreement; However, it is often done in the cases as set forth above. It is certainly *not recommended* in cases where the parties are *unknown to* each other or the *"first time around".* It can also be open to "difficult" *to resolve arguments* if disagreement develops after the fact.

2. Letter Type Agreement

It is strongly recommended that at least this type of written agreement be entered into between the parties involved. A letter from the client to the reviewer, and accepted by the reviewer, may constitute a written contract of employment. I f a client is sincere, the reviewer can almost always secure such a letter agreement, and the fundamental information as to review requirements can best be furnished by the client, rather than the reviewer. However, the reviewer *can often assist the client* in preparation of such an agreement, so that a complete agreement is reached, eliminating further questions.

This type of agreement is normally preceded by an information discussion and an informal agreement as to the requirements, fees, etc. As *a minimum,* such an agreement should include the following:

1. Parties involved
2. Appraisal to be reviewed
3. Location of property
4. Type of review required - *with details of requirements*
5. Authorization to proceed with review
6. Fee to be charged
7. Number of copies of review required
8. Time of delivery of review
9. Acceptance by Reviewer
10. Other information and authorization which may be essential to the assignment

An example of such a letter agreement is shown in Exhibit B. This example letter agreement is for a formal type of review of a detailed narrative appraisal report. An agreement for a lesser type review of a short form or form type review report would naturally require much less detailed specifications.

EXHIBIT B

EXAMPLE - Letter Type Agreement to Perform Reviewing Services

April 16th, 1986   Timbucktoo Development Corporation
Suite 10, Downtown Building
Timbucktoo, California

Mr. Jacob Smith, CRA
101 West "K" Street
Timbucktoo, California

Dear Mr. Smith:

In compliance with our informal discussion of April 15th, 1986 concerning the appraisal reviewing requirements for this organization, you are authorized to proceed in the preparation of an appraisal review in accordance with the following:

1. Appraisal report to be reviewed, dated March 15, 1986 prepared by Richard Free, contract appraiser for this organization, copy of which is enclosed herewith.
2. The property is Moonlight Building, situated at 200 21st Street, Timbucktoo, California, owned by Joe T Tanner.
3. The appraisal review you are to prepare is to be a detailed formal review - narrative type, in writing, which is to include, but is not limited to, a complete discussion, reviewing comments and recommendations concerning the following:
   a. Form and presentation of report.
   b. Conformance to acceptable appraisal principles and practices.
   c. Delineation of appraisal agreement.
   d. Scope of the appraisal investigation made.
   e. Factual data considered.

f. Analysis of techniques and data utilized by the Appraiser.

g. Reasoning and logic of the appraisal process utilized.

h. Appraisers qualifications.

i. Discussions held with the appraiser.

j. Reasonableness of the valuation conclusion reached.

k. Reviewers conclusion and recommendations.

l. Certification and signature of reviewing appraiser.

4. A field review of the property involved, as well as all comparable data utilized and other influencing factors is , the results of which are to be included in your reviewing comments.

5. Three copies of your review are to be furnished.

Both the property owner and the appraiser have been advised of your assignment, for this organization, and you are authorized to consult with either of them, as may be necessary to perform your assignment.

In accordance with our discussion of April 15, 1986, the subject review shall be submitted no later than ten days after your acceptance of this agreement. Also, your statement for reviewing services, in the amount of Five Hundred Dollars ($500.00) is to be submitted along with your review which will be paid immediately upon delivery.

Feel free to call upon me for any further information you require, or questions which you may have in the course of your review.

Your signature of approval and acceptance of this letter agreement, with date, should be inserted in the lower left hand corner on the second copy of this letter, to be returned to me, which will confirm our mutual understanding of this agreement.

Very truly yours,

TIMBUCKTOO DEVELOPMENT CORPORATION

S. Randy Tandy, Vice President
Chief Real Estate Operations

Accepted:
April 20th, 1986
By: S. Jacob Smith, CRA

Note: The reviewer should have a copy of this agreement prior to commencing work.

Formal Contract Type

The formal written contact is a *legal document* and is normally used by all Federal agencies, many other governmental agencies, and many larger private organizations. They are usually required by the organization's regulations. Quite lengthy and standard contracts are prepared by their legal counsel rather than by the reviewer.

Each agency or organization has its own form, own conditions, own specifications, own performance standards and special clauses. State agency contracts will differ from Federal agency contracts. No two agencies in the same bureaucracy will have exactly the same contract form, although many of the clauses will be similar. Most Federal Government contracts have clauses which relate to numerous Federal laws or regulations which have been passed through the years such as:

a. Covenant against contingent fees
b. Officials not to benefit
c. Buy American Act
d. Compliance with Civil Rights Act

e. Work Hours Act

f. Equal opportunity affirmative action program

g. And, many more

These contracts are often in fine print, and before signing the contract, it is extremely important that the reviewing appraiser read it very carefully and be sure that he understands each and every paragraph or clause. If he does not understand any particular clause, he should consult the agency for clarification before he signs it. This type of formal contract must be executed by the contractor/reviewing appraiser and the contracting officer who is authorized to act for the organization. The reviewing appraiser should also be certain that he or she has *received a copy of the contract,* executed by the contracting officer, for his or her own records, prior *to proceeding with the review.* The fact that the contractor/reviewer has executed the contract and returned it to the agency is not *authorization to proceed.* Many times, in the interim of sending out the contract to the contractor and execution by the agency, the agency changes its mind, changes the specifications or a long delay may be involved in securing official approval to execute or the obligation of funds for payment. There are certain items which the contractor/review appraiser should be especially cognizant of, in addition to the normal "boiler plate". They are as follows:

1. *Type of report required and specifications* for preparation—be sure they are clear and you understand them.

2. *Time element*—In connection with this, most agencies operate on certain project "deadlines" and the appraisal review is only one of the factors in the "chain" of development. The time element is thus extremely important, and the reviewer must remember that *promptness is a "must".* In the event that unforeseen circumstances develop whereby the review cannot be completed on time, the reviewer should contact the ontracting officer *well in advance*—explain the situation and see if an *extension of time* may be granted . Any extension

should be obtained in writing.

3. *Fee to be paid*—Does this include all the contractor's costs, supplies, materials, etc. ? Or is there some special contingencies or additional expenses allowed? When and how will this fee be paid?

4. Clause of condition involving confidentiality of a report. Usually, the contractor/reviewer or any of his staff is restricted *from divulging information* to anyone other than authorized representatives of the agency.

5. Conditions upon which the agency can *make changes* in the specifications, *content or scope* of the requirements *after execution* of the contract and prior to the delivery of the review.

6. Conditions of *liability and penalties* imposed upon the contractor/reviewer if *he fails to perform*—late penalty.

7. Conditions of termination of the contract in whole or in part.

8. Procedure for settlement of disputes which may arise under the contract.

9. Restrictions on assignment of contract.

There are no "standard" type specifications for appraisal reviewing, used in such contracts. Each organization's are probably somewhat different, and are "geared" to their special needs. In some cases, they use a standard contract form for services to which the specifications for the particular service is added as a part of the contract. Exhibit C includes an example of such an attached contract specification.

Other Types of Contracts

Extended Multiple Reviewing Contract

In some instances, a reviewing appraiser may be hired on a consultant type basis to do all of an organizations appraisals reviewing over an extended period of time, either on a flat fee per report, or on a per diem basis. These contracts may have an upper limit of total amount of fees over the period of the contract.

Administration is the successful ingredient of any contract or agreement for reviewing services.

1. *Timeliness*—On the part of the principal in the execution of the contract, and on the part of the contractor in completing his review.

2. *Consultation*—Availability of the contracting officer to resolve any problems or questions which the reviewer may have in connection with the performance of the review and the reviewer should take advantage of this, and use it if he does have any questions, before the execution of the contract or during its performance.

3. *Promptness*—Upon the part of the contracting officer in payment of the fee, after the review is satisfactorily completed and promptness upon the part of the reviewing appraiser in submitting his review.

EXHIBIT C

EXAMPLE—Specifications for Appraisal Report Review as Part of a Formal Contract

SPECIFICATIONS

An appraisal report review to be prepared in a professional manner from the standpoint of meeting accepted professional appraisal reviewing practices and techniques. This appraisal review and analysis, of the subject appraisal report to be reviewed, shall be made from the standpoint of its meeting established contract specifications and requirements of (NAME *of organization),* as well as conformity to acceptable appraisal practices and techniques, scope of the appraisal investigation made, factual data considered, reasoning and logic of the appraisal processes utilized, and reasonableness of the valuation conclusions reached by the appraiser.

The reviewing report is to include reviewing comments, exceptions to and/or discussion of the following major factors, but not limited thereto:

1. Form and presentation of report
2. Delineation of assignment
3. Analysis of techniques and data utilized
    a. Factual data considered
    b. Factual errors or omissions
    c. Reasoning and logic of appraisal process utilized
    d. Reconciliation and reasonableness of conclusions reached. i.e.; Adequacy of the report
4. Appraiser's qualifications
5. Field review made
6. Discussions with appraiser
7. Other valuation reports considered
8. Reviewers conclusions and recommendations
9. Appraisal contract data
    a. Contract number
    b. Contract date
    c. Time element
    d. Date received
    e. Appraisal fee
    f. Recommendation for payment of fee
10. Certification of reviewing appraiser

Summary

1. There are no standard or established "set fees" for reviewing.
2. Fees should be based on time involved; professional qualifications; experience and actual expenses involved.
3. A preliminary estimate should be made prior to accepting any assignment.
4. A low fee is not always assurance that you will be awarded the assignment.
5. An oral agreement is not the recommended type.
6. A written agreement either letter type or formal contract is preferable.
7. There are certain items in a contract which a reviewer should be especially cognizant of.

CHAPTER SEVEN

COMMON ERRORS AND DEFICIENCIES IN APPRAISAL REPORTS

Socrates said that "a knowledge of our own ignorance is the first step toward true knowledge," - and Caleridge said, "We cannot comprehend our knowledge until we first comprehend his ignorance".

The following list of common errors and deficiencies has been compiled through extensive research and survey. They were completed in the following categories:

1. Contractual
2. Data
3. Premises and Techniques
4. Report Production

Contractual

Appraisal Requests Not Clear, Complete, or Correct

The contracting officer or client may be inexperienced as to appraisal procedures or legal ramifications in complex appraisal cases and without professional help (appraisal and possibly legal) may ask for values which are not what they really want or the wording is ambiguous or data inaccurate.

Contract Specifications Not Followed

Too often appraisals are submitted that do not meet the specifications of the contract. This is due in part to the appraiser not carefully reading the contract while preparing the report.

Appraisers Not Accustomed to Client's Requirements or Procedures

Many appraisers become accustomed to writing appraisal reports for one type of client and find it difficult to meet requirements of a client requiring a substantially different type report. An example might be a condemnation attorney wanting only a "bare-bones" report for trial purposes and General Services Administration which needs a fully documented report.

Appraisers Using Less Experienced Help Without Adequate Supervision or Review

Some appraisers because of their professional designations or wide reputation are solicited for appraisals in preference to less experienced appraisers and the appraisal is then prepared by a staff member or other appraiser with apparently little, if any, review or supervision from the contract appraiser. As a result, the reports are often sub-standard for a well-qualified appraiser and the client feels gypped. The appraiser's responsibility is to thoroughly understand the contract specifications, the client's requirements and furnish a professional appraisal report. The reviewer's responsibility is to see that the contractual specifications have been substantially complied with in the report.

Failure to Offer Opportunity to Owner to Inspect Property

In appraisals for the Federal government it is necessary to offer the owner an opportunity to jointly inspect the property with the appraiser.

Failure to Include Critical Factors in Limiting Conditions

It is critical that factors be included in the Limiting Conditions those factors which affect valuation conclusions.

Data

Material Not Related to the Appraisal Problem

Appraisals are often loaded with "Chamber of Commerce" type data that the appraiser fails to relate to the subject appraisal problem. If the material is pertinent, it should be related to the subject. If not, leave it out.

Neighborhood Trends

Sufficient data should be included to indicate the neighborhood conditions and trends that would affect the present or future value of the property. This should include economic, demographic, and neighborhood analysis.

Inadequate History of the Subject Property

The historical background of a property is extremely helpful to a reader who is not familiar with the property. This background aids the reader greatly in understanding the appraiser's value conclusions.

Inadequate or Incomplete Improvement Description

Description of improvements should be such that the reader will have a good idea of the construction, conditions, and general appearance of the improvements. Good photos also tell much.

Errors in Land or Building Areas

Mistakes are frequently found in land or building areas. Care should be exercised by both appraiser and reviewer to insure the accuracy of the property areas. An example of a possible error would be of a high-rise building where the superstitious owner left out the 13th floor and the appraiser did not thoroughly check the building or plans.

Lack of Adequate Market Research

Appraisers who are after the "fast buck" frequently fail to make a thorough search of the market for sales or leases. In an active market there is little excuse for not having good current sales or leases to support the value conclusions.

Using Un-Comparable Comparables

The extreme of using inadequate comparable data is the use of comparables that are so far different from the subject that large adjustments are necessary. This is particularly hazardous in court cases as this opens the gate to wild speculations by the opposing side. The sales may be cited as having been considered but not used.

Failure to Fully Analyze Comparable Data

Even though a large number of comparables have been listed in the report, this is of little help to the reviewer without a thorough analysis and comparison of each with the subject. As an example, 20 land sales from $150.00 per acre to $1,500.00 per acre without analysis and comparison with the subject.

Different Methods of Area Measurements Between Comparables and Subject

Consistency is the key word in comparing comparable areas and the subject area - gross to gross, net to net, full floor to full floor, net rentable to net rentable. Substantial errors may result if this rule is not followed and proper adjustment made.

Inconsistent Adjustment Patterns

It is not uncommon for an appraiser to make an adjustment in one approach, say the cost approach, for some feature or lack of feature in the subject by possibly capitalizing loss of rent and completely ignoring it in the other approaches used.

To Follow Through in the Analysis on Data in the Factual

Again. Consistency is the key. Be sure the analysis of data has been reflected in the value conclusions.

Making Unsupported Adjustments

Percentage or dollar adjustments without supportive evidence is not very convincing. If at all possible, adjustments should be supported for such items as time, easements, etc. with facts and figures. If this is not possible, then convincing rationale should be furnished.

Failure to Properly Consider Restrictions

Restrictions can greatly affect values and should not be ignored or taken for granted. Windfall profits have resulted from changes in zoning. The probability of zoning changes should be carefully considered and possibly value estimates given based on present as well as probable zoning.

Legal or Title Problems Not Reflected

Any title or legal items which affect the value should be adequately researched and reflected.

Inadequate Discussion of "Highest and Best Use"

The highest and best use is the very heart of the appraisal. Probably more and greater divergencies in value conclusions result from differences in the highest and best use concepts than any other single factor in appraising. The highest and best use of some typical properties is obvious. However, if the highest and best use is considered to be something other than its original intended use or present use, it is deserving of careful study and thorough discussion.

Improvement Value Not Supportable Under Highest and Best Use

Where the highest and best use for the property calls for a use other than the current use or improvements other than the existing improvements, the improvements will usually contribute only salvage value or incur demolition costs and these estimates should be included.

Personal Property Items Included in Cost Approach

Usually only items of equipment lending support to the building are included in the building costs. Other items are listed as "Personal Property."

Inadequate Support of Costs

Items such as cost to cure, deferred maintenance or obsolescence should be supported by estimates of the appraiser from reliable cost standards or by estimates from engineers, contractors, etc.

Deficiencies in Income Items

Income and expense statements sometimes fail to include all items needed such as management, vacancy, replacement reserves, etc.

Assumption of Future Appreciation

Any future predictions of appreciation or depreciation should be supported by past trends or logical and reasonable rationale.

Inconsistencies Between the Approaches to Value

Frequently appraisers are not consistent in the approaches used relating to such factors as economic life, depreciation, net returns, etc. This obviously damages the credibility of the report and the Appraiser and should be avoided.

Inadequate Correlation

The strengths and weaknesses of each approach used should be discussed as well as reasons for not using any one approach.

Values Not Consistent With Highest and Best Use

Occasionally appraisers will use approaches to value based on a use other than the stated highest and best use. This usually occurs where there is a change of use or conversion. This should only be done as a backup to the approach based on the highest and best use and not as a substitute.

Lack of Clarity or Explanation

Often the reviewer does not understand the appraiser's rationale or reasoning. When asked, the appraiser often explains it very satisfactorily in a few words. appraisers should bear in mind that the reader may know only what is read in the report and a few words or a short paragraph can clarify much in the reader's mind.

Unsupported Capitalization Rates

With the exception of the highest and best use, probably no other factor affects the value conclusion more than the capitalization rate in the income approach.

In these times of controlled economy and fluctuating interest rates, it is of the greatest importance that the capitalization rates used be supported by the market and sound reasoning.

Using Techniques and Procedures Not Applicable To Problem

Many techniques and procedures are great tools but are fitted for specific uses and when misused can produce rather sad results. An example might be multiple regression which, if used on 1,000 properties, might produce excellent results but if used on five, could be disaster.

Relying Too Heavily on Mathematical Exercises, Formulas

Many mathematical exercises, formulas, curves, etc. have and are being written about, taught, and expounded upon. Some are good, some have limited use, and some have questionable value when presented in lectures or publications, are sometimes grabbed or to and used by appraisers who may not have a clear understanding of the technique or circumstances under which it should be used and end up with results that are far from sound. There is no substitute for sound judgment based upon research and experience; otherwise, we can be replaced by the computer. All untried theories and formulas should be tested in the fires of reason and good common sense.

Inconsistent Updating

The updated appraisal, whether a substantial change in value has occurred or not, should indicate to the reviewer that the appraiser is familiar with the current market and the current condition of the property. If there is a substantial change in value, it should be well supported. Negotiations may be in progress, the board of directors may have met and concurred in the original report, so any change must be convincing and defensible.

Report Production

Typing, Grammatical, and Punctuation Errors

The appraisal report is the appraiser's product and will be judged to a greater or lesser degree by its appearance. If the report is full of typographical, grammatical, and punctuation errors, the appraiser loses credibility, especially in the eyes of a casual reader.

Mathematical Errors

Errors in math do frequently appear in the best of appraisals. If mathematical changes have been made after the rough draft has been prepared, the figures often appear throughout the report, making it difficult to correct all of them. The appraiser should be doubly careful to check all figures and the reviewer should also check to insure no mistakes have been made.

Poorly Reproduced Copies

Reports that are poorly reproduced not only give a poor appearance but at times are difficult, if not impossible, to read. This is especially true of carbon copies. Care should be exercised by the Appraiser to have all copies neat and legible. Attractive covers are desirable but elaborate covers and logos do not hide a poor quality appraisal. In large appraisals, more than one volume makes for easier handling by the reader.

Poor Format

Some agencies develop their own format and should be followed by the appraiser. In narrative reports the one that leads the reviewer step by step in the thought process to the conclusions is the ideal. Having to flip pages back and forth and search through the report in reviewing takes time.

Poor Exhibits

Exhibits such as maps, photos, etc., are sometimes of little value to the reviewer because of the poor quality or because they are not relevant.

Maps should be prepared so the properties can be located without difficulty. Photos should be of a quality that the reviewer can have a reasonably good idea of the type, construction, and condition of the subject and comparable properties.

Summary

The results of this study will assist the appraiser in preparing a more acceptable report and aid the reviewer in distinguishing some of the most common errors and deficiencies.

In summary of some of the most common "Errors and Deficiencies":

1. Requests not clear, complete or correct.
2. Contract specifications not followed.
3. Typing, Grammatical, and Punctuation Errors.
4. Mathematical Errors.
5. Poorly reproduced copies.
6. Poor Exhibits - Quality and Relevance.
7. Poor Format.
8. Appraisers not accustomed to clients' requirements or procedures.
9. Loading appraisal with "Chamber of Commerce" type data without relating factual data to subject.
10. Inadequate history of property.
11. Errors in land or building areas (no 13th floor).
12. Failure to properly consider zoning or potential zoning and other restrictions affecting value.
13. Inadequate discussion of "highest and best use".
14. Not adequately searching market for sales and leases.
15. Using comparables too far afield in size and use, which in

condemnation, can open gate to wild speculation.
16. Failure to fully analyze and adjust all comparable data.
17. Abundant sales or rental data with little or no discussion relating these to the "subject".
18. Not using same methods of measurement between comparables and subject and the method used should be clear and concise.
19. Inconsistent adjustment patterns.
20. Relying on mathematical exercises, formulas, curves; i. e., regressions, Stanford learning curves, Dilmore depth curve, etc.
21. Failure to follow through in the analysis on data in the factual presentation.
22. Values derived on assumptions not consistent with the highest and best use statement.
23. Inconsistencies between cost, market, and income approaches relating to economic life, depreciation, net returns, etc.
24. Making unsupported adjustments; i.e., time, for easements, etc.
25. Using techniques and procedures not appropriate to the problem.
26. Capitalization rates not current or adequately supported from market.
27. Lack of clarity or explanation of appraiser's reasoning or procedures.
28. Appraisers using less experienced help without adequate supervision or review.
29. Updating inconsistent with the original findings.
    a. Going through the motions of updating without making any changes.
    b. Making substantial changes with weak justification.

CHAPTER EIGHT

APPRAISAL PURPOSE AND THE REVIEWER

Introduction

Appraisal reports often follow a standardized format which has been developed to demonstrate that the appraiser has considered all of the factors which may be pertinent to the value conclusion. The reviewer must be cognizant of the problem which may arise due to the report format being more standardized or general than the nature of the appraisal problem itself. The reviewer must hold foremost in the review process a conceptualization of the purpose or objective which motivated the report as well as a framework of analysis which is designed on the specific characteristics of the problem at hand. This chapter presents two ways of looking at the review process. The first is an informal topology of the various motivations and objectives inherent in the appraisal process. This approach attempts to point out some of the common analytic pitfalls associated with different types of appraisal situations. The second approach involves a more formal treatment of the nature of the risk faced by real estate investors.

Scope of the Appraisal Process

The historical distinction between appraisals, as an estimate of the fair market value, and the feasibility study, as a more comprehensive analysis of the financial and market viability of a proposed project or major acquisition, has become increasingly blurred in recent years. The majority of recent appraisal assignments have included elements of feasibility analysis or full scale feasibility studies within appraisals of proposed developments and acquisitions.

During this period, which saw the typical appraisal report take on added complexity, another trend has been quite pronounced, namely the increasing participation in the market by institutions organizations who are generally involved in large scale real estate investments. As this group is currently the focus of appraisal review activity, and as the group is more than likely to be involved with projects which require feasibility type analysis as well as traditional appraisals, the focus of this chapter will be on this expanded definition of the appraisal process. Therefore, the term appraisal report will be considered to include the concept of feasibility analysis. In the same vein, the terms appraiser and analyst will be used interchangeably throughout the chapter.

Types of Appraisal Reports and Concerns of the Reviewer

A list of the various types of appraisal reports a reviewer might encounter would be too cumbersome to deal with in the scope of this chapter. Instead, a typology is offered which groups appraisal activity according to the overall purpose which is served by the investigation. While by no means exhaustive, such a typology might included our categories: Financial Reporting, Financial Decision-Making, Litigation and Investment Decision-Making. Working within this typology the reviewer must ascertain that the special nature of any given appraisal assignment has been treated successfully. Included below are a series of points the reviewer should keep in mind when dealing with the various types of reports.

Financial Reporting

Reports are often generated to comply with requests or requirements of regulatory agencies such as the Securities and Exchange

Commission, State Commissioners of Corporations, and State Departments of Real Estate. For example, blind pool syndicates and real estate investment trusts are often required to file independent appraisals of their property acquisitions. Requirements of the SEC may lead to reports being generated during the course of mergers and acquisitions by publicly-held companies. In the case of regulatory reports, the reviewer must make certain that the content and format of the report meet regulatory requirements. Such agencies are notorious for developing reporting formats which could baffle the mind of Solomon and try the patience of Job. Despite this problem, the reviewer is responsible for insuring that the client is not deterred or delayed from its objectives by errors of form. It is not safe to assume that the analyst has met the proper guidelines: the reviewer must determine that this has been done. Many public agencies request data which is far different from that found in the standard report format. The reviewer must determine that all of the data requested, if available, has been supplied . The analytic processes and conclusions in regulatory reports flow from objectives which are quite unlike those of an investor. Regulatory agencies are charged with protection of the public; directly, by preventing misrepresentation; and indirectly, by monitoring the behavior of organizations and their principals. The reviewer should keep these objectives in mind when evaluating such a report. It is the reviewer's ethical responsibility to determine that financial and fiscal relationships contrary to public policy are not represented in a misleading manner. It is also the reviewer's responsibility to determine that the data and analysis presented in the report are legitimate and straightforward and that the conclusions are not presented in such a way as to lessen any unfavorable aspect.

Financial Decision Making

Internal use of appraisals, pricing studies, and market surveys are becoming the norm for large development organizations, as well as for non-real estate companies whose activities put them in the real estate market as a sideline.

Some typical independent reports commissioned by a large developer would include market pricing analysis, estimation of rent schedules, analysis of capital structure and selection of optimum financing techniques. The analyst plays a role in all of these activities and must often look beyond the standard analysis used in estimating fair market value. Internal reports of this nature are, by definition, unlike standard format appraisals. The reviewer should be certain that the analyst has taken into account the specific circumstances of the client organization and has incorporated them into the analysis and conclusions. The individual capital structure, operating efficiencies, tax situation, and marketing capabilities of the organization are clearly influential in the decision-making process and should be allowed for in the analysis.

In the case of acquisitions and mergers, the acquiring firm often needs to determine the value of newly acquired assets and then must make decisions regarding their retention, disposition, or financial restructuring. Real property holdings of this type are subject to strategies which are not those of the ordinary investor. Again, the analysis must be cast in the organizational context and should speak to the unique characteristics of the situation. Perhaps the greatest service that the analyst and the reviewer can provide such a client is the ability to combine the insights gained from standard format work with those engendered by the specific context of the assignment.

Litigation

The number of possible types of analysis required in litigation is limited only by the range of litigious behavior in our society.

There are civil actions regarding historical values, partial damages, adherence to contractual terms and many others. Governments enter the picture through condemnation, property and income tax disputes, and many other areas. The legal arena is one which often requires that the analysis be carried out under a set of suppositions which are highly artificial and potentially misleading. This is one area in which the reviewer's role could be critically important yet often goes unfilled. Attorneys for litigants often rely on an analyst's report without having it reviewed by a competent professional. There are two aspects of the litigation appraisal process which are extremely important. First, the analyst is expected to uncover data, analyze it, arrive at conclusions, and present the supporting arguments skillfully and forcefully. It is a fact, however, that any three analysts can, and often do, arrive at three different conclusions. Second, the litigation process is an adversary one, and the attorney must expect that the conclusions of any given analyst are subject to disputation. Because of this situation, the reviewer should be involved in this process on two fronts. First, as in any review situation, he or she should render a judgment regarding the validity and suitability of the analysis. Second, and perhaps more important, the reviewer should be able to provide the attorney with a concise statement on the likely alternatives to the analysis which might be presented, an outline of their rationale, and an independent opinion as to their relative merits. This is not to say that the analyst or reviewer should forsake independence, but that the reviewer should provide a comprehensive analysis of the potential viewpoints which may be at odds with the analyst's.

Investment Decision Making

The realm of investment decision-making with respect to real property assets encompasses the greatest variety of appraisal and analysis. Investors, both individual and institutional, require analysis to make purchase and sale decisions. Developers require feasibility studies, both market and economic. Developers also frequently look for advice on development configuration, staging, expected absorption rates, and many other forms of input to the investment decision. Another type of investor, the Lender, typically makes *NO* investment decision regarding real estate without some form of analysis by the appraiser. The lender's viewpoint is radically different from the developer's, even though they look at the same transaction or development. The needs of the lender require different assumptions about the market, the local economy, and the viability of any given product. In order to determine the proper elements of the appraisal analysis, characterize the nature and extent of the risk faced by the investor. Risk is the basic concept of investment analysis, and can be separated into various categories depending on its nature. The reviewer, by reference to the specific nature of the risk in any given investment, can then determine if the analysis speaks directly to the relevant factors which influence the amount of risk of the investment and by extension, the expected rates of return and the project's present value.

Specifically, the analyst and the reviewer need to be concerned with *market risk, operating risk,* and the *degree of risk concentration.* Due to the number of possible combinations of these three factors and their possible categorizations, the information about them is presented in matrix form in the following tables.

Table 1 and Table 2 (see page 131) depict the combination of Market and Operating risk levels and the Degree of Risk Concentration in several types of real estate development. Table 1 deals with lender participants in such projects, while Table 2 deals with investor participants of several types in the same projects. As used in the tables, the definition of market and operating risk vary somewhat. In the case of lender participants, market risk is defined as the probability of loss under conditions of lack of marketability of the proposed project. In the case of lenders, the concept of loss is assumed to be synonymous with default. Each type of lender represented in the table has a characteristic risk exposure in each type of project which is described as low or high to indicate the probability of such a loss due to lack of marketability. In the case of investors, the probability of loss due to market risk is based on a concept of loss which ranges from suboptimal

Table 1

LENDER PARTICIPANT

KEY

	Market Risk
	Operating Risk
	Degree of Risk Concentration

PROPERTY TYPE	CONSTRUCTION LENDER	TAKEOUT LENDER	SWING LENDER
Single Family Homes	High, High, Concentrated	Low, Low, Dispersed	High, High, Concentrated
Condominiums	High, High, Concentrated	Low, Low, Dispersed	High, High, Concentrated
Apartments	Low, High, Concentrated	High, Medium, Concentrated	High, High, Concentrated
Office Buildings	Low, High, Concentrated	High, Low, Concentrated	High, High, Concentrated
Office Buildings w/Major Tenants Committed	Low, Medium, Dispersed	Low, Low, Dispersed	Low, High, Dispersed
Retail Commercial	Low, High, Concentrated	High, Low, Concentrated	High, High, Concentrated
Retail Commercial w/Major Tenants Committed	Low, Medium, Dispersed	Low, Low, Dispersed	Low, High, Dispersed
Industrial	Low, High, Concentrated	High, Low, Concentrated	High, High, Concentrated
Industrial w/Major Tenants Committed	Low, Medium, Dispersed	Low, Low, Dispersed	Low, High, Concentrated

Table 2

KEY: Market Risk / Operating Risk / Degree of Risk Concentration

PROPERTY TYPE	EQUITY PARTICIPANT		JOINT-VENTURE PARTNERS		LAND LEASE HOLDERS	
	DEVELOPER	INVESTOR	INVESTOR	SUBORDINATED LANDOWNER/ PARTNER	UNSUBORDINATED	SUBORDINATED
Single Family Homes	High, Variable Concentrated	High, High Concentrated	High, High Concentrated	Same as Investor	Low, High Concentrated	High, High Concentrated
Condominiums	High, Variable Concentrated	High, High Concentrated	High, High Concentrated	"	Low, High Concentrated	High, High Concentrated
Apartments	High, Variable Concentrated	High, High Concentrated	High, High Concentrated	"	Low, High Concentrated	High, High Concentrated
Office Buildings	High, Variable Concentrated	High, High Concentrated	High, High Concentrated	"	Low, High Concentrated	High, High Concentrated
Offices w/Major Tenants Committed	Low, Medium Dispersed	Low, Medium Dispersed	Low, Medium Dispersed	"	Low, Medium Dispersed	Low, Medium Dispersed
Retail Commercial	High, Variable Concentrated	High, High Concentrated	High, High Concentrated	"	Low, High Concentrated	High, High Concentrated
Retail Commercial w/Major Tenants Committed	Low, Medium Dispersed	Low, Medium Dispersed	Low, Medium Dispersed	"	Low, Medium Dispersed	Low, Medium Dispersed
Industrial	High, Variable Concentrated	High, High Dispersed	High, High Dispersed	"	Low, High Concentrated	High, High Concentrated
Industrial w/Major Tenants Committed	Low, Medium Dispersed	Low, Medium Dispersed	Low, Medium Dispersed	"	Low, Medium Dispersed	Low, Medium Dispersed

returns to default and total loss of investment. Market risk is the first entry in each of the boxes found in the tables. Operating risk is defined as the probability of loss due to instability in the financial condition of the principal or the inability or failure of the principal to perform as expected. In the case of lenders, loss is assumed to be synonymous with default, while an investor's loss could range from suboptimal returns to default and total loss. Operating risk is the second entry in each of the boxes found in the tables. The degree of concentration of both types of risk is expressed as a composite ranging from concentrated to dispersed. This is essentially the number of eggs in one basket argument. Concentrated risk would indicate that the investor or lender's participation rides on a single entity and that entity's response to market and internal conditions. Dispersed risk would indicate that the participant can rely on a large number of factors, each subject to varying degrees of operating risk or market risk. The Degree of Risk Concentration is the last entry in each of the boxes. A comprehensive example would be; from Table 1, a comparison of two lenders' risk exposure in two projects, a condominium development and an apartment building. In the case of the condominium, the construction lender faces high market risk because the construction loan typically remains in force until the units are sold and individual escrows are closed (with a commensurate reduction in construction loan principal). The construction lender faces a high operating risk because the stability of the loan during the construction and sales process is dependent on the financial health and business vitality of the developer. For the same reason, the construction lender's risk is concentrated in the developer and dependent on his ability to run a healthy business, successfully complete construction, and sell the units. By contrast, the condominium takeout lender's position is one of relatively low market risk since funds are not advanced until the units are sold, and operating risk is spread across the individual buyers and their personal financial condition which is subject to scrutiny at the time of advancing the takeout. Also, the risk is dispersed on the operating side by the above, and to some degree on the market side since the lender can expect that individual unit owners will have different tenure horizons so that a defaulted unit can be introduced into an orderly market flow. In the case of apartment buildings, the construction lender faces a relatively low market risk so long as the takeout is conditional only upon the issuance of a certificate of occupancy. In recent years, however, it has become increasingly common for takeout lenders to require a fixed percentage of accomplished rent-up before advancing the takeout. In this case, both construction and takeout lenders share the market risk. The in Table 1 do not assume such arrangements. The operating risk to the construction lender is high since the conditions are the same as in the condominium project with respect to the lender's reliance on the strength and ability of the developer. By the same token the lender's risk is concentrated in the developer. The apartment takeout lender faces a high market risk in the absence of a rent-up clause, since there is some probability of funding a loan on an empty apartment building with uncertain rental prospects. It is assumed that the operating risk to this lender is moderate since the lender has the opportunity to make a careful scrutiny of the project and the developer at the time of the loan commitment. The risk is concentrated since the lender can look only to the owner/developer whose performance under the loan is subject to factors extraneous to the encumbered property.

Due to the differing nature of the exposure to market and operating risk, as well as the different degrees of concentration of risk, each type of project and each type of participant requires careful analysis of certain critical points before making a decision. The nature of these critical points changes with the level and concentration of each type of risk. Following is a brief discussion of these critical points under the various risk conditions.

High Operating Risk:

The analysis should contain a heavy component which is borrower or investor specific, as well as project specific. Projected absorption rates, project cash flow projections, developer track records, and the financial and operating history of comparable projects should be major features of the analysis.

High Market Risk:

The analysis should be project relying heavily on analysis of market feasibility, pricing schedules and their competitiveness, projected absorption rates, project compatibility with the existing market, and potential resale behavior.

Concentrated Risk:

The critical points here are project and/or investor specific. The emphasis in analysis of high market risk and high operating risk situations is also equally relevant to a situation of high concentration.

Dispersed Risk:

Evaluation of dispersed risk situations needs to be heavily market specific rather than project specific. Near term and intermediate term economic trends which will impact nationally or locally on the relevant buyer or borrower group need to be analyzed carefully and expanded beyond the standard brief introductory sections of the typical appraisal/feasibility report. In the case of dispersion achieved through the lease guarantee of a regional or national tenant, the analysis should include careful review of the tenant's financial statements. The study of trends in the tenant's industry is also recommended. In the more general case, careful attention must be paid to industry-wide or regional demand and supply analysis for the product in question, be it homes or storefronts. Many lenders and investors have lost substantial investments in projects which were "perfect" from the standpoint of the strength of the developer and the marketability of the product because they failed to apprehend the near-term future for the market in its entirety.

Low Market Risk and Low Operating Risk:

For any number of reasons, a specific investment may enjoy low market risk, low operating risk, or both. It is the reviewer's task to be certain that such a characterization is legitimate, and that the analyst's report or the reviewer's evaluation contain a discussion of the reasons for, and a justification of that characterization.

Summary

It is the reviewer's role to provide insight and evaluation. Merely checking off the contents of a report against a standard format worksheet does not fulfill the demands of this role. Rather, the reviewer must think carefully about the particular nature of the appraisal assignment and the motivations and objectives of the client organization. The reviewer must determine that the report does, in fact, speak to these particular circumstances to the same degree that it meets general standards of value analysis. Beyond the level of objectives and motivations, one of the reviewer's most powerful tools is the ability to analyze the nature and extent of risk faced by the client organization. Only by fully understanding the risk can the reviewer determine if the report answers relevant questions and examines the critical variables.

While the standardized report format has done much to spread professional standards throughout the industry, it can be dangerously misleading in the absence of careful consideration of all of the specifics of the appraisal situation.

CHAPTER NINE

ENVIRONMENTAL CONCERNS FOR THE REVIEW APPRAISER

In recent years environmental problems have become a major factor in real estate valuation. Virtually any property, should it be found to have an environmental problem, can become worthless or even a major liability to it's owner, the lender, or anyone involved in the sale or ownership of the property. It is no longer uncommon for a $200,000 property to have a $1 million environmental hazard. The review appraiser must become familiar with the various types of environmental problems as well as with the information and terminology used in environmental assessment reports. The reviewer should also know how to resource information about a property if none is presented with the appraisal. As growing concerns about these issues cause the parties involved in a real estate transaction to insist on environmental data, the appraiser must be prepared to help provide it. The Environmental Assessment Association was formed to provide real estate professionals, such as Review Appraisers, with a resource for information and education. The following information is excerpted from some of their publications. The Environmental Assessment Association has defined the different levels of Environmental Inspection as follows:

Phase 1: Present condition of the site and signs of possible spills, discharge, use and storage of hazardous waste, and other signs are included in a Phase 1 Inspection. These are obtained through a visual inspection. Some clients may ask for or require other information which may include a review of available documents and information regarding the property.

If information or visible signs indicate that an environmental hazard may exist or a problem has previously occurred, then a Phase 2 **audit** should be conducted. No laboratory tests are used in the Phase 1 Inspection.

Phase 2: Following a Phase 1 inspection a determination will have been made, through direct observation and readily available means, if there is a likelihood that hazardous materials are or have been on the property or if releases of these materials have or are occurring. A Phase 2 Environmental Audit involves a sampling of on-site materials and laboratory testing. The recommendation to start a Phase 2 audit depends on several important factors. It will be up to the judgement of the Environmental Inspector as well as the parties involved in the transaction when suggesting further investigation and testing. Some of the factors that need to be considered are:

- the nature of the property
- the quantity and quality of the information available from the Phase 1 inspection - the strength of the evidence that hazardous materials did or currently exist on the property - the likelihood that humans or the environment were or are being exposed to hazardous materials

A Phase 2 level of Environmental Inspection concentrates on determining the occurrence or presence of an environmental hazard. It can be time consuming and expensive so carefully consider all the appropriate factors before making a decision.

Phase 3: The Phase 3 Environmental Audit measures the extent of the environmental hazard and its impacts on the property and human safety. Tests on surface water, ground water and soil are usually performed. Cleanup processes are also recommended in this phase. Real estate transactions are being subjected to increasing scrutiny regarding the presence of hazardous substances and their potential liabilities and cleanup costs. Failure to provide this scrutiny has left many lenders and property owners with the cost of addressing conditions of which they were totally unaware and which they did not cause. Land that has a high potential for hazardous materials problems include industrial and manufacturing properties, land fills, railroad yards, oil field and refinery areas, gas stations and dry-cleaning facilities, vehicle maintenance shops and agricultural land.

Many residential properties have been built on land that once was used for other purposes and may contain hazardous materials. In addition, many residential properties are near enough to a contaminated property or a source of contamination that there may be hazardous materials present caused by leaking, runoff, discharge or seepage through soil over a period of time. The Comprehensive Environmental Response, Compensation and Liability Act of 1980 (CERCLA), also known as Superfund, was created to provide the authority and a source of funding for cleaning-up hazardous materials released into the environment. The Superfund Amendments and Reauthorization Act of 1986 (SARA) contains provisions defining who is liable to pay for cleanup of contamination caused by past activities. The current legislative, regulatory and judicial climate has provided notice to property buyers, developers and lending institutions of the environmental risks associated with purchasing property. In some cases, the cost of cleaning-up a hazardous waste site can far exceed the value of the property. This risk, as well as the "innocent purchaser" defense established by SARA, has created the need for special, professional assessments of environmental conditions at the time of each real estate transaction. Buyers, sellers and lenders need to be aware of liability provisions outlined under CERCLA/SARA and must take appropriate steps to satisfy the elements of the innocent-purchaser defense or, where contamination is found, to obtain data for negotiating the costs associated with cleanup within the terms of the transaction. A Phase One Environmental Inspection can provide the information needed to satisfy these requirements, at a fraction of the cost of the potential liability. A Phase I environmental inspector can pinpoint problem areas and recommend further inspection or the inspector may find no evidence of environmental contaminants. CERCLA defines four categories of persons who are financially responsible for hazardous waste cleanup:

- Present owners & operators
- Past owners & operators
- Transporters of hazardous substances
- Generators of hazardous substances

In addition, recent court cases and rulings have shown others to be at risk with regard to responsibility for environmental problems. These have included persons and companies providing appraisals, home inspections and title information. Also at risk are past and present lien holders and persons or companies involved with any business operated from the property. The following sections explain various types of hazardous substances and how to identify them when inspecting a property.

Hazardous Wastes:

The term hazardous substances refers to a large variety of chemical, biological, and radioactive substances. These substances pose health and safety risks to the environment, humans, vegetation and wildlife. Hazardous materials have a potential to cause contamination to a property or its surroundings should they be released into the environment by a spill, fire or intentional disposal. The improper disposal of hazardous substances can also result in contamination of soil, groundwater, or surface water.

Asbestos:

Asbestos is a mineral fiber found in rocks. There are several kinds of asbestos fibers, all of which are fire resistant and extremely durable. These qualities made asbestos very useful in construction and industry. Between 1900 and 1972 asbestos was commonly used in many kinds of buildings. In the 1970's, however, the use of asbestos was first restricted and was gradually phased out of use in building materials. It was discovered that the inhalation of asbestos fibers can cause various types of cancer, as well as asbestosis (a serious degenerative lung disease). The danger posed by asbestos is through the breathing of asbestos fibers, which most often escape into the air when "firable" asbestos begin to deteriorate on the surface it has been applied to. (Asbestos is called "firable" if it crumbles easily when subjected to hand pressure.) Although the dangers associated with the use of asbestos have been evident for quite some time, asbestos' superior fire resisting and insulating abilities practically dictated its use until very recently. Between 1900 and 1980, it has been estimated that more than 30 million tons of asbestos were used in the U.S.

Water Supplies:

There are some obvious and not-so-obvious problems that can occur with the water supply to a property. The first thing that needs to be determined is the source of the water supply - is it provided by a city water service or is it well-water. Municipal water supplies are usually safe and clean. However, some recent studies have shown that there are serious quality problems with some water supplies from municipalities. If the water is brought up from a well on or near the property, it probably will go through a filtration system but may not be as safe as municipal supplies.

Radon Gas:

Radon is a radioactive gas which is produced when certain

natural radioactive minerals break down or decay. These natural minerals are always present in the environment in slight amounts and are found in increased quantities in particular geologic deposits . Radon gas further decays into smaller particles known as radon "daughters" or progeny, which can attach to soil or dust particles in the air. As these particles are inhaled, the daughter products can be deposited on the lining of the lung and subsequently decay or emit radioactive particles. This radioactive decay damages lung tissue and causes cellular changes which may transform normal cells into cancer cells. There are certain areas of the country where the incidence of radon is very high. In the state of Pennsylvania, for example, of over 30,000 homes tested, 55% had levels of radon considered potentially dangerous. There is no way to determine which homes or buildings might have high levels of radon. Two adjacent structures can have completely different levels of radon, which is dependent on the structure of the subsurface rocks. It is believed that entry of the gas occurs through slab cracks and leaks, and through porous building materials. The highest radon readings are usually found in the lowest levels of a structure and decrease significantly on the first and second floors. Fortunately, curing a structure of radon gas is relatively easy and inexpensive once the problem has been discovered. It is simply a process of sealing the cracks and crevices that allow the gas to leak in or creating a way to vent the gas out of the structure.

Lead Based Paint:

Over the course of the past few years, the federal government has strengthened its regulation of lead products. Recognizing that lead can be extremely toxic, can impair physical and mental development of young children and can apparently lead to increases in high blood pressure in adults, the Environmental Protection Agency, the Department of Housing and Urban Development and the Consumer Product Safety Commission have moved to restrict people's exposure to lead. The presence of old lead-based paint in housing represents the most significant hazard remaining for lean poisoning, particularly for young children. The most common means of exposure is young children eating peeled and flaking pieces of paint, which is a significant problem in inner-city, lower-income areas where housing may be older and poorly maintained. Lead poisoning can also result from children having access to surfaces that have perfectly intact lead-based paint covering them, yet are chewable (e.g., door edging, banisters, etc.). It is estimated that a total of 30 to 40 million older homes around the country contain lead-based paint.

Underground Storage Tanks:

Underground Storage Tank (UST) registration is required for all tanks containing regulated substances (all petroleum products) that are not already listed as hazardous "wastes." Look for existing records or registrations with the state UST section.

Any tanks already having held one of these substances needs a site assessment and proper closure. This means an investigation into the ground below the tanks and any connected pipelines and the filling of the tank with an inert material or the removal (with inspection) to a proper safe location. Any materials held in the tanks need to be property disposed of also.

Waste Sites:

This is a broad category that incorporates quite a range of possible problems. A waste site can be defined as property engaged in storing, producing or transporting waste, chemicals or hazardous substances. The inspector must determine if a property not only is being used as a waste site, but if there is any visible environmental damage as a result of this use.

Polychlorinated Biphenyls - (PCB'S)

Polychlorinated Biphenyls are toxic molecules, which when ingested, attach themselves to human fat tissue and act as possible carcinogens. There is little evidence that PCB's are harmful to humans unless they are ingested. Most often PCB's are found in electrical equipment such as transformers, ballasts in fluorescent lighting, circuit breakers and switch gears. PCB's may also exist in hydraulic fluids found in heavy equipment. The danger of PCB's develops when the oils or fluids containing the PCB's leak out and contaminate the soil and ground water when they are no longer in use. If the equipment is in good condition and the PCB's are contained within it, there is little danger to humans.

There are many things that may be considered as environmental hazards which don't fit easily into specific categories. Some of these would include abandoned vehicles or heavy equipment, abandoned buildings, the storage or disposal of any quantity of anything which may be composed of or contain hazardous materials. Keep in mind that it is often only large numbers or quantities of objects or materials that pose a hazard.

PART II

**Review Appraisal
Guidelines
and Examples**

CHAPTER TEN

DETAILED APPRAISAL REVIEW AND APPROVAL

EXHIBIT 1:

EXAMPLE: DETAILED APPRAISAL REVIEW AND APPROVAL

Appraisal Review and Analysis

Mr. Joseph Nelson
General Manager
Real Estate Division

In compliance with your request, and in accordance with my authority, I have carefully reviewed the attached appraisal report which covers 109,798 square feet of vacant land situated on North Adams. Subject report as of June 1, 1986 was prepared by: John Doe, an Associate Appraiser of Denver, Colorado   I have reviewed the subject report from the standpoint of meeting established specifications and requirements, as well as conforming to acceptable professional appraisal practices and techniques; scope of the appraisal investigation; factual data considered; reasoning and logic of the appraisal process and reasonableness of the valuation conclusion of: $680,000.00.

Form and Presentation:

This appraisal meets all Contract Requirements, as well as accepted appraisal standards for analytical narrative appraisal reports.

Deliniation of Assignment:

The appraiser's have adequately delineated the purpose of the report; described the property; substantiated the highest and best use; and set forth limiting conditions and assumptions. The following assumptions are recited as being of major importance in connection with the valuation:

(I) That Rio Grande Drive will be properly graded and surfaced. Concrete curbs and gutter, will be installed by others.

(2) That all required utilities will be provided to the site, at the cost of seller.

(3) That the rear terraced portion and steep embankment on the site is not usable.

(4) A 15' sewer line traverses the site, which is not defined or a recorded easement, and it is assumed any such right of way to be fifteen feet in width.

(5) That there is no adverse soil conditions.

Factual Data Considered

The Appraiser's have adequately presented and considered the economics, general area, trends and environmental influences of the area and neighborhood. Subject is situated in an outlying neighborhood which is mostly vacant land. Local governmental planning is attempting to shift governmental and commercial interests to this area, away from the downtown tourist oriented area. The population has doubled in the past five years, and the local government rewrote the zoning manual to control and limit the growth, which has affected development. The energy crisis has also created a moratorium on natural gas hookups, which restricts developments. The subject adjoins an existing sewer plant which is a detrimental influence. However, it is expected that the use of this plant will be phased out in the not-too-distant future. The existing zoning is for service, commercial and industrial use which is also a specially planned area. The highest and best use determined by the appraiser was to be for commercial usage in nature, which is concurred by the review. The unusable rear area has been estimated by the appraiser to be approximately 30,445 square feet, or approximately 28% of the total site area. No mineral value was indicated.

Factual Errors or Omissions

No computational or other factual errors or omissions were noted.

Reasoning and Logic of Appraisal Process Utilized

The valuation of subject property has been based upon off site improvements installed at the cost of others. The appraiser also went into the history of subject ownership, which indicated a sale at $2.45 per square foot on the total acquisition of 19.546 acres; a sale of 8.082 acres of the larger ownership at $5.43 per square foot in September of 1983 and another sale of 11.496 acres in September of 1973 at $3.49 per square foot. The appraisers have also taken cognizance of a pending sale of a corner parcel located adjacent to the subject for a super market, at a reported price of $8.25 per square foot, comprising of 2 acres. The appraisers have eliminated the cost and income approaches as being inapplicable, which is concurred in. A diligent search of the market was made, and some 36 sales indices were utilized in the market approach to value. These sales indicated a range of $2.45 to $22.67 per square foot in the period of 1980 to 1985 of site areas comprising .07 to 19.54 acres.

Because of location and size, it was their opinion that the subject tended toward the lower indicators.

After careful comparative analysis with the subject and after utilizing "bracketing procedures", the appraiser narrowed this range to $2.45 to $8.93, and further to $5.43 to $8.50 per square foot. This analysis was carefully done and the conclusions are concurred in by the reviewer.

The appraiser segregated the site area into three categories:

A. —Level usable area.
B. —Steep upper terrace—unusable area.
C. —Sewer Main Right-of-Way area.

From the analysis they have made, the appraisers concluded the following valuation, under their initial premise:

A. —$8.00 per square foot = $592,824.00
B. —$2.00 per square foot = $60,890.00
C. —$4.00 per square foot = $21,000.00
                          TOTAL $674,714.00

A rationale under "C" was that the right-of-way area surface could be utilized for parking purposes A second premise was used whereby the cost of relocation of the sewer line was considered. This indicated the following valuation:

Area's A & C @ $8.00 per square foot	$634,824.00
Area B at $2.00 per square foot	$ 60,890.00
Subtotal	$695,714.00
Less the estimated cost of	
relocating the sewer line	$10,000.00
Total	$685,714.00

The relocation cost of $10,000.00 was based upon an estimate obtained from a contractor and appears to be adequately justified. In the final analysis, the appraisers concluded a valuation of $680,000.00 for an average value of $6.19 per square foot.

Reconciliation and Reasonableness of Conclusion Reached

From my reviewing analysis, it is my considered judgment

that the estimated valuation of $680,000.00 is a fair and reasonable estimate of the property's probable market value.

Adequacy of Report

It is my opinion that this appraisal is adequate for the purpose intended.

Appraisers Qualifications

The appraiser's are indicated to be well qualified and experienced in the appraisal of such properties in this area, and the quality of their report so indicated.

Field Review

None made.

Appraiser Discussion (Conference)

None considered necessary.

OFFER TO SELL

The owners have offered the subject property at $800,000 which indicates an overall per square foot price of approximately $7.29.

REVIEWER'S CONCLUSIONS AND RECOMMENDATIONS

A. It is my recommendation that the appraised valuation of $680,000.00 be approved as being fair and just compensation for the subject property, including all off-site streets and utilities.

B It is recommended that the Appraisers fee of $1,500 be paid as having satisfactorily met contract requirements.

CONTRACT DATA

1. Contract Number	06-9218-75-PT41
2. Date Of Contract	July 7th, 1986
3. Time Element	60 Days
4. Date Received	August 5th, 1986
5. Appraisal Fee	$1,500.00

BY:_____

William S. Brown, C.R.A.
Reviewing Appraiser

DETAILED APPRAISAL REVIEW AND DISAPPROVAL WITH ATTACHED FIELD REPRESENTATIVE REVIEW FORM

EXHIBIT 2

EXAMPLE: DETAILED APPRAISAL REVIEW AND DISAPPROVAL WITH ATTACHED FIELD REPRESENTATIVE REVIEW FORM

Appraisal Review and Analysis

In compliance with your request, and in accordance with my authority, I have carefully reviewed the attached appraisal report which covers 30,643 square feet of land area, and a two story building with a basement facility of approximately 26,379 square feet of floor area, situated on Main Street in Bangor, Maine. Subject report as of March 15th, 1987, was prepared by John Doe, Appraiser, Boston, Massachusetts.

I have reviewed the subject report from the standpoint of meeting established specifications and requirements, as well as conforming to acceptable professional appraisal practices and techniques; scope of the appraisal investigation; factual data considered; reasoning and logic of the appraisal process and reasonableness of the valuation conclusion of $270,000.00.

FORM AND PRESENTATION

The appraisal meets contract requirements, as well as accepted standards for analytical narrative appraisal reports.

DATE: 4/24/87
SUBJECT: Field Appraisal Review & Analysis
PROJECT: Bangor, Maine-Existing Administrative Facility
CONTRACT APPRAISER: John Doe

1. I have reviewed the above referenced appraisal, and I will concur in the Appraiser's valuation estimate of: $_____;
   with the following comments: N/A
2. 1 have reviewed the above referenced appraisal and I do not concur in the Appraiser's valuation estimate of: $270,000.00 for the following reasons:

The appraisal is well presented and convincing, except for the capitalization rate of 91/2% which was used on the income approach. This is all-important, and I believe that no prudent investor would pay $270,000.00 for this marginal property in the hope of obtaining 91/2% on his investment. I do not believe that properties such as warehouses, sold in Portland, have comparability to the subject. I also see little relationship of the subject to the office building in Bangor, located at 4th Avenue and 16th Street. It is clear that the greater risk involved in the subject should promise a greater return, say 12% to 16%.

3. It is recommended that the Appraiser's fee of: $2,500.00

☑ Be Paid

☐ Not be paid at this time for the following reasons or subject to the following being submitted:
4. Other Remarks: Suggest contact with Appraiser regarding cap

rate and his comments obtained prior to final estimate of value.

BY: _____

    Paul Jones, Real Estate Representative

    December 27th, 1986

Deliniation of Assignment

The appraisers have adequately delineated the purpose of the report; described the property; and set forth limiting conditions and assumptions. With respect to the appraiser's conclusions concerning highest and best use, the reviewer takes issue with the soundness of this conclusion which will later be discussed.

Analasys Techniques and Data Utilized

Factual Data Considered

The appraisers have presented and considered the economics, general area, trends and environmental influences of the area and neighborhood. Bangor is supported mainly by an agricultural economy with the government being the largest employer in the county. The city has the highest per capita income in the State. Future growth is estimated to be steady, with good potential. The subject is located in the old downtown area of Bangor, which has definitely and seriously been on the decline. Local efforts were made to revitalize the area with the "Bangor Mall" renovation project, to combat this downtown deterioration and the outflux of merchants. However, this has been unsuccessful. Some 27% of the stores were vacant in 1986, with numerous additional vacancies since then. The area south of the subject is a dilapidated residential area of which many buildings have been demolished. Business trends have been to the south. Demand for space in this area is extremely limited, and with the increasing supply of convertible office space in vacant buildings, the market has been further affected. The appraiser's have also indicated that it is highly improbable that the area will ever regain prominence, based upon the size of the city, rate of growth and the trend of growth.

With this economic picture, it can be concluded that conversion and private economic usage of the subject property is highly improbable at this time. It is indicated that irrespective of its age, the facility is considered to be in excellent condition, including the installed equipment.

Factual Errors or Omissions

No computational or other factual errors or omissions were noted.

Reasoning and Logic of Appraisal Process Utilized

The appraisers concluded that there is no economic need for the facility for private market usage. However, they indicated that it is highly improbable that this structure will be demolished within the next 40 years. This conclusion appears to be reasonable, based upon the factual data. They have based their conclusion of highest and best usage and value concept upon the premise that the most likely user, and only tenancy capable of occupying the structure, will be some governmental type agency, desiring a large quantity of office space and one who is politically motivated for this location. The reviewer has taken exception to this premise upon the basis of factual economic data presented for the area. Also, there was really no support presented—"Market-wise" for such usage. The questionable premise was discussed with the appraiser. His explanation, in effect, was that this was not based upon a market analysis, indicating a need by such agencies, as well as ability, to pay market value for such space. It was predicated mainly upon a subjective assumption that the city would endeavor to acquire this property for governmental usage in order to further revitalize the "Bangor Mall" area. While during the original concept of a new Administrative Facility, there was some interest in a trade of the subject for the proposed facility on city owned property. Such is apparently no longer being actively considered. It is my considered opinion that the appraiser's determination of usage is not adequately substantiated by factual market analysis, and therefore rests upon thin ice. It is, therefore, not a very reasonable assumption. In support of their value conclusion, the Appraiser's have considered the accepted approaches to value, which will be separately commented upon by the reviewer.

Land Value—Market Approach

The value of the subject site is directly related to surrounding property values, and the ability to return a positive cash flow. The many properties vacated, and the poor likelihood of improvement has resulted in declining value of the remaining properties. Some eleven (11) sales indices were utilized during a span of 1971 to 1983. These ranged in- size from 1,520 to 117,000 square feet, and ranged in price from .36 to $4.41 per square foot. Of these sales, the Appraiser's concluded a "bracket" value of .42 per square foot on sales 2 and 3, to an upper limit of .69 under sale 6. From this, the Appraiser's concluded a valuation of .56 per square foot, or $17,200 being the median. They also indicated this to be a "speculators gamble" to some degree. Upon the factual economic conditions of the area and trends, this estimate is concurred in as being reasonably indicative of the land's probable market value. In the Site Planning Report, the valuation for land was estimated at $1.35 per square foot, or $43,000, which in my opinion, is quite high under the current conditions.

Cost Approach to Value

The structure is a reinforced concrete two story building with a full basement, constructed in 1933 and is in excellent physical condition. The first floor could be partitioned into office space without difficulty, and the second floor is already divided into offices. The appraisers consider it improbable that the structure would be demolished within the next 40 years. The appraiser's eliminated the use of the cost approach as being an inappropriate technique for the subject property. The property being an over-improvement with substantial obsolescence, depreciation is difficult to estimate and can only be reflected in the income approach.

While the reviewer is in agreement that the property is an over-improvement, construction-wise, and that there is substantial depreciation, I cannot agree with their premise of non-use of this approach. Their income approach, as will be further discussed, is weak, and under these circumstances, the cost approach should have been utilized for further support. It is also my opinion that this technique, correctly executed, would show a valuation substantially below their value conclusion of $270,000.00. Also, for this type of property, and under the current circumstances, the remaining physical value of the structure would be most indicative of value to any potential user.

Market Approach—Overall Property

The appraisers presented some five sales. And one offering of a retail store property, which have taken place in the area from to 1983. Most of these were smaller properties and the range of price per square foot of the building indicated .50 to $6.11. The appraisers discounted these sales as not being meaningful as indicators of the comparative value for the subject. Therefore, no value was indicated under this approach.

The reviewer generally concurs with their conclusion concerning this approach. However, using even the upper limit of these indices, a valuation of $100,000 or more below the appraiser's valuation conclusion of $270,000 would be indicated.

Income Approach to Value

The approach to value was utilized as the appraiser's *only* basis for market value.

The appraisers utilized some 19 leases of government and non-government space in various office buildings in Bangor. These ranged from approximately $2.00 to $6.60 per square foot, per year. From an analysis, and considering the location and quality, the appraisers estimated the economic rent as follows:

Basement: $2.25 per square foot per year
First floor: $4.25 per square foot per year
1st Floor Mezzanine: $3.75 per square foot per year
Second Floor: $3.75 per square foot per year

This resulted in a gross income of $69,759. If anything, in my opinion, this is probably on the high side, considering economic conditions of the area. In order to attract adequate occupancy, any rental rate would have to be quite low, possibly lower than they have established. The basis for the expenses appears to be adequately substantiated. The total expenses, approximating 59%, appears to be reasonable for such a property. The estimated net operating income of $25,694.00 compares to $27,509, as estimated in the Site Report. The appraisers utilized a capitalization rate of 9.5%. This was based upon an indication of a Savings & Loan Company acquisition in Bangor, which indicated an 8.3%, and two J.C. Penny warehouses in Portland. The reviewer takes exception to this rate, as being probably low for such a property. This matter was discussed with the appraiser. He indicated that this rate was based on the assumption of governmental usage and predicated upon the city probably taking the property in its entirety. He also indicated that if one were to assume multiple ownership under the general market, a much higher cap-rate would have to be used. Some question is also raised by the reviewer, as to the comparability of the cap-rate support properties to the subject property. It is my considered opinion that to assume city acquisition of the subject property at such a price, is a precarious assumption. Based upon this income approach, the appraisers concluded a market valuation of $270,000.00. This compares with a valuation of $172,000.00 estimated in the site planning report. From the analysis I have made of this approach, there is considerable doubt in my mind as to its being reliably indicative of the probable market value of the subject property for disposal purposes.

Correlation and Reasonableness of Conclusion Reached

From the review and analysis I have made, it is my considered judgment that the estimated valuation of $270,000.00 is probably quite high, and has not been substantiated and justified beyond a reasonable doubt. In arriving at this conclusion, the reviewer has given consideration to the field appraisal review and analysis, dated April 24th, 1987, prepared by Paul Jones, Real Estate Representative, which is attached herewith. I concur in his conclusions and recommendations. Mr. Jones prepared the previous valuation in the site report.

Adequacy of Report

It is my opinion that his report is adequate from the standpoint of being well presented and having satisfied the contract; although I do not concur in the valuation conclusion reached. From this standpoint, it is not adequate for disposition purposes at this time. It is therefore recommended that a second appraisal be obtained prior to disposition of this property.

Appraiser's Qualifications

Appraiser John Doe is known by the undersigned to be an extremely well qualified and experienced appraiser in the New England Area.

Field Review

None made by the Reviewer.

Appraiser Discussion (Conference)

As previously mentioned, certain factors were discussed with the appraiser in the course of preparing this review.

Site Report

Under the Site Selection Report, dated November 1986, prepared by Paul Jones, Real Estate Representative, the value for disposal purposes was estimated to be $172,000. Under review, dated December 9, 1986, the undersigned took some exception to this valuation conclusion; however, it is probably more indicative of value than that estimated by the appraisal.

Offer To Sell

No offer has been obtained in connection with the disposal of this property.

Reviewer's Conclusions And Recommendations

A. It is my recommendation that the appraised valuation of $270,000.00 *not* be approved at this time, for disposal purposes.
B. It is further recommended that a second appraisal be obtained, from a well qualified appraiser, prior to disposition of the subject property.
C. It is recommended that the appraiser's fee of $2,500 be paid, as having satisfactorily met their contract requirements.

ADDITIONAL DATA

Appraisal Contract Number: #07-8742-67-Q-2C8T
Date of Contract: February 14th, 1987 (Transmittal February 24)
Time Allowed: 30 days
Date Received: April 1987 (Note: Delay in submission was caused by a request from this office to defer this appraisal and complete another contract first.)
Fee: $2.500.00

By _____
        William S. Brown CRA
        Reviewing Appraiser

Concurred_____
        William S. Johnson
        Manager, Real Estate Section

COMMENTS:

The subject USPS - owned property is located in the old downtown area of Bangor, which has been in a serious economic decline. Right now, 27% of the stores in the downtown area are presently vacant. Demand for office space in the area is extremely limited, and there is no economic need for additional private market usage of office space. The appraiser has based his highest and best usage and value conception upon the premise of Governmental type agency usage. His usage is not substantiated by factual market analysis. Therefore, I do not agree with his assumption, nor do I agree with his appraised value of $270,000.

I concur with William S. Brown CRA, that the appraised value of $270,000 should not be approved and that a second appraisal be obtained prior to disposal of this property.

CHAPTER TWELVE

CONSOLIDATED REVIEWING STATEMENT

TWO APPRAISALS

EXHIBIT 3:

EXAMPLE:—Consolidated Reviewing Statement

Two Appraisals

Mr. Ralph Mason, Director
Real Estate Division

In connection with the above referenced project, attention is directed to the following:

1. Appraisal Report, dated September 27, 1986, prepared by Smith Associates, Chicago, Illinois, wherein the valuation of the subject property was estimated to be $10,000,000.
2. Appraisal Review and Analysis, dated November 12, 1986, prepared by William S. Brown, C.R.A., Reviewing Appraiser on number one above.
3. Joint Appraisal Report, dated December 19, 1984, prepared by Walter Grignon and Paul Bertrand (both of Chicago, Illinois) wherein the valuation of the subject property was estimated to be $11,250,000.
4 . Appraisal Review and Analysis dated January by William S. Brown, CRA, Reviewing Appraiser on number three above.

PURPOSE

The purpose of this reviewing statement is to make a comparative analysis of the two separate appraisals prepared on this project, and to arrive at certain resulting conclusions and recommendations. We have had the benefit of valuation opinions from three well qualified, experienced appraisers on such properties in this area. The conclusions which they have reached should, in effect, indicate the probable market value of the subject property, beyond a reasonable doubt. In considering this, it is fully realized that appraising is not an exact science.

Comparative Analysis

The Smith report basically utilized the cost approach to estimate the market value of the subject property. The Grignon-Bertrand report utilized all three accepted approaches, but places greatest reliance upon the income and market approaches to value. The various individual factors or approaches will be separately, comparatively analyzed.

DATE: 4/24/87

SUBJECT: Field Appraisal Review & Analysis

PROJECT: Bangor, Maine--Existing Administrative Facility

CONTRACT APPRAISER: John Doe

1. I have reviewed the above referenced appraisal, and I concur in the appraiser's valuation estimate of $XX.xx with the following comments: N/A

2. I have reviewed the above referenced appraisal, and I do not concur in the appraiser's valuation estimate of: $270,000.00 for the following reasons:

The appraisal is well presented and convincing, except for the capitalization rate of 9 1/2% which was used on the income approach. This is all important, and I believe that no prudent investor would pay $270,000 for this marginal property in the hope of obtaining 9 1/2% on his investment. I do not believe that properties such as warehouses sold in Portland have comparability to the subject. Also, I see little relationship of the subject to the office building in Bangor at 4th Avenue and 16th Street. It is clear that the greater risk involved in the subject should promise a greater return, say 12% to 16%.

3. It is recommended that the appraiser's fee of $2,500.00

☑ Be Paid

☐ Not Be paid

at this time For the following reasons, or subject to the following being submitted:
4. Other Remarks: Suggest contact with appraiser regarding: cap rate and his comments obtained prior to final estimate of value.
By **Paul Jones,** Real Estate Representative
December 27, 1986

Cost Approach to Value

Land Value

Smith concluded a land value of $3.67 per square foot, or $3,184,000, which compares to $5.02 per square foot or $4,350,000 estimated in the second appraisal. Mr. Smith utilized four (4) sales in the area, of which all except one was considered in the second report. The second report considered 14 sales, and as such, in my opinion, considered a broader spectrum of the market. In a conference with Mr. Smith on November- 21st, 1986 in Chicago, he intimated that he probably could have gone higher on his land value. Giving consideration to the above, it is my considered opinion that the second appraisal estimate of $5.02 is better substantiated and justified, and is more realistically indicative of the probable market value.

Replacement Cost

The replacement cost, as estimated by Appraiser Smith, is $7,402,348 or $23.95 per square foot. However, this is without architectural fees and building changes. The second appraisal estimated replacement at $8,345,000 or $27.00 per square foot including fees and charges. Deducting fees and charges of 10% of the cost estimate is $7,584,869 or $24.54 per square foot. The two appraisals' basic costs therefore compare quite closely. These basic costs on the Smith appraisal were also previously checked by Mr. Grignon and Mr. Bertrand, and were considered to be reasonably indicative.

There is a difference in the two appraisals on architectural fees and building charges, which divergence was to some degree caused by the method used. Smith figured his costs after deducting over-improvement? And 7% was used versus 10% in the second appraisal.

Depreciation

Smith used a 6% physical depreciation? Or $429,544, as compared to the second appraisal of 6%, or $500,700. The difference, which is not excessive, results from the base used. Appraiser Smith estimated the amount of over-improvement to $710,625. The second appraisal estimated functional obsolescence to be $751,050. While the two appraisals used different premises, in effect, they are both functional obsolescence and are thus in quite close proximity and therefore can be considered realistic and acceptable.

Cost Approach Estimate

The final cost approach estimate of the Smith appraisal is $9,913,529, including land value, as compared to $11,450,000 in the second appraisal. The major difference is in the land value. Utilizing the higher land value of $4,350,000 of the second appraisal on Mr. Smith's depreciated replacement cost of $7,159,073, a valuation of $11,500,000 rounded, or virtually the same would be indicated.

It is therefore my considered opinion that a valuation of $11,500,000, under the cost approach, is a fair and reasonable indication of the "upper limit" of value for the subject property and both appraisals are compatible in this respect.

Market Approach

The Smith appraisal did not utilize the market approach; since in his opinion it was not indicative of market value on such a unique property. No comparative analysis can be made on this approach with the second appraisal. In my review of this report on November 22, 1986, I stressed that this was one of the weaknesses of Mr. Smith's appraisal. The second appraisal estimated the valuation of the subject property under this approach to be $11,000,000 to $11,000,000, with a final conclusion of $11,250,000. My comments concerning this approach were covered in my review of the second appraisal, dated January 22, 1987. This valuation could be considered a value to a "market user" of the property as is.

Income Approach

The rentable area used in both reports were the same. The average rental value used by Smith was .27 per square foot, and in the second appraisal, .30 per square foot was used. This is relatively close, and in my opinion, an acceptable difference. Both appraisals utilized a 10% capitalization rate, which appears to be justified and substantiated. Both appraisals considered the undeveloped vacant area as excess to the properties' needs, and added the value to the income value. This is concurred in as being a reasonable premise. Appraiser Smith used a lesser value per square foot for this undeveloped parcel, which resulted in an approximately $96,800 lesser value. Both appraisers in their initial submission, did not include any item for expenses, to which the reviewer took exception. Mr. Smith submitted a revision which changed his original valuation of $10,081,600 to $8,889,600. No supplemental revision has yet been obtained on the second appraisal, which will be covered under supplemental review when received. Adjusting Mr. Smith's income valuation upward for a higher land value on the vacant parcel would indicate a valuation of approximately $10,000,000. Reducing the second appraisal some, for an item of expenses would reduce the valuation to at least $11,200,000 or less. From this analysis, it is my considered opinion that a fair and reasonable estimate of the property's probable market value is $10,000,000 to $11,000,000 under the income approach.

CONCLUSIONS

From the comparative analysis I have made, I have reached the following conclusions:

Three Valuation Approaches

From the three approaches used by both Appraisers, I have concluded the following as being reasonable estimates:

1. Cost Approach	$11,500,000
2. Market Approach	$11,250,000
3. Income Approach	$10,000,000 to $11,000,000

Correlation

These value estimates fall in the usually accepted theoretical indications of value, which are: under normal conditions, the cost approach indicates the upper limit of value and the income approach indicates the lower limit of value. From this, it could be concluded that the subject property has a range of market value of $ 10,000,000 to $ 11,500,000.

Other Factors of Consideration

1. The valuation of $11,250,000, as estimated in the second appraisal, has basically been estimated on the highest and best use for a "market user", who would purchase, and be able to use the subject property, as it is presently developed and

equipped, as a research and development facility. In effect, this is indicative of the "maximum value" the property would have on the market. Considering a wider spectrum of the market, its value could be somewhere below this amount.

2. An appraisal, especially of a large, unique facility such as this, is an economic analysis under conditions of uncertainty and its findings can be expressed only in probabilistic terms. No Appraiser is capable of making a prediction of probable selling price in the form of a precise figure. At best, he can define a range of prices within which the selling price would probably fall, and, in some cases, he may have sufficient data to express his judgment at various points within this range. The valuation of a property of this complex nature, in my opinion, cannot therefore be expressed as an "exact figure", as is theoretically desirable. In the case in question, it may not be the most practical or logical.

Owning to the many variable factors present, in my opinion, a "range of value" is probably more logical and realistic.

3. Theoretically, an appraisal for "market value" is based upon the "highest and best use", which in this particular case has been determined to be a "market user" who could utilize the property to its "full activity", as is. The purpose of an appraisal is to estimate the most probable selling price. When considering the value to a "user" in the market, this can be a widely variable amount. The question in any purchaser's mind is not necessarily *what he may pay,* but more, *what he should pay,* when considering his own requirements, as well as the property itself, and to its fitting his needs. Therefore, while market value, theoretically may be one thing, value to a particular user may be something entirely different. This factor must be kept in retrospect especially considering the U.S. Postal Service's particular requirements and use, as to what the value may be to them.

RECOMMENDATIONS

Based upon the comparative review and analysis I have made, the following are my considered recommendations:

A. The market value of the subject property lies within a range of $10,000,000 to $11,500,000 for negotiating purposes.

B. Discretion should be used as to the actual amount, offered or paid, depending upon the "use value" of the subject facility.

By: _____
      William S. Brown, CRA
      Reviewing Appraiser

Concurred: _____
      Raymond Stone
      Real Estate Director

APPRAISAL QUALITY AND VARIANCE REPORT FOR INDIVIDUAL PROPERTY REVIEWS:

FANNIE MAE

FORM DA 388

Appraisal Quality Report: Fannie Mae

Form DA 388

The Federal National Mortgage Association has been at the forefront of using appraisal review as a principal method of quality control, Fannie Mae Form DA388 is an appraisal review report that is used internally by Fannie Mae offices for quality control purposes. NARA/MU has reviewed this form and considers it a good example of a checklist type of appraisal review. It can easily be adapted for general appraisal review purposes.

APPRAISAL QUALITY AND VARIANCE REPORT FOR INDIVIDUAL PROPERTY REVIEWS:

Lending Institution _____

Lender's Address _____

Name of Borrower_____

Property Address_____

Certificate or Loan Number _____

Original Appraisal $ _____ Date_____

Lender's Appraiser_____

Address_____

    (City & State)

Spot-Check Appraisal $ _____Date_____

Spot-Check Appraiser _____

Address_____

    (City & State)

Variance between original approval and the spot-check appraiser's value conclusion %_____ $ _____

Comments on the quality, completeness, consistency, accuracy, and valuation techniques of the lender's appraisal report:

_____

_____

_____

_____

_____

_____

_____

_____

_____

_____

_____

_____

Comments on the spot-check appraisal; is the spot-check appraiser's analysis of the original appraisal convincing and accurate?

_____

_____

_____

_____

_____

_____

_____

_____

_____

Summary of action taken (if necessary):

_____

_____

_____

_____

_____

_____

_____

_____

_____

_____

EXHIBIT 5

Appraisal Review Tracking Report Data Base Outlline

The following is an appraisal quality control data base outline that can be utilized in constructing an appraisal review tracking report. It contains basic information that is useful to management in spotting appraisal problems and evaluating the effectiveness of the company's appraisal quality control efforts.

Building a Quality Control Appraisal Review Tracking Report

1. Borrower's Name(s)
2. Address of Property
3. Certificate or Loan Number
4. Branch Office
5. Loan Officer's or lender's Name
6. Appraiser's Name and I.D. number
7. Sales Price
8. Appraised Value
9. Date of Appraisal
10. Spot-Check Appraiser's Name and I.D. Number
11. Spot-Check Value
12. Spot-Check Date
13. Date Reviewed by Underwriting/Quality Control
14. Variance (% and $ Amount)
15. Is the Appraisal Satisfactory or Unsatisfactory
16. Appraisal Quality Rating (Poor, Fair, Good, Very Good, Excellent)
17. Action Taken (If Any)

CHAPTER FOURTEEN

SPOT CHECK APPRAISER COVER LETTER AND REVIEW FORMS

EXHIBIT 6

SPOT CHECK APPRAISER COVER LETTER AND REVIEW FORMS

This appraisal cover letter and review form can be sent to the spot-check appraiser along with a copy of the original appraisal report when making a spot-check appraisal request. The company underwriter will compare the original appraisal with the spot-check analysis in order to form an opinion with respect to the quality of both the original appraisal and the spot-check analysis.

SPOT-CHECK APPRAISER COVER LETTER (SAMPLE)

Re: Spot-check appraisal request information

Dear (Appraiser)

(Company Name) is requesting a spot-check review on the above named property. Attached is a copy of the original appraisal as well as the company's "Appraisal Review Form". Please review the enclosed appraisal report and complete the "Appraisal Review Form" in accordance with (Company Name) spot-check review requirements. Our spot-check review procedures are as follows:

1. The appraiser will visit the subject property and take a picture of the subject. Photo will be attached to the "Appraisal Review Form". This is a "drive-by review" rather than a full property inspection.
2. Also, the spot-check appraiser will include a list of comparables used in arriving at an opinion of value. Comparables must be all closed sales. List of comparable sales will include sales date, sales price, address, distance from subject, design, room count and gross square foot living area. A sheet for comparable sales is attached to the "Appraisal Review Form".
3. Appraiser will review the original appraisal and fill in the "Appraiser Review Form".
4. Submit the completed "Appraiser Review Form", photograph, and list of comparables along with a cover letter stating a value range for the subject property, as well as it's most probable selling price.

Since this is a "drive-by review", which does not require an inspection or filling out the FNMA/FHLMC form or providing a variety of attachments, (Company Name) appraisal fee is $_____.

In brief, we would like you to review the original appraisal based upon your knowledge of the subject area as well as three well selected comparable sales. The comparables should be recent, closed sales or similar properties from the subject neighborhood. In completing the assignment, the appraiser will simply follow the above four steps., Since real property provides security for the loan, (Company Name) is concerned with the quality of the appraisal reports and spot-check review it receives. We are interested in obtaining insight into the value and marketability of each property underwritten. Quality information enables the company to determine appropriate loan to value ratios and make prudent risk decisions. We expect that each spot-check assignment will be thoughtfully handled.

We look forward to receiving your review and hope that the future will provide a pleasant association between your firm and (Company Name). If at present or in the future you have any questions, please feel free to contact my office.

Very truly yours,

EXHIBIT 7

RESIDENTIAL APPRAISAL REVIEW FORM

Lending Institution _____

Lender's Address _____

Name of Borrower _____

Property Address _____

Loan Number _____

Appraised Value $ _____ Date _____

Lender's Appraiser _____ Phone _____

Appraiser's Address _____

Review Appraiser _____ Phone _____

Reviewer's Address _____

FORMAT AND PRESENTATION | LENDER SECTION

	YES	NO	N/A		YES	NO	N/A
1. Is the Appraisal format in conformance with company appraisal requirements?	☐	☐	☐	2. Is the lender section of the report complete and accurate?	☐	☐	☐

NEIGHBORHOOD SECTION

	YES	NO	N/A		YES	NO	N/A
3. Does the neighborhood section provide the reviewer an adequate understanding with respect to locational factors, growth rate and economic trends, property values, housing supply, marketing time, land use, price ranges, convenience to employment and amenities, adequacy of utilities and recreational facilities, property compatibility, appearance of properties, detrimental conditions and marketability?				5. Are comments in the neighborhood section relevant and do they give insight into those conditions which positively or negatively affect the appraised properties value and marketability?	☐	☐	☐
	☐	☐	☐	6. Have all fair and poor ratings in the neighborhood section been explained?	☐	☐	☐
4. Does the appraisal report enable the reviewer to spot healthy growth patterns or trends that may indicate a deteriorating neighborhood with limited market appeal?	☐	☐	☐	7. If marketing time is over six months, has the appraiser commented on the reasons for slow market conditions in the subject area?	☐	☐	☐
				8. If the market is slow, has the appraiser indicated whether or not this has resulted in a decline in values?	☐	☐	☐
				9. Is the neighborhood section of the report completed and accurate?	☐	☐	☐

Reviewer's Comments _____

SITE SECTION

	YES	NO	N/A		YES	NO	N/A
10. Has the appraiser commented on unfavorable site factors?	☐	☐	☐	13. Does the appraiser indicate the subject's zoning and whether or not the subject conforms with present zoning requirements?	☐	☐	☐
11. Does the appraiser indicate whether or not the subject property meets all the criteria for a desirable lot in the area?	☐	☐	☐	14. Has the appraiser accurately indicated the dimensions and size of the subject lot?	☐	☐	☐
12. Has the appraiser addressed and commented on problems relating to poor drainage, flood conditions, adverse easements, encroachments or other detrimental factors?	☐	☐	☐	15. Does the appraisal report reveal whether or not site improvements and services to the site are adequate and acceptable in the market place?	☐	☐	☐
				16. Is the site section of the appraisal report complete and accurate?	☐	☐	☐

Reviewer's Comments _____

IMPROVEMENTS SECTION

	YES	NO	N/A		YES	NO	N/A
17. If the subject property is a condominium, are the project improvements and project rating sections complete and accurate?	☐	☐	☐	adequate equipment and amenities, limit the value and market appeal of the subject?	☐	☐	☐
18. Did the appraiser comment on physical and functional inadequacies and indicate whether or not repairs and modernization are needed?	☐	☐	☐	25. If there is evidence of dampness, termites or settlement, did the appraiser comment on these factors?	☐	☐	☐
19. Has the appraiser explained fair or poor improvement ratings?	☐	☐	☐	26. Has the appraiser provided the reviewer with a clear and accurate understanding of the physical and functioning attributes of the subject property?	☐	☐	☐
20. Does the appraiser indicate whether or not factors receiving poor or fair ratings, adversely affect the property's marketability?	☐	☐	☐	27. Is the property rating section accurate as well as consistent with other data contained in the report?	☐	☐	☐
21. Have factor's relating to age, condition, quality or construction, finish and equipment, as well as size and utility been properly handled?	☐	☐	☐	28. Has the appraiser presented information on construction features in a manner that gives an accurate and adequate view of the subject property?	☐	☐	☐
22. Has the appraiser given serious attention to structural problems?	☐	☐	☐	29. Has information relating to the improvement been well handled?	☐	☐	☐
23. Did the appraiser comment on unusual layouts, peculiar floor plans, inadequate equipment and amenities?	☐	☐	☐	30. In the reviewer's opinion, is the descriptive section of the appraisal report (page one) acceptable?	☐	☐	☐
24. Has the appraiser indicated whether or not factors relating to unusual layouts, peculiar floor plans, in-				31. Has appraiser required all needed repairs?	☐	☐	☐
				32. Is the improvement section of the report complete and accurate?	☐	☐	☐

Reviewer's Comments _____

COST SECTION

	YES	NO	N/A		YES	NO	N/A
33. Are the appraiser's measurements for gross living area correct?	☐	☐	☐	preciation appear reasonable in light of the subject's age, condition, state of modernization, size, utility, and location?	☐	☐	☐
34. Has the appraiser commented on functional and economic obsolescence?	☐	☐	☐	37. Is the estimate of land value appropriate?	☐	☐	☐
35. In estimating reproduction costs, has the appraiser used cost figures that are appropriate for the local market?	☐	☐	☐	38. Are the appraiser's mathematical calculations accurate?	☐	☐	☐
36. Do figures for physical, functional and economic de-				39. Is the budget analysis section accurate and complete (if condo)?	☐	☐	☐
				40. Is the cost section complete and accurate?	☐	☐	☐

Reviewer's Comments _____

Review Form No. 2002
Revised 1/86

EXHIBIT 8

RESIDENTIAL APPRAISAL REVIEW NARRATIVE FORM

Lending Institution _____

Lender's Address _____

Name of Borrower _____

Property Address _____

Loan Number _____

Appraised Value $ _____ Date _____

Lender's Appraiser _____ Phone _____

Appraiser's Address _____

Review Appraiser _____ Phone _____

Reviewer's Address _____

REVIEW ANALYSIS

1. Does the appraisal report present a consistent and convincing anaylsis? _____

2. Are there serious omissions, false information, faulty reasoning or the possibility of calculated deception? _____

3. Comment on the report's quality, completeness, consistency and accuracy _____

4. Do you agree with the appraiser's value conclusion? Comment on the adequacy of the appraiser's value analysis as well as the soundness of the value conclusion? _____

5. If there is a difference between your opinion and that of the appraiser, what is the reason for the difference? _____

6. Does it appear that the subject property has been over appraised? Comment on your opinion of value and the appraiser's opinion of value: _____

7. How would you rate the appraisal report with respect to overall quality (poor, fair, good, very good, excellent)? _____

REVIEWER'S SUMMARY

Recommendation:

☐ Accept as is   ☐ Accept when revised-See items # _____

☐ Have another appraisal prepared by someone else   ☐ Other

Comments: _____

Field Review was made   ☐ YES   ☐ NO

Sales price $ _____ Appraisers Value $ _____ Reviewers Recommendation $ _____

Reviewer's Signature _____ Title _____ Date of Review _____

Reviewer's Signature _____ Title _____ Date of Review _____

See Attached ☐

Review Form No. 2004
Revised 1/88

MARKET ANALYSIS SECTION

	YES	NO	N/A			YES	NO	N/A
41. Has the appraiser selected his or her comparables from the subject neighborhood?	☐	☐	☐	56. Does the appraiser's final value conclusion relate for the adjusted comparables?		☐	☐	☐
42. If not, has the appraiser explained why comparables were selected from a different neighborhood?	☐	☐	☐	57. Has the appraiser selected good market data and handled it well?		☐	☐	☐
43. In your opinion, are the comparables really similar with respect to location, site, design and style, quality and amenities, as well as size and utility?	☐	☐	☐	58. Has the appraiser commented on the subject's marketability?		☐	☐	☐
If no, Comp. # _____ needs to be replaced.				59. Does the appraiser's marketability information appear to be accurate?		☐	☐	☐
44. Are all of the comparables recent sales of similar properties from the subject neighborhood?	☐	☐	☐	60. Has the appraiser avoided the appearance of backing into any or all of the approaches to value?		☐	☐	☐
45. If the comparables are over three months old, has the appraiser explained why he or she failed to use recent sales?	☐	☐	☐	61. Is there clarity with respect to the appraiser's reasoning?		☐	☐	☐
46. Are room counts and square foot areas of the subject and comparables and similar?	☐	☐	☐	62. Can you read the appraisal report, step by step, and arrive at the same conclusion of value as the appraiser?		☐	☐	☐
47. Do the sale prices of the comparables correlate and indicate comparability?	☐	☐	☐	63. Does the appraiser appear to be an individual offering an independent and impartial third party opinion of value rather than an advocate?		☐	☐	☐
48. Do the prices per square foot of the comparables correlate and indicate comparability?	☐	☐	☐	64. Are all the required photographs attached and do they adequately show the subject and surrounding properties?		☐	☐	☐
49. Has the appraiser bracketed his or her sales data (before making adjustments)?	☐	☐	☐	65. Is other needed illustrative material attached and properly completed?		☐	☐	☐
50. Do time adjustments, for date of sale, appear reasonable in light of market trends and current market conditions?	☐	☐	☐	66. If the appraiser is using computer generated data, are the facts and comments in the report accurate and applicable to the subject and comparable properties?		☐	☐	☐
51. Has the appraiser avoided numerous adjustments?	☐	☐	☐	67. Does it appear that the appraiser has clearly thought through this process rather than using a computer as a substitute?		☐	☐	☐
52. Has the appraiser adjusted all three comparables in a reasonable and consistent manner?	☐	☐	☐					
53. Are total gross adjustments exceeding 25% of the comparable's sales price and individual line adjustments exceeding 10% of the comparable's sales price adequately explained and justified?	☐	☐	☐	68. Has the appraiser identified which comparable(s) are the most relevant?		☐	☐	☐
54. Are the appraiser's mathematical calculations accurate?	☐	☐	☐	69. Is the market analysis section complete and accurate?		☐	☐	☐
55. Is there a convincing value range with respect to the three adjusted comparables— In brief, are the adjusted value conclusions reasonably similar?	☐	☐	☐					

Reviewer's Comments _____

_____

_____

INCOME APPROACH SECTION

	YES	NO	N/A			YES	NO	N/A
70. Has the income approach been completed?	☐	☐	☐	72. Is supporting data valid and correctly analysed?		☐	☐	☐
71. Has supporting data been submitted?	☐	☐	☐					

Reviewer's Comments _____

_____

_____

RECONCILIATION SECTION

	YES	NO	N/A			YES	NO	N/A
73. In your opinion, has the appraiser proven his or her case?	☐	☐	☐	76. Is it clear which approach to value was given the most weight in the final estimate of value?		☐	☐	☐
74. Do you concur with the value conclusion of the appraiser, based upon data contained within the report?	☐	☐	☐	77. Is the final estimate of value weighted by the most appropriate approach to value?		☐	☐	☐
75. Are the appraiser's comments and final reconciliation of value adequate and does the appraisal give insight into the value and marketability of the subject property?	☐	☐	☐	78. Is the appraiser's value conclusion reasonable?		☐	☐	☐
				79. Has the appraiser signed the report and typed his or her name under the signature?		☐	☐	☐
				80. Is there a phone number on the report and/or cover letter which would enable the reviewer to contact the appraiser and clarify a questionable appraisal report?		☐	☐	☐

Reviewer's Comments _____

_____

_____

REVIEWER'S SUMMARY

Appraisal report was: Good ☐   Fair ☐   Poor ☐

Recommendation:

☐ Accept as is   ☐ Accept when revised–See items # _____

☐ Have another appraisal perpared by someone else   ☐ Other

Comments: _____

_____

_____

_____

Field Review was made   ☐ YES   ☐ NO

Sales price $_____   Appraisers Value $_____   Reviewers Recommendation $ _____

Reviewer's Signature_____   Title_____   Date of Review_____

Reviewer's Signature_____   Title_____   Date of Review_____

See Attached ☐

Review Form No. 2002
Revised 1/88

TIPS ON PROTECTING YOUR COMPANY FROM APPRAISAL AND OTHER TYPES OF REAL ESTATE RISK

EXHIBIT 9

Tips on Protecting Your Company From Appraisal and Other Types of Real Estate Risk

How can financial institutions protect themselves from risk?

1. Implement appraisal, project, and loan quality control programs. Ascertain reasons for company losses and design programs to address problems.
2. Maintain a market analysis capability. Attention should be given to areas experiencing economic problems. Particular concern must be directed to overbuilt markets where investor speculation and creative financing schemes are apparent.
3. Develop tracking and monitoring systems that will reveal areas that need to be addressed. Tracking and monitoring are part of a company's defense system. Financial require tracking and monitoring systems in order to protect and direct themselves.
4. Train underwriters so that they will be able to intelligently review appraisal reports. This task is part of the company's ongoing educational efforts.
5. Tie appraisers to underwriting. Encourage your organization to relate appraisers to an underwriting, appraisal, or quality control department. The appraisal is an underwriting tool and

not a sales tool. Sales people in financial institutions should not be allowed to select appraisers and order appraisal reports. Again, sales and appraising don't mix. In fact, mixing the two has perverted the appraisal process.

6. Require narrative appraisals on custom homes and high risk properties. The FNMA/FHLMC forms are not adequate for custom homes and high risk properties which present special risks. On certain types of properties and loans? Financial institutions need a more in-depth look at the real estate providing security for the loan, as well as a more in-depth at the surrounding market. Narrative appraisals will cost more than form appraisals but, considering the chance of loss involved in high risk and high dollar properties, they are a bargain.

7. Don't give appraisers the sales price of a property being appraised unless the appraisal request is part of the company's spot-check program. Lending institutions should be encouraged not to divulge the sales price to the appraiser. If you give the appraiser the sales price, then 95% to 98% of the time this is exactly what you will get back.

8. There should be a complete separation between sales and underwriting departments. Sales departments must not be allowed to control, direct, or pressure underwriting personnel. In brief, underwriting should be allowed to fulfill its mission.

9. In your contacts with appraisers, let them know you want quality appraisal reports. Financial institutions will have to convince appraisers that they will be rewarded for doing good quality work. In recent years, the system has rewarded poor quality work and punished appraisers doing good quality work.

10. Counsel with appraisers who do questionable work and attempt to get them to improve the quality of their appraisers. Counseling has a positive effect on the quality of submitted appraisal work and will resolve most problems.

11. Monitor appraisal reports and eliminate appraisers who consistently do poor quality work. If an appraiser continues to submit poor quality work after counseling, use the services of

another appraiser.

12. If an appraiser is consistently doing poor quality and/or unethical work, submit the poor quality reports to the ethics committee of the appraisal society of which the appraiser is a member.

13. Quality control, appraisal, and underwriting departments in financial institutions should relate directly to senior management. It is recommended that these departments be headed by individuals who have vice presidential titles.

14. Review questionable appraisal reports before the loan is underwritten. Don't be afraid to get a second opinion. Engage in preventative medicine. We always wind up doing post mortems. Preventative medicine is preferable.

15. Develop a policy on business decisions. A policy is needed on business decisions that will allow underwriting to honestly and objectively perform its task. There are situations where the rejection of a loan or project will affect a business relationship. However, it is appropriate for sales managers to approach senior management, preferably the President, with respect to overriding an underwriting decision. If an approval is granted to sales on a loan or project that was rejected by underwriting, then the sales person involved should have to sign the file and be instructed that such loans will be tracked. The file will state that the loan was rejected by underwriting and give the reasons for rejection. Sales and senior management will indicate that they have approved the loan based on a business decision.

Reviewing Appraisal's Responsibilities; Objectives and the Role of the Reviewer

1. Autonomy: How can the review appraiser attain that position? Here are some procedures which you may wish to follow:

    a.) Establish all independent appraisal review section. This section shall not be answerable to those in acquisition, mortgage production etc. as they may have different motives than the review appraisal section.

b.) Your Conclusions: Justify and substantiate your opinions. Others may challenge your statements if they are not well thought out and communicated.

c.) If your position is correct and no new data is brought forth, and management wants to make a decision that will override your recommendations, do not create bad feelings that may last. Restate your case, pointing out the protective functions you are as a reviewer. Inform management that you would like your recommendation to remain in the file so that if something happens years from now, your position will be clear.

2. There are different theories about the appraisal process, and as a result, it has been exceedingly difficult to distinguish between unsound valuations made by honest intentioned appraisers, and actual fraudulent valuations. This is one of the reviewer's functions, to see that the valuation is based on sound Judgment. It is difficult to distinguish between a good appraisal that may be well supported and a poor appraisal that has lots of apparent support, but is quite inadequate. The appraiser must secure appraisals that are well substantiated and contain a reasonableness in the appraisal logic. This procedure will insure that the appraisals have met the contracted requirements and provide management with the data they need to make important decisions.

4. The reviewer must act in a supervisory capacity over the appraiser. It is suggested that the appraiser be told the appraisal report will be reviewed.

5. The reviewer should point out to the appraiser that the report must be defensible. After all, many times it ends up that way— that is, "on trial."

6. Should the reviewer have any contradictory "circumstantial data" that the appraiser may not have discussed, it should be presented to the appraiser for appropriate comments.

7. The reviewer should give the appraiser the opportunity to "defend" the valuation conclusions should there be doubts as to the reasonableness of the conclusions. There may be good reasons for the valuation conclusion, but they were not communicated in the report.
8. Be sure from the beginning that the appraiser knows your authority as a reviewer.
9. The reviewer should be diplomatic and discuss controversial data professionally with the appraiser.
10. The reviewer should see that the appraisal is in compliance with the assignment and is in conformity with generally accepted appraisal practices. Minor items should be pointed out to the appraiser so in future assignments, the report can be improved. Do not get put in the position of having the appraiser call you a "nit picker". Bring small or insignificant items to the appraiser's attention telling the appraiser you will not require a correction on the report, but the items must be mentioned in your review, as it is your responsibility to look for all items minor or major. Point out, too many minor items can turn into a major problem.
11. When apparent conflicting data or methodology exists, bring it to the attention of the appraiser at once. The sooner the confrontation, the sooner the problem can be resolved.
12. In conflicting situations, give the appraiser the opportunity to fully explain his or her positions after you have made your known.
13. The reviewer should get his or her thoughts together before calling the appraiser to discuss a problem. If the appraiser knows you have given the problem serious thought, the results of the conversation may be greatly improved.
14. Giving the appraiser the "benefit of the doubt" on occasions is okay, but remember it is your review that management will be looking at, and if you are not completely satisfied, it may make your position (and professionalism) very weak.
15. The reviewer should be able to comprehend the valuation data

presented and make a recommendation from the submitted report.

16. The reviewer should remind the appraiser that they are for a "common goal"—that is, to obtain a well and substantiated report that can be used to assist management in the decisions that will be made.
17. The reviewer should know his function in an assignment. It is the reviewer's responsibility to interpret the appraisal report for management.
18. The reviewer should not become the appraiser in the assignment. If there are serious doubts or other problems, get another appraisal opinion, do not become the appraiser.
19. The rreviewer should not "second guess" the appraiser. If doubt exists, call the appraiser for clarification.
20. The reviewer should avoid having "preconceived valuation opinions." Let the appraisal report do the work.
21. The reviewer should examine the appraisal report in its entirety, not just one or two sections of the report. The reviewer should be convinced of the appraisal's validity, rationality, and its "truth" in the marketplace.
22. The reviewer should look for mistakes in the report. In many situations the reviewer is the "Last Defense" before some type of action is taken based on the appraisal report.
23. The reviewer should be careful not to influence the appraiser in the valuation report. The reviewer's job is to clarify the report, not influence the appraiser. There are many stories of appraisers who were later confronted about the report and then state they were influenced by the reviewer. Do not get put in this position.
24. The reviewer may, after seeing an appraisal report that doesn't meet the needs of the assignment, appraise the property. It must be remembered that in this situation, the reviewer becomes the appraiser and that if a review function is to be carried out, this report must be revised and cannot be reviewed by the person performing the appraisal.

25. The reviewer should always "document" the file in writing after every conversation with the appraiser or others. This procedure is very valuable as time passes and memories fade.
26. The reviewer's function is not only to review the report, but also review the experience, qualifications, and professionalism of the appraiser.

COMMON ERRORS AND DEFICIENCIES IN APPRAISAL REPORTS

The following list of appraisal problems have been presented to direct the underwriter's attention to important appraisal considerations. An understanding of these items can help the underwriter and/or reviewer to spot poor quality appraisal reports. The common errors and deficiencies listed below are the most common problems faced by individuals whose daily task is to review residential appraisal reports.

1. *Subject and comparables not located anywhere each other.* Good comparables are recent sales of similar properties from the subject neighborhood. Frequently, appraisers use comparables that are located many miles from the subject property.
2. *Comparables that are not comparable.* Frequently, comparable data is inadequate because the comparables are not even remotely similar to the subject. Poor selection of market data is one of the worst problems financial institutions experience in reviewing appraisal reports.
3. *Old comparables.* Again, proper appraisal practice requires that the appraiser select recent sales of similar properties from the subject neighborhood.
4. *Over-appraised properties.* Over-appraised properties are one of the chief concerns of the financial community because they increase the magnitude of our loss when a default occurs.

5. *Missing or inaccurate information?* Often, appraisers leave out vital information that is important in the loan underwriting process. Many a property has been underwritten that would have been rejected if the appraisal report were accurate.

6. *Failure to bracket sales data.* Appraisers should find comparables that are a little better than the subject, those that are not quite as good, as well as properties that fall between these poles. This will allow the appraiser to establish a range and allow him or her, by adjustments, to find a point within the range where the subject property can be placed.

7. *Consistently listing sales price as market value.* Sales price and market value are two different concepts. Many appraisers are now backing into the market approach to value.

8. *Excessive adjustments.* Large adjustments indicate that the appraiser has selected inappropriate market data. This can result in properties being over-appraised. When properties are substantially over-appraised, the companies loss can also be substantial.

9. *Using construction cost figures to indicate the subject property's "Fair Market Value."* Cost does not necessarily equal value. Attempting to justify a loan based upon construction costs is risky. Construction costs may not be supported in the marketplace.

10. *Handwritten appraisal reports.* A professional appraisal report should be typed, with the appraiser's name typed under his or her signature. Handwritten reports are hard to read. Frequently, they are illegible.

11. *Inconsistent Adjustment Patterns.* Appraisers sometimes adjust value factors in an inconsistent manner without any explanation of why similar features are given dissimilar adjustments.

12. *Lack of clarity with respect to the appraiser's reasoning procedures.* An appraisal report is supposed to be a logical document that you can read, step by step, and come to the same conclusion as the appraiser.

I 3. Report is inadequate with respect to neighborhood data and trends. Often, important information on the neighborhood is missing. Inadequate or missing information Can lead the underwriter to make decisions that are contrary to the company's underwriting guidelines.

14. Report is too short or brief to adequately cover the property being appraised. The appraiser should spend the time and effort necessary to adequately describe and appraise the subject being appraised. If the form does not contain enough space to explain special property features or problems connected with the property and/or market, the appraiser should use additional pages to cover topics that cannot be adequately described on the appraisal form.

15. Positive or negative features of the property are not mentioned. I he appraiser should clarify both positive and negative features of the subject property. How can the underwriter make an intelligent decision if he or she does not know the strong or weak points associated with the subject property. Underwriting is a judgmental process. The underwriter needs to know the factors that positively or adversely affect the value and marketability of the subject property.

I 6. Missing photographs or photographs that do not adequately show the subject property and it's surroundings. When the underwriter's vision is limited due to poor quality photographs, so is the underwriter's judgment. The underwriter, in underwriting a loan, is trying to see. In a variety of ways, the appraiser is literally the underwriter's eyes and ears.

17. Errors in reports. Errors may exist in the appraisal report due to faulty or missing information, as well as from inappropriate handling of market or other data.

18. Making unsupportable adjustments. Many appraisal reports lack credibility because the appraiser's adjustments are illogical, as well as unconvincing.

19. Properties that lack marketability. Appraisers often fail to comment on marketability. This is important, especially when there are apparent marketability problems within a given geographic area. The underwriter's or reviewer's job with respect to appraising, is to secure acceptable appraisal reports; reports that meet standards set by professional appraisal societies. The underwriter and reviewer are the company's last defense before the loan is underwritten. Thus, the underwriter/reviewers's task is one of quality control. In reviewing appraisal reports, companies are attempting to protect themselves from an unreasonable degree of risk. Financial institutions should expect to take risks. However, the risks should be normal.

The underwriter/reviewer is responsible for the quality of appraisal reports submitted to the company. This is a vitally important role as the company is relying on appraisal reports for making decisions on whether or not to finance real property. In brief, should the institution accept or reject certain projects and end loans. The work of the underwriter/reviewer is critical in making such decisions, good quality appraisal reports will enable financial institutions to make sound decisions. Poor quality reports may cause a company to approve loans that would have been rejected had the appraisal reports been complete, consistent and accurate. The underwriter/reviewer's major task is to ensure that financial institutions engage in underwriting rather than overwriting.

CHAPTER SIXTEEN

REVIEWING GUIDELINES FOR THE UNIFORM RESIDENTIAL APPRAISAL REPORT

SUBJECT SECTION

1. The appraiser should complete the subject section of the report utilizing information supplied by the client as well as from data contained in the appraiser's own reference materials. Information should be verified by reviewing tax bills, plats of survey and other recognized real estate records and source books.
2. Check census tract, map references and zip code numbers. These items are frequently left out of the report. Missing information in any section of the report is a sign that the appraiser has not handled the appraisal assignment in a thorough and thoughtful manner.
3. It is the appraiser's responsibility to complete the form in its entirety except for the box titled "Lender Discretionary Use." The purpose of this box is to encourage lenders to provide closing dates to comparable sales reporting services. If the lender completes this section, it should do so after the loan settlement.
4. If the appraiser has checked the box De Minimus PUD, the appraiser must provide the monthly homeowner's association fee for De Minimus PUD units. In addition, the appraiser must describe the project amenities in the "Neighborhood" section and address their effect on marketability and value.

Property Description & Analysis **UNIFORM RESIDENTIAL APPRAISAL REPORT** File No.

SUBJECT		
Property Address	Census Tract	LENDER DISCRETIONARY USE
City County State	Zip Code	Sale Price $
Legal Description		Date
Owner/Occupant	Map Reference	Mortgage Amount $
Sale Price $ Date of Sale	PROPERTY RIGHTS APPRAISED	Mortgage Type
Loan charges/concessions to be paid by seller $	Fee Simple	Discount Points and Other Concessions
R.E. Taxes $ Tax Year HOA $/Mo.	Leasehold	Paid by Seller $
Lender/Client	Condominium (HUD/VA)	
	De Minimis PUD	Source

NEIGHBORHOOD

LOCATION	Urban	Suburban	Rural	NEIGHBORHOOD ANALYSIS	Good	Avg.	Fair	Poor
BUILT UP	Over 75%	25-75%	Under 25%	Employment Stability				
GROWTH RATE	Rapid	Stable	Slow	Convenience to Employment				
PROPERTY VALUES	Increasing	Stable	Declining	Convenience to Shopping				
DEMAND/SUPPLY	Shortage	In Balance	Over Supply	Convenience to Schools				
MARKETING TIME	Under 3 Mos.	3-6 Mos.	Over 6 Mos.	Adequacy of Public Transportation				

PRESENT LAND USE %	LAND USE CHANGE	PREDOMINANT	SINGLE FAMILY HOUSING	Recreation Facilities				
Single Family ___	Not Likely	OCCUPANCY	PRICE AGE $ (000) (yrs)	Adequacy of Utilities				
2-4 Family ___	Likely	Owner		Property Compatibility				
Multi-family ___	In process	Tenant	Low	Protection from Detrimental Cond.				
Commercial ___	To: ___	Vacant (0-5%)	High	Police & Fire Protection				
Industrial ___		Vacant (over 5%)	Predominant	General Appearance of Properties				
Vacant ___			—	Appeal to Market				

Note: Race or the racial composition of the neighborhood are not considered reliable appraisal factors.
COMMENTS: _____

SITE

Dimensions		Topography
Site Area	Corner Lot	Size
Zoning Classification	Zoning Compliance	Shape
HIGHEST & BEST USE: Present Use	Other Use	Drainage

UTILITIES	Public	Other	SITE IMPROVEMENTS	Type	Public	Private	View
Electricity			Street				Landscaping
Gas			Curb/Gutter				Driveway
Water			Sidewalk				Apparent Easements
Sanitary Sewer			Street Lights				FEMA Flood Hazard Yes* No
Storm Sewer			Alley				FEMA* Map/Zone

COMMENTS (Apparent adverse easements, encroachments, special assessments, slide areas, etc.): _____

IMPROVEMENTS

GENERAL DESCRIPTION	EXTERIOR DESCRIPTION	FOUNDATION	BASEMENT	INSULATION
Units	Foundation	Slab	Area Sq. Ft.	Roof
Stories	Exterior Walls	Crawl Space	% Finished	Ceiling
Type (Det./Att.)	Roof Surface	Basement	Ceiling	Walls
Design (Style)	Gutters & Dwnspts.	Sump Pump	Walls	Floor
Existing	Window Type	Dampness	Floor	None
Proposed	Storm Sash	Settlement	Outside Entry	Adequacy
Under Construction	Screens	Infestation		Energy Efficient Items:
Age (Yrs.)	Manufactured House			
Effective Age (Yrs.)				

ROOM LIST

ROOMS	Foyer	Living	Dining	Kitchen	Den	Family Rm.	Rec. Rm.	Bedrooms	# Baths	Laundry	Other	Area Sq. Ft.
Basement												
Level 1												
Level 2												

Finished area **above** grade contains: Rooms; Bedroom(s); Bath(s); Square Feet of Gross Living Area

INTERIOR

SURFACES	Materials/Condition	HEATING	KITCHEN EQUIP.	ATTIC	IMPROVEMENT ANALYSIS	Good	Avg.	Fair	Poor
Floors		Type	Refrigerator	None	Quality of Construction				
Walls		Fuel	Range/Oven	Stairs	Condition of Improvements				
Trim/Finish		Condition	Disposal	Drop Stair	Room Sizes/Layout				
Bath Floor		Adequacy	Dishwasher	Scuttle	Closets and Storage				
Bath Wainscot		COOLING	Fan/Hood	Floor	Energy Efficiency				
Doors		Central	Compactor	Heated	Plumbing-Adequacy & Condition				
		Other	Washer/Dryer	Finished	Electrical-Adequacy & Condition				
		Condition	Microwave		Kitchen Cabinets-Adequacy & Cond.				
Fireplace(s) #		Adequacy	Intercom		Compatibility to Neighborhood				

AUTOS

CAR STORAGE	Garage	Attached	Adequate	House Entry	Appeal & Marketability				
No. Cars	Carport	Detached	Inadequate	Outside Entry	Estimated Remaining Economic Life				Yrs.
Condition	None	Built-In	Electric Door	Basement Entry	Estimated Remaining Physical Life				Yrs.

Additional features: _____

COMMENTS

Depreciation (Physical, functional and external inadequacies, repairs needed, modernization, etc.): _____

General market conditions and prevalence and impact in subject/market area regarding loan discounts, interest buydowns and concessions: _____

Freddie Mac Form 70 10/86 (10 ch)   Fannie Mae Form 1004 10/86

Valuation Section   **UNIFORM RESIDENTIAL APPRAISAL REPORT**   **File No.**

Purpose of Appraisal is to estimate Market Value as defined in the Certification & Statement of Limiting Conditions.

COST APPROACH

BUILDING SKETCH (SHOW GROSS LIVING AREA ABOVE GRADE)

If for Freddie Mac or Fannie Mae, show only square foot calculations and cost approach comments in this space

ESTIMATED REPRODUCTION COST - NEW - OF IMPROVEMENTS:

Dwelling	Sq. Ft. @ $ _____	= $ _____
	Sq. Ft. @ $ _____	= _____
Extras		= _____
		= _____
Special Energy Efficient Items	_____	= _____
Porches, Patios, etc.	_____	= _____
Garage/Carport _____	Sq. Ft. @ $ _____	= _____
Total Estimated Cost New		= $ _____

	Physical	Functional	External
Less			

Depreciation _____ = $ _____
Depreciated Value of Improvements .... = $ _____
Site Imp. "as is" (driveway, landscaping, etc.) = $ _____
ESTIMATED SITE VALUE .... = $ _____
(If leasehold, show only leasehold value.)
INDICATED VALUE BY COST APPROACH .... = $ _____

(Not Required by Freddie Mac and Fannie Mae)

Does property conform to applicable HUD/VA property standards? ☐ Yes ☐ No

If No, explain: _____

Construction Warranty	☐ Yes ☐ No
Name of Warranty Program	_____
Warranty Coverage Expires	_____

The undersigned has recited three recent sales of properties most similar and proximate to subject and has considered these in the market analysis. The description includes a dollar adjustment, reflecting market reaction to those items of significant variation between the subject and comparable properties. If a significant item in the comparable property is superior to, or more favorable than, the subject property, a minus (−) adjustment is made, thus reducing the indicated value of subject; if a significant item in the comparable is inferior to, or less favorable than, the subject property, a plus (+) adjustment is made, thus increasing the indicated value of the subject.

SALES COMPARISON ANALYSIS

ITEM	SUBJECT	COMPARABLE NO. 1		COMPARABLE NO. 2		COMPARABLE NO. 3	
Address							
Proximity to Subject							
Sales Price	$		$		$		$
Price/Gross Liv. Area	$	$		$		$	
Data Source							
VALUE ADJUSTMENTS	DESCRIPTION	DESCRIPTION	+ (−) $ Adjustment	DESCRIPTION	+ (−) $ Adjustment	DESCRIPTION	+ (−) $ Adjustment
Sales or Financing Concessions							
Date of Sale/Time							
Location							
Site/View							
Design and Appeal							
Quality of Construction							
Age							
Condition							
Above Grade Room Count	Total / Bdrms / Baths	Total / Bdrms / Baths		Total / Bdrms / Baths		Total / Bdrms / Baths	
Gross Living Area	Sq. Ft.	Sq. Ft.		Sq. Ft.		Sq. Ft.	
Basement & Finished Rooms Below Grade							
Functional Utility							
Heating/Cooling							
Garage/Carport							
Porches, Patio, Pools, etc.							
Special Energy Efficient Items							
Fireplace(s)							
Other (e.g. kitchen equip., remodeling)							
Net Adj. (total)		☐ + ☐ − $		☐ + ☐ − $		☐ + ☐ − $	
Indicated Value of Subject		$		$		$	

Comments on Sales Comparison: _____

INDICATED VALUE BY SALES COMPARISON APPROACH .... $ _____

INDICATED VALUE BY INCOME APPROACH (If Applicable) Estimated Market Rent $ _____ /Mo. x Gross Rent Multiplier _____ = $ _____

This appraisal is made ☐ "as is" ☐ subject to the repairs, alterations, inspections or conditions listed below ☐ completion per plans and specifications.

Comments and Conditions of Appraisal: _____

RECONCILIATION

Final Reconciliation: _____

This appraisal is based upon the above requirements, the certification, contingent and limiting conditions, and Market Value definition that are stated in

☐ FmHA, HUD &/or VA instructions.

☐ Freddie Mac Form 439 (Rev. 7/86)/Fannie Mae Form 1004B (Rev. 7/86) filed with client _____ 19 ____ ☐ attached.

I (WE) ESTIMATE THE MARKET VALUE, AS DEFINED, OF THE SUBJECT PROPERTY AS OF _____ 19 ____ **to be $** _____

I (We) certify: that to the best of my (our) knowledge and belief the facts and data used herein are true and correct; that I (we) personally inspected the subject property, both inside and out, and have made an exterior inspection of all comparable sales cited in this report; and that I (we) have no undisclosed interest, present or prospective therein.

Appraiser(s) SIGNATURE _____   Review Appraiser SIGNATURE _____ ☐ Did ☐ Did Not

NAME _____   (if applicable) NAME _____   Inspect Property

Freddie Mac Form 70 10/86 (12 ch.)   Fannie Mae Form 1004 10/86

Property Description & Analysis **UNIFORM RESIDENTIAL APPRAISAL REPORT** File No.

SUBJECT

Property Address	
City	County	State	Zip Code ②
Legal Description	
Owner/Occupant	Map Reference
Sale Price $ ① Date of Sale	
Loan charges/concessions to be paid by seller $	
R.E. Taxes $ Tax Year HOA $/Mo	
Lender/Client	

LENDER DISCRETIONARY USE
Sale Price $
Date
Mortgage Amount $ ③
Mortgage Type
Discount Points and Other Concessions
Paid by Seller $
Source

PROPERTY RIGHTS APPRAISED
Fee Simple
Leasehold ④
Condominium (HUD/VA)
De Minimis PUD

NEIGHBORHOOD

LOCATION	Urban	Suburban	Rural
BUILT UP	Over 75%	25-75%	Under 25%
GROWTH RATE	Rapid	Stable	Slow
PROPERTY VALUES	Increasing	Stable	Declining
DEMAND/SUPPLY	Shortage	In Balance	Over Supply
MARKETING TIME	Under 3 Mos. ⑤	3-6 Mos. ⑥	Over 6 Mos.

PRESENT LAND USE % — LAND USE CHANGE — PREDOMINANT OCCUPANCY — SINGLE FAMILY HOUSING
Single Family ___ Not Likely — Owner — PRICE $(000) — AGE (yrs)
2-4 Family ___ Likely — Tenant
Multi-family ___ In process — Vacant (0-5%) — Low
Commercial ___ To: — Vacant (over 5%) — High
Industrial ___ — Predominant —
Vacant ___ —

NEIGHBORHOOD ANALYSIS   Good Avg Fair Poor ⑧
Employment Stability
Convenience to Employment
Convenience to Shopping
Convenience to Schools
Adequacy of Public Transportation
Recreation Facilities
Adequacy of Utilities
Property Compatibility
Protection from Detrimental Cond.
Police & Fire Protection
General Appearance of Properties
Appeal to Market

Note: Race or the racial composition of the neighborhood are not considered reliable appraisal factors.
COMMENTS: ⑦

SITE

Dimensions	Topography
Site Area Corner Lot	Size
Zoning Classification Zoning Compliance	Shape
HIGHEST & BEST USE: Present Use Other Use	Drainage

UTILITIES   Public   Other   SITE IMPROVEMENTS   Type   Public   Private   View
Electricity — Street — Landscaping
Gas — Curb/Gutter — Driveway
Water — Sidewalk — Apparent Easements
Sanitary Sewer — Street Lights — FEMA Flood Hazard   Yes*   No
Storm Sewer — Alley — FEMA* Map/Zone

COMMENTS (Apparent adverse easements, encroachments, special assessments, slide areas, etc.):

IMPROVEMENTS

GENERAL DESCRIPTION	EXTERIOR DESCRIPTION	FOUNDATION	BASEMENT	INSULATION
Units	Foundation	Slab	Area Sq. Ft.	Roof
Stories	Exterior Walls	Crawl Space	% Finished	Ceiling
Type (Det./Att.)	Roof Surface	Basement	Ceiling	Walls
Design (Style)	Gutters & Dwnspts.	Sump Pump	Walls	Floor
Existing	Window Type	Dampness	Floor	None
Proposed	Storm Sash	Settlement	Outside Entry	Adequacy
Under Construction	Screens	Infestation		Energy Efficient Items:
Age (Yrs.)	Manufactured House			
Effective Age (Yrs.)				

ROOM LIST

ROOMS	Foyer	Living	Dining	Kitchen	Den	Family Rm.	Rec. Rm.	Bedrooms	# Baths	Laundry	Other	Area Sq. Ft.
Basement												
Level 1												
Level 2												

Finished area above grade contains: Rooms;   Bedroom(s);   Bath(s);   Square Feet of Gross Living Area

INTERIOR

SURFACES	Materials/Condition	HEATING	KITCHEN EQUIP.	ATTIC	IMPROVEMENT ANALYSIS	Good Avg Fair Poor
Floors		Type	Refrigerator	None	Quality of Construction	
Walls		Fuel	Range/Oven	Stairs	Condition of Improvements	
Trim/Finish		Condition	Disposal	Drop Stair	Room Sizes/Layout	
Bath Floor		Adequacy	Dishwasher	Scuttle	Closets and Storage	
Bath Wainscot		COOLING	Fan/Hood	Floor	Energy Efficiency	
Doors		Central	Compactor	Heated	Plumbing-Adequacy & Condition	
		Other	Washer/Dryer	Finished	Electrical-Adequacy & Condition	
		Condition	Microwave		Kitchen Cabinets-Adequacy & Cond.	
Fireplace(s) #		Adequacy	Intercom		Compatibility to Neighborhood	

AUTOS

CAR STORAGE: Garage   Attached   Adequate   House Entry   Appeal & Marketability
No. Cars   Carport   Detached   Inadequate   Outside Entry   Estimated Remaining Economic Life   Yrs.
Condition   None   Built-In   Electric Door   Basement Entry   Estimated Remaining Physical Life   Yrs.
Additional features:

COMMENTS

Depreciation (Physical, functional and external inadequacies, repairs needed, modernization, etc.):

General market conditions and prevalence and impact in subject/market area regarding loan discounts, interest buydowns and concessions:

Freddie Mac Form 70   10/86   (10 ch)   Fannie Mae Form 1004   10/86

NEIGHBORHOOD SECTION

5. The neighborhood section of the appraisal report should be complete and accurate. Location is a critical factor with respect to a property's value and marketability. Information in this section is also vitally important as financial institutions must evaluate loan packages based upon their underwriting standards. Complete and accurate information is necessary in order to make sound underwriting decisions. What a company doesn't know *can* hurt it!

6. Factors in the neighborhood section must be carefully handled by the appraiser. Since financial institutions are concerned with risk, underwriters working for these organizations are attempting to visualize both the neighborhood and surrounding market in order to spot healthy growth patterns versus undesirable trends that may indicate a deteriorating neighborhood with limited market appeal. For example, a property located in an over-built area where values are steeply declining and marketing time is lengthy may be an unacceptable risk to a financial institution.

7. Comments in the neighborhood section must be relevant and give insight into those factors which positively or negatively affect the appraised property's marketability. A neighborhood should be acceptable to a large enough segment of buyers to support an active market. In brief, a property should have potential for long-term acceptance and be relatively free of detrimental conditions.

8. All fair and poor ratings in the neighborhood analysis section must be explained. Negative factors may adversely affect the value and long-term marketability of a property. The ratings on the appraisal form have been specially selected to represent items that are important to buyers in the market place. Low rating need to be addressed since financial institutions are concerned with market strength over a long period of time.

Exhibit B. Neighborhood Section

| Property Description & Analysis | UNIFORM RESIDENTIAL APPRAISAL REPORT | File No. | |

SUBJECT

Property Address		Census Tract	LENDER DISCRETIONARY USE	
City	County	State	Zip Code	Sale Price $
Legal Description				Date
Owner/Occupant		Map Reference		Mortgage Amount $
Sale Price $	Date of Sale	PROPERTY RIGHTS APPRAISED	Mortgage Type	
Loan charges/concessions to be paid by seller $		☐ Fee Simple	Discount Points and Other Concessions	
R.E. Taxes $	Tax Year	HOA $/Mo.	☐ Leasehold	Paid by Seller $
Lender/Client		☐ Condominium (HUD/VA)		
		☐ De Minimis PUD	Source	

NEIGHBORHOOD

LOCATION	☐ Urban	☐ Suburban	☐ Rural	NEIGHBORHOOD ANALYSIS	Good Avg Fair Poor
BUILT UP	☐ Over 75%	☐ 25-75%	☐ Under 25%	Employment Stability	☐☐☐☐
GROWTH RATE	☐ Rapid	☐ Stable	☐ Slow	Convenience to Employment	☐☐☐☐
PROPERTY VALUES	☐ Increasing	☐ Stable	☐ Declining	Convenience to Shopping	☐☐☐☐
DEMAND/SUPPLY	☐ Shortage	☐ In Balance	☐ Over Supply	Convenience to Schools	☐☐☐☐
MARKETING TIME	☐ Under 3 Mos	☐ 3-6 Mos	☐ Over 6 Mos	Adequacy of Public Transportation	☐☐☐☐

(11) (12) (10)

PRESENT LAND USE %	LAND USE CHANGE	PREDOMINANT	SINGLE FAMILY HOUSING	Recreation Facilities	☐☐☐☐
Single Family	Not Likely ☐	OCCUPANCY	PRICE AGE	Adequacy of Utilities	☐☐☐☐
2-4 Family	Likely ☐	Owner ☐	$ (000) (yrs)	Property Compatibility	☐☐☐☐
Multi-family	In process ☐	Tenant ☐		Protection from Detrimental Cond.	☐☐☐☐
Commercial	To:	Vacant (0-5%) ☐		Police & Fire Protection	☐☐☐☐
Industrial		Vacant (over 5%) ☐	Predominant	General Appearance of Properties	☐☐☐☐
Vacant			—	Appeal to Market	☐☐☐☐

Note: Race or the racial composition of the neighborhood are not considered reliable appraisal factors.

COMMENTS: (9)

SITE

Dimensions			Topography	
Site Area		Corner Lot	Size	
Zoning Classification		Zoning Compliance	Shape	
HIGHEST & BEST USE: Present Use		Other Use	Drainage	

UTILITIES	Public	Other	SITE IMPROVEMENTS	Type	Public	Private	View	
Electricity			Street				Landscaping	
Gas			Curb/Gutter				Driveway	
Water			Sidewalk				Apparent Easements	
Sanitary Sewer			Street Lights				FEMA Flood Hazard Yes* No	
Storm Sewer			Alley				FEMA* Map/Zone	

COMMENTS (Apparent adverse easements, encroachments, special assessments, slide areas, etc.):

IMPROVEMENTS

GENERAL DESCRIPTION	EXTERIOR DESCRIPTION	FOUNDATION	BASEMENT	INSULATION
Units	Foundation	Slab	Area Sq. Ft.	Roof
Stories	Exterior Walls	Crawl Space	% Finished	Ceiling
Type (Det./Att.)	Roof Surface	Basement	Ceiling	Walls
Design (Style)	Gutters & Dwnspts.	Sump Pump	Walls	Floor
Existing	Window Type	Dampness	Floor	None
Proposed	Storm Sash	Settlement	Outside Entry	Adequacy
Under Construction	Screens	Infestation		Energy Efficient Items:
Age (Yrs.)	Manufactured House			
Effective Age (Yrs.)				

ROOM LIST

ROOMS	Foyer	Living	Dining	Kitchen	Den	Family Rm.	Rec. Rm.	Bedrooms	# Baths	Laundry	Other	Area Sq. Ft.
Basement												
Level 1												
Level 2												

Finished area **above** grade contains: Rooms; Bedroom(s); Bath(s); Square Feet of Gross Living Area

INTERIOR

SURFACES	Materials/Condition	HEATING	KITCHEN EQUIP.	ATTIC	IMPROVEMENT ANALYSIS	Good Avg Fair Poor
Floors		Type	Refrigerator ☐	None ☐	Quality of Construction	☐☐☐☐
Walls		Fuel	Range/Oven ☐	Stairs ☐	Condition of Improvements	☐☐☐☐
Trim/Finish		Condition	Disposal ☐	Drop Stair ☐	Room Sizes/Layout	☐☐☐☐
Bath Floor		Adequacy	Dishwasher ☐	Scuttle ☐	Closets and Storage	☐☐☐☐
Bath Wainscot		COOLING	Fan/Hood ☐	Floor ☐	Energy Efficiency	☐☐☐☐
Doors		Central	Compactor ☐	Heated ☐	Plumbing-Adequacy & Condition	☐☐☐☐
		Other	Washer/Dryer ☐	Finished ☐	Electrical-Adequacy & Condition	☐☐☐☐
		Condition	Microwave ☐		Kitchen Cabinets-Adequacy & Cond.	☐☐☐☐
Fireplace(s)	#	Adequacy	Intercom ☐		Compatibility to Neighborhood	☐☐☐☐

AUTOS

CAR STORAGE:	Garage	Attached	Adequate ☐	House Entry ☐	Appeal & Marketability	☐☐☐☐
No. Cars	Carport	Detached	Inadequate ☐	Outside Entry ☐	Estimated Remaining Economic Life	Yrs.
Condition	None	Built-In	Electric Door ☐	Basement Entry ☐	Estimated Remaining Physical Life	Yrs.

Additional features:

COMMENTS

Depreciation (Physical, functional and external inadequacies, repairs needed, modernization, etc.):

General market conditions and prevalence and impact in subject/market area regarding loan discounts, interest buydowns and concessions:

Freddie Mac Form 70 10/86 (10 ch.)   Fannie Mae Form 1004 10/86

9. The appraiser should comment when the neighborhood is experiencing a decline in values. Due to a loss in equity, a property located in a neighborhood or area where values are declining may present a financial institution with a high and perhaps unacceptable risk. Financial organizations expect that loan amortization will keep up with or exceed any decline in prices. Therefore, stable or rising property values with average or above ratings for the improvements are important considerations in underwriting any given loan.

10. Residential properties that are near the top or above the top of the neighborhood value range may present a high risk to financial institutions. The appraiser should comment on properties that are valued at 90% or more of the highest property value in the neighborhood. Such properties may represent over improvements and be difficult to sell in a reasonable length of time. The appraiser's comments can clarify whether or not a property lacks marketability because it represents an over improvement for the area.

11. When there is an over supply of housing this factor must be addressed by the appraiser. An over supply of housing is a critical factor as it may result in limited marketability and produce a decline in values. Financial institutions in underwriting loans in overbuilt markets can experience substantial losses. Frequently, appraisal reports fail to inform financial institutions of declining values and marketability problems. Financial organizations wish to obtain insight into the reasons for market rejection in a given geographic area or neighborhood.

12. The appraiser should comment when marketing time is over six months. A lengthy marketing time poses special problems as it reflects a slow market and usually declining values. In a slow or declining market, the borrowers may be placed in a position where it is impossible for them to dispose of their property. An erosion in values can result in a substantial loss for the financial institution.

Exhibit C. Site Section

Property Description & Analysis **UNIFORM RESIDENTIAL APPRAISAL REPORT** File No.

SUBJECT

Property Address			Census Tract	LENDER DISCRETIONARY USE
City	County	State	Zip Code	Sale Price $
Legal Description				Date
Owner/Occupant			Map Reference	Mortgage Amount $
Sale Price $	Date of Sale		PROPERTY RIGHTS APPRAISED	Mortgage Type
Loan charges/concessions to be paid by seller $			Fee Simple	Discount Points and Other Concessions
R.E. Taxes $	Tax Year	HOA $/Mo.	Leasehold	Paid by Seller $
Lender/Client			Condominium (HUD/VA)	
			De Minimis PUD	Source

NEIGHBORHOOD

LOCATION	Urban	Suburban	Rural	NEIGHBORHOOD ANALYSIS	Good	Avg.	Fair	Poor
BUILT UP	Over 75%	25-75%	Under 25%	Employment Stability				
GROWTH RATE	Rapid	Stable	Slow	Convenience to Employment				
PROPERTY VALUES	Increasing	Stable	Declining	Convenience to Shopping				
DEMAND/SUPPLY	Shortage	In Balance	Over Supply	Convenience to Schools				
MARKETING TIME	Under 3 Mos.	3-6 Mos.	Over 6 Mos.	Adequacy of Public Transportation				

PRESENT LAND USE %	LAND USE CHANGE	PREDOMINANT	SINGLE FAMILY HOUSING	Recreation Facilities				
Single Family	Not Likely	OCCUPANCY	PRICE / AGE	Adequacy of Utilities				
2-4 Family	Likely	Owner	$ (000) (yrs)	Property Compatibility				
Multi-family	In process	Tenant		Protection from Detrimental Cond.				
Commercial	To:	Vacant (0-5%)	Low	Police & Fire Protection				
Industrial		Vacant (over 5%)	High	General Appearance of Properties				
Vacant			Predominant	Appeal to Market				

Note: Race or the racial composition of the neighborhood are not considered reliable appraisal factors.
COMMENTS:

SITE

Dimensions		Topography	
Site Area		Size	
Zoning Classification	Corner Lot z(16)ompliance	Shape	
HIGHEST & BEST USE: Present Use	Other Use	Drainage	

UTILITIES	Public	Other	SITE IMPROVEMENTS	Type	Public	Private	View	
Electricity			Street				Landscaping	
Gas			Curb/Gutter				Driveway	
Water			Sidewalk				Apparent Easements	(15)
Sanitary Sewer			Street Lights				FEMA Flood Hazard	Yes* No
Storm Sewer			Alley				FEMA* Map/Zone	

COMMENTS (Apparent adverse easements, encroachments, special assessments, slide areas, etc.) (13) (14)

IMPROVEMENTS

GENERAL DESCRIPTION	EXTERIOR DESCRIPTION	FOUNDATION	BASEMENT	INSULATION
Units	Foundation	Slab	Area Sq. Ft.	Roof
Stories	Exterior Walls	Crawl Space	% Finished	Ceiling
Type (Det./Att.)	Roof Surface	Basement	Ceiling	Walls
Design (Style)	Gutters & Dwnspts.	Sump Pump	Walls	Floor
Existing	Window Type	Dampness	Floor	None
Proposed	Storm Sash	Settlement	Outside Entry	Adequacy
Under Construction	Screens	Infestation		Energy Efficient Items:
Age (Yrs.)	Manufactured House			
Effective Age (Yrs.)				

ROOM LIST

ROOMS	Foyer	Living	Dining	Kitchen	Den	Family Rm.	Rec. Rm.	Bedrooms	# Baths	Laundry	Other	Area Sq. Ft.
Basement												
Level 1												
Level 2												

Finished area above grade contains: Rooms; Bedroom(s); Bath(s); Square Feet of Gross Living Area

INTERIOR

SURFACES	Materials/Condition	HEATING		KITCHEN EQUIP.	ATTIC	IMPROVEMENT ANALYSIS	Good	Avg.	Fair	Poor
Floors		Type		Refrigerator	None	Quality of Construction				
Walls		Fuel		Range/Oven	Stairs	Condition of Improvements				
Trim/Finish		Condition		Disposal	Drop Stair	Room Sizes/Layout				
Bath Floor		Adequacy		Dishwasher	Scuttle	Closets and Storage				
Bath Wainscot		COOLING		Fan/Hood	Floor	Energy Efficiency				
Doors		Central		Compactor	Heated	Plumbing-Adequacy & Condition				
		Other		Washer/Dryer	Finished	Electrical-Adequacy & Condition				
		Condition		Microwave		Kitchen Cabinets-Adequacy & Cond.				
Fireplace(s) #		Adequacy		Intercom		Compatibility to Neighborhood				
CAR STORAGE:	Garage	Attached		Adequate	House Entry	Appeal & Marketability				
No. Cars	Carport	Detached		Inadequate	Outside Entry	Estimated Remaining Economic Life				Yrs.
Condition	None	Built-In		Electric Door	Basement Entry	Estimated Remaining Physical Life				Yrs.

Additional features:

COMMENTS

Depreciation (Physical, functional and external inadequacies, repairs needed, modernization, etc.):

General market conditions and prevalence and impact in subject/market area regarding loan discounts, interest buydowns and concessions:

Freddie Mac Form 70 10/86 (10 ch.)   Fannie Mae Form 1004 10/86

SITE SECTION

13. Unfavorable site factors must be commented on by the appraiser. Financial institutions wish to know that site features such as size, shape and topography, etc. are acceptable in the market place. In brief, a site should meet all the criteria for a desirable lot in the area. A poor lot may result in poor marketability for the subject property.

14. The appraisal report should explain the affect on marketability of any unfavorable site conditions such as adverse easements, encroachments or other detrimental factors.

15. Problems relating to poor drainage and/or flood conditions must be dealt with by the appraiser in the comment section or attachments. If the appraiser indicates that the property is located in a Special Flood Hazard Area—as identified by the Federal Emergency Management Agency (FEMA)—the map number and designated zone must be noted. A financial institution may need to seek additional information to determine if the degree of risk is acceptable.

16. The appraiser should verify zoning for the subject and surrounding properties and give careful consideration to the appraisal property's highest and best use. If the improvements do not represent a legal, conforming use under the current zoning classification, the appraiser must clarify whether the subject's use is "legal non-conforming" or "illegal." The underwriter may wish to clarify non-compliance with zoning regulations, as non-compliance may have a significant impact on value and marketability.

Exhibit D. Improvements Section

Property Description & Analysis **UNIFORM RESIDENTIAL APPRAISAL REPORT** File No.

SUBJECT

Property Address	Census Tract	LENDER DISCRETIONARY USE
City County State	Zip Code	Sale Price $
Legal Description		Date
Owner/Occupant	Map Reference	Mortgage Amount $
Sale Price $ Date of Sale	PROPERTY RIGHTS APPRAISED	Mortgage Type
Loan charges/concessions to be paid by seller $	☐ Fee Simple	Discount Points and Other Concessions
R.E. Taxes $ Tax Year HOA $/Mo.	☐ Leasehold	Paid by Seller $
Lender/Client	☐ Condominium (HUD/VA)	
	☐ De Minimis PUD	Source

NEIGHBORHOOD

LOCATION	☐ Urban	☐ Suburban	☐ Rural	NEIGHBORHOOD ANALYSIS	Good	Avg.	Fair	Poor
BUILT UP	☐ Over 75%	☐ 25-75%	☐ Under 25%	Employment Stability	☐	☐	☐	☐
GROWTH RATE	☐ Rapid	☐ Stable	☐ Slow	Convenience to Employment	☐	☐	☐	☐
PROPERTY VALUES	☐ Increasing	☐ Stable	☐ Declining	Convenience to Shopping	☐	☐	☐	☐
DEMAND/SUPPLY	☐ Shortage	☐ In Balance	☐ Over Supply	Convenience to Schools	☐	☐	☐	☐
MARKETING TIME	☐ Under 3 Mos.	☐ 3-6 Mos.	☐ Over 6 Mos.	Adequacy of Public Transportation	☐	☐	☐	☐

PRESENT LAND USE %	LAND USE CHANGE	PREDOMINANT	SINGLE FAMILY HOUSING	Recreation Facilities	☐	☐	☐	☐
Single Family ___	Not Likely ☐	OCCUPANCY	PRICE $ (000) / AGE (yrs)	Adequacy of Utilities	☐	☐	☐	☐
2-4 Family ___	Likely ☐	☐ Owner		Property Compatibility	☐	☐	☐	☐
Multi-family ___	In process ☐	☐ Tenant		Protection from Detrimental Cond	☐	☐	☐	☐
Commercial ___	To:	☐ Vacant (0-5%)	Low	Police & Fire Protection	☐	☐	☐	☐
Industrial ___		☐ Vacant (over 5%)	High	General Appearance of Properties	☐	☐	☐	☐
Vacant ___			Predominant	Appeal to Market	☐	☐	☐	☐

Note: Race or the racial composition of the neighborhood are not considered reliable appraisal factors.

COMMENTS:

SITE

Dimensions				Topography	
Site Area			Corner Lot	Size	
Zoning Classification			Zoning Compliance	Shape	
HIGHEST & BEST USE: Present Use			Other Use	Drainage	

UTILITIES	Public	Other	SITE IMPROVEMENTS	Type	Public	Private	View	
Electricity	☐		Street		☐	☐	Landscaping	
Gas	☐		Curb/Gutter		☐	☐	Driveway	
Water	☐		Sidewalk		☐	☐	Apparent Easements	
Sanitary Sewer	☐		Street Lights		☐	☐	FEMA Flood Hazard	Yes* ___ No ___
Storm Sewer	☐		Alley		☐	☐	FEMA* Map/Zone	

COMMENTS (Apparent adverse easements, encroachments, special assessments, slide areas, etc.):

IMPROVEMENTS

GENERAL DESCRIPTION	EXTERIOR DESCRIPTION	FOUNDATION	BASEMENT	INSULATION
Units	Foundation	Slab	Area Sq Ft	Roof ☐
Stories	Exterior Walls	Crawl Space	% Finished	Ceiling ☐
Type (Det./Att.)	Roof Surface	Basement	Ceiling	Walls ☐
Design (Style)	Gutters & Dwnspts ⟨22⟩	Sump Pump	Walls	Floor ☐
Existing	Window Type	Dampness	Floor	None ☐
Proposed	Storm Sash	Settlement	Outside Entry	Adequacy
Under Construction	Screens	Infestation		Energy Efficient Items
Age (Yrs.)	Manufactured House			
Effective Age (Yrs.)				

ROOM LIST

ROOMS	Foyer	Living	Dining	Kitchen	Den	Family Rm	Rec Rm	Bedrooms	# Baths	Laundry	Other	Area Sq Ft
Basement												
Level 1												
Level 2												

Finished area **above** grade contains ___ Rooms. ___ Bedroom(s). ___ Bath(s). ___ Square Feet of Gross Living Area

INTERIOR

SURFACES	Materials/Condition	HEATING		KITCHEN EQUIP	ATTIC	IMPROVEMENT ANALYSIS	Good	Avg	Fair	Poor
Floors		Type		Refrigerator ☐	None ☐	Quality of Construction	☐	☐	☐	☐
Walls		Fuel		Range/Oven ☐	Stairs ☐	Condition of Improvements	☐	☐	☐	☐
Trim/Finish		Condition		Disposal ☐	Drop Stair ☐	Room Sizes/Layout	☐	☐	☐	☐
Bath Floor		Adequacy		Dishwasher ☐	Scuttle ☐	Closets and Storage	☐	☐	☐	☐
Bath Wainscot		COOLING		Fan/Hood ☐	Floor ☐	Energy Efficiency	☐	☐	☐	☐
Doors		Central		Compactor ☐	Heated ☐	Plumbing-Adequacy & Condition	☐	☐	☐	☐
		Other		Washer/Dryer ☐	Finished ☐	Electrical-Adequacy & Condition	☐	☐	☐	☐
		Condition		Microwave ☐		Kitchen Cabinets-Adequacy & Cond	☐	☐	☐	☐
Fireplace(s) #		Adequacy		Intercom ☐		Compatibility to Neighborhood	☐	☐	☐	☐

AUTOS

CAR STORAGE	Garage ☐	Attached ☐	Adequate ☐	House Entry ☐	Appeal & Marketability	☐	☐	☐	☐
No. Cars ___	Carport ☐	Detached ☐	Inadequate ☐	Outside Entry ☐	Estimated Remaining Economic Life	___ Yrs
Condition ___	None ☐	Built-In ☐	Electric Door ☐	Basement Entry ☐	Estimated Remaining Physical Life	___ Yrs

Additional features ⟨19⟩

COMMENTS

Depreciation (Physical, functional and external inadequacies, repairs needed, modernization, etc.) ⟨17⟩ ⟨20⟩ ⟨21⟩

General market conditions and prevalence and impact in subject/market area regarding loan discounts, interest buydowns and concessions

Freddie Mac Form 70 10/86 (10 ch) Fannie Mae Form 1004 10/86

(18)

IMPROVEMENT SECTION (etc.)

17. The appraiser must comment on functional and physical in-adequacies and indicate when repairs or modernization are needed. Serious attention must be given to structural problems.

18. Fair or poor ratings for improvements must be explained. Such factors may adversely affect the property's long-term market-ability. They may also limit the buyer's commitment to the property and loan.

19. Over and under-improvements deserve special comments. An over-improvements represents a higher risk than typical properties in the neighborhood. Further, their construction cost may be greater than their market value. Since cost and value can be quite different, the appraiser's value conclusion should reflect and be consistent with market information. When appraising recently built custom homes, the appraiser should be careful not to confuse the concept of cost with the concept of value.

20. The appraiser should comment on unusual layouts, peculiar floor plans, inadequate equipment and amenities. These factors limit value and market appeal and are important to the underwriter in determining the property's suitability for long-term high ratio financing.

21. If the appraiser is using computer generated data, facts and comments on the report must be applicable to the subject and comparable properties. Each property is unique. Therefore, comments and factual data will vary depending on the nature of the property. The appraiser should avoid using the computer to produce cookie-cutter appraisal reports. A computer is a tool to aid the appraiser. It is not to be used as a substitute for thinking.

22. If there is evidence of dampness, termites or settlement, the appraiser must comment on these factors as such conditions require careful documentation. In brief, the financial institu-

Exhibit E. Cost Approach Section

Valuation Section   **UNIFORM RESIDENTIAL APPRAISAL REPORT**   File No.

Purpose of Appraisal is to estimate Market Value as defined in the Certification & Statement of Limiting Conditions

COST APPROACH

BUILDING SKETCH (SHOW GROSS LIVING AREA ABOVE GRADE)
If for Freddie Mac or Fannie Mae, show only square foot calculations and cost approach comments in this space

(23)

ESTIMATED REPRODUCTION COST-NEW-OF IMPROVEMENTS

Dwelling	Sq. Ft. @ $	= $
	Sq. Ft. @ $	=
Extras (24)		=
Special Energy Efficient Items		=
Porches, Patios, etc		=
Garage/Carport	Sq. Ft. @ $	=
Total Estimated Cost New		= $

	Physical	Functional	External
Less			
Depreciation			= $

Depreciated Value of Improvements	= $
Site Imp "as is" (driveway, landscaping, etc.)	= $
ESTIMATED SITE VALUE	= $
(If leasehold, show only leasehold value)	
INDICATED VALUE BY COST APPROACH	= $

(Not Required by Freddie Mac and Fannie Mae)
Does property conform to applicable HUD/VA property standards? ☐ Yes ☐ No
If No, explain:

Construction Warranty ☐ Yes ☐ No
Name of Warranty Program
Warranty Coverage Expires

The undersigned has recited three recent sales of properties most similar and proximate to subject and has considered these in the market analysis. The description includes a dollar adjustment, reflecting market reaction to those items of significant variation between the subject and comparable properties. If a significant item in the comparable property is superior to, or more favorable than, the subject property, a minus (−) adjustment is made, thus reducing the indicated value of subject; if a significant item in the comparable is inferior to, or less favorable than, the subject property, a plus (+) adjustment is made, thus increasing the indicated value of the subject.

SALES COMPARISON ANALYSIS

ITEM	SUBJECT	COMPARABLE NO. 1		COMPARABLE NO. 2		COMPARABLE NO. 3	
Address							
Proximity to Subject							
Sales Price	$		$		$		$
Price/Gross Liv. Area	$		$		$		$
Data Source							
VALUE ADJUSTMENTS	DESCRIPTION	DESCRIPTION	+ (−)$ Adjustment	DESCRIPTION	+ (−)$ Adjustment	DESCRIPTION	+ (−)$ Adjustment
Sales or Financing Concessions							
Date of Sale/Time							
Location							
Site/View							
Design and Appeal							
Quality of Construction							
Age							
Condition							
Above Grade Room Count	Total | Bdrms | Baths	Total | Bdrms | Baths		Total | Bdrms | Baths		Total | Bdrms | Baths	
Gross Living Area	Sq. Ft.	Sq. Ft.		Sq. Ft.		Sq. Ft.	
Basement & Finished Rooms Below Grade							
Functional Utility							
Heating/Cooling							
Garage/Carport							
Porches, Patio, Pools, etc.							
Special Energy Efficient Items							
Fireplace(s)							
Other (e.g. kitchen equip., remodeling)							
Net Adj. (total)		☐ + ☐ −	$	☐ + ☐ −	$	☐ + ☐ −	$
Indicated Value of Subject			$		$		$
Comments on Sales Comparison:							

RECONCILIATION

INDICATED VALUE BY SALES COMPARISON APPROACH .... $
INDICATED VALUE BY INCOME APPROACH (If Applicable) Estimated Market Rent $ _____ /Mo. x Gross Rent Multiplier _____ = $
This appraisal is made ☐ "as is" ☐ subject to the repairs, alterations, inspections or conditions listed below ☐ completion per plans and specifications.
Comments and Conditions of Appraisal:

Final Reconciliation:

This appraisal is based upon the above requirements, the certification, contingent and limiting conditions, and Market Value definition that are stated in
☐ FmHA, HUD &/or VA instructions.
☐ Freddie Mac Form 439 (Rev. 7/86)/Fannie Mae Form 1004B (Rev. 7/86) filed with client _____ 19 ___ ☐ attached.
I (WE) ESTIMATE THE MARKET VALUE, AS DEFINED, OF THE SUBJECT PROPERTY AS OF _____ 19 ___ **to be $** _____
I (We) certify: that to the best of my (our) knowledge and belief the facts and data used herein are true and correct; that I (we) personally inspected the subject property, both inside and out, and have made an exterior inspection of all comparable sales cited in this report; and that I (we) have no undisclosed interest, present or prospective therein.

Appraiser(s) SIGNATURE _____   Review Appraiser SIGNATURE _____ ☐ Did ☐ Did Not
            NAME _____   (if applicable) NAME _____   Inspect Property

Freddie Mac Form 70 10/86 (12 ch)   Fannie Mae Form 1004 10/86

tion's underwriters will have to determine the severity of the condition, etc.

COST APPROACH SECTION

23. In estimating the cost approach, the appraiser should show measurements and state the subject's total gross living area. The form does not provide sufficient space, the gross living area calculations can be shown on the floor plan sketch either within the cost approach section or in the exhibit section of the report.

24. In estimating reproduction costs, the appraiser should use cost figures that are appropriate for the local market. Further, the appraiser should attempt to be as accurate as possible with land costs as the value of land in proportion to the value of the total property is an important underwriting consideration.

Exhibit F. Sales Comparison Section

UNIFORM RESIDENTIAL APPRAISAL REPORT   File No.

Valuation Section

Purpose of Appraisal is to estimate Market Value as defined in the Certification & Statement of Limiting Conditions.

COST APPROACH

BUILDING SKETCH (SHOW GROSS LIVING AREA ABOVE GRADE)
It for Freddie Mac or Fannie Mae, show only square foot calculations and cost approach comments in this space.

ESTIMATED REPRODUCTION COST - NEW - OF IMPROVEMENTS:

Dwelling	Sq. Ft. @ $	= $
	Sq. Ft. @ $	=
Extras		=
		=
Special Energy Efficient Items		=
Porches, Patios, etc.		=
Garage/Carport	Sq Ft @ $	=
Total Estimated Cost New		= $

	Physical	Functional	External
Less			
Depreciation			= $
Depreciated Value of Improvements			= $
Site Imp. "as is" (driveway, landscaping, etc.)			= $
ESTIMATED SITE VALUE			= $
(If leasehold, show only leasehold value.)			
INDICATED VALUE BY COST APPROACH			= $

(Not Required by Freddie Mac and Fannie Mae)
Does property conform to applicable HUD/VA property standards? ☐ Yes ☐ No
If No, explain:

Construction Warranty ☐ Yes ☐ No
Name of Warranty Program
Warranty Coverage Expires

SALES COMPARISON ANALYSIS

The undersigned has recited three recent sales of properties most similar and proximate to subject and has considered these in the market analysis. The description includes a dollar adjustment, reflecting market reaction to those items of significant variation between the subject and comparable properties. If a significant item in the comparable property is superior to, or more favorable than, the subject property, a minus (−) adjustment is made, thus reducing the indicated value of subject. If a significant item in the comparable is inferior to or less favorable than, the subject property, a plus (+) adjustment is made, thus increasing the indicated value of the subject.

ITEM	SUBJECT	COMPARABLE NO 1	COMPARABLE NO 2	COMPARABLE NO 3
Address		(25)	(27)	(28)
Proximity to Subject				
Sales Price	$	$	$	$
Price/Gross Liv. Area	$ ☑	$ ☑	$ ☑	$ ☑
Data Source				

VALUE ADJUSTMENTS	DESCRIPTION	DESCRIPTION	+ (−)$ Adjustment	DESCRIPTION	+ (−)$ Adjustment	DESCRIPTION	+ (−)$ Adjustment
Sales or Financing Concessions				(26)			
Date of Sale/Time							
Location							
Site/View	(31)						
Design and Appeal							
Quality of Construction							
Age							
Condition							
Above Grade	Total · Bdrms · Baths	Total · Bdrms · Baths		Total · Bdrms · Baths		Total · Bdrms · Baths	
Room Count							
Gross Living Area	Sq Ft	Sq Ft		(29) Sq Ft		Sq Ft	(32)
Basement & Finished Rooms Below Grade							
Functional Utility							
Heating/Cooling							
Garage/Carport							
Porches, Patio, Pools, etc							
Special Energy Efficient Items							
Fireplace(s)							
Other (e.g. kitchen equip., remodeling)							
Net Adj. (total)		☐ + ☐ − $		☐ + ☐ − $		☐ + ☐ − $	
Indicated Value of Subject		$		$		$	

Comments on Sales Comparison (30)

INDICATED VALUE BY SALES COMPARISON APPROACH $
INDICATED VALUE BY INCOME APPROACH (If Applicable) Estimated Market Rent $ _____ /Mo. x Gross Rent Multiplier _____ = $
This appraisal is made ☐ "as is" ☐ subject to the repairs, alterations, inspections or conditions listed below ☐ completion per plans and specifications.
Comments and Conditions of Appraisal:

Final Reconciliation:

RECONCILIATION

This appraisal is based upon the above requirements, the certification, contingent and limiting conditions, and Market Value definition that are stated in
☐ FmHA, HUD &/or VA instructions.
☐ Freddie Mac Form 439 (Rev. 7/86)/Fannie Mae Form 1004B (Rev. 7/86) filed with client _____ 19 ___ ☐ attached.
I (WE) ESTIMATE THE MARKET VALUE, AS DEFINED, OF THE SUBJECT PROPERTY AS OF _____ 19 ___ to be $
I (We) certify: that to the best of my (our) knowledge and belief the facts and data used herein are true and correct; that I (we) personally inspected the subject property, both inside and out, and have made an exterior inspection of all comparable sales cited in this report; and that I (we) have no undisclosed interest, present or prospective therein.

Appraiser(s) SIGNATURE _____
NAME _____

Review Appraiser SIGNATURE _____
(if applicable) NAME _____ ☐ Did ☐ Did Not Inspect Property

Freddie Mac Form 70 10/86 (12 ch)

Fannie Mae Form 1004 10/86

ANALYSIS SECTION

25. An appraiser should not enter cost data into the market approach to value. For example, adjustments for gross living area should reflect what buyers are paying in the market place for specific value elements. Such adjustments should not represent preselected cost data which is applied equally to all types of living space.

26. All comparables must be recently closed sales of similar properties from the subject neighborhood. Good appraisal reports all have one thing in common: the appraiser has selected good comparable data which has been well handled.

27. The appraiser must avoid using old comparables. Sales should have occurred within the last three months. Any sales that are over three months old must be explained. Markets change, and sometimes swiftly. Therefore, it is important that appraisers use the most recent sales available.

28. Comparables must be similar in design and style. They should contain, if possible, the same room count and approximate square foot area. Dissimilar properties should not be used as comparables.

29. All sales should be transactions that have closed. The appraiser should not adjust contracts or listings. A meeting of the minds in a real estate transaction involves something more than a sales contract. It involves the ability to go to the closing table and complete the transaction. Recorded data can be adequately verified and has a much higher degree of validity than word of mouth information from brokers and builders. Contracts frequently do not make it to closing. When they do, details of the transactions sometimes change before closing. In brief, contracts may not reflect a property's market value.

30. If the appraiser has obtained contract or listing data which the appraiser feels deserves consideration, this information can be placed in the comment or addenda section of the report.

31. Except for rural locations, all sales must be from the neigh-

Exhibit F. Sales Comparison Section (continued)

Valuation Section

UNIFORM RESIDENTIAL APPRAISAL REPORT   File No.

Purpose of Appraisal is to estimate Market Value as defined in the Certification & Statement of Limiting Conditions.

COST APPROACH

BUILDING SKETCH (SHOW GROSS LIVING AREA ABOVE GRADE)
If for Freddie Mac or Fannie Mae show only square foot calculations and cost approach comments in this space.

ESTIMATED REPRODUCTION COST-NEW-OF IMPROVEMENTS:

Dwelling _____ Sq. Ft. @ $ _____ = $ _____
_____ Sq. Ft. @ $ _____ = _____
Extras _____ = _____
Special Energy Efficient Items _____ = _____
Porches, Patios, etc. _____ = _____
Garage/Carport _____ Sq. Ft. @ $ _____ = _____
Total Estimated Cost New _____ = $ _____

| | Physical | Functional | External |
Less
Depreciation _____ = $ _____
Depreciated Value of Improvements _____ = $ _____
Site Imp. "as is" (driveway, landscaping, etc.) _____ = $ _____
ESTIMATED SITE VALUE _____ = $ _____
(If leasehold, show only leasehold value.)
INDICATED VALUE BY COST APPROACH _____ = $ _____

(Not Required by Freddie Mac and Fannie Mae)
Does property conform to applicable HUD/VA property standards? ☐ Yes ☐ No
If No, explain:

Construction Warranty ☐ Yes ☐ No
Name of Warranty Program _____
Warranty Coverage Expires _____

The undersigned has recited three recent sales of properties most similar and proximate to subject and has considered these in the market analysis. The description includes a dollar adjustment, reflecting market reaction to those items of significant variation between the subject and comparable properties. If a significant item in the comparable property is superior to, or more favorable than, the subject property, a minus (−) adjustment is made, thus reducing the indicated value of subject. If a significant item in the comparable is inferior to, or less favorable than, the subject property, a plus (+) adjustment is made, thus increasing the indicated value of the subject.

SALES COMPARISON ANALYSIS

ITEM	SUBJECT	COMPARABLE NO. 1		COMPARABLE NO. 2		COMPARABLE NO. 3	
Address							
Proximity to Subject							
Sales Price	$	$		$ (33)		$	
Price/Gross Liv Area	$ ☑	$ ☑		$ ☑		$ ☑	
Data Source							
VALUE ADJUSTMENTS	DESCRIPTION	DESCRIPTION	+(−)$ Adjustment	DESCRIPTION	+(−)$ Adjustment	DESCRIPTION	+(−)$ Adjustment
Sales or Financing Concessions							
Date of Sale/Time			(34)		(35)		
Location							
Site/View							
Design and Appeal							
Quality of Construction							
Age							
Condition							
Above Grade	Total Bdrms Baths	Total Bdrms Baths		Total Bdrms Baths		Total Bdrms Baths	
Room Count							
Gross Living Area	Sq. Ft.	Sq. Ft.		Sq. Ft.		Sq. Ft.	
Basement & Finished Rooms Below Grade							
Functional Utility							
Heating/Cooling							
Garage/Carport							
Porches, Patio, Pools, etc							
Special Energy Efficient Items							
Fireplace(s)							
Other (e.g. kitchen equip. remodeling)							
Net Adj. (total)		☐+ ☐− $	(36)	☐+ ☐− $		☐+ ☐− $	
Indicated Value of Subject		$		$		$	
Comments on Sales Comparison							

INDICATED VALUE BY SALES COMPARISON APPROACH _____ $ _____
INDICATED VALUE BY INCOME APPROACH (If Applicable) Estimated Market Rent $ _____ /Mo. x Gross Rent Multiplier _____ = $ _____
This appraisal is made ☐ "as is" ☐ subject to the repairs, alterations, inspections or conditions listed below ☐ completion per plans and specifications.
Comments and Conditions of Appraisal:

Final Reconciliation:

RECONCILIATION

This appraisal is based upon the above requirements, the certification, contingent and limiting conditions, and Market Value definition that are stated in
☐ FmHA, HUD &/or VA instructions.
☐ Freddie Mac Form 439 (Rev. 7/86)/Fannie Mae Form 1004B (Rev. 7/86) filed with client _____ 19 ____ ☐ attached.
I (WE) ESTIMATE THE MARKET VALUE, AS DEFINED, OF THE SUBJECT PROPERTY AS OF _____ 19 ____ to be $ _____
I (We) certify: that to the best of my (our) knowledge and belief the facts and data used herein are true and correct; that I (we) personally inspected the subject property, both inside and out, and have made an exterior inspection of all comparable sales cited in this report; and that I (we) have no undisclosed interest, present or prospective therein.

Appraiser(s) SIGNATURE _____ Review Appraiser SIGNATURE _____ ☐ Did ☐ Did Not
NAME _____ (if applicable) NAME _____ Inspect Property

Freddie Mac Form 70 10/86 (12 ch)   Fannie Mae Form 1004 10/86

Exhibit G. Reconciliation Section

UNIFORM RESIDENTIAL APPRAISAL REPORT

Valuation Section | File No.

Purpose of Appraisal is to estimate Market Value as defined in the Certification & Statement of Limiting Conditions

COST APPROACH

BUILDING SKETCH (SHOW GROSS LIVING AREA ABOVE GRADE)
If for Freddie Mac or Fannie Mae show only square foot calculations and cost approach comments in this space

ESTIMATED REPRODUCTION COST–NEW–OF IMPROVEMENTS:

Dwelling	Sq. Ft. @ $	= $
	Sq. Ft. @ $	=
Extras		=
		=
Special Energy Efficient Items		=
Porches, Patios, etc.		=
Garage/Carport	Sq. Ft. @ $	=
Total Estimated Cost New	....	= $

	Physical	Functional	External
Less			
Depreciation			= $

Depreciated Value of Improvements .... = $
Site Imp. "as is" (driveway, landscaping, etc.) = $
ESTIMATED SITE VALUE .... = $
(If leasehold, show only leasehold value.)
INDICATED VALUE BY COST APPROACH .... = $

(Not Required by Freddie Mac and Fannie Mae)
Does property conform to applicable HUD/VA property standards? ☐ Yes ☐ No
If No, explain:

Construction Warranty ☐ Yes ☐ No
Name of Warranty Program
Warranty Coverage Expires

The undersigned has recited three recent sales of properties most similar and proximate to subject and has considered these in the market analysis. The description includes a dollar adjustment, reflecting market reaction to those items of significant variation between the subject and comparable properties. If a significant item in the comparable property is superior to, or more favorable than, the subject property, a minus (–) adjustment is made, thus reducing the indicated value of subject. If a significant item in the comparable is inferior to, or less favorable than, the subject property, a plus (+) adjustment is made, thus increasing the indicated value of the subject.

SALES COMPARISON ANALYSIS

ITEM	SUBJECT	COMPARABLE NO. 1		COMPARABLE NO. 2		COMPARABLE NO. 3	
Address							
Proximity to Subject							
Sales Price	$		$		$		$
Price/Gross Liv. Area	$	$		$		$	
Data Source							
VALUE ADJUSTMENTS	DESCRIPTION	DESCRIPTION	+ (–)$ Adjustment	DESCRIPTION	+ (–)$ Adjustment	DESCRIPTION	+ (–)$ Adjustment
Sales or Financing Concessions							
Date of Sale/Time							
Location							
Site/View							
Design and Appeal							
Quality of Construction							
Age							
Condition							
Above Grade	Total Bdrms Baths	Total Bdrms Baths		Total Bdrms Baths		Total Bdrms Baths	
Room Count							
Gross Living Area	Sq. Ft.	Sq. Ft.		Sq. Ft.		Sq. Ft.	
Basement & Finished Rooms Below Grade							
Functional Utility							
Heating/Cooling							
Garage/Carport							
Porches, Patio, Pools, etc.							
Special Energy Efficient Items							
Fireplace(s)							
Other (e.g. kitchen equip., remodeling)							
Net Adj. (total)			+ ☐ – $		+ ☐ – $		+ ☐ – $
Indicated Value of Subject			$		$		$
Comments on Sales Comparison:							

INDICATED VALUE BY SALES COMPARISON APPROACH .... $
INDICATED VALUE BY INCOME APPROACH (If Applicable) Estimated Market Rent $ _____ /Mo. x Gross Rent Multiplier _____ = $
This appraisal is made ☐ "as is" ☐ subject to the repairs, alterations, inspections or conditions listed below ☐ completion per plans and specifications
Comments and Conditions of Appraisal:

RECONCILIATION

Final Reconciliation:

This appraisal is based on the above requirements, the certification, contingent and limiting conditions, and Market Value definition that are stated in
☐ FmHA, HUD &/or VA instructions
☐ Freddie Mac Form 439 (Rev. 7/86)/Fannie Mae Form 1004B (Rev 7/86) filed with client _____ 19 ___ ☐ attached
I (WE) ESTIMATE THE MARKET VALUE, AS DEFINED, OF THE SUBJECT PROPERTY AS OF _____ 19 ___ **to be $**
I (We) certify that to the best of my (our) knowledge and belief the facts and data used herein are true and correct; that I (we) personally inspected the subject property, both inside and out, and have made an exterior inspection of all comparable sales cited in this report; and that I (we) have no undisclosed interest, present or prospective therein

Appraiser(s) SIGNATURE _____ Review Appraiser SIGNATURE _____ ☐ Did ☐ Did Not
NAME _____ (if applicable) NAME _____ Inspect Property

Freddie Mac Form 70 10/86 (12 ch) Fannie Mae Form 1004 10/86

borhood. A range of one mile will usually encompass the neighborhood for most properties. The appraiser should be familiar with the neighborhood boundaries. However, it is always good practice to find properties as close to the subject as possible.

32. Appraisers must not engage in excessive adjusting. Large adjustments indicate that the comps are not comparable. Large upward adjustments can be a clue that the appraiser is pumping value. Total gross adjustments on all comparables must not exceed 25% of the sales price. Individual line adjustments must not be greater than 10% of the sales price. In brief, the appraiser's adjustments should be realistic.

33. The appraiser should attempt to bracket the sales data before making adjustments. In brief, find properties that are a little better than the subject and those that are not quite as good, as well as a range in between. This will enable the appraiser to establish a tight value range. Proper bracketing aids the appraiser in producing a convincing appraisal report.

34. Time adjustments must reflect the market. The appraiser should avoid making upward adjustments in a flat or declining market. This can result in a property being substantially over appraised.

35. Sales and financing concessions must be properly handled by the appraiser. The value of giveaway items such as cars and boats must also be explained in the appraisal report. The area for the sales for financing concession data for the subject property is shaded in the sales comparison analysis adjustment grid. The appraiser must state the specific information for the property in the "subject" section or in the "comments" section on the first page. Also, the appraiser must include the specific sales or financing concession information for the comparable sales—such as the mortgage amount, interest rate, loan type, and any loan fees or concessions that the seller paid. For special or creative financing or for sales concessions, the comparable sales must be adjusted to the market at

the time of the comparable sales, not to the subject property. No adjustments are necessary for those costs that are normally paid by sellers because of tradition or law in a market area—these costs are readily identifiable since the seller pays them in virtually all sales transactions. Special or creative financing adjustments can be made to a comparable property by comparing the financing terms offered by a third party institutional lender that is not involved in the property or transaction. Any adjustment should not be calculated on a mechanical dollar-for-dollar cost for the financing or concession—the dollar amount of any adjustment should approximate the market's reaction to the financing or concessions based on the appraiser's judgment.

36. The appraiser will check the appropriate boxes and complete the comments and reconciliation sections under the sales comparison grid. The appraisal must be based on the definition of market value, that is stated in the Certification and Statement of Limiting Conditions. If the Freddie Mac Form 439 (Rev. 7/86) and Fannie Mae Form 1004B (Rev. 7/86) have not been filed with the Lender, it should be attached to the Appraisal Report currently being submitted.

RECONCILIATION

37. Personal property must not be included in the market value of the subject. Chattel property is not eligible for mortgage financing.

38. If the appraiser has selected good comparable market data and handled it well, the adjusted sales should fall into a tight range. The final conclusion of value should relate to the adjusted comparables. It is appropriate for the appraiser to base a value conclusion on the adjusted value of the best comparable.

39. The appraiser will type his or her name under the signature.

COMMENTS

Required Documentation in support of the Uniform Residential Appraisal Report include:

- Clear, descriptive photographs that show the front of each comparable property. The appropriate property address should be indicated on each photograph;
- Clear, descriptive photographs that show the front and back of the subject property, as well as one that shows a street scene;
- A floor plan sketch that identifies and shows the location of all rooms, interior walls, and interior and exterior doors. Exterior building dimensions are also required, but interior room dimensions are not necessary. Although the floor plan sketch should closely resemble the subject property, it does not need to be drawn to scale;
- An area map that shows the location of the subject property and of all comparables that the appraiser used;
- Single Family Comparable Rent Schedule for single-family investment properties if the property is rented;
- Certificate of Completion & Recertification of Value (if applicable), and;
- Any other data that is necessary to provide a complete appraisal report.

The appraisal report should give a concise and precise picture of the neighborhood, site, improvements, value and marketability of the subject property. Backing into the approaches to value, based upon the sales price of the subject, is unacceptable appraisal practice. Value is not intrinsic to the property being appraised but is derived from what other similar properties in the subject neighborhood have sold for recently. In brief, sales price and market value are two different concepts.

These guidelines are not to be utilized by appraisers for the purpose of telling financial institutions what the appraiser thinks financial institutions want to hear, but are to be used to accurately reflect the subject's value and marketability. A responsible financial organization is interested in the truth and expects appraisal reports to have substance. The appraiser's task is to provide an independent third party opinion of value. In short, the appraiser is not an advocate trying to make deals work.

Appraisal reports should be utilized by appraisers and financial institutions as underwriting and not sales tools. Any financial institution that is serious about managing risk will separate sales and appraisal functions by tying appraisers to underwriting, appraisal or quality control departments rather than sales departments. Sales and appraising don't mix. In fact, it is the mixing of the two that has distorted the appraisal process.

CHAPTER SEVENTEEN

COMMERCIAL APPRAISAL REVIEW CHECK LIST

This check list is intended to be an approach to reviewing a commercial appraisal report using a series of questions as a guide to what should be answered in the various subsections of an appraisal. The areas focused upon are representative of the most common issues encountered in reviewing commercial appraisals.

FORMAT AND PRESENTATION

- Has the purpose of the appraisal been stated?
- Does the appraisal report contain a definition of market value?
- Did the appraiser properly identify the subject property?
- Has the appraiser identified the property rights involved in the appraisal assignment?
- Are salient features of subject identified?
- Does the appraisal report contain a certificate of limited conditions that are reasonable, not so extensive and protective as to make the contents of the report meaningless?
- Does the appraisal report set forth all relevant data and analytical process in arriving at highest and best use?
- Has the appraiser described the zoning for the subject and comparable properties?
- Have taxes, special assessments as well as expected tax increases been included in the appraisal report?
- Is illustrative and other data contained in the addendum complete and acceptable?
- Does it appear the appraiser has the experience and qualifications to undertake the appraisal assignment?

CITY OR REGIONAL DESCRIPTION

- Is the economical vitality of the city dependent upon one or two particular industries?
- Does the appraisal report enable the reviewer to spot healthy growth patterns within the region and city or trends that may indicate deterioration and perhaps limited market appeal for the subject property?
- How current is the city and regional data contained in the appraisal report?
- When employing secondary data or forecasts, has the appraiser provided commentary as to his/her evaluation of this secondary source?
- Are comments on the region or city relevant and do they give insight into conditions which positively or negatively affect the appraised properties value and marketability?

NEIGHBORHOOD DESCRIPTION

- How old is the neighborhood and what is the composition?
- How does the property rank in terms of its ability to compete with comparable properties?
- Are there any adverse influences encroaching upon or infiltrating the neighborhood?
- How accessible is the neighborhood to major thoroughfares, shopping facilities and restaurants?

SITES ANALYSIS

- Has the appraiser commented on unfavorable site factors?
- Has the appraiser examined the market data for support of the estimation of marketing time?
- How does the marketing time of the sales correlate with the market exposure time of the competitive offerings?
- Does the appraiser's analysis of the marketing period employ both sales and offerings?

- In the analysis of the historical market exposure of a sale, does the appraiser recognize the environment that existed at the time of the sale?
- Was the subject inspected by the persons signing the appraisal report?
- Has the "Four Way Test" of comparability been applied by the appraisal report?
  1. The time of sale is reasonably similar.
  2. The location of sale is reasonably comparable.
  3. The sale is a bonafide voluntary arms length transaction.
  4. The characteristics to the subject property are similar.
- In the reviewer's opinion, has the appraiser properly handled the market approach to value?

INCOME APPROACH

- Has the appraiser accurately listed gross income for the subject and comparables?
- Did the appraiser verify the income data?
- Does the expense data appear to be accurate?
- Has there been an adequate accounting of annual expenses such as those incurred for light, heat, water, gas, fuel, insurance, etc.?
- Was the expense data verified by the appraiser?
- Have the appropriate adjustments been made for expense items?
- Has the appraiser properly deducted operating expenses from effective gross income to arrive at a net income figure?
- Have items charged to repairs been capitalized and depreciated?
- Did the appraiser properly capitalize net income expectancy into an estimate of market value?

DESCRIPTION OF IMPROVEMENTS

- Does the appraiser's description enable the reviewer to clearly visualize the subject property and its attributes and limitations?
- Did the appraiser comment on physical and functional inadequacies and indicate whether or not repairs and modernization are needed?
- Does the appraiser consider effective age as well as chronological age?
- Have the factors relating to condition, quality of construction, finish and equipment, as well as size and utility been properly handled?
- Has the appraiser given attention to structural problems?
- Has the appraiser adequately dealt with the subject's physical, functional and economic obsolescence?

VALUATION ANALYSIS (APPROACH TO VALUE) COST APPROACH

- Has land been valued as if vacant and unimproved?
- If the land contains improper improvements and is not available for its highest and best use, has the appraiser made adjustments to reflect demolition and other costs to make it available for proper development?
- Does the appraiser identify the source of cost information and his confidence in the reliability of the source?
- Did the appraiser state whether the improvements have been valued on the basis of the properties reproduction or replacement cost?
- Do figures for physical, functional and economic depreciation appear reasonable in light of the subject's age, condition, state of modernization, size and vitality, location, etc.?
- Has the appraiser deducted all forms of depreciation from his

or her estimate of construction costs new?
- Are the appraiser's mathematical calculations accurate?
- In the reviewer's opinion, has the appraiser properly handled the cost approach to value?

MARKET APPROACH

- Do the adjustments appear reasonable in terms of contributory value?
- How does the implied contributory value compare with the cost and income approaches to value?
- Is there an internal integrity to the appraiser's adjustments? (Bias or pattern of inconsistency?)
- Did the adjustments consider the motivations of the buyer, the cash flow variances, ability to debt service and effects of various debt structuring?
- Was cash equivalency employed?
- Did the appraiser indicate whether or not the subject and comparable properties were offered on the open market?
- Has the appraiser selected good data and handled it well?
- Did the appraiser comment on the subject's marketability?
- Does the appraiser's information and analysis appear to be accurate?
- Does the appraiser in his or her analysis appear to be backing into any or all of the approaches to value?
- Is there a lack of clarity with respect to the appraiser's reasoning?
- Does the appraiser appear to be an advocate rather than an individual offering an independent or impartial third party opinion of value?
- Are the appraiser's comments and final reconciliation of value adequate and does the appraisal give insight into the value and marketability of the subject property?
- Is the appraiser's final value conclusion supported by cost, income and market data approaches to value?

- Is the appraiser's value conclusion reasonable?
- Has the appraiser failed to prove his or her case?
- Do you wind up with a different value conclusion than the appraiser, based upon data contained within the report?
- Does it appear the subject property has been over appraised?

SUMMARY QUESTIONS FOR THE REVIEWER

- How would you rate the appraisal report with respect to overall quality? (Poor, Fair, Good, Very Good, Excellent)
- Does the appraisal report present a consistent and convincing analysis?
- Are there serious omissions, false information, faulty reasoning or the possibility of calculated deception?
- Do you agree with the appraiser's value conclusion?
- If there is a difference between your opinion and that of the appraiser, what is the reason for the difference?
- Is the appraisal report acceptable or unacceptable? Why is it acceptable or unacceptable?

CHAPTER EIGHTEEN

LIMITED APPRAISAL RESTRICTED REPORTS

In the wake of the failure of the savings and loan system in the eighties, the appraisal profession has been heavily regulated. Standards of Practice, designed to produce better appraisal reports, instead became too cumbersome for some types of appraisal assignments. The market of appraisal users was overwhelmed by the requirements that appraisers had to follow. That market however, has decided to speak.

The market has made it known loud and clear that it now wants shorter, simpler and more quickly transmitted appraisal reports. The lending industry in particular has attempted to make this point for some time by calling for such products as appraisal updates and recertification of value reports.

The current trend was codified in 1994 when the lending industry was able to persuade the federal lending regulators to increase the de miniums threshold to $250,000 and to create a new appraisal product called the Evaluation of Real Property Collateral. This abbreviated appraisal report was to be used in federally related mortgage transactions below the de miniums threshold.

The appraisal profession responded with massive changes to the Uniform Standards of Professional Appraisal Practice (USPAP) that included redefining appraisal and the development of different reporting options for appraisals.

Types of Appraisal

There are two types of appraisals; Complete and Limited. Complete appraisals are those prepared according to the all of the binding requirements and specific guidelines found in Standard 1 of the USPAP.

The profession now acknowledges that there are those appraisal assignments that call for something less than or different from what Standard 1 calls for. In those cases, the appraiser prepare a Limited appraisal, that is one prepared when the appraiser has departed from the specific guidelines found in Standard 1.

In order to prepare a Limited appraisal, the appraiser must invoke the departure provision of the USPAP which includes detailing the departures in the appraisal report. It is important to note that the reliability of the appraisal ~~increases~~ *Decreases* with the amount of departure taken.

Types of Appraisal Reports

The USPAP now allows for three reporting options; the Self-Contained Report, the Summary Report and the Restricted Report. The content of each of these reports is virtually the same. The only real difference between the three is the level of presentation of the data, guided by the terms describe, summarize and state.

For example, in a Self-contained report, the highest and best use analysis might run for two pages. In the Summary report, it could be only two paragraphs and in the Restricted report, it could be done in only two sentences.

The Restricted report is called such because it is some limited in its presentation of data that its use is restricted to the client only, as others might be misled from trying to use it. A prominent restricted use state is required in these types of the reports.

The ingredients of each reporting option are found in Standard 2, Rule 2-2 (exhibit A, page xxx). Appraisers may not

Exhibit A
STANDARDS RULE 2-2 REPORT COMPARISON CHART

The essential difference among the three options is in the use and application of the terms **describe summarize** and **state. Describe** is used to connote a comprehensive level of detail in the presentation of information. **Summarize** is used to connote a more concise presentation of information. State is used to connote the minimal presentation of information.

a) Self-Contained Appraisal Report	b) Summary Appraisal Report	c) Restriced Appraisal Report
i. identify and describe the real estate being appraised	i. identify and provide a summary description of the real estate being appraised.	i. identify and describe the real estate being appraised
ii. state the real property interest being appraised	ii. state the real property interest being appraised	ii. state the real property interest being appraised
iii. state the purpose and intended use of the appraisal	iii. state the purpose and intended use of the appraisal	iii. state the purpose and intended use of the appraisal
iv. define the value to be estimated	iv. define the value to be estimated	iv. state the reference a definition of the value to be estimated
v. state the effective date of the appraisal and the date of the report	v. state the effective date of the appraisal and the date of the report	v. ~~describe~~ the effective date of the appraisal and the date of the report
vi. state the extent of the process of collecting, confirming and reporting data Comment: the full extent of the process should be apparent to the reader in the contents of the report	vi. summarize the extent of the process of collecting, confirming and reporting data Comment: the full extent of the process should be apparent to the reader in the contents of the report	vi. describe the extent of the process of collecting, confirming and reporting data Comment: the full extent of the process should be apparent to the reader in the contents of the report
vii. state all assumptions and limiting conditions that affect the analyses, opinions and conclusions	vii state all assumptions and limiting conditions that affect the analyses, opinions and conclusions.	vii. state all assumptions and limiting conditions that affect the analyses, opinions and conclusions
viii. describe the information considered, a the appraisal procedures followed, and the reasoning that supports the analyses, opinions and conclusions	viii. summarize the information considered, the appraisal procedures followed, and the reasoning that supports the analyses, opinions, and conclusions	viii state the appraisal procedures followed, state the value conclusion and reference the existence of specific file information in support of the conclusion
ix. describe the appraiser's opinion of the highest and best use of the real estate, when such an opinion is necessary and appropriate	ix. summarize the appraiser's opinion of the highest and best use of the real estate, when such an opinion is necessary and appropriate	ix state the appraiser's opinion of the highest and best use of the real estate, when such an opinion is necessary and appropriate
x. explain and support the exclusion of any of the usual valuation approaches	x. explain and support the exclusion of any of the usual valuation approaches	x. state the exclusion of any of the usual valuation approaches
xi. describe any additional information that may be appropriate to show compliance with, or clearly identify and explain permitted departures from the specific guidelines of Standard 1	xi. summarize any additional information that may be appropriate to show compliance with or clearly identify and explain permitted departures from the specific guidelines of Standard 1	xi. contain a prominent use restriction that limits reliance on the report to the client and warns that the report cannot be understood properly without additional information in the workfile of the appraiser, and clearly identify and explain any permitted departures from the specific guidelines of Standard 1
xii. include a signed certification in accordance with Standards Rule 2-3	xii include a signed certification in accordance with Standard Rule 2-3	xii. include a signed certification in accordance with Standards Rule 2-3

Explanatory Comments have not been included in this chart, except for excerpt of Comment on vi.

deviate from these ingredient lists and the lists should serve as the basis for reviewing any kind of appraisal report.

Either a Complete appraisal or Limited appraisal can be reported in any of three reports and the report must clearly state what type of appraisal and what type of report the reader has before them. In the case of a Complete appraisal-Restricted report the appraiser will be conducting all the research and analysis called for but will be reporting very little of it to the client. Therefore, it is important that the appraiser maintain a full work file on all appraisals regardless of what reporting option is used. The workfile should be available for review.

Evaluations

Evaluations as called for by the federal lending regulators are Restricted reports and can be either Complete or Limited appraisals. More often than not, they are Limited appraisals. These are usually form reports with a wide variety of forms being used for this purpose. One of the more popular ones is the Freddie Mac 704 form which was originally designed for low value second mortgages. Other forms abound, having been promulgated by lenders, software vendors and appraisers.

One of the best forms in current use for evaluations is one being used in Freddie Mac's automated underwriting system (see exhibit B-1 & 2, page xxx). It is perhaps the one that is most compliant with the requirements of the USPAP. It even includes a space to address departure, an item that most appraisers fail to include in the preparation of a Limited appraisal.

The form begins with a clear statement denoting the report as a Limited appraisal-Restricted report with a restricted use statement. The subject section is typical of most forms in the identification of the property and the property rights to be appraised.

The neighborhood section is very much like that of the URAR. However it does ask the appraiser to address the property's compatibility to the neighborhood, convenience to public facilities,

THE SCOPE OF THE LIMITED APPRAISAL

This Limited Appraisal and Restricted Appraisal Report is based on an inspection of the neighborhood, subject property, and the analysis of information gathered from public or private records that may have an influence on the value of the property. Use and reliance upon this report is restricted to the client. Anyone else using the report is an unintended user.

DEFINITION OF MARKET VALUE: The most probable price which a property should bring in a competitive and open market under all conditions requisite to a fair sale, the buyer and seller, each acting prudently, knowledgeably and assuming the price is not affected by undue stimulus. Implicit in this definition is the consummation of a sale as of a specified date and the passing of title from seller to buyer under conditions whereby: (1) buyer and seller are typically motivated; (2) both parties are well informed or well advised, and each acting in what he considers his own best interest; (3) a reasonable time is allowed for exposure in the open market; (4) payment is made in terms of cash in U.S. dollars or in terms of financial arrangements comparable thereto; and (5) the price represents the normal consideration for the property sold unaffected by special or creative financing or sales concessions granted by anyone associated with the sale.

STATEMENT OF LIMITING CONDITIONS AND APPRAISER'S CERTIFICATION

CONTINGENT AND LIMITING CONDITIONS: The appraiser's certification that appears in this report is subject to the following conditions:

1. The appraiser will not be responsible for matters of a legal nature that affect either the property being valued or the title to it. The appraiser assumes that the title is good and marketable and, therefore, will not render any opinions about the title. The property is valued on the basis of it being under responsible ownership.

2. Any sketch that may be included in the report to show approximate dimensions of the improvements (and) the sketch is included only to assist the reader of the report in visualizing the property and understanding the appraiser's determination of its size.

3. The appraiser has examined the available flood maps that are provided by the Federal Emergency Management Agency (or other data sources) and has noted in the appraisal report whether the subject site is located in an identified Special Flood Hazard Area. Because the appraiser is not a surveyor, he or she makes no guarantees, express or implied, regarding this determination.

4. The appraiser will give no testimony or appear in court because he or she made a valuation of the property in question, unless specific arrangements to do so have been made beforehand.

5. If the cost approach is utilized, the value of the land is estimated at its highest and best use and the improvements at their contributory value. These separate valuations of the land and improvements must not be used in conjunction with any other report and are invalid if they are so used.

6. Unless otherwise noted in this report, an interior and complete exterior inspection of the subject property has not been completed. Only observable adverse conditions (such as, needed repairs, depreciation, the presence of hazardous wastes, toxic substances, etc.) noted during the inspection of the subject property or that the appraiser became aware of during the normal research involved in performing the limited appraisal are contained herein. Unless otherwise stated in the report, the appraiser has no knowledge of any hidden or unapparent conditions of the property or adverse environmental conditions (including the presence of hazardous wastes, toxic substances, etc.) that would make the property more or less valuable, and has assumed that there are no such conditions and makes no guarantees or warranties, express or implied, regarding the condition of the property. The appraiser will not be responsible for any such conditions that do exist or for any engineering or testing that might be required to discover whether such conditions exist. Because the appraiser is not an expert in the field of environmental hazards, the report must not be considered as an environmental assessment of the property.

7. The appraiser obtained the information, estimates, and opinions that were expressed in the appraisal report from sources that he or she considers to be reliable and believes them to be true and correct. The appraiser does not assume responsibility for the accuracy of such items that were furnished by other parties.

8. The appraiser will not disclose the contents of the appraisal report except as provided for in the Uniform Standards of Professional Appraisal Practice.

9. If the appraiser has based his or her report and valuation conclusion for an appraisal that is subject to satisfactory completion, repairs, or alterations, it is under the assumption that completion of the improvements will be performed in a workmanlike manner.

10. The appraiser must provide his or her prior written consent before the lender/client specified in the appraisal report can distribute the report (including conclusions about the property value, the appraiser's identity and professional designations, and references to any professional appraisal organizations or the firm with which the appraiser is associated) to anyone other than the borrower; the mortgagee or its successors and assigns; the mortgage insurer; consultants; professional appraisal organizations; any state or the District of Columbia; except that the lender/client may distribute the property description section of the report only to data collection or reporting service(s) without having to obtain the appraiser's prior written consent. The appraiser's written consent and approval must also be obtained before the appraisal can be conveyed by anyone to the public through advertising, public relations, news, sales, or other media.

APPRAISERS CERTIFICATION: The Appraiser certifies and agrees that:

1. I have researched the subject market area and have selected a minimum of three recent sales of properties most similar and proximate to the subject property for consideration in the sales comparison analysis and have made a dollar adjustment when appropriate to reflect the market reaction to those items of significant variation. If a significant item in a comparable property is superior to , or more favorable than, the subject property, I have made a negative adjustment to reduce the adjusted sales price of the comparable and, if a significant item in a comparable property is inferior to, or less favorable than the subject property, I have made a positive adjustment to increase the adjusted sales price of the comparable.   Unless included as an addendum to this report, the adjustment grid is retained in the workfile of the appraiser.

2. I have taken into consideration the factors that have an impact on value in my development of the estimate of market value in the report. I have not knowingly withheld any significant information from the report and I believe, to the best of my knowledge, that all statements and information in the report are true and correct.

3. I stated in the report only my own personal, unbiased, and professional analysis, opinions, and conclusions, which are subject only to the contingent and limiting conditions specified in this form.

4. I have no present or prospective interest in the property that is the subject of this report, and I have no present or prospective personal interest or bias with respect to the participants in the transaction. I did not base, either partially or completely, my analysis and/or the estimate of market value in the appraisal report on the race, color, religion, sex, handicap, familial status, or national origin of either the prospective owners or occupants of the subject property or of the present owners or occupants of the properties in the vicinity of the subject property.

5. I have no present or contemplated future interest in the subject property, and neither my current or future employment nor my compensation for performing this appraisal is contingent on the appraised value of the property.

6. I was not required to report a predetermined value or direction in value that favors the cause of the client or any related party, the amount of the value estimate, the attainment of a specific result, or the occurrence of a subsequent event in order to receive my compensation and/or employment for performing the report. I did not base the report on a requested minimum valuation, a specific valuation, or the need to approve a specific mortgage loan.

7. I completed this report in conformity with the Uniform Standards of Professional Appraisal Practice that were adopted and promulgated by the Appraisal Standards Board of The Appraisal Foundation and that were in place as of the effective date of this report. I certify that I have both the knowledge and experience required to perform this assignment competently. I acknowledge that an estimate of a reasonable time for exposure in the open market is a condition in the definition of market value and the estimate I developed is consistent with the marketing time noted in the neighborhood section of this report, unless I have otherwise stated in the addendum to the report.

8. The extent of the inspection process (exterior and/or interior) with respect to the subject of the report is noted on page 1 of the report and/or in a separate addendum. Unless otherwise noted in the report or an attached addendum, the appraiser has not inspected the exterior of the properties listed as comparables in this report. I have noted any observable, apparent or known adverse conditions in the subject improvements, on the subject site, or on any site within the immediate vicinity of the subject property of which I am aware and have made adjustments for these adverse conditions in my analysis of the property value to the extent that I had market evidence to support them. I have also commented about the effect of the adverse conditions on the marketability of the subject property.

9. I personally prepared all conclusions and opinions about the real estate that were set forth in the report. If I relied on significant professional assistance from any individual(s) in the performance of the report or the preparation of the report, I have named such individual(s) and disclosed the specific tasks performed by them in an attached addendum to this report. I certify that any individual so named is qualified to perform the tasks. I have not authorized anyone to make a change to any item in the report; therefore, if an unauthorized change is made to the report, I will take no responsibility for it.

SUPERVISORY APPRAISER'S CERTIFICATION: If a supervisory appraiser signed the report, he or she certifies and agrees that: I directly supervise the appraiser who prepared the appraisal report, have reviewed the report, agree with the statements and conclusions of the appraiser, agree to be bound by the appraiser's certifications above, and am taking full responsibility for this report.

ADDRESS OF PROPERTY APPRAISED: _____

APPRAISER: **SUPERVISORY APPRAISER (only if required)**

Signature: _____   Signature: _____

Name: _____   Name: _____

Date Signed: _____   Date Signed: _____

State Certification #:_____   State Certification #:_____

or State License #:_____   or State License #: _____

State: _____   State: _____

Expiration Date of Certification or License: _____   Expiration Date of Certification or License: _____

                                                           ☐ Did   ☐ Did Not Inspect Property

Subject Inspection: Subject Inspection:
☐ Interior and Exterior ☐ Exterior Only   ☐ Interior and Exterior ☐ Exterior Only

REAL ESTATE EVALUATION ANALYSIS
(Restricted Appraisal Report for 1–4 Family Properties)

Extent of the Appraisal Process. The purpose of this limited appraisal is to estimate the market value of the subject property as of the effective date of the appraisal. The extent of the process of collecting, confirming, and reporting data used in this analysis includes a physical inspection of the neighborhood, subject property (interior and/or exterior), and the analysis of information gathered from public or private records that may have an influence on the value of the property. Unless otherwise noted the appraiser is to perform an exterior-only (drive-by) inspection of the subject property. Use and reliance upon this report is restricted to the client. Anyone else using the report is an unintended user.

SUBJECT

Property Address _____ City _____
County _____ State _____ Zip _____ Census Tract _____ MSA # _____
Borrower _____ Property Rights Appraised: ☐ Fee ☐ Leasehold
Property Type: ☐ Single Family ☐ PUD ☐ Condo ☐ 2–4 Units Appraiser/Address _____
Client _____

NEIGHBORHOOD

					Typical	Atypical
Location	☐ Urban	☐ Suburban	☐ Rural			
Built Up	☐ Over 75%	☐ 25% to 75%	☐ Under 25%	Property Compatibility	☐	☐
Growth Rate ☐ Fully Dev.	☐ Rapid	☐ Steady	☐ Slow	Convenience to Public Facilities	☐	☐
Property Values	☐ Increasing	☐ Stable	☐ Declining	General Appearance of Properties	☐	☐
Market Time	☐ Under 3 Mo.	☐ 3 to 6 Mo.	☐ Over 6 Mo.	Appeal to Market	☐	☐
Predominant Occupancy	☐ Owner	☐ Tenant	___ % Vacant			

Similar Property Price Range $ ____ to $ ____ Age ____ yrs. to ____ yrs.

Note: Race or racial composition of the neighborhood is not considered as a reliable evaluation factor. _____

SITE

Highest and Best Use: ☐ Present Use ☐ Other (specify) _____
Zoning Compliance: ☐ Legal ☐ Legal non-conforming (grandfathered use) ☐ Illegal ☐ No Zoning

Utilities	Public	Other		Briefly describe and rate:
Electricity	☐	_____	Topo	_____
Gas	☐	_____	Size	_____
Water	☐	_____	Shape	_____
Sanitary Sewer	☐	_____	View	_____
	Underground Elec. & Tel. ☐ Yes ☐ No		Drainage	_____

Describe visible easements, if any, affecting subject property _____
Is the property located in a FEMA-Identified Special Flood Hazard Area? ☐ No ☐ Yes FEMA Flood Zone _____
FEMA Map No. _____ Effective Date _____

IMPROVEMENTS

				Typical	Atypical
Design _____		Exterior Condition		☐	☐
Type _____		Interior Condition	☐ N/A	☐	☐
Exterior Walls _____ Roof _____		Overall Livability		☐	☐
Approximate Age (Actual) ____ Yrs. (Effective) ____ Yrs.		Appeal to Marketability		☐	☐

Comments _____

INTERIOR

Comments and Interior Description (if available): _____

No. of Rooms ____ No. of Bedrooms ____ No. of Baths ____ Gross Living Area ____ Sq.Ft.
Parking Facilities: ☐ Garage ☐ Carport ☐ Open ☐ None ____ Cars
Interior description and room count provided by: _____

MARKET DATA ANALYSIS

COMPARABLE SALES

ITEM	COMPARABLE #1	COMPARABLE #2	COMPARABLE #3
Address			
Proximity to Subject			
Sale Price	$	$	$
Date of Sale			
Overall Comparison to Subject	☐ Superior ☐ Equal ☐ Inferior	☐ Superior ☐ Equal ☐ Inferior	☐ Superior ☐ Equal ☐ Inferior
Data/Verification Sources			

Note: Unless attached as an addendum, supporting documentation for the above Market Data Analysis Summary, including full description of comparables, adjustments, etc. are maintained in the appraiser's file and are available for review upon request. Addendum attached ☐ Yes ☐ No _____
COMMENTS: _____

Comment on any departure(s) from the specific guidelines USPAP and any limitations in addition to those disclosed in the attached Statement of Limiting Conditions and Appraiser's Certification. _____

One year sale, listing and/or offering history: _____
Cost Approach Summary: ☐ Not applicable. Comment: _____
☐ Included in an attached addendum. Indicated Value by Cost Approach is $ _____
Income Approach Summary: ☐ Not applicable. Comment: _____
☐ Included in an attached addendum. Indicated Value by Income Approach is $ _____

RECONCILIATION

FINAL RECONCILIATION: _____

The appraisal is made ☐ "as is" ☐ "subject to" repairs, alterations, inspections, or conditions listed in an attached addendum.
The purpose of this limited appraisal is to estimate the market value of the real property that is the subject of this report, based on the above conditions and the certification, contingent and limiting conditions, and market value definition that are stated in the attached Statement of Limiting Conditions and Appraiser's Certification, Form #0105-080-B (Revised 8/94). This is a limited appraisal only and has been prepared for the exclusive, confidential use of the above reference client. The report cannot be understood properly without additional information that is contained in the workfile of the appraiser. The information shown on this report is derived from an inspection of the neighborhood, subject property, and other sources considered reliable.
I (we) estimate the Market Value, as defined, of the Real Property that is the subject of this Evaluation, as of _____
(which is the Date of Inspection and the Effective Date of this Report) to be $ _____

Appraiser Name: _____ Supervisory Appraiser Name: _____
Signature: _____ Date: _____ Signature: _____ Date: _____
☐ License, or ☐ Certification # _____ ☐ License, or ☐ Certification # _____
Subject Inspection: ☐ Interior and Exterior ☐ Exterior Only ☐ Interior and Exterior ☐ Exterior Only ☐ Did Not Inspect

Attach descriptive photographs of subject property and street scene. Form #0105-080

general appearance of properties and appeal to the market. Note that these ratings are typical and atypical.

The evaluation form does not provide a comments section like the URAR, since it is a restricted report.

The site section addresses highest and best use and zoning compliance. However, the appraiser does not need to provide the zoning classification, nor is it necessary to provide dimensions or area of the site. Utilities to the site must be noted, but off-site improvements are not required. The site is described with brief comments about topography, size, shape, view and drainage. The only other data required for the site is the FEMA flood information and the reporting of any visible easements. A search of public records to determine other easements that might not be visible is not necessary.

The improvements section calls for brief descriptions of the design, type of dwelling, exterior walls and roof. The appraiser must also state the actual and the effective age of the improvements and rank the exterior and interior condition, overall livability and appeal to marketability as typical or atypical. Comment sections are provided for further clarification of the general condition of the improvements.

Basic information is required when completing the interior section of the evaluation form. Room count should be completed according to the Fannie Mae method; bathrooms, utility rooms and foyers are not included in the total number of rooms. The gross living area should be calculated only through accurate measurement of the improvements and should include only gross living area, that is the portion that is heated and cooled. Parking facilities should also be checked. Note that the appraiser is asked how the interior description and room count was obtained. Since this form is sometimes used for drive-by inspections, it should be noted that the appraiser did or did not inspect the interior of the property.

The market data analysis section offers a short grid to list three comparable sales. However, dollar adjustments are not required.

This does not mean that the appraiser is relieved of making comparison with dollar adjustments or providing full description of the comparable sales. Appraisers are required to keep this data in the appraisal workfile. The wording of this form states as such. It is suggested that appraisers ask clients in these types of appraisal assignments whether they want such data in the appraisal report.

Special emphasis should be placed on the verification of comparable sales data as called for in the grid. Comments should also be written to provide the client with some insight into the appraiser's analysis of the sales data presented.

As previously mentioned, limited appraisals require the appraiser to comment on any departure from the USPAP and to list any other limiting conditions that might affect the outcome of the appraisal. Appraisers should be explicit in denoting which specific guidelines from which they departed and give reasons why they chose to do so.

A sales history of the subject property as called for in the reconciliation section is required for any type of appraisal and any type of report. It makes a good lead-in for the reconciliation of the three approaches to value and appraisers are asked to explain why an approach was not used or to provide the indicated value by that approach. A statement about the appraiser's reasoning should be given to explain the final estimate.

Finally, be sure that the evaluation provides an estimate of value, an effective date and the appraiser's signature and license or certification number.

Addenda material should be kept to a minimum because it defeats the purpose of the restricted report. However, the appraiser's certification and Limiting conditions, signed and dated is a must.

It's worth mentioning again that maintenance of a complete file of all of the appraiser's data collection and analysis is imperative. Even those items not transmitted in the report must be on file with the appraiser and available for review if called for.

Another popular form for use of communicating evaluations is the Freddie Mac 704 form (see exhibit C). Although this was not the use that was intended when the form was created, many lenders like the form for use in evaluations. Its field report section is completed according to the guidelines found elsewhere in this chapter for completion of the assessment validation. The comparable sales data is adjusted as in a formal appraisal performed on the URAR, only with less comment required.

Collateral Assessment Products

In addition to the use of the evaluation, Freddie Mac's automated underwriting system also uses two non-appraisal products, the curbside inspection and the assessment validation. Along with the evaluation, the three are referred to collateral assessment products.

The curbside inspection and the assessment validation do not call for the preparer to provide an estimate of value and therefore are not considered appraisals under the currently accepted definition of appraisal. However, they are prepared more often than not by an appraiser.

The curbside inspection (see Exhibit D, page xxx) is just what it says it is; an exterior inspection of the subject property. It does not address value. Instead, it addresses the fraud factor--is there a structure on this parcel of real property? The form used asks for a minimum amount of information about the neighborhood and refers to the classifications of data in this section as indicators. These categories cannot be answered without a physical inspection of the neighborhood and/or some knowledge of the neighborhood.

The form also provides a section for comments on the subject amenities. The comments should fully describe the improvements based upon an exterior inspection only and should delineate both all positive and negative characteristics visible to the preparer from the exterior inspection. These comments should support

Freddie Mac
Federal
Home Loan
Mortgage
Corporation
Owned by America's
Savings Institutions

Second Mortgage
Property Value Analysis Report

(This form may be used if the second mortgage will not exceed
$15,000 and value is based on "as is" condition.)

BORROWER/SUBJECT PROPERTY INFORMATION

Borrower _____ Census Tract _____ Map Reference _____

Property Address _____ Check One: ☐ SF ☐ PUD ☐ Condo ☐ 2-4 Units

City _____ County _____ State _____ Zip Code _____

Phone No. Res. _____ Loan Amount Requested $ _____ Term _____ Months _____ Owner's Estimate of Value $ _____

No. of Rooms	No. of Bedrooms	No. of Baths	Family Room or Den	Gross Living Area	Garage/Carport (Specify Type & Number)	Porches, Patio or Pool (Specify)	Central Air
			☐ Yes ☐ No	Sq Ft			☐ Yes ☐ No

FIELD REPORT

NEIGHBORHOOD

						Good	Avg.	Fair	Poor
Location	☐ Urban	☐ Suburban	☐ Rural						
Built Up	☐ Over 75%	☐ 25% to 75%	☐ Under 25%	Property Compatibility		☐	☐	☐	☐
Growth Rate	☐ Fully Dev ☐ Rapid	☐ Steady	☐ Slow	General Appearance of Properties		☐	☐	☐	☐
Property Values	☐ Increasing	☐ Stable	☐ Declining	Appeal		☐	☐	☐	☐
Demand/Supply	☐ Shortage	☐ In Balance	☐ Oversupply						
Marketing Time	☐ Under 3 Months	☐ 4-6 Months	☐ Over 6 Months						

Present Land Use _____ % 1 Family _____ % 2-4 Family _____ % Apts _____ % Condo _____ % Commercial _____ % Industrial _____ % Vacant _____ %

Change in Present Land Use ☐ Not Likely ☐ Likely ☐ Taking Place From _____ To _____

Predominant Occupancy ☐ Owner ☐ Tenant _____ % Vacant

Single Family Price Range $ _____ To $ _____ Predominant Value $ _____

Single Family Age _____ Years To _____ Years Predominant Age _____ Yrs

Note: Freddie Mac does not consider race or the racial composition of the neighborhood to be reliable appraisal factors.

Comments including those factors, favorable or unfavorable, affecting marketability (e.g. public parks, schools, view, noise) _____

SUBJECT PROPERTY

Approximate Year Built 19 _____ No. Units _____ No. Stories _____

Type (detached, duplex, semi-det etc.) _____

Design (rambler, split level, etc.) _____

Exterior Walls Material _____ Roof Material _____

Is the property located in a HUD-identified Special Flood Hazard Area? ☐ No ☐ Yes

Special Energy Efficient Items _____

PROPERTY RATING	Good	Avg.	Fair	Poor
Condition of Exterior	☐	☐	☐	☐
Compatibility to Neighborhood	☐	☐	☐	☐
Appeal and Marketability	☐	☐	☐	☐

Comments (favorable or unfavorable including any deferred maintenance) _____

MARKET COMPARABLE ANALYSIS PRIOR TO IMPROVEMENT

ITEM	SUBJECT	COMPARABLE NO. 1		COMPARABLE NO. 2		COMPARABLE NO. 3	
Address							
Proximity to Subject							
Sales Price	$	$		$		$	
VALUE ADJUSTMENTS	DESCRIPTION	DESCRIPTION	+ (-) $ Adjustment	DESCRIPTION	+ (-) $ Adjustment	DESCRIPTION	+ (-) $ Adjustment
Date of Sale/Time							
Location							
Site/View							
Age							
Condition							
Above Grade	Total Bdrms Baths	Total Bdrms Baths		Total Bdrms Baths		Total Bdrms Baths	
Room Count							
Gross Living Area	Sq Ft	Sq Ft		Sq Ft		Sq Ft	
Heating/Cooling							
Garage/Carport							
Porches, Patio, Pools, etc.							
Special Energy Efficient Items							
Other (e.g. kitchen equip., remodeling)							
Net Adj. (total)		+ - $		+ - $		+ - $	
Indicated Value of Subject		$		$		$	

General Comments _____

The information shown on this report is derived from an inspection of the neighborhood and exterior inspection of the subject property and market comparables. The estimated market value is based upon this information and the knowledge of the undersigned. This report is not to be construed as an appraisal report.

ESTIMATED MARKET VALUE $ _____ as of _____ 19 _____

Completed By _____ Title _____

Signature _____ Date _____ , 19 _____

CURBSIDE INSPECTION FORM

Case No.
File No.
Transaction No.

SUBJECT

APN:
Property Type:
Style:

Street Address:
City: _____ State: ___ Zip: _____

Garage: ☐ Yes ☐ No
Carport:
Other Parking:
Basement: ☐ Yes ☐ No
Legal Description:

NEIGHBORHOOD

Neighborhood Information:

A. Property values indicator
☐ Increasing
☐ Stable
☐ Declining

B. Marketing time indicator
☐ 3 months or less
☐ 3 to 6 months
☐ Over 6 months

C. Single family dwelling unit indicator
☐ Yes
☐ No

D. Property typical of NBHD indicator
☐ Yes
☐ No

E. Deferred maintenance indicator
☐ Yes
☐ No

F. Inventory
☐ High
☐ Medium
☐ Low

AMENITIES/CONDITION

Subject Amenities/Condition Comments: (Please provide any significant negative/positive property characteristics):

_____
_____
_____
_____
_____
_____
_____
_____
_____
_____

ADVERSE PROPERTY INDICATORS

Adverse Property Indicators:

A. Ineligible property
☐ Not single family residential
☐ Not improved land
☐ Not located

B. Neighborhood market conditions
☐ Adverse market conditions in subject neighborhood

C. Site
☐ Adverse easement
☐ Adverse encroachment
☐ Adverse zoning

D. Depreciation condition
☐ Atypical physical
☐ Atypical functional
☐ Atypical external

E. Subject property condition
☐ Significant repairs needed
☐ ATypical quality of construction
☐ Atypical remodeling/additions
☐ Subsidence
☐ Special study zone
☐ Pest Infestation

F. Adverse environment condions
☐ Hazardous waste
☐ Toxic substances
☐ Environmental problems

G. Miscellaneous
☐ Other
☐ Utilities inadequate
☐ Road maintenance required or questionable ingress/egress
☐ Atypical offsite improvements

H. Typical water for the neighborhood is
☐ Public
☐ Private

I. Water for the subject property is
☐ Public
☐ Private

J. Typical sewer in the neighborhood is
☐ Public
☐ Private

K. Sewer for the subject property is
☐ Public
☐ Private

L. Typical roads for the neighborhood are
☐ Public
☐ Private

M. Roads for the subject property are
☐ Public
☐ Private
☐ Unable to determine

RECONCILIATION

APPRAISER:
Signature
Name
Date Report Signed
State Certification # _____ State
Or State License # _____ State

SUPERVISORY APPRAISER (ONLY IF REQUIRED):
Signature
Name
Date Report Signed:
State Certification # _____ State
Or State License # _____ State

CURBSIDE INSPECTION REPORT LIMITING CONDITIONS

Case No.
File No.
Transaction No.

Purpose of the Curbside Report: The purpose of this curbside service is to provide the client with an indication of any observable adverse conditions that affect the property's marketability. The market indicators presented may or may not be indicative of the neighborhood range and are not intended to reflect a specific value range for the subject of this report. The objective of the client is to utilize this information to make decisions as to the overall marketability of the subject property in relation to locationally similar properties in order to establish lending parameters. The referenced sales information is not to be considered as an indication of value for the captioned property and should not be utilized for any purpose requiring either an appraisal or an appraisal review.

THE SCOPE OF THE CURBSIDE REPORT

This consultation consists of obtaining information regarding the subject property and the neighborhood, by performing a curbside inspection and a drive through the neighborhood. The objective of the client is to utilize this information to make decisions as to the overall marketability of the subject property in relation to locationally similar properties in order to establish lending parameters.

STATEMENT OF LIMITING CONDITIONS AND ANALYST'S CERTIFICATION

CONTINGENT AND LIMITING CONDITIONS: The analyst's certification that appears in this report is subject to the following conditions:

1. The analyst will not be responsible for matters of a legal nature that affect either the subject property or the title to it. The analyst assumes that the title is good and marketable and, therefore, will not render any opinions about the title. The property is analyzed on the basis of it being under responsible ownership.

2. The analyst will give no testimony or appear in court because he or she performed this consultation, unless specific arrangements to do so have been made beforehand.

3. Unless otherwise noted in the report, the inspection is limited to an exterior inspection of the subject property and neighborhood. The analyst has noted only those adverse conditions (such as needed repairs, depreciation, the presence of hazardous waste, toxic substances, etc.) that he or she became aware of during the normal research involved in preforming the analysis contained herein. Unless otherwise stated in the report, the analyst has no knowledge of any hidden or unapparent conditions of the property or adverse environmental conditions (including the presence of hazardous wastes, toxic substances, etc.) that would make the property more or less valuable, and has assumed that there are no such conditions and makes no guarantees or warrantees, express or implied, regarding the condition of the property. The analyst will not be responsible for any such conditions that do exist or for any engineering or testing that might be required to discover whether such conditions exist. Because the analyst is not an expert in the field of environmental hazards, the report must not be considered as an environmental assessment of the property.

4. The analyst obtained the information contained in the consultation report from sources that he or she considers to be reliable and believe them to be true and correct. The analyst does not assume responsibility for the accuracy of such items that were furnished by other parties.

5. The analyst will not disclose the contents of the report except as provided for in the Uniform Standards of Professional Appraisal Practice.

6. The analyst must provide his or her prior written request before the lender/client can distribute the report (including any conclusions, the analyst's identity and professional designations, and references to any professional organizations or the firm in which the analyst is associated) to anyone other than the borrower, the mortgagee, or its successors and assigns; the mortgage insurer, consultants; professional appraisal organizations; any state or the district of Columbia; except that the lender/client may distribute the property description section of the report only to data collection or reporting service(s) without having to obtain the analyst's prior written consent. The analyst does not assume responsibility obtained before the report can be conveyed by anyone to the public through advertising, public relations, news, sales, or other media.

ANALYST'S CERTIFICATION: The analyst certifies that

1. I have completed an inspection of the neighborhood and a curbside inspection of the subject property.

2. I have not knowingly withheld any significant information from the consultation report and I believe, to the best of my knowledge, that all statements and information in the report are true and correct.

3. I stated in the curbside inspection report only my own personal, unbiased, and professional analysis, opinions, and conclusions which are subject only to the . ntingent and limiting conditions specified in this form.

4. I have no present or prospective interest in the property that is the subject of this report, and I have no present or prospective personal interest or bias with respect to the participants in the transaction. I did not base, either partially or completely, my analysis on the race, color, religion, sex, handicap, familial status, or national origin of either the prospective owners or occupants of the subject property or of the present owner or occupants of the properties in the vicinity of the subject property. I have no present or contemplated future interest in the subject property, and neither my current or future employment nor my compensation for performing this analysis is contingent on the results attained.

5. My compensation is not contingent on an action or event resulting from the analysis, opinions, or conclusions in, or the use of, this report. I was not required to a predetermined conclusion that favors the cause of the client or in any related party, the attainment of a specified result, or the occurence of a subsequent event in order to receive my compensation and/or employment for performing the consulting assignment.

6. I performed this consulting assignment in conformity with the Uniform Standards of Professional Appraisal Practice that were adopted and promulgated by the Appraisal Standards Board of the Appraisal Foundation and that were in place as of the effective date of this analysis.

7. Unless otherwise noted in the report, the extent of the inspection of the subject property is limited to an exterior only inspection.

8. I personally prepared all conclusions and opinions about the real estate that were set forth in consultation report. If I called on significant professional assistance from any individual(s) in the performance of the analysis or the preparation of the report, I have named such individual(s) and disclosed the specific tasks performed by them in an attached addendum to this report. I certify that any individual as named is qualified to perform the tasks. I have not authorized anyone to make a change to any item in the report, therefore, if any unauthorized change is made to the report, I will take no responsibility for it.

Address of Property Inspected: _____

APPRAISER:		SUPERVISORY APPRAISER (ONLY IF REQUIRED):	
Signature		Signature	
Name		Name	
Date Report Signed		Date Report Signed	
State Certification #	State	State Certification #	State
Or State License #	State	Or State License #	State
Expiration Date of Certification/License:		Expiration Date of Certification/License:	

Extent of Inspection ☐ Exterior Only ☐ Interior and Exterior and coincide with the responses checked in the adverse property Indicators in the following section.

The items found in the adverse property Indicators permit the preparer of the inspection to highlight for the client items that would indicate the need for some other type of report or the need to stop the transaction at that point. Responses to the items in this section use the words adverse and atypical to describe certain features about the improvements.

First, the preparer must indicate whether the property is ineligible, that is, it is not a single family residence, there are no improvements at all or the property could not be located by the preparer. This is required because this service was designed for single family residences for the Freddie Mac program.

Next, the preparer must indicate if there are any adverse market conditions in the subject property. In order to respond, the preparer must look at the neighborhood through the eyes of a typical buyer and have an understanding of those conditions which would discourage a potential buyer from purchasing in that neighborhood. For example, airport noise, high voltage power lines and the like, may or may not be adverse factors in that particular market. As always, racial and ethnic composition should not be a consideration in determining adverse marketing conditions.

Site data asks for adverse easements, encroachments and zoning. Based upon the physical inspection only, this would include such items as a neighbor's fence or retainer wall or overhang restricting the rights of ownership of the subject property, enjoyment of the property and marketability.

Adverse zoning would be changes to non-residential uses.

The depreciation of the improvements, physical, functional and external are only noted if they are atypical. Examples would include severe roof damage, multiple broken windows, excessive paint peeling, dry rot or structural defects. Functional depreciation usually includes both function and quality of construction and materials. Since this is an exterior inspection only, adverse functional depreciation will more than likely be based mainly on factor of quality of construction and materials. This item should be considered in relation to other properties in the neighborhood. External depreciation should be considered in terms of its affect on the marketability of the property.

Under the category of Subject property condition, the need for significant repairs relates to the impact on marketability and habitability. The lender may eventually require a final inspection for repairs. If construction does not meet minimum building codes and does not conform with neighboring properties, then the preparer should check the box for atypical quality of construction. If remodeling or additions are not architecturally congruent with the original structure then the appraiser should indicate atypical remodeling/addition on the form. Also prompting a response on this section would be an improvement that resulted in significant over-improvement. The preparer should also consider if the remodeling is amateurish or has an impact on marketability.

Subsidence notations on the curbside inspection would be based upon any noted in the physical inspection and known problems in the area.

Special study zones such as earthquake zones, flooding zones and the like should be noted as well.

Pest infestation notations would be based upon both the presence of pests and/or visible signs of pest damage.

As with most property transactions in today's market, the preparer must address environmental conditions affecting the subject property. The preparer must consider the permanency of the hazard and the proximity to the subject and the neighborhood. Marketability is the main consideration in determining how to respond to this section of the report.

Miscellaneous items to consider include adequacy of utilities to the subject property, particularly in comparison to other properties; road maintenance, especially ingress and egress.

Other sections of the report ask the preparer to note whether water, sewer and roads for the subject and the neighborhood are public or private.

Again, keep in mind that the curbside inspection does not result in an estimate of value and is based only on an exterior inspection of the subject property.

The assessment validation (see Exhibit E) is not an appraisal either. However, it does provide the client a range of value for the neighborhood using a search of recent comparable sales. In addition to the comparable sales research the preparer is required to conduct a field study which could include an interior inspection as well as an exterior and neighborhood inspection.

When completing the section on borrower/subject property information section, count the rooms according to the Fannie Mae method, remembering that bathrooms, utility rooms and foyers are not included in the total room count. As gross living area is to be provided, accurate measurements of the exterior requirements must be taken.

The Field report section includes both neighborhood data and subject property data. The neighborhood data is quite similar to that found on the URAR except for a section asking for ratings of property compatibility, general appearance of properties and appeal to market. A comment section is also provided. Here, the appraiser should discuss neighborhood factors, both favorable and unfavorable, which affect marketability. Subject property data includes actual age, type, design, exterior and roof material. The property is also rated for condition of the exterior, compatibility to the neighborhood and appeal and marketability. A comment section allows for further coverage on factors both favorable and unfavorable about the subject.

Note that the comparable sales data does not allow for adjustments of the comparable's sale price. Comparables chosen for the assessment validation should be current sales, with as much conformity to the subject property as possible. The comment section of this form should provide an explanation of the comparable sales data.

Both the assessment validation and the curbside inspection are accompanied by a specifically worded Certification and Lim-

ASSESSMENT VALIDATION

Borrower/Subject Property Information

File Number: _____   Case Number: _____   Transaction Number: _____

Borrower: _____

Property Address: _____

City: _____   County: _____   State: _____   Zip Code: _____

No. of Rooms	No. of Bedrooms	No. of Baths	Family Room or Den ☐ Yes ☐ No	Gross Living Area Sq. Ft.	Garage/ Carport	Porches, Patio or Pool	Central Air ☐ Yes ☐ No

Field Report

NEIGHBORHOOD

Location	☐ Urban	☐ Suburban	☐ Rural		Good	Avg.	Fair	Poor

Location   ☐ Urban   ☐ Suburban   ☐ Rural
Built Up   ☐ Over 75%   ☐ 25% to 75%   ☐ Under 25%   Property Compatibility   ☐ ☐ ☐ ☐ (Good Avg. Fair Poor)
Growth Rate   ☐ Fully Dev.   ☐ Rapid   ☐ Steady   ☐ Slow   General Appearance of Properties   ☐ ☐ ☐ ☐
Property Values   ☐ Increasing   ☐ Stable   ☐ Declining   Appeal to Market   ☐ ☐ ☐ ☐
Demand/Supply   ☐ Shortage   ☐ In Balance   ☐ Over Supply
Marketing Time   ☐ Under 3 Mos. ☐ 3–6 Mos.   ☐ Over 6 Mos.
Present Land Use   ☐ 1 Family ☐ 2–4 Family   ☐ Apts.   ☐ Condo   ☐ Commercial   ☐ Industrial   ☐ Vacant   ☐ PUD
Change in Present Land Use   ☐ Not Likely   ☐ Likely   ☐ Taking Place From
Predominant Occupancy   ☐ Owner   ☐ Tenant   _____ % Vacant
Price Range $ _____ to $ _____ $ _____ Predominant Value
Age _____ yrs. to _____ yrs. Predominate Age _____ yrs.

Note: Race or the racial composition of the neighborhood is not considered to be a reliable factor in this analysis.
Comments including those factors, favorable or unfavorable, affecting marketability (e.g., public parks, schools, view, noise):

_____
_____
_____
_____

SUBJECT PROPERTY

Approximate Year Built: _____   No. Units: _____   No. Stories: _____

	Good	Avg.	Fair	Poor

PROPERTY RATING
Type (detached, duplex, semi/det., etc.): _____   Condition of Exterior   ☐ ☐ ☐ ☐
Design (rambler, split level, etc.): _____   Compatibility to Neighborhood ☐ ☐ ☐ ☐
Exterior Wall Material: _____   Roof Material: _____ Appeal and Marketability   ☐ ☐ ☐ ☐
Comments (favorable or unfavorable including any deferred maintenance):

_____
_____
_____
_____

Comparable Sales Search

The requested sales search has resulted in the selection of the following three recent transactions to depict a sales price range for properties similar to the subject property in the subject neighborhood.
The purpose of this search is to provide an indication of the prevalent sales price range for reasonably similar properties in the subject's neighborhood. The referenced sales information is not to be considered as an indication of value for the captioned property and should not be utilized for any purpose requiring either an appraisal or an appraisal review.

ITEM	SUBJECT	SALE 1	SALE 2	SALE 3
Address				
Proximity to Subject				
Square Foot Area				
Sale Date				
Sale Price				
Sale Price/Sq.Ft.				
Comments:				

_____
_____
_____
_____

This is a report of subject property data and relevant market data only and is not to be construed as an appraisal report.

ANALYST:
Signature _____
Name _____
Date Report Signed _____
State Certification # _____   State _____
Or State License # _____   State _____

Assessment Validation Report Limiting Conditions

Purpose of the Consultation: The purpose of this consultation service is to provide the client with an indication: of the prevalent sales price range for reasonably similar residential properties in the subject neighborhood, or competing neighborhood(s) in proximity to the subject property. The market indicators presented may or may not be indicative of the neighborhood range and are not intended to reflect a specific value range for the subject of this report. The objective of the client is to utilize this information to make decisions as to the overall marketability of the subject property in relation to locationally similar properties in order to establish lending parameters. The referenced sales information is not to be considered as an indication of value for the captioned property and should not be utilized for any purpose requiring either an appraisal or an appraisal review.

THE SCOPE OF THE CONSULTING REPORT

This consultation consists of obtaining information regarding the subject property and the neighborhood, verifying the information through public and/or private records, and researching local data sources for three recent sales of relatively similarity, and presenting a summary of the relevant data. The objective of the client is to utilize this informatoin to make decisions as to the overall marketability of the subject property in relation to locationally similar properties in order to establish lending parameters.

STATEMENT OF LIMITING CONDITIONS AND ANALYST'S CERTIFICATION

CONTINGENT AND LIMITING CONDITIONS: The analyst's certification that appears in this report is subject to the following conditions:

1. The analyst will not be responsible for matters of a legal nature that affect either the subject property or the title to it. The analyst assumes that the title is good and marketable and, therefore, will not render any opinions about the title. The property is analyzed on the basis of it being under responsible ownership.

2. The analyst will give no testimony or appear in court because he or she performed this consultation, unless specific arrangements to do so have been made beforehand.

3. Unless otherwise noted in the report, the inspection is limited to an exterior only inspection, and no interior physical inspection of the subject property has been completed. The analyst has noted only those adverse conditions (such as needed repairs, depreciation, the presence of hazardous waste, toxic substances, etc.) that he or she became aware of during the normal research involved in performing the analysis are contained herein. Unless otherwise stated in the report, the analyst has no knowledge of any hidden or unapparent conditions of the property or adverse environmental conditions (including the presence of hazardous wastes, toxic substances, etc.) that would make the property more or less valuable, and has assumed that there are no such conditions and makes no guarantees or warranties, express or implied, regarding the condition of the property. The analyst will not be responsible for any such conditions that do exist or for any engineering or testing that might be required to discover whether such conditions exist. Because the analyst is not an expert in the field of environmental hazards, the report must not be considered as an environmental assessment of the property.

4. The analyst obtained the information contained in the consultation report from sources that he or she considers to be reliable and believe them to be true and correct. The analyst does not assume responsibility for the accuracy of such items that were furnished by other parties.

5. The analyst will not disclose the contents of the report except as provided for in the Uniform Standards of Professional Appraisal Practice.

6. The analyst must provide his or her prior written consent before the lender/client can distribute the report (including any conclusions, the analyst's identity and professional designations, and references to any professional appraisal organizations or the firm in which the analyst is associated) to anyone other than the borrower, the mortgagee or its successors and assigns; the mortgage insurer; consultants; professional appraisal organizations; any state or the District of Columbia; except that the lender/client may distribute the property description section of the report only to data collection or reporting service(s) without having to obtain the analyst's prior written consent. The analyst's written consent and approval must also be obtained before the report can be conveyed by anyone to the public through advertising, public relations, news, sales, or other media.

ANALYST'S CERTIFICATION: The analyst certifies and agrees that:

1. I have researched the subject market area and have selected a minimum of three recent sales or properties that appear to be proximate to the subject property for consideration in this analysis.

2. I have not knowingly withheld any significant information from the consultation report and I believe, the best of my knowledge, that all statements and information in the report are true and correct.

3. I stated in the consultation report only my personal, unbiased, and professional analysis, opinions, and conclusions, which are subject only to the contingent and limiting conditions specified in this form.

4. I have no present or prospective interest in the property that is the subject of this report, and I have no present or prospective personal interest or bias with respect to the participants in the transaction. I did not base, either partially or completely, my analysis on the race, color, religion, sex, handicap, familial status, or national origin of either the prospective owners or occupants of the subject property or of the present owners or occupants of the properties in the vicinity of the subject property. I have no present or contemplated future interest in the subject property, and neither my current or future employment nor my compensation for performing this analysis is contingent on the results attained.

6. My compensation is not contingent on an action or event resulting from the analysis, opinions, or conclusions in, or the use of, this report. I was not required to a predetermined conclusion that favors the cause of the client or in any related party, the attainment of a specified result, or the occurrence of a subsequent event in order to receive my compensation and/or employment for performing the consulting assignment.

7. I performed this consulting assignment in conformity with the Uniform Standards or Professional Appraisal Practice that were adopted and promulgated by the Appraisal Standards Board of the Appraisal Foundation and that were in place as of the effective date of this analysis.

8. Unless otherwise noted in the report, the extent of the inspection of the subject property is limited to an exterior only inspection.

9. I personally prepared all conclusions and opinions about the real estate that were set forth in the consultation report. If I called on significant professional assistance from any individual(s) in the preparation of the analysis or the preparation of the report, I have named such individual(s) and disclosed the specific tasks performed by them in an attached addendum to this report. I certify that any individual as named is qualified to perform the tasks. I have not authorized anyone to make a change to any item in the report, therefore, if any unauthorized change is made to the report, I will take no responsibility for it.

Address of Property Analyzed: _____

APPRAISER:

Signature _____

Name _____

Date Report Signed _____

State Certification # _____ State _____

Or State License # _____ State _____

Expiration Date of Certification/License: _____

Extent of Inspection ☐ Exterior Only ☐ Interior and Exterior iting Conditions. Note that the preparer of the report is referred to as an analyst and the reports are referred to as consultations.

In the Freddie Mac transaction, more often than not, the first assignment will be to call for the curbside inspection. If the property is atypical in too many categories or in some other way, does not fit the program's criteria, then an upgrade will be called for. This would be the assessment validation or it might call for going further to evaluation or even a formal appraisal prepared on the URAR. The underwriters at Freddie Mac will make this decision.

It is important for both field appraisers and reviewers to differentiate between those services that are appraisals and those that are not.

PART III

Appraisal Review

CHAPTER NINETEEN

REVIEWING THE SINGLE FAMILY RESIDENCE

Introduction

The estimate of value of a single family residence may be more difficult to predict with reasonable accuracy than estimating the value of a multimillion dollar commercial property due to the unpredictably of the market players. Single family purchasers and sellers are often times unsophisticated, uninformed, and are occasionally forced to act under pressure. Therefore, many sales do not fall within the common definition of "market value". This, in turn, results in several judgments which a review appraiser must make.

Appraising is not an exact science and this is the most important concept that a reviewer must keep in mind at all times. Pinpoint judgment is not included in the duties of a reviewer. Rather, the establishment of levels or probabilities of acceptance or of reasonableness should be the methodology used.

A review appraiser must recognize and must have shared common problems experienced by most field appraisers to be objective in a judgment capacity. In addition, the reviewer must be an expert in appraisal theory. The review process is analogous to a courtroom trial in several ways. First of all, the facts in any number of legal cases, or properties, will never be the same. Second, the facts or the testimony is presented differently by each counsel, or appraiser, as the case may be. Third, courtroom procedures, or the appraisal form, are used as the basis for the presentation of the facts of testimony. Fourth, case law, or appraisal theory, is used as the basis for the verdict. Finally, the judge or the review appraiser arrives at a final conclusion and acts on that decision. Therefore, for any appraisal, the reviewer reads the appraisal facts, weighs the valuation procedures, consults "case law" on appraisal theory, and then arrives at a final conclusion of value.

In the remainder of this discussion, several rules of thumb or definitions are presented and may appear to be a set of rules or ultimate solutions to reviewing appraisals. However, the intention here is merely to provide opinions based on several years of reviewing single family appraisals and to uncover some controversial issues. By no means should a review appraiser attempt to subscribe to a predetermined set of formulas. Rather, common sense should rule the review process.

Forms

Like an author, the duty of a field appraiser is to lead a potential reader logically through the report. The final conclusion must be well supported and documented. First of all, an appraisal must contain a description section and a valuation section. The description should contain all neighborhood information, a detailed outline of the subject property in both quantitive and qualitative terms, and certain observations or judgments regarding its physical characteristics. The valuation section must contain market extracted support in the form of either comparable sales, a market related gross income multiplier analysis, and/or a cost approach. The review appraiser is either aided or handicapped by the detail and adaptability of the form to the type of property under appraisal.

The Uniform Residential Appraisal Report (FHLMC Form #70/FNMA Form #1004) is one appraisal form which is all-encompassing with provisions for a large amount of detailed information that is vital for a complete understanding of the property for any reader. Generally, it could be said that if the report is fully completed with detailed information, the reviewer should be presented with a realistic synopsis of a property. However, all of the lines and boxes do not have to be filled out, as some items may not be applicable or may be inappropriate for the property in ques-

Property Description & Analysis **UNIFORM RESIDENTIAL APPRAISAL REPORT** File No. _____

SUBJECT

Property Address			Census Tract	
City	County	State	Zip Code	
Legal Description				
Owner/Occupant			Map Reference	
Sale Price $	Date of Sale			PROPERTY RIGHTS APPRAISED
Loan charges/concessions to be paid by seller $				Fee Simple
R.E. Taxes $	Tax Year	HOA $/Mo.		Leasehold
Lender/Client				Condominium (HUD/VA)
				De Minimis PUD

LENDER DISCRETIONARY USE

Sale Price	$ _____
Date	
Mortgage Amount	$ _____
Mortgage Type	
Discount Points and Other Concessions	
Paid by Seller	$ _____
Source	

NEIGHBORHOOD

LOCATION	Urban	Suburban	Rural
BUILT UP	Over 75%	25-75%	Under 25%
GROWTH RATE	Rapid	Stable	Slow
PROPERTY VALUES	Increasing	Stable	Declining
DEMAND/SUPPLY	Shortage	In Balance	Over Supply
MARKETING TIME	Under 3 Mos.	3-6 Mos.	Over 6 Mos.

PRESENT LAND USE	%	LAND USE CHANGE	PREDOMINANT OCCUPANCY
Single Family	___	Not Likely	Owner
2-4 Family	___	Likely	Tenant
Multi-family	___	In process	Vacant (0-5%)
Commercial	___	To: ___	Vacant (over 5%)
Industrial	___		
Vacant	___		

SINGLE FAMILY HOUSING

PRICE $ (000)	AGE (yrs)
Low	
High	
Predominant	
—	

NEIGHBORHOOD ANALYSIS	Good	Avg.	Fair	Poor
Employment Stability				
Convenience to Employment				
Convenience to Shopping				
Convenience to Schools				
Adequacy of Public Transportation				
Recreation Facilities				
Adequacy of Utilities				
Property Compatibility				
Protection from Detrimental Cond.				
Police & Fire Protection				
General Appearance of Properties				
Appeal to Market				

Note: Race or the racial composition of the neighborhood are not considered reliable appraisal factors.
COMMENTS _____

SITE

Dimensions		
Site Area	Corner Lot	
Zoning Classification	Zoning Compliance	
HIGHEST & BEST USE: Present Use	Other Use	

Topography	
Size	
Shape	
Drainage	
View	
Landscaping	
Driveway	
Apparent Easements	
FEMA Flood Hazard	Yes* ___ No ___
FEMA* Map/Zone	

UTILITIES	Public	Other	SITE IMPROVEMENTS	Type	Public	Private
Electricity			Street			
Gas			Curb/Gutter			
Water			Sidewalk			
Sanitary Sewer			Street Lights			
Storm Sewer			Alley			

COMMENTS (Apparent adverse easements, encroachments, special assessments, slide areas, etc.): _____

IMPROVEMENTS

GENERAL DESCRIPTION	EXTERIOR DESCRIPTION	FOUNDATION	BASEMENT	INSULATION
Units	Foundation	Slab	Area Sq. Ft.	Roof
Stories	Exterior Walls	Crawl Space	% Finished	Ceiling
Type (Det./Att.)	Roof Surface	Basement	Ceiling	Walls
Design (Style)	Gutters & Dwnspts.	Sump Pump	Walls	Floor
Existing	Window Type	Dampness	Floor	None
Proposed	Storm Sash	Settlement	Outside Entry	Adequacy
Under Construction	Screens	Infestation		Energy Efficient Items:
Age (Yrs.)	Manufactured House			
Effective Age (Yrs.)				

ROOM LIST

ROOMS	Foyer	Living	Dining	Kitchen	Den	Family Rm.	Rec. Rm.	Bedrooms	# Baths	Laundry	Other	Area Sq. Ft.
Basement												
Level 1												
Level 2												

Finished area **above** grade contains: ___ Rooms; ___ Bedroom(s); ___ Bath(s); ___ Square Feet of Gross Living Area

INTERIOR

SURFACES	Materials/Condition
Floors	
Walls	
Trim/Finish	
Bath Floor	
Bath Wainscot	
Doors	

Fireplace(s) ___ # ___

HEATING	
Type	
Fuel	
Condition	
Adequacy	
COOLING	
Central	
Other	
Condition	
Adequacy	

KITCHEN EQUIP	
Refrigerator	
Range/Oven	
Disposal	
Dishwasher	
Fan/Hood	
Compactor	
Washer/Dryer	
Microwave	
Intercom	

ATTIC	
None	
Stairs	
Drop Stair	
Scuttle	
Floor	
Heated	
Finished	

IMPROVEMENT ANALYSIS	Good	Avg.	Fair	Poor
Quality of Construction				
Condition of Improvements				
Room Sizes/Layout				
Closets and Storage				
Energy Efficiency				
Plumbing-Adequacy & Condition				
Electrical-Adequacy & Condition				
Kitchen Cabinets-Adequacy & Cond.				
Compatibility to Neighborhood				
Appeal & Marketability				

AUTOS

CAR STORAGE					
Garage	Attached	Adequate	House Entry	Estimated Remaining Economic Life	Yrs.
No. Cars	Carport	Detached	Inadequate	Outside Entry	Estimated Remaining Physical Life	Yrs.
Condition	None	Built-In	Electric Door	Basement Entry		

Additional features: _____

COMMENTS

Depreciation (Physical, functional and external inadequacies, repairs needed, modernization, etc.): _____

General market conditions and prevalence and impact in subject/market area regarding loan discounts, interest buydowns and concessions: _____

Freddie Mac Form 70 10/86   Fannie Mac Form 1004 10/86

Valuation Section **UNIFORM RESIDENTIAL APPRAISAL REPORT** File No.

Purpose of Appraisal is to estimate Market Value as defined in the Certification & Statement of Limiting Conditions

COST APPROACH

BUILDING SKETCH (SHOW GROSS LIVING AREA ABOVE GRADE)
If for Freddie Mac or Fannie Mae show only, square ft of calculations and cost approach comments in this space.

ESTIMATED REPRODUCTION COST - NEW - OF IMPROVEMENTS

Dwelling	Sq Ft is $	= $
	Sq Ft a $	=
Extras		=
		=
Special Energy Efficient Items		=
Porches, Patios, etc		=
Garage/Carport	Sq Ft a $	=
Total Estimated Cost New		= $
	Physical Functional External	
Less		
Depreciation		= $
Depreciated Value of Improvements		= $
Site Imp "as is" (driveway, landscaping, etc)		= $
ESTIMATED SITE VALUE		= $
(If leasehold, show only leasehold value)		
INDICATED VALUE BY COST APPROACH		= $

(Not Required by Freddie Mac and Fannie Mae)
Does property conform to applicable HUD/VA property standards? ☐ Yes ☐ No
If No, explain

Construction Warranty ☐ Yes ☐ No
Name of Warranty Program
Warranty Coverage Expires

The undersigned has recited three recent sales of properties most similar and proximate to subject and has considered these in the market analysis. The description includes a dollar adjustment, reflecting market reaction to those items of significant variation between the subject and comparable properties. If a significant item in the comparable property is superior to or more favorable than, the subject property, a minus (-) adjustment is made, thus reducing the indicated value of subject, if a significant item in the comparable is inferior to, or less favorable than, the subject property, a plus (+) adjustment is made, thus increasing the indicated value of the subject.

SALES COMPARISON ANALYSIS

ITEM	SUBJECT	COMPARABLE NO. 1		COMPARABLE NO 2		COMPARABLE NO 3	
Address							
Proximity to Subject							
Sales Price	$		$		$		$
Price/Gross Liv. Area	$	$		$		$	
Data Source							
VALUE ADJUSTMENTS	DESCRIPTION	DESCRIPTION	+ (-)$ Adjustment	DESCRIPTION	+ (-)$ Adjustment	DESCRIPTION	+ (-)$ Adjustment
Sales or Financing Concessions							
Date of Sale/Time							
Location							
Site/View							
Design and Appeal							
Quality of Construction							
Age							
Condition							
Above Grade Room Count	Total Bdrms Baths	Total Bdrms Baths		Total Bdrms Baths		Total Bdrms Baths	
Gross Living Area	Sq Ft	Sq Ft		Sq Ft		Sq Ft	
Basement & Finished Rooms Below Grade							
Functional Utility							
Heating/Cooling							
Garage/Carport							
Porches, Patio, Pools, etc							
Special Energy Efficient Items							
Fireplace(s)							
Other (e.g. kitchen equip., remodeling)							
Net Adj. (total)		☐+ ☐- $		☐+ ☐- $		☐+ ☐- $	
Indicated Value of Subject			$		$		$

Comments on Sales Comparison

INDICATED VALUE BY SALES COMPARISON APPROACH .... $

INDICATED VALUE BY INCOME APPROACH (If Applicable) Estimated Market Rent $ _____ /Mo x Gross Rent Multiplier _____ = $

This appraisal is made ☐ "as is" ☐ subject to the repairs, alterations, inspections or conditions listed below ☐ completion per plans and specifications.

Comments and Conditions of Appraisal

RECONCILIATION

Final Reconciliation

This appraisal is based upon the above requirements, the certification, contingent and limiting conditions, and Market Value definition that are stated in

☐ FmHA, HUD &/or VA instructions.
☐ Freddie Mac Form 439 (Rev 7/86)/Fannie Mae Form 1004B (Rev 7/86) filed with client _____ 19 ____ ☐ attached.
I (WE) ESTIMATE THE MARKET VALUE, AS DEFINED, OF THE SUBJECT PROPERTY AS OF _____ 19 ____ **to be $**

I (WE) certify that to the best of my (our) knowledge and belief the facts and data used herein are true and correct, that I (we) personally inspected the subject property, both inside and out, and have made an exterior inspection of all comparable sales cited in this report; and that I (we) have no undisclosed interest, present or prospective therein.

Appraiser(s) SIGNATURE _____
NAME _____

Review Appraiser SIGNATURE _____
(if applicable) NAME _____

☐ Did ☐ Did Not
Inspect Property

Freddie Mac Form 70 10/86 **1004**

Fannie Mae Form 1004 10/86

tion. In such instances, the field appraiser may wish to insert the words "not applicable". Finally, review appraisers should encourage field appraisers to add amendments to the appraisal form to elaborate on certain problems or unusual circumstances.

Appearance

Review appraisers must demand a legible report which is professional in appearance. A review appraiser can sometimes assess the credibility of the field appraiser if the report is filled with grammatical errors, punctuation mistakes, misspelled words, or smudges on the report pages. A form report need not be typed, but should be neatly written or printed. Abbreviations should be avoided to avoid misinterpretation. Additional comments should not be squeezed into a predesignated section of the form when an addendum could be used. Errors often occur, especially in the adjustment section of the market approach. Therefore, all calculations supplied by the field appraiser should be carefully scrutinized. Despite the argument that neat and legible appraisals may reflect the meticulousness of the field appraiser, just having all of the "i's" dotted and the "t's" crossed does not mean that the appraisal is acceptable.

Photographs and Supporting Illustrations

Photographs are usually necessary since the reviewer needs to establish a visual reference. Furthermore, a photo may verify the physical description contained in the report. Rear and side photos of the improvement may add a further visual reference, but typically are not necessary unless for unusual conditions. Street scenes are good, but an astute field appraiser can select a camera angle which obscures an adjacent detrimental property. Oblique aerial photos are invaluable as they will give the reader a "bird's eye" view of the location in reference to the surrounding area and land uses. Aerial photos are typically not justified for a single family residential appraisal, however. Site plans or plot plans are informative, but may not be necessary in platted or subdivided areas where lots are similar and conforming. Unusual properties involving such conditions as setback violations, shared driveways? High ground coverage, restrictive or adverse easements, etc., are situations where a site plan may be helpful. Subdivision or plat map requirements should be adhered to in similar situations. Area or city location maps, census tract maps, zip code maps, etc. may be helpful, especially if the review appraiser is not familiar with a particular community or neighborhood. Supporting data and photos of comparables should be required in unusual circumstances and in cases where the accurate determination of value is extremely important. However, the photos and multiple listing information may not be as revealing as the field appraiser's observations.

Plans and specifications on proposed dwellings may be important, especially where the structure has an unconventional architectural design. In the case of tract development, if the field appraiser has inspected the model home, he or she should be qualified to value a proposed dwelling of the same design, despite the fact that there may be upgrades and minor alterations. In all cases, the review appraiser must be acquainted with the construction materials, design, finish items, site improvements, etc., with each locale as well as the costs. Field inspection trips and discussions with local building contractors are suggested as the most successful way to bridge this gap.

Quality Control Procedures

An astute review appraiser will quickly learn that reliance upon the field appraisal report may lead to inaccurate value conclusions. Field appraisers have been known to produce false property information or to select a subset of inappropriate market comparables. If an appraisal appears highly questionable, the review appraiser should consider a field inspection trip to analyze the situation firsthand. If a trend is detected in reference to a particular appraiser, lending institution, geographic location, property type, or dwelling age, a personal inspection is certainly necessary. Meetings are suggested with field appraisers in order to capture as much of their local real estate knowledge as possible, as well as to assess their professionalism. In addition, an inspection of the field appraisers' offices and files may be enlightening. Where field inspections and appraiser contact are not possible, the use of spot check appraisals may aid in the review process. The selection of field review appraisers is vital to maintain a level of independence. The detail of a field review will vary depending upon the importance of the case. Drive-by inspections are sufficient where the purpose of the review is to verify the property description and location or to verify the existence of comparable sales that were presented by the field appraiser. Where the establishment of value is important, each independent field review appraiser must fully inspect the property and must not consult with the original field appraiser.

Conditions and Pertinent Information

The review appraiser must be aware of the following assumptions, conditions and other vital information before the review can begin:

1. Property address and legal description
2. Property rights appraised (fee simple, leasehold, condo, etc.)
3. Effective date of the appraisal
4. Date the property was inspected
5. Contingent events or circumstance such as:
    a. subject to zoning change
    b. subject to repairs or alterations
    c. subject to completion in a workmanship manner according to plans and specifications
6. A copy of a statement of limiting conditions
7. Sales or financing concessions

8. Definition of market value

Location

The review appraiser is normally very interested in the property location information which ranges from the macro market to the micro market. Because real estate is fixed in location, value is largely determined by the impact of external market forces and, in particular, the forces of supply and demand. Both the field appraiser and the review appraiser must identify the forces at work, measure the broad impact on the macro market, on the micro market, and, in particular, on the property being appraised. Although there are quantitative formulas available, the typical appraiser will rely on mass media to evaluate these environmental, political, economic, or social factors. These determinants are difficult to measure, especially in advance. However, we are all familiar with examples of the following phenomena on the real estate market:

1. Gas rationing
2. Double digit inflation rates
3. Double digit interest rates
4. Smog, pollution, weather conditions
5. Taxes and public services
6. Industry strikes, layoffs, expansion
7. Population migration
8. Neighborhood revitalization
9. Recreational development

Not every area of the United States has experienced an inflation in residential values over the past decade. Why have some sections of the country witnessed an increase of residential property values of 20% while other areas have struggled through a decline? These are important factors which a review appraiser must be familiar with. National real estate publications, newspapers, and other periodicals are the most convenient method for the review appraiser to keep reasonably informed.

A review appraiser who may be reviewing local property appraisals certainly must be aware of all factors which would affect the local real estate market. Other reviewers, however, may be hundreds or thousands of miles from the subject property. In such cases, it is suggested that the review appraiser keep in close contact with all forms of public media, conduct personal inspections, and consult with local experts.

Neighborhood Location

The questions of neighborhood description and definition have certainly come under close scrutiny over the past decade, especially in the residential sector, as outgrowths of various government legislation such as the Fair Housing Act of 1968, the Civil Rights Act of 1964 the Home Loan Disclosure Act, and the Equal Credit Opportunity Act. Unfortunately, discrimination has been and continues to be a reality in housing. Several court decisions such as Trifficante v. Metropolitan Life Insurance Company; Lauffman v. Oakley Building and Loan Company; Harrison v. Heinzeroth Mortgage Company; and Griggs v. Duke Power Company have concentrated on housing discrimination as related to the lending industry.

An appraiser must objectively evaluate the economic, social, political, and physical forces of a neighborhood, as well as other significant determinants which have an impact on the valuation process. As indicated previously, real estate is a fixed asset with external forces continually influencing it. The appraiser must recognize these factors and evaluate the impact on the neighborhood. The recognition and evaluation, however, must be objective and must be unbiased with reference to race, color, religion, sex, national origin or other minority group. To quote the "Policy Statement: SREA Educational Professional Concepts Relating to Neighborhood Analysis and the Formation for an Opinion of Value of Properties Located in Residential Settings" which appeared in the March 21, 1979 issue of Appraisal Brief:

> "...neighborhood factors and forces, being in a constant of change, must be observed, recorded and analyzed with the recognition that some of those factors and forces are not readily susceptible to quantitative analysis. Extreme care must be taken in articulating and considering any factor or force which is not easily measured.
>
> The responsible appraiser must recognize that the dynamic interplay of neighborhood forces and factors directly affects the opinions and hence the behavior of buyers and sellers of property within a neighborhood setting. These opinions, like the neighborhood dynamics, are constantly changing."

One important point must be made here—racial, religious, or ethnic composition may or may not have a relationship on value, neighborhood stability, or compatibility. We subscribe to the principle that there is no predetermined relationship of value with race, religion, color, or national origin, etc. Any correlation must be well documented or supported without bias. Similarly, a property's convenience to shopping, adequacy of public transportation, availability of public utilities, for example, may or may not have a direct relationship with value, neighborhood stability, or compatibility. Any statement suggesting that it did must be supported with strong market data, and also without bias.

How does one define a neighborhood? Traditional definitions indicate that the neighborhood is defined by physical boundaries, political boundaries, or land use. The "extent" of a neighborhood, its size, or other measurements are the judgment of the field appraiser based on observations and experience in the marketplace. For most appraisers, the definition of a neighborhood must be a homogeneous area and therefore, somewhat limited in size. To others, it may encompass a large geographic area composed of a variety of land uses.

The review appraiser must receive a clear definition of neighborhood from the field appraiser. Principally, the review appraiser must be made aware of all supportable factors which have a direct external influence on the subject property. Such factors must be unbiased with respect to minorities as discussed above. The State of California Department of Savings and Loan has described proximity to the subject property in consideration of "localized factor" (the neighborhood) in Subchapter 241 Chapter 2, Title 10, California Administration Code—"Guidelines Relating to Fair Lending" as "only those blocks and sides of blocks that are likely to most directly impact on the security property". The following exhibit, used in subchapter of the "code", illustrates the shaded areas as the subject property with the dark lines representing those block sides which might most directly impact upon the subject property.

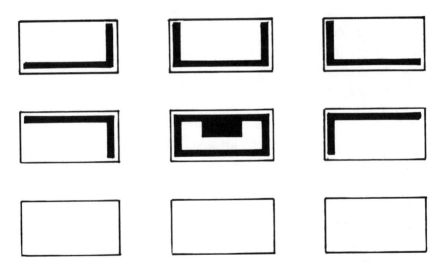

I would strongly suggest that the review appraiser emphasize to the field appraiser that the neighborhood be defined in the appraisal and that all comments stated indicate only those external forces which have a direct impact upon the subject property. I subscribe to the theory that the neighborhood be defined to as small a geographic area as possible and, hopefully, to the definition stated by the California Department of Savings and Loans.

The review appraiser is normally interested in locational factors which promote stability, compatibility, or other measurements of market acceptance. The Uniform Residential Appraisal Report form recognizes the following factors which appear to be categorized by physical or measurable descriptions:

1. Urban/suburban/rural
2. Percentage built up
3. Percent land use by type
4. Occupancy types
5. Marketing time
6. Value trends
7. Changes in land use
8. Single family age

The several factors which follow are normally based on the appraiser's judgment:

1. Growth rate
2. Demand/supply
3. Employment stability
4. Convenience to employment
5. Convenience to shopping
6. Convenience to schools
7. Adequacy of transportation
8. Recreation facilities
9. Adequacy of utilities
10. Protection from detrimental influences

11. Project compatibility
12. Police & fire protection
13. General appearance of property
14. Appeal to market.

In terms of the physical items, the review appraiser will be most interested in such items as present land use by type, marketing time, value trends, change in land use, and single family price range. Where a possible question arises from negative descriptions, the review appraiser will look to the judgment section in order to determine how the field appraiser has interpreted this situation. If a problem is apparent, the field appraiser must describe in appropriate detail the effect, if any, on the subject property. Furthermore, these problems should be treated consistently throughout the remainder of the report and supported with market evidence.

The review appraiser must be alert to the fact that the field appraiser may have a certain bias or that the market information contained in the report may be inaccurate. Hence, questions related to the 14 items listed above under the judgmental category must be probed, if not properly defined or described in proper detail. Ultimately, the review appraiser should look to the last item, "appeal to market", as the field appraiser may be somewhat concerned by isolated circumstances, but overall feels that the subject property evidences adequate marketability, or adequate security if it involves a mortgage.

For a proposed dwelling in a large residential project, the review appraiser must question the feasibility of the development in terms of location, price range, competition, potential demand, amenities, accessibility, etc. Many field appraisers may be unprepared to make an accurate judgment in this area unless they have several years of experience upon which to base it. The period of the mid-1970's dramatically evidenced this phenomenon. To properly evaluate the success of a proposed project, the resale market in the immediate vicinity must give unqualified evidence as to the strength of the demand/supply situation in terms of breadth and depth.

The review appraiser, in interpreting neighborhood factors, must always weigh the specific influence, if any, on the subject property. This is one area upon which the experience and judgment of the field appraiser is most important. Confidence in the ability of the field appraiser is generally the most effective way for the review appraiser to receive assurance that the neighborhood is properly defined.

The Site

The review appraiser must be supplied with the following information to objectively evaluate the subject site:

1. Lot dimensions and shape
2. Current, proposed, or probable future zoning
3. Public services and utilities
4. Off-site information
5. Topography, view, drainage
6. Easements or encroachments

The review appraiser must first analyze the site, as if vacant and available for any use, to determine its highest and best use. Then, the determination must be made if the present use is the same as the highest and best use. If the existing use is an under-utilization of the land, there should be concern and a further investigation is suggested. If an over-utilization is present, normally a potential problem exists and the review appraiser should look to the market analysis of the field appraiser to determine its severity.

In terms of the six items listed above, the review appraiser must reference any unusual circumstance by its effect upon market value. A site, for example, may be shaped like a pretzel, but still have no loss in value, per unit of value cited, as evidenced by the market. Although there may be no detrimental conditions, the field appraiser is obligated to complete in as sufficient detail as possible, all descriptions of site information.

Improvement Description

Review appraisers must be given an adequate description of the dwelling unit and site improvements. Photos, as indicated, are vital in visualizing the improvement if the description is inadequate.

Normally, the field appraiser will supply the following items:

1. age of dwelling,
2. number of units,
3. type and design,
4. exterior wall and roof materials,
5. windows and door materials,
6. insulation,
7. foundation and basement description,
8. room list,
9. gross living area,
10. equipment (built-in),
11. mechanical items,
12. floor, wall, trim finish,
13. special features/finish/improvements or other items,
14. attics,
15. porches, (enclosed areas not included in living area)
16. garage or other on-site buildings,
17. on-site improvements (landscape, fence, patio, deck, pool, etc.)

As listed on the Uniform Residential Appraisal Report Form, the following judgment factors will be the basis of the Review appraiser's interpretation of the subject property as acceptable security as related to the market:

1. quality of construction,
2. condition of improvements,
3. room size/layout,
4. closets and storage,
5. adequacy of insulation,
6. adequacy and condition of plumbing,
7. adequacy and condition of electrical,
8. adequacy of kitchen cabinets,
9. compatibility to neighborhood,
10. overall livability,
11. appeal and marketability,
12. remaining economic life

The four items a review appraiser must concentrate on in reference to an overall evaluation are the following:

1. Compatibility to neighborhood
2. Overall livability
3. Appeal and marketability
4. Remaining years of economic life

All judgments of the field appraiser must be supported by market evidence as discussed in the location section. The review appraiser reserves the right to challenge all such opinions. In addition, consistency must be recognized on the part of the field appraiser throughout the report, including the valuation section.

In terms of "neighborhood compatibility", the review appraiser must be aware that potential problems exist where surrounding properties have a negative or detrimental influence on the subject. On the other hand, higher valued dwellings or proximate sites having a higher utilization may have a positive influence on the subject property despite the fact that compatibility is lacking.

The factor of overall livability" generally pertains to the functional utility of the home in terms of market acceptance and current demand/supply determinants. The judgment of "appeal and marketability" is highly correlated with overall livability.

The remaining economic life of a dwelling may have a small correlation with actual physical age. Homes can be easily rehabilitated, remodeled, or renovated to provide a continuing basis for market acceptance and livability. Remaining economic life is often treated in relation to the properties located in the immediate neighborhood which exhibit a direct influence on the subject property. Abandonment, vandalism, deferred maintenance, etc. may have a detrimental effect on the subject. On the other hand, revitalization of a neighborhood may have the opposite effect and will prolong the economic life of a dwelling. In terms of a neighborhood definition in this regard, the State of California interpretation, as earlier alluded to in this chapter, appears to be most applicable. The traditional definition of neighborhood evolution (formation, equilibrium, and disintegration) is being questioned in terms of today's market.

The review appraiser must assume that the subject dwelling has been properly measured and the correct living area determined. Dwelling measurements cannot be verified unless another independent appraisal is conducted. The determination of living area is, however, an area of interpretation.

Typically, all areas above ground which are finished, enclosed, and heated can be treated as living area. Enclosed, but unheated porches and unfinished, but heated attics cannot be considered as living space. These areas could be given some contributory value, nonetheless, as supported in the market. Finished basements generally will not be recognized fully as living area due to degrees of disutility associated with below-ground space. Again, contributory value will be recognized if market determined. Split-level homes require special market segmentation since some below-ground space can be recognized as full living area.

When rooms are counted, again only above-ground finished areas should be included. A room can be defined as a distinctly separate space having a minimum of 80 to 100 square feet. In defining living areas and room counts, the subject and the comparables must be dealt with on equal terms and assumptions.

The Cost Approach

The cost approach should normally be given little consideration in the support of the final value estimate unless the property is of a unique type, design, or construction. Many of the assumptions made in the cost approach, such as all forms of depreciation and the land value estimate, are subject to questionable assumptions. Furthermore, many of these assumptions are ultimately based on market information and observation which is contained in other sections of the report.

If the improvements involve unique construction materials or architectural design, it is suggested that local contractors be contacted as sources of cost information rather than rely upon cost manuals or modifiers. Even if the property is of a conventional design and cost manuals are utilized, the field appraiser must be ultimately familiar with the cost manual specifications and utilize the current modifiers. In terms of the land valuation, residential appraisers search the market for vacant land sales except in developing areas. Normally, the land value is derived through a "back door" approach or through a residual, as typically in existing neighborhoods there are no comparable vacant land sales available.

Sales Comparison Analysis

The direct sales comparison approach employs the principle of substitution, or the substitution of alternative properties for the subject as the basis of the determination of value. The market is dependent upon the actions of buyers and sellers who are often irrational. But based on probabilities and measured through experience and sound appraisal judgement value can be determined within acceptable limits via statistical interpretation by the review appraiser.

As direct sales comparison approach begins with the selection of a relevant subset of similar properties. The he subset may range from a subset of one to several handled. The review appraiser will typically prefer all least three comparables to establish a statistical base of reference. Adjustments are them made, via market observation by comparing components of the selected market sales to the subject property. In cases where a value cannot attached to a component by isolating market reaction cost may be used as a limit.

The direct sales comparison approach is defined by the following steps:

1. The review appraiser must be given the specific location of each comparable sale (legal description or street address). In addition, listing identification numbers, public recording, information, or other sale identification may be required by the review appraiser to verify each sale.

2. Proximity to the subject property is an important point in the selection of comparable properties. The review appraiser should select sales within the subject neighborhood in order to avoid adjustments for locational differences. Often times, where appreciation is negligible, current sales outside of the subject neighborhood could be overlooked for the selection of older sales within the subject neighborhood. Where the review appraiser is unfamiliar with the specific property location, street maps should be obtained in order to pinpoint the location of all comparables used. Field appraisers have been known to select properties outside of the subject neighborhood to justify the sales price or inflate a property value.

3. The sale price of the comparables must be verified by the field appraiser by contacting the principals of the transactions. Prices are normally reflected in dollars rounded off to the nearest hundred dollars. For example, sale prices reflecting such figures as $47,237 may not meet the criteria of a market transaction and should therefore be verified. Sale prices of

the comparables should normally reflect a range slightly above and slightly below the final appraised value of the subject property. This is because another convenient method used to support a higher value for a property is to select higher valued properties as comparables for the subject. Negative adjustments are much more easily supported than larger positive adjustments and will arouse less suspicion.

4. Price per square foot of living area may be a good rule of thumb to select possible comparable sales, but will rarely be a means of arriving at a final value estimate. Value per square foot is generally inaccurate since it compares only living area and avoids amenity packages, condition, quality of construction, age, design, sales concessions and so on.

5. The date of sale is a vital piece of information, especially in contemporary markets where appreciation may be as much as 2% per month. First of all, all comparables should reflect a date of sale. The effective date should be the date the sale was negotiated rather than the date it was closed. This means that contracts could be accepted as reliable indications of value. Generally, however, the review appraiser will prefer to see which have been closed. Nevertheless, contracts may be very reliable indicators of value in certain situations where closed sales are unavailable.

   The adjustments for appreciation, or depreciation where appropriate, must be based on verifiable market evidence. Typically, real estate organizations publish area or regional statistics on appreciation rates which can be used as rules of thumb. Where field appraisers are very active in a particular area, one can rely on their judgment. Normally, adjustments are based on percentages with the resulting dollar figure rounded to the nearest $100, $500, or $1,000, depending on the market. The comparables must be adjusted to the effective date of the appraisal. The review appraiser will find it necessary to check for consistency among these adjustments for each sale.

6. Location adjustments should not be necessary if the

comparables are selected within the subject neighborhood. Newer differences will exist and the review appraiser will normally not have a basis to evaluate the adjustment. The reviewer may want to check the street map or aerial, if included, to locate possible sources of difference. In any event, the review appraiser should be suspicious if the location adjustment exceeds 5% of the sale price, especially if it is a positive adjustment, and should question the field appraisal.

7. The site adjustment should be nominal, especially if the comparables are located in the subject neighborhood. In areas of homogeneity such as an established subdivision adjustments will be made on the basis of front footage. For irregular shaped parcels, adjustments can be based on square footage or some other market extracted basis. Site adjustments will be crucial on rural properties involving a large parcel or on properties which have a view amenity. In these cases, land sale comparables may be requested by the reviewer.

8. Design and appeal adjustments are based solely upon the judgment of the field appraiser. The review appraiser will be interested in the magnitude of such adjustments.

9. Quality of construction, age, and condition will also be based totally on the field appraiser's opinions and experience. If the comparables are representatively selected, such adjustments will not be large. Normally, unless the field appraiser has personally inspected each comparable, such adjustments will be token only. Unique features, such as decorating, probably should not be recognized since personal tastes between buyers and sellers are seldom similar. The field appraiser should, therefore, reflect differences only where the subject or the comparable is definitely below market standards for condition or decorating. If a significant amount of repairs is required, the cost of such work will set the upper limit for the dollar adjustment.

10. Room count adjustments should be based only on rooms included in the living area of the dwelling, as previously dis-

cussed. Typically included are common areas such as a living room, kitchen, dining room, family room and den; bedrooms; and bathrooms (bathrooms should be rounded to the nearest 1/2 bath). Other areas such as finished basement rooms, dining nooks, 1/4 baths, etc. should not be recognized fully as rooms or as full baths, respectively, and may be adjusted under a miscellaneous category. Comparables should typically reflect similar room counts, bedroom counts, and baths. Recognition of a room can usually be determined by size or by its utility.

Adjustments must be market determined. In some neighborhoods, demand can be distinguished between three and four bedroom homes, and so on. In subdivisions characterized by split-level homes or bi-level dwellings, lower-level finished rooms could be accepted as living area if demonstrated by the market.

11. Gross living area is an important criteria for comparable selection. Although prospective buyers normally do not physically measure a home, they typically make objective judgments concerning the size of the rooms. Unless the appraiser is using comparables which have been actually measured, the living areas listed under multiple listing sale sheets must be questioned, especially where the comparable is irregular in shape or has some overlapping levels. Where the measurements of a comparable are questionable, the only alternative will be to actually measure the sales or to verify through public records.

Adjustments for differences in living area are also market determined. An adjustment based on construction costs per square foot is normally very unreliable, especially where the property is not new. The safest method is to select comparables of the same size range as the subject property.

12. Basements, porches, patios, pools, etc. will differ in approach, depending upon geographic location, climate, price range, and buyer preference. Basements, for example, are typically re-

quired in the Midwest and in northern sections of the country. Homes without basements characteristically are difficult to sell in these areas, and functional disutility will be attached in those locations evidencing market demand for basements.

Other site improvements such as pools, tennis courts, or other custom items are typically stratified by price range or location. For example, $300,000 homes in Phoenix will typically have pools. A $300,000 home without a pool, therefore, must be adjusted at a market determined rate which will approach the replacement cost as a limit. On the other hand adjustments between homes with and without pools in Minneapolis, for example, will probably be in the range of 50% of its replacement cost since the market is not well stratified for homes with pools in a northern climate.

Garages and carports are generally in demand at any price range and location. In the northern climates, the difference in value between a property with no garage and one with a garage will probably be greater than the difference in a southern climate location. In any event, the adjustment must be market determined and must not exceed cost.

13. Other improvements generally include such items as air conditioning, fireplaces, built-in appliances, energy features, etc. As previously discussed, adjustments for these items must be market determined.

14. Sales concessions and financing may be the most debatable section of adjustments. Specifically, how does one account for points paid by the seller for VA or FHA financing, for a land contract or other owner financed transaction, for chattel items included in the sale, for developers who provide favorable financing secured by points or fees paid to a lending institution, or for distressed projects offering sale concessions? In each of the above situations, the purchaser indirectly pays for each of these incentives. Therefore, the appraiser must take into account concessions and financing involved in each of the comparable transactions and apply it to what is typical

in the market. If the appraisal of the subject property is connected with a sale, the final valuation must be contingent upon the financing or concession utilized in that transaction, if not typical of the market. Furthermore, the appraiser must explore the possibilities of another sale occurring under those same conditions. If the possibilities are remote, the appraiser must adjust for the terms of the sale. The review appraiser must pay particular attention to these factors in periods of tight money".

One such case which I have found most interesting is associated with a distressed project or a "workout" situation. In such cases, developers or interim owners may be providing incentives in the form of reduced interest rates, homeowner fee waivers, no closing costs, promotional gifts, or cash rebates. In such cases, the appraiser must evaluate whether the existing owner, or typical owner, would be able to provide the same incentives on a resale basis. If not, the following rules of thumb are suggested:

a. For interest rate subsidies, capitalize the difference between the market rate and the contract rate over the typical holding period of a residence.
b. For homeowner fees or other subsidies, take the present value of such amounts over the period of months or years applicable.
c. For rebates, points, or other promotional items, adjust for the actual dollars involved.
d. In particularly distressed markets, the appraiser may make negative adjustments for the date of sale due to holding costs.

The terms of a sale is an important item in the market comparison approach. A major error of many appraisers is to consider each comparable as a conventional transaction. All comparable sales should be verified with the parties of the transaction or the realtors for these reasons.

The field appraiser will normally rely on one or two sales as being most comparable to the subject and, therefore, most reliable as a prediction of value. These dates will typically be ones with the least number of adjustments, the most recent sales, the proximate sales to the subject, and so on. The review appraiser can normally make this determination objectively by examining the comparable description and adjustments.

The comparables may not necessarily be within a narrow range of adjusted value when compared to the subject. To reiterate, one sale may be given the greatest consideration despite the fact that the other sale may be several thousand dollars different. However, the review appraiser is encouraged to challenge the field appraiser when such differences occur.

The Income Approach

The income approach is a misnomer when applied to single family properties. First of all, even if rents on single family residences are available, this approach is actually market determined through the gross rent multiplier approach. GRM (Gross Rent Multiplier) may be applied either to a monthly market rent or to an annual rent, and is determined simply by dividing the sale price of a comparable by its monthly or annual rent. Single family properties are typically not rented and, therefore, this entire approach may not even be applicable to most properties. However, in subdivisions or areas characterized by rental occupancy and where residences are purchased as investment opportunities, the gross rent multiplier approach may be more valid than the direct sales comparison approach through adjustments. This chapter has concentrated only on single family residences. Two to eight family dwellings are often categorized with single units. The gross rent multiplier is an excellent indication of value for properties of this type and, in most instances, should be given the greatest weight in the final value determination.

Summary

In conclusion, lets reiterate the opening comments regarding the function of a review appraiser and to emphasize the objectivity which that position requires. Appraising is not an exact science and, therefore, review appraising is not an exact science. The reviewer is obligated to exhibit knowledge of appraisal theory and to practice consistency in judgment. The reviewer must rely upon wisdom, equity, and integrity in reaching the final conclusion.

CHAPTER TWENTY

REVIEWING A CONDOMINIUM APPRAISAL REPORT

Appraising condominiums can be a very challenging task. The condominium market has shown itself to be a volatile market at times and it can be a much more difficult market to read than the single family home market. This has been very evident during the 1980's as the depressed nature of the condominium market in some areas has resulted in some erratic sale prices and some rapidly dropping values. The condominium market has not followed the value trends of the single family home market in many cases, but has headed off in a direction all of its own. This problem is compounded because condominiums themselves are simply different from single family homes, as evidenced by the fact that condominium appraisals are done on a different form than single family home appraisals. One of the results of this volatile market and the overall differences between condominiums and single family homes is that there tends to be more appraisal errors and a greater problem with faulty appraisals on condominiums than is usually seen with single family home appraisals.

This chapter is intended to provide some insights into reviewing a condominium appraisal report, centering on those areas that most commonly result in errors. When appraisers begin to make errors in certain categories, it tends to raise questions as to how familiar they are with the condominium form and how thorough of a job they have done on the entire report. Reviewers and appraisers should make sure that these particular areas are adequately covered if they apply to the subject property being appraised. The standard individual condominium or PUD unit appraisal form is

APPRAISAL REPORT — INDIVIDUAL ☐ CONDOMINIUM OR ☐ PUD UNIT   File No ___

Borrower ___ Census Tract ___ Map Reference ___
Unit No ___ Address ___ Project Name/Phase No ___
City ___ County ___ State ___ Zip Code ___
Actual Real Estate Taxes $ ___ (yr) Sales Price $ ___ Property Rights Appraised ☐ Fee ☐ Leasehold
Loan Charges to be Paid by Seller $ ___ Other Sales Concessions ___
Lender/Client ___ Lender's Address ___
Occupant ___ Appraiser ___ Instructions to Appraiser ___
☐ FNMA 1073A required   ☐ FHLMC 465 Addendum A required   ☐ FHLMC 465 Addendum B required

NEIGHBORHOOD

Location	☐ Urban	☐ Suburban	☐ Rural	
Built Up	☐ Over 75%	☐ 25% to 75%	☐ Under 25%	
Growth Rate ☐ Fully Developed	☐ Rapid	☐ Steady	☐ Slow	
Property Values	☐ Increasing	☐ Stable	☐ Declining	
Demand/Supply	☐ Shortage	☐ In Balance	☐ Oversupply	
Marketing Time	☐ Under 3 Mos	☐ 4-6 Mos	☐ Over 6 Mos	

Present Land Use ___ % 1 Family ___ % 2-4 Family ___ % Apts ___ % Condo
___ % Commercial ___ % Industrial ___ % Vacant
Change in Present Land Use ☐ Not Likely ☐ Likely* ☐ Taking Place*
*From ___ To ___
Predominant Occupancy ☐ Owner ☐ Tenant ___ % Vacant
Condominium Price Range $ ___ to $ ___ Predominant $ ___
Age ___ yrs to ___ yrs Predominant ___ yrs
Single Family Price Range $ ___ to $ ___ Predominant $ ___
Age ___ yrs to ___ yrs Predominant ___ yrs
Describe potential for additional Condo/PUD units in nearby area ___

NEIGHBORHOOD RATING	Good	Avg	Fair	Poor
Adequacy of Shopping	☐	☐	☐	☐
Employment Opportunities	☐	☐	☐	☐
Recreational Facilities	☐	☐	☐	☐
Adequacy of Utilities	☐	☐	☐	☐
Property Compatibility	☐	☐	☐	☐
Protection from Detrimental Conditions	☐	☐	☐	☐
Police and Fire Protection	☐	☐	☐	☐
General Appearance of Properties	☐	☐	☐	☐
Appeal to Market	☐	☐	☐	☐

	Distance	Access or Convenience			
Public Transportation		☐	☐	☐	☐
Employment Centers		☐	☐	☐	☐
Neighborhood Shopping		☐	☐	☐	☐
Grammar Schools		☐	☐	☐	☐
Freeway Access		☐	☐	☐	☐

NOTE: FHLMC/FNMA do not consider race or the racial composition of the neighborhood to be reliable appraisal factors
Describe those factors, favorable or unfavorable affecting marketability (e g public parks schools noise view mkt area population size and financial ability) ___

SITE

Lot Dimensions (if PUD) ___ Sq Ft ☐ Corner Lot Project Density When Completed as Planned ___ Units/Acre
Zoning Classification ___ Present improvements ☐ do ☐ do not conform to zoning regulations
Highest and best use ☐ Present use ☐ Other (specify) ___

	Public	Other (Describe)	OFF-SITE IMPROVEMENTS			
Elec	☐		Street Access	☐ Public	☐ Private	
Gas	☐		Surface ___			
Water	☐		Maintenance	☐ Public	☐ Private	
San Sewer	☐		☐ Storm Sewer	☐ Curb/Gutter		
	☐ Underground Elect & Tel		☐ Sidewalk	☐ Street Lights		

Project Ingress/Egress (adequacy) ___
Topo ___
Size/Shape ___
View Amenity ___
Drainage/Flood Conditions ___
Is the property located in a HUD identified Special Flood Hazard Area? ☐ No ☐ Yes
Comments (including any easements encroachments or other adverse conditions) ___

PROJECT IMPROVEMENTS

	☐ Existing Approx Year Built 19 ___ Original Use ___	
	☐ Condo ☐ PUD ☐ Converted (19 ___)	
TYPE	☐ Proposed ☐ Under Construction	
PROJECT	☐ Elevator ☐ Walk-up No of Stories ___	
	☐ Row or Town House ☐ Other (specify) ___	
	☐ Primary Residence ☐ Second Home or Recreational	

If Completed No Phases ___ No Units ___ No Sold ___
If Incomplete Planned No Phases ___ No Units ___ No Sold ___
Units in Subject Phase Total ___ Completed ___ Sold ___ Rented ___
Approx No Units for Sale Subject Project ___ Subject Phase ___
Exterior Wall ___ Roof Covering ___ Security Features ___
Elevator No ___ Adequacy & Condition ___ Soundproofing Vertical ___ Horizontal ___
Parking Total No Spaces ___ Ratio ___ Spaces/Unit ___ Type ___ No Spaces of Guest Parking ___
Describe common elements or recreational facilities ___
Are any common elements, rec facilities or parking leased to Owners Assoc? ___ If yes, attach addendum describing rental terms and options

PROJECT RATING	Good	Avg	Fair	Poor
Location	☐	☐	☐	☐
General Appearance	☐	☐	☐	☐
Amenities and Recreational Facilities	☐	☐	☐	☐
Density (units per acre)	☐	☐	☐	☐
Unit Mix	☐	☐	☐	☐
Quality of Constr (mat'l & finish)	☐	☐	☐	☐
Condition of Exterior	☐	☐	☐	☐
Condition of Interior	☐	☐	☐	☐
Appeal to Market	☐	☐	☐	☐

SUBJECT UNIT

☐ Existing ☐ Proposed ☐ Under Constr Floor No ___ Unit Livable Area ___ Basement ___ % Finished ___
Parking for Unit No ___ Type ___ ☐ Assigned ☐ Owned Convenience to Unit ___

Room List	Foyer	Liv	Din	Kit	Bdrm	Bath	Fam	Rec	Lndry	Other
Basement										
1st Level										
2nd Level										

Floors	☐ Hardwood	☐ Carpet over ___	☐ ___
Int Walls	☐ Drywall	☐ Plaster	☐ ___
Trim/Finish	☐ Good	☐ Average	☐ Fair ☐ Poor
Bath Floor	☐ Ceramic	☐ ___	☐ Wainscot ☐ Ceramic ___

Windows (type) ___ ☐ Storm Sash ☐ Screens ☐ Combo
Kitchen Equip ☐ Refrig ☐ Range/Oven ☐ Fan/Hood ☐ Washer ☐ Dryer
☐ Intercom ☐ Disposal ☐ Dishwasher ☐ Microwave ☐ Compactor
HEAT Type ___ Fuel ___ Cond ___
AIR COND ☐ Central ☐ Other ___ ☐ Adequate ☐ Inadequate
☐ Earth Sheltered Housing Design ☐ Solar Design/Landscape ☐ Solar Space Heat/Air Cond ☐ Solar Hot Water
☐ Flue Damper ☐ Elec /Mech Gas Furn Ignition ☐ Auto Setback Thermostat ☐ Dble /Triple Glazed Windows ☐ Caulk/Weatherstrip
INSULATION (state R-Factor if known) ☐ Walls ___ ☐ Ceiling ___ ☐ Floor ___ ☐ Roof/Attic ___ ☐ Water Heater ___
If rehab proposed, do plans and specs provide for adequate energy conservation? ___ If no, attach description of modification needed
ENERGY EFFICIENCY APPEARS ☐ High ☐ Adequate ☐ Low Energy Audit ☐ Yes (attach if available) ☐ No
COMMENTS (special features, functional or physical inadequacies, modernization or repairs needed etc) ___

UNIT RATING	Good	Avg	Fair	Poor
Condition of Improvement	☐	☐	☐	☐
Room Sizes and Layout	☐	☐	☐	☐
Adequacy of Closets and Storage	☐	☐	☐	☐
Kit Equip Cabinets & Workspace	☐	☐	☐	☐
Plumbing Adequacy and Condition	☐	☐	☐	☐
Electrical Adequacy and Condition	☐	☐	☐	☐
Adequacy of Soundproofing	☐	☐	☐	☐
Adequacy of Insulation	☐	☐	☐	☐
Location within Project or View	☐	☐	☐	☐
Overall Livability	☐	☐	☐	☐
Appeal and Marketability	☐	☐	☐	☐

Est Effective Age ___ to ___ yrs
Est Remaining Economic Life ___ to ___ yrs

BUDGET ANALYSIS

Unit Charge $ _____ /Mo x 12 = $ _____ /Yr ($ _____ /Sq Ft /year of livable area) Ground Rent (if any) $ _____ /yr

Utilities included in unit charge ☐ None ☐ Heat ☐ Air Cond ☐ Electricity ☐ Gas ☐ Water ☐ Sewer

Note any fees, other than regular Condo/PUD charges, for use of facilities _____

To properly maintain the project and provide the services anticipated, the budget appears ☐ High ☐ Adequate ☐ Inadequate

Compared to other competitive projects of similar quality and design subject unit charge appears ☐ High ☐ Reasonable ☐ Low

Management Group ☐ Owners Association ☐ Developer ☐ Management Agent (identify) _____

Quality of Management and its enforcement of Rules and Regulations appears ☐ Superior ☐ Good ☐ Adequate ☐ Inadequate

Special or unusual characteristics in the Condo/PUD Documents or otherwise known to the appraiser, that would affect marketability (if none, so state)

Comments

COST APPROACH

NOTE: FHLMC does not require the cost approach in the appraisal of condominium or PUD units

Cost Approach (to be used only for detached, semi-detached, and town house units)

Reproduction Cost New _____ Sq Ft @ $ _____ per Sq Ft = $ _____

Less Depreciation: Physical $ _____ Functional $ _____ Economic $ _____ (_____)

Depreciated Value of Improvements _____

Add Land Value (if leasehold, show only leasehold value—attach calculations) _____

Pro-rata Share of Value of Amenities $ _____

Total Indicated Value ☐ FEE SIMPLE ☐ LEASEHOLD $ _____

Comments regarding estimate of depreciation and value of land and amenity package _____

The appraiser, whenever possible, should analyze two comparable sales from within the subject project. However, when appraising a unit in a new or newly converted project, at least two comparables should be selected from outside the subject project. In the following analysis, the comparable should always be adjusted to the subject unit and not vice versa. If a significant feature of the comparable is superior to the subject unit, a minus (−) adjustment should be made to the comparable; if such a feature of the comparable is inferior to the subject, a plus (+) adjustment should be made to the comparable.

MARKET DATA ANALYSIS

LIST ONLY THOSE ITEMS THAT REQUIRE ADJUSTMENT

ITEM	Subject Property	COMPARABLE NO 1		COMPARABLE NO 2		COMPARABLE NO 3	
Address-Unit No							
Project Name							
Proximity to Subj							
Sales Price	$	$		$		$	
Price/Living Area	$	$		$		$	
Data Source							
	DESCRIPTION	DESCRIPTION	+ (−) $ Adjustment	DESCRIPTION	+ (−) $ Adjustment	DESCRIPTION	+ (−) $ Adjustment
Date of Sale and Time Adjustment							
Location							
Site/View							
Design and Appeal							
Quality of Constr							
Age							
Condition							
Living Area, Room Count & Total	Total : B-rms : Baths	Total : B-rms : Baths		Total : B-rms : Baths		Total : B-rms : Baths	
Gross Living Area	Sq Ft	Sq Ft		Sq Ft		Sq Ft	
Basement & Bsmt							
Finished Rooms							
Functional Utility							
Air Conditioning							
Storage							
Parking Facilities							
Common Elements and Recreation Facilities							
Mo. Assessment							
Leasehold/Fee							
Special Energy Efficient Items							
Other (e g fire-places, kitchen equip., remodeling)							
Sales or Financing Concessions							
Net Adj (total)		☐ Plus ☐ Minus : $		☐ Plus ☐ Minus : $		☐ Plus ☐ Minus : $	
Indicated value of Subject		$		$		$	

Comments on Market Data Analysis _____

☐ INDICATED VALUE BY MARKET DATA APPROACH $ _____

☐ INDICATED VALUE BY INCOME APPROACH (If applicable) Economic Market Rent $ _____ /Mo x Gross Rent Multiplier _____ = $ _____

This appraisal is made ☐ "as is" ☐ subject to repairs, alterations, or conditions listed below ☐ subject to completion per plans and specifications

Comments and Conditions of Appraisal _____

Final Reconciliation: _____

Construction Warranty ☐ Yes ☐ No Name of Warranty Program _____ Warranty Coverage Expires _____

This appraisal is based upon the above requirements, the certification, contingent and limiting conditions, and Market Value definition that are stated in

☐ FHLMC Form 439 (Rev 10/78)/FNMA Form 1004B (Rev 10/78) filed with client _____ 19____ ☐ attached

I ESTIMATE THE MARKET VALUE, AS DEFINED, OF SUBJECT PROPERTY AS OF _____ 19____ to be $ _____

Appraiser(s) _____ Review Appraiser (if applicable) _____

Date Report Signed _____ 19____ ☐ Did ☐ Did Not Physically Inspect Property

FHLMC Form 465 9/10   REVERSE   L   FNMA Form 1073 9/80

Exhibit A. To be completed by Lender

APPRAISAL REPORT — INDIVIDUAL ☐ CONDOMINIUM OR ☐ PUD UNIT   File No

To be completed by Lender

Borrower _____ Census Tract _____ Map Reference _____
Unit No _____ Address _____ Project Name·Phase No _____
City _____ County _____ State _____ Zip Code _____
Actual Real Estate Taxes $ _____ (yr) Sales Price $ _____ Property Rights Appraised ☐ Fee ☐ Leasehold
Loan Charges to be Paid by Seller $ _____ Other Sales Concessions _____
Lender/Client _____ Lender's Address _____
Occupant _____ Appraiser _____ Instructions to Appraiser _____
☐ FNMA 1073A required   ☐ FHLMC 465 Addendum A required   ☐ FHLMC 465 Addendum B required

NEIGHBORHOOD

				NEIGHBORHOOD RATING	Good	Avg	Fair	Poor
Location	☐ Urban	☐ Suburban	☐ Rural	Adequacy of Shopping	☐	☐	☐	☐
Built Up	☐ Over 75%	☐ 25% to 75%	☐ Under 25%	Employment Opportunities	☐	☐	☐	☐
Growth Rate ☐ Fully Developed	☐ Rapid	☐ Steady	☐ Slow	Recreational Facilities	☐	☐	☐	☐
Property Values	☐ Increasing	☐ Stable	☐ Declining	Adequacy of Utilities	☐	☐	☐	☐
Demand/Supply	☐ Shortage	☐ In Balance	☐ Oversupply	Property Compatibility	☐	☐	☐	☐
Marketing Time	☐ Under 3 Mos	☐ 4-6 Mos	☐ Over 6 Mos	Protection from Detrimental Conditions	☐	☐	☐	☐

Present Land Use ___ % 1 Family ___ % 2-4 Family ___ % Apts ___ % Condo ___ % Commercial ___ % Industrial ___ % Vacant
Change in Present Land Use ☐ Not Likely ☐ Likely* ☐ Taking Place* *From ___ To ___
Predominant Occupancy ☐ Owner ☐ Tenant ___ % Vacant
Condominium Price Range $ ___ to $ ___ Predominant $ ___
Age ___ yrs to ___ yrs Predominant ___ yrs
Single Family Price Range $ ___ to $ ___ Predominant $ ___
Age ___ yrs to ___ yrs Predominant ___ yrs
Describe potential for additional Condo PUD units in nearby area _____

	Distance	Access or Convenience
Police and Fire Protection		
General Appearance of Properties		
Appeal to Market		
Public Transportation		
Employment Centers		
Neighborhood Shopping		
Grammar Schools		
Freeway Access		

NOTE: FHLMC/FNMA do not consider race or the racial composition of the neighborhood to be reliable appraisal factors
Describe those factors, favorable or unfavorable, affecting marketability (e g public parks, schools noise view mkt area population size and financial ability)

SITE

Lot Dimensions (if PUD) _____ Sq Ft ☐ Corner Lot   Project Density When Completed as Planned ___ Units/Acre
Zoning Classification _____   Present improvements ☐ do ☐ do not conform to zoning regulations
Highest and best use ☐ Present use ☐ Other (specify) _____

OFF SITE IMPROVEMENTS
	Public	Other (Describe)			
Elec	☐		Street Access	☐ Public	☐ Private
Gas	☐		Surface		
Water	☐		Maintenance	☐ Public	☐ Private
San Sewer	☐		☐ Storm Sewer	☐ Curb Gutter	
	☐ Underground Elect & Tel		☐ Sidewalk	☐ Street Lights	

Project ingress Egress (adequacy) _____
Topo _____
Size Shape _____
View Amenity _____
Drainage Flood Conditions _____
Is the property located in a HUD identified Special Flood Hazard Area? ☐ No ☐ Yes
Comments (including any easements encroachments or other adverse conditions) _____

PROJECT IMPROVEMENTS

TYPE	☐ Existing Approx Year Built 19 ___ Original Use ___		
	☐ Condo ☐ PUD ☐ Converted (19 ___)		
PROJECT	☐ Proposed ☐ Under Construction		
	☐ Elevator ☐ Walk-up No of Stories ___		
	☐ Row or Town House ☐ Other (specify) ___		
	☐ Primary Residence ☐ Second Home or Recreational		

If Completed No Phases ___ No Units ___ No Sold ___
If Incomplete Planned No Phases ___ No Units ___ No Sold ___
Units in Subject Phase Total ___ Completed ___ Sold ___ Rented ___
Approx No Units for Sale Subject Project ___ Subject Phase ___
Exterior Wall _____ Roof Covering _____ Security Features _____
Elevator No ___ Adequacy & Condition _____ Soundproofing Vertical _____ Horizontal _____
Parking Total No Spaces ___ Ratio ___ Spaces Unit ___ Type ___ No Spaces of Guest Parking ___
Describe common elements or recreational facilities _____
Are any common elements rec facilities or parking leased to Owners Assoc ? ___ If yes attach addendum describing rental terms and options

PROJECT RATING	Good	Avg	Fair	Poor
Location	☐	☐	☐	☐
General Appearance	☐	☐	☐	☐
Amenities and Recreational Facilities	☐	☐	☐	☐
Density (units per acre)	☐	☐	☐	☐
Unit Mix	☐	☐	☐	☐
Quality of Constr (mat'l & finish)	☐	☐	☐	☐
Condition of Exterior	☐	☐	☐	☐
Condition of Interior	☐	☐	☐	☐
Appeal to Market	☐	☐	☐	☐

SUBJECT UNIT

☐ Existing ☐ Proposed ☐ Under Constr   Floor No ___ Unit Livable Area ___ ☐ Basement ___ % Finished _____
Parking for Unit No ___ Type ___ ☐ Assigned ☐ Owned   Convenience to Unit _____

Room List	Foyer	Liv	Din	Kit	Bdrm	Bath	Fam	Rec	Lndry	Other
Basement										
1st Level										
2nd Level										

Floors ☐ Hardwood ☐ Carpet over ___
Int Walls ☐ Drywall ☐ Plaster ___
Trim/Finish ☐ Good ☐ Average ☐ Fair ☐ Poor
Bath Floor ☐ Ceramic ___ Wainscot ☐ Ceramic
Windows (type) ___ ☐ Storm Sash ☐ Screens ☐ Combo
Kitchen Equip ☐ Refrig ☐ Range Oven ☐ Fan Hood ☐ Washer ☐ Dryer
☐ Intercom ☐ Disposal ☐ Dishwasher ☐ Microwave ☐ Compactor
HEAT Type ___ Fuel ___ Cond ___
AIR COND ☐ Central ☐ Other ___ ☐ Adequate ☐ Inadequate
☐ Earth Sheltered Housing Design ☐ Solar Design Landscape ☐ Solar Space Heat Air Cond ☐ Solar Hot Water
☐ Flue Damper ☐ Elec Mech Gas Furn Ignition ☐ Auto Setback Thermostat ☐ Dble Triple Glazed Windows ☐ Caulk/Weatherstrip
INSULATION (state R Factor if known) ☐ Walls ☐ Ceiling ☐ Floor ☐ Roof Attic ☐ Water Heater
If rehab proposed do plans and specs provide for adequate energy conservation? ___ If no, attach description of modification needed
ENERGY EFFICIENCY APPEARS ☐ High ☐ Adequate ☐ Low   Energy Audit ☐ Yes (attach if available) ☐ No
COMMENTS (special features functional or physical inadequacies modernization or repairs needed etc) _____

UNIT RATING	Good	Avg	Fair	Poor
Condition of Improvement	☐	☐	☐	☐
Room Sizes and Layout	☐	☐	☐	☐
Adequacy of Closets and Storage	☐	☐	☐	☐
Kit Equip Cabinets & Workspace	☐	☐	☐	☐
Plumbing Adequacy and Condition	☐	☐	☐	☐
Electrical Adequacy and Condition	☐	☐	☐	☐
Adequacy of Soundproofing	☐	☐	☐	☐
Adequacy of Insulation	☐	☐	☐	☐
Location within Project or View	☐	☐	☐	☐
Overall Livability	☐	☐	☐	☐
Appeal and Marketability	☐	☐	☐	☐

Est Effective Age ___ to ___ yrs
Est Remaining Economic Life ___ to ___ yrs

FHLMC Form 465 9/80   ATTACH DESCRIPTIVE PHOTOGRAPHS OF SUBJECT PROPERTY AND STREET SCENE   FNMA Form 1073 9/80

the FHLMC Form 465/FNMA Form 1073 (9/80) and this study covers reviewing this form. Each section of this chapter refers to the specific sections of the FHLMC/FNMA form as printed on its left-hand margin. To help follow the comments made below, the FHLMC/FNMA form is reproduced and has been coded with a series of circled numbers that correspond with each section of the form.

TO BE COMPLETED BY THE LENDER

1. Most condominium complexes are single phase complexes. When the complex is a multi-phase complex, the phase that the subject unit is in should be noted. The condominium Declaration (also called the C, C & Rs) will provide the appraiser with this information. Sometimes the information will be found in amendments to the Declaration that are filed when succeeding phases are built.
2. Most condominiums are appraised as Fee Simple; that is, they have full ownership of the land and improvements. However, it is not unusual in some areas of the country for complexes to lease the land that the improvements are on. The appraiser and reviewer should be knowledgeable as to when a condominium needs to be appraised as a Leasehold. Whether a complex is Fee Simple or Leasehold should be stated in the Declaration.

Exhibit B. Site

APPRAISAL REPORT — INDIVIDUAL ☐ CONDOMINIUM OR ☐ PUD UNIT   File No

Borrower	Census Tract ___ Map Reference
Unit No ___ Address	Project Name/Phase No
City	County ___ State ___ Zip Code
Actual Real Estate Taxes $ ___ (yr) Sales Price $	Property Rights Appraised ☐ Fee ☐ Leasehold
Loan Charges to be Paid by Seller $ ___ Other Sales Concessions	
Lender/Client	Lender's Address
Occupant ___ Appraiser	Instructions to Appraiser

☐ FNMA 1073A required   ☐ FHLMC 465 Addendum A required   ☐ FHLMC 465 Addendum B required

NEIGHBORHOOD

Location	☐ Urban	☐ Suburban	☐ Rural
Built Up	☐ Over 75%	☐ 25% to 75%	☐ Under 25%
Growth Rate ☐ Fully Developed	☐ Rapid	☐ Steady	☐ Slow
Property Values	☐ Increasing	☐ Stable	☐ Declining
Demand/Supply	☐ Shortage	☐ In Balance	☐ Oversupply
Marketing Time	☐ Under 3 Mos	☐ 4-6 Mos	☐ Over 6 Mos

Present Land Use ___ % 1 Family ___ % 2-4 Family ___ % Apts ___ % Condo
___ % Commercial ___ % Industrial ___ % Vacant

Change in Present Land Use ☐ Not Likely ☐ Likely* ☐ Taking Place*
*From ___ to ___

Predominant Occupancy ☐ Owner ☐ Tenant ___ % Vacant

Condominium Price Range $ ___ to $ ___ Predominant $ ___
Age ___ yrs to ___ yrs Predominant $ ___ yrs

Single Family Price Range $ ___ to $ ___ Predominant $ ___
Age ___ yrs to ___ yrs Predominant ___ yrs

Describe potential for additional Condo/PUD units in nearby area ___

NEIGHBORHOOD RATING

	Good	Avg	Fair	Poor
Adequacy of Shopping	☐	☐	☐	☐
Employment Opportunities	☐	☐	☐	☐
Recreational Facilities	☐	☐	☐	☐
Adequacy of Utilities	☐	☐	☐	☐
Property Compatibility	☐	☐	☐	☐
Protection from Detrimental Conditions	☐	☐	☐	☐
Police and Fire Protection	☐	☐	☐	☐
General Appearance of Properties	☐	☐	☐	☐
Appeal to Market	☐	☐	☐	☐

	Distance	Access or Convenience
Public Transportation		
Employment Centers		
Neighborhood Shopping		
Grammar Schools		
Freeway Access		

NOTE: FHLMC/FNMA do not consider race or the racial composition of the neighborhood to be reliable appraisal factors.

Describe those factors, favorable or unfavorable, affecting marketability (e.g. public parks, schools, noise, view, mkt. area, population size and financial ability)

SITE

Lot Dimensions (if PUD) ___ Sq. Ft ___ ☐ Corner Lot   Project Density When Completed as Planned ___ Units/Acre

Zoning Classification ___ Present improvements ☐ do ☐ do not conform to zoning regulations

Highest and best use ☐ Present use ☐ Other (specify) ___

	Public	Other (Describe)
Elec	☐	
Gas	☐	
Water	☐	
San Sewer	☐	
	☐ Underground Elect. & Tel	

OFF-SITE IMPROVEMENTS

Street Access	☐ Public ☐ Private
Surface	
Maintenance	☐ Public ☐ Private
☐ Storm Sewer	☐ Curb/Gutter
☐ Sidewalk	☐ Street Lights

Project Ingress-Egress (adequacy) ___
Topo ___
Size-Shape ___
View Amenity ___
Drainage/Flood Conditions ___
Is the property located in a HUD identified Special Flood Hazard Area? ☐ No ☐ Yes

Comments (including any easements, encroachments or other adverse conditions) ___

PROJECT IMPROVEMENTS

☐ Existing Approx. Year Built 19 ___ Original Use ___
☐ Condo ☐ PUD ☐ Converted (19 ___)

TYPE ☐ Proposed ☐ Under Construction
PROJECT ☐ Elevator ☐ Walk up No. of Stories ___
☐ Row or Town House ☐ Other (specify) ___
☐ Primary Residence ☐ Second Home or Recreational

If Completed ___ No. Phases ___ No. Units ___ No. Sold ___
If Incomplete Planned No. Phases ___ No. Units ___ No. Sold ___
Units in Subject Phase Total ___ Completed ___ Sold ___ Rented ___
Approx. No. Units for Sale Subject Project ___ Subject Phase ___

Exterior Wall ___ Roof Covering ___ Security Features ___
Elevator No ___ Adequacy & Condition ___ Soundproofing Vertical ___ Horizontal ___
Parking Total No. Spaces ___ Ratio ___ Spaces/Unit ___ Type ___ No. Spaces of Guest Parking ___
Describe common elements or recreational facilities ___
Are any common elements, rec. facilities or parking leased to Owners Assoc.? ___ If yes, attach addendum describing rental, terms and options

PROJECT RATING

	Good	Avg	Fair	Poor
Location	☐	☐	☐	☐
General Appearance	☐	☐	☐	☐
Amenities and Recreational Facilities	☐	☐	☐	☐
Density (units per acre)	☐	☐	☐	☐
Unit Mix	☐	☐	☐	☐
Quality of Constr. (mat'l & finish)	☐	☐	☐	☐
Condition of Exterior	☐	☐	☐	☐
Condition of Interior	☐	☐	☐	☐
Appeal to Market	☐	☐	☐	☐

SUBJECT UNIT

☐ Existing ☐ Proposed ☐ Under Constr. Floor No ___ Unit Livable Area ___ Basement ___ % Finished ___
Parking for Unit No ___ Type ___ ☐ Assigned ☐ Owned   Convenience to Unit

Room List	Foyer	Liv	Din	Kit	Bdrm	Bath	Fam	Rec	Lndry	Other
Basement										
1st Level										
2nd Level										

Floors	☐ Hardwood	☐ Carpet over ___ ☐ ___
Int. Walls	☐ Drywall	☐ Plaster
Trim/Finish	☐ Good	☐ Average ☐ Fair ☐ Poor
Bath Floor	☐ Ceramic	☐ Ceramic ☐ Wainscot ☐ Ceramic ☐ ___
Windows (type)		☐ Storm Sash ☐ Screens ☐ Combo
Kitchen Equip	☐ Refrig	☐ Range-Oven ☐ Fan/Hood ☐ Washer ☐ Dryer
☐ Intercom	☐ Disposal	☐ Dishwasher ☐ Microwave ☐ Compactor
HEAT Type ___ Fuel ___ Cond ___
AIR COND ☐ Central ☐ Other ___ ☐ Adequate ☐ Inadequate

☐ Earth Sheltered Housing Design ☐ Solar Design/Landscape ☐ Solar Space Heat/Air Cond ☐ Solar Hot Water
☐ Flue Damper ☐ Elec./Mech. Gas Furn. Ignition ☐ Auto. Setback Thermostat ☐ Dble./Triple Glazed Windows ☐ Caulk/Weatherstrip
INSULATION (state R Factor if known) ___ Walls ___ Ceiling ___ Floor ___ ☐ Roof/Attic ___ Water Heater ___
If rehab proposed, do plans and specs provide for adequate energy conservation? ___ If no, attach description of modification needed
ENERGY EFFICIENCY APPEARS ☐ High ☐ Adequate ☐ Low   Energy Audit ☐ Yes (attach, if available) ☐ No
COMMENTS (special features, functional or physical inadequacies, modernization or repairs needed, etc.) ___

UNIT RATING

	Good	Avg	Fair	Poor
Condition of Improvement	☐	☐	☐	☐
Room Sizes and Layout	☐	☐	☐	☐
Adequacy of Closets and Storage	☐	☐	☐	☐
Kit. Equip. Cabinets & Workspace	☐	☐	☐	☐
Plumbing Adequacy and Condition	☐	☐	☐	☐
Electrical Adequacy and Condition	☐	☐	☐	☐
Adequacy of Soundproofing	☐	☐	☐	☐
Adequacy of Insulation	☐	☐	☐	☐
Location within Project or View	☐	☐	☐	☐
Overall Livability	☐	☐	☐	☐
Appeal and Marketability	☐	☐	☐	☐
Est. Effective Age				___ to ___ yrs
Est. Remaining Economic Life				___ to ___ yrs

FHLMC Form 465 9/80   ATTACH DESCRIPTIVE PHOTOGRAPHS OF SUBJECT PROPERTY AND STREET SCENE   FNMA Form 1073 9/80

SITE

3. In a multi-phase complex it should be noted whether the lot size is for the entire complex or for just the subject phase. Some phases of a complex are completely different in design from another phase in the same complex and factors such as density can be quite different. The first phase of a complex may consist of townhouse style units with a density of eight units per acre and the second phase may be a three story, elevator building with a density of thirty units per acre.

 If the subject is a PUD unit, it is going to own its own lot and the lot dimensions and site size for this lot needs to be listed. It would also be beneficial if the entire site size for the project was included in the Site Comments.

Exhibit C. Project Improvements

APPRAISAL REPORT — INDIVIDUAL ☐ CONDOMINIUM OR ☐ PUD UNIT File No

Borrower	Census Tract __ Map Reference
Unit No __ Address	Project Name/Phase No
City	County __ State __ Zip Code
Actual Real Estate Taxes $ __ (yr.) Sales Price $	Property Rights Appraised ☐ Fee ☐ Leasehold
Loan Charges to be Paid by Seller $ __ Other Sales Concessions	
Lender/Client __ Lender's Address	
Occupant __ Appraiser __ Instructions to Appraiser	
☐ FNMA 1073A required	☐ FHLMC 465 Addendum A required ☐ FHLMC 465 Addendum B required

				NEIGHBORHOOD RATING	Good	Avg	Fair	Poor
Location	☐ Urban	☐ Suburban	☐ Rural	Adequacy of Shopping	☐	☐	☐	☐
Built Up	☐ Over 75%	☐ 25% to 75%	☐ Under 25%	Employment Opportunities	☐	☐	☐	☐
Growth Rate ☐ Fully Developed	☐ Rapid	☐ Steady	☐ Slow	Recreational Facilities	☐	☐	☐	☐
Property Values	☐ Increasing	☐ Stable	☐ Declining	Adequacy of Utilities	☐	☐	☐	☐
Demand/Supply	☐ Shortage	☐ In Balance	☐ Oversupply	Property Compatibility	☐	☐	☐	☐
Marketing Time	☐ Under 3 Mos	☐ 4-6 Mos	☐ Over 6 Mos	Protection from Detrimental Conditions	☐	☐	☐	☐
Present Land Use __ % 1 Family __ % 2-4 Family __ % Apts __ % Condo				Police and Fire Protection	☐	☐	☐	☐
__ % Commercial __ % Industrial __ % Vacant				General Appearance of Properties	☐	☐	☐	☐
Change in Present Land Use ☐ Not Likely	☐ Likely*	☐ Taking Place*		Appeal to Market	☐	☐	☐	☐
*From __ To __								

Predominant Occupancy	☐ Owner	☐ Tenant	__ % Vacant		Distance	Access or Convenience
Condominium Price Range $ __ to $ __ Predominant $				Public Transportation		☐
Age __ yrs to __ yrs Predominant __ yrs				Employment Centers		☐
Single Family Price Range $ __ to $ __ Predominant $				Neighborhood Shopping		☐
Age __ yrs to __ yrs Predominant __ yrs				Grammar Schools		☐
Describe potential for additional Condo/PUD units in nearby area				Freeway Access		☐

NOTE: FHLMC/FNMA do not consider race or the racial composition of the neighborhood to be reliable appraisal factors.

Describe those factors, favorable or unfavorable, affecting marketability (e.g. public parks, schools, noise, view, mix, area, population size and financial ability)

Lot Dimensions (if PUD) __ × __ Sq. Ft. ☐ Corner Lot	Project Density When Completed as Planned __ Units/Acre
Zoning Classification	Present improvements ☐ do ☐ do not conform to zoning regulations
Highest and best use ☐ Present use ☐ Other (specify)	

	Public	Other (Describe)	OFF-SITE IMPROVEMENTS	Project Ingress/Egress (adequacy)
Elec	☐		Street Access ☐ Public ☐ Private	Topo
Gas	☐		Surface	Size/Shape
Water	☐		Maintenance ☐ Public ☐ Private	View Amenity
San Sewer	☐		☐ Storm Sewer ☐ Curb/Gutter	Drainage/Flood Conditions
	☐ Underground Elect. & Tel		☐ Sidewalk ☐ Street Lights	Is the property located in a HUD identified Special Flood Hazard Area? ☐ No ☐ Yes

Comments (including any easements, encroachments or other adverse conditions)

	PROJECT RATING	Good	Avg	Fair	Poor
☐ Existing Approx Year Built 19 __ Original Use __	Location	☐	☐	☐	☐
☐ Condo ☐ PUD ☐ Converted (19 __)	General Appearance	☐	☐	☐	☐
TYPE ☐ Proposed ☐ Under Construction	Amenities and Recreational Facilities	☐	☐	☐	☐
PROJECT ☐ Elevator ☐ Walk-up No. of Stories __	Density (units per acre)	☐	☐	☐	☐
☐ Row or Town House ☐ Other (specify) __	Unit Mix	☐	☐	☐	☐
☐ Primary Residence ☐ Second Home or Recreational	Quality of Constr. (mat'l & finish)	☐	☐	☐	☐
If Completed No. Phases __ No. Units __ No. Sold __	Condition of Exterior	☐	☐	☐	☐
If Incomplete Planned No. Phases __ No. Units __ No. Sold __	Condition of Interior	☐	☐	☐	☐
Units in Subject Phase Total __ Completed __ Sold __ Rented __	Appeal to Market	☐	☐	☐	☐
Approx No. Units for Sale Subject Project __ Subject Phase __					

Exterior Wall __ Roof Covering __ Security Features	
Elevator No __ Adequacy & Condition __ Soundproofing Vertical __ Horizontal	
Parking Total No. Spaces __ Ratio __ Spaces/Unit __ Type __ No. Spaces of Guest Parking	
Describe common elements or recreational facilities	
Are any common elements, rec facilities or parking leased to Owners Assoc.? __ If yes, attach addendum describing rental terms and options	

☐ Existing ☐ Proposed ☐ Under Constr Floor No __ Unit Livable Area __ ☑ Basement __ % Finished __ ☑										
Parking for Unit No __ Type __ ☐ Assigned ☐ Owned Convenience to Unit										

Room List	Foyer	Liv	Din	Kit	Bdrm	Bath	Fam	Rec	Lndry	Other
Basement										
1st Level										
2nd Level										

	UNIT RATING	Good	Avg	Fair	Poor
Floors ☐ Hardwood ☐ Carpet over __ ☐	Condition of Improvement	☐	☐	☐	☐
Int. Walls ☐ Drywall ☐ Plaster __	Room Sizes and Layout	☐	☐	☐	☐
Trim/Finish ☐ Good ☐ Average ☐ Fair ☐ Poor	Adequacy of Closets and Storage	☐	☐	☐	☐
Bath Floor ☐ Ceramic __	Kit. Equip., Cabinets & Workspace	☐	☐	☐	☐
Windows (type) __ ☐ Wainscot ☐ Ceramic __	Plumbing Adequacy and Condition	☐	☐	☐	☐
☐ Storm Sash ☐ Screens ☐ Combo	Electrical Adequacy and Condition	☐	☐	☐	☐
Kitchen Equip ☐ Refrig ☐ Range/Oven ☐ Fan/Hood ☐ Washer ☐ Dryer	Adequacy of Soundproofing	☐	☐	☐	☐
☐ Intercom ☐ Disposal ☐ Dishwasher ☐ Microwave ☐ Compactor	Adequacy of Insulation	☐	☐	☐	☐
HEAT Type __ Fuel __ Cond __	Location within Project or View	☐	☐	☐	☐
AIR COND ☐ Central ☐ Other ☐ Adequate ☐ Inadequate	Overall Livability	☐	☐	☐	☐
☐ Earth Sheltered Housing Design ☐ Solar Design/Landscape ☐ Solar Space Heat/Air Cond	Appeal and Marketability	☐	☐	☐	☐
☐ Flue Damper ☐ Elec./Mech Gas Furn Ignition ☐ Auto Setback Thermostat ☐ Dble./Triple Glazed Windows ☐ Caulk/Weatherstrip	Est Effective Age __ to __ yrs
INSULATION (state R-Factor if known) __ Walls __ Ceiling __ Floor __	Est Remaining Economic Life __ to __ yrs
☐ Solar Hot Water					
☐ Roof/Attic ☐ Water Heater					

If rehab proposed, do plans and specs provide for adequate energy conservation? __ If no, attach description of modification needed

ENERGY EFFICIENCY APPEARS	☐ High	☐ Adequate	☐ Low	Energy Audit ☐ Yes (attach if available)	☐ No

COMMENTS (special features, functional or physical inadequacies, modernization or repairs needed, etc.)

FHLMC Form 465 9/80   ATTACH DESCRIPTIVE PHOTOGRAPHS OF SUBJECT PROPERTY AND STREET SCENE   FNMA Form 1073 9/80

PROJECT IMPROVEMENTS

4. The information concerning the subject complex, its number of phases, and the subject phase needs to be filled out completely as factors such as the number of units sold, the number rented, and the number for sale can affect loan eligibility, particularly the ability to sell the loan on the secondary mortgage market. Leaving these spaces blank or stating N/A or unknown is not an acceptable approach. When the number of units rented is stated for a multi-phase complex, it should be clarified as to whether this is the number rented in the entire project or if it is the number for just the subject phase. Both numbers should probably be provided as the percentage of rentals in a complex is quite important to the secondary mortgage market. Some of the information is in the Declaration and in other cases it will be necessary to contact the Homeowner's Association, its management firm, and/or the manager of the complex, if there is one.

   Other categories such as Number Spaces for Guest Parking and Soundproofing should be filled in with specific information if at all possible, not with generalities such as average or adequate. Simply stating adequate for Number Spaces for Guest Parking does not really tell a reviewer anything. Stating ten spaces as being adequate gives a reviewer something to base that judgment on.

SUBJECT UNIT

5. A unit's Livable Area square footage that is listed in the Declaration should not be relied upon. In most cases this square footage is supposed to be based on interior wall dimensions as that is what the condominium unit actually owns. Unfortunately, it is not uncommon for the condominium Declaration to list square footages that are not based on interior dimensions. The listed square footage at times has been calculated

Exhibit D. Subject Unit

APPRAISAL REPORT — INDIVIDUAL ☐ CONDOMINIUM OR ☐ PUD UNIT   File No

Borrower _____
Unit No _____ Address _____   Census Tract _____ Map Reference _____
City _____   Project Name/Phase No _____
_____ County _____   State _____ Zip Code _____
Actual Real Estate Taxes $ _____ (yr) Sales Price $ _____   Property Rights Appraised ☐ Fee ☐ Leasehold
Loan Charges to be Paid by Seller $ _____ Other Sales Concessions _____
Lender/Client _____   Lender's Address _____
Occupant _____ Appraiser _____ Instructions to Appraiser _____
☐ FNMA 1073A required   ☐ FHLMC 465 Addendum A required   ☐ FHLMC 465 Addendum B required

Location	☐ Urban	☐ Suburban	☐ Rural	NEIGHBORHOOD RATING	Good	Avg	Fair	Poor
Built Up	☐ Over 75%	☐ 25% to 75%	☐ Under 25%	Adequacy of Shopping	☐	☐	☐	☐
Growth Rate ☐ Fully Developed	☐ Rapid	☐ Steady	☐ Slow	Employment Opportunities	☐	☐	☐	☐
Property Values	☐ Increasing	☐ Stable	☐ Declining	Recreational Facilities	☐	☐	☐	☐
Demand/Supply	☐ Shortage	☐ In Balance	☐ Oversupply	Adequacy of Utilities	☐	☐	☐	☐
Marketing Time	☐ Under 3 Mos	☐ 4-6 Mos	☐ Over 6 Mos	Property Compatibility	☐	☐	☐	☐

Present Land Use ___ % 1 Family ___ % 2-4 Family ___ % Apts ___ % Condo
___ % Commercial ___ % Industrial ___ % Vacant
Change in Present Land Use ☐ Not Likely ☐ Likely* ☐ Taking Place*
*From _____ To _____

Predominant Occupancy ☐ Owner ☐ Tenant ___ % Vacant
Condominium Price Range $ ___ to $ ___ Predominant $ ___
Age ___ yrs to ___ yrs Predominant ___ yrs
Single Family Price Range $ ___ to $ ___ Predominant $ ___
Age ___ yrs to ___ yrs Predominant ___ yrs

Protection from Detrimental Conditions ☐ ☐ ☐ ☐
Police and Fire Protection ☐ ☐ ☐ ☐
General Appearance of Properties ☐ ☐ ☐ ☐
Appeal to Market ☐ ☐ ☐ ☐

	Distance	Access or Convenience
Public Transportation		☐ ☐ ☐ ☐
Employment Centers		☐ ☐ ☐ ☐
Neighborhood Shopping		☐ ☐ ☐ ☐
Grammar Schools		☐ ☐ ☐ ☐
Freeway Access		☐ ☐ ☐ ☐

Describe potential for additional Condo/PUD units in nearby area _____

NOTE: FHLMC/FNMA do not consider race or the racial composition of the neighborhood to be reliable appraisal factors.
Describe those factors, favorable or unfavorable, affecting marketability (e.g. public parks, schools, noise, view, mar. area, population size and financial ability) _____

Lot Dimensions (if PUD) _____ • _____ Sq Ft ☐ Corner Lot   Project Density When Completed as Planned ___ Units/Acre
Zoning Classification _____   Present improvements ☐ do ☐ do not conform to zoning regulations
Highest and best use ☐ Present use ☐ Other (specify) _____

	Public	Other (Describe)	OFF-SITE IMPROVEMENTS	Project Ingress/Egress (adequacy) _____
Elec	☐		Street Access ☐ Public ☐ Private	Topo _____
Gas	☐		Surface _____	Size/Shape _____
Water	☐		Maintenance ☐ Public ☐ Private	View Amenity _____
San Sewer	☐		☐ Storm Sewer ☐ Curb/Gutter	Drainage/Flood Conditions _____
		☐ Underground Elect & Tel	☐ Sidewalk ☐ Street Lights	Is the property located in a HUD identified Special Flood Hazard Area? ☐ No ☐ Yes

Comments (including any easements, encroachments or other adverse conditions) _____

☐ Existing Approx Year Built 19 ___ Original Use _____
☐ Condo ☐ PUD ☐ Converted (19 ___)
TYPE ☐ Proposed ☐ Under Construction
PROJECT ☐ Elevator ☐ Walk-up No. of Stories _____
☐ Row or Town House ☐ Other (specify) _____
☐ Primary Residence ☐ Second Home or Recreational

If Completed No. Phases ___ No Units ___ No Sold ___
If Incomplete Planned No Phases ___ No Units ___ No Sold ___
Units in Subject Phase Total ___ Completed ___ Sold ___ Rented ___
Approx No Units for Sale Subject Project ___ Subject Phase ___

Exterior Wall _____ Roof Covering _____ Security Features _____
Elevator No ___ Adequacy & Condition _____ Soundproofing Vertical _____ Horizontal _____
Parking Total No Spaces ___ Ratio ___ Spaces/Unit Type _____ No Spaces of Guest Parking _____
Describe common elements or recreational facilities _____
Are any common elements, rec. facilities or parking leased to Owners Assoc? _____ If yes, attach addendum describing rental, terms and options

PROJECT RATING	Good	Avg	Fair	Poor
Location	☐	☐	☐	☐
General Appearance	☐	☐	☐	☐
Amenities and Recreational Facilities	☐	☐	☐	☐
Density (units per acre)	☐	☐	☐	☐
Unit Mix	☐	☐	☐	☐
Quality of Constr (mat'l & finish)	☐	☐	☐	☐
Condition of Exterior	☐	☐	☐	☐
Condition of Interior	☐	☐	☐	☐
Appeal to Market	☐	☐	☐	☐

☐ Existing ☐ Proposed ☐ Under Constr Floor No _____ Livable Area _____ Basement ___ % Finished _____
Parking for Unit No ___ Type _____ ☐ Assigned ☐ Owned   Convenience to Unit _____

Room List	Foyer	Liv	Din	Kit	Bdrm	Bath	Fam	Rec	Lau	Other	UNIT RATING	Good	Avg	Fair	Poor
Basement											Condition of Improvement	☐	☐	☐	☐
1st Level											Room Sizes and Layout	☐	☐	☐	☐
2nd Level											Adequacy of Closets and Storage	☐	☐	☐	☐

Kit Equip Cabinets & Workspace ☐ ☐ ☐ ☐
Plumbing Adequacy and Condition ☐ ☐ ☐ ☐
Electrical Adequacy and Condition ☐ ☐ ☐ ☐
Adequacy of Soundproofing ☐ ☐ ☐ ☐
Adequacy of Insulation ☐ ☐ ☐ ☐
Location within Project or View ☐ ☐ ☐ ☐
Overall Livability ☐ ☐ ☐ ☐
Appeal and Marketability ☐ ☐ ☐ ☐
Est Effective Age ___ to ___ yrs
Est Remaining Economic Life ___ to ___ yrs

Floors ☐ Hardwood ☐ Carpet over _____ ☐ _____
Int Walls ☐ Drywall ☐ Plaster _____
Trim/Finish ☐ Good ☐ Average _____ ☐ Fair ☐ Poor
Bath Floor ☐ Ceramic _____ Wainscot ☐ Ceramic ☐ _____
Windows (type) _____ ☐ Storm Sash ☐ Screens ☐ Combo
Kitchen Equip ☐ Refrig ☐ Range Oven ☐ Fan Hood ☐ Washer ☐ Dryer
☐ Intercom ☐ Disposal ☐ Dishwasher ☐ Microwave ☐ Compactor
HEAT Type _____ Fuel _____ Cond _____
AIR COND ☐ Central ☐ Other _____ ☐ Adequate ☐ Inadequate
☐ Earth Sheltered Housing Design ☐ Solar Design Landscape ☐ Solar Space Heat Air Cond ☐ Solar Hot Water
☐ Flue Damper ☐ Elec/Mech Gas Furn Ignition ☐ Auto Setback Thermostat ☐ Dble Triple Glazed Windows ☐ Caulk/Weatherstrip
INSULATION (state R Factor if known) ☐ Walls ___ ☐ Ceiling ___ ☐ Floor ___ ☐ Roof Attic ___ ☐ Water Heater ___
If rehab proposed do plans and specs provide for adequate energy conservation? _____ If no attach description of modification needed _____
ENERGY EFFICIENCY APPEARS ☐ High ☐ Adequate ☐ Low   Energy Audit ☐ Yes (attach if available) ☐ No
COMMENTS (special features, functional or physical inadequacies, modernization or repairs needed, etc.) _____

FHLMC Form 465 9/80   ATTACH DESCRIPTIVE PHOTOGRAPHS OF SUBJECT PROPERTY AND STREET SCENE   FNMA Form 1073 9/80

on building plan dimensions, which are based on exterior dimensions and the middle of common party walls, areas that are not owned in Fee Simple by the unit. The resulting square footage is usually about six to seven percent greater than the square footage based on interior dimensions. At other times the listed square footage includes decks, exterior storage lockers, and/or garages. The appraiser should only be listing actual Livable Area square footage.

When there is an obvious discrepancy between the Declaration square footage and the interior Livable Area square footage, the appraiser should explain the reason for this discrepancy. Examining the plans filed with the Declaration will often times clarify the reason for this type of discrepancy.

6. A unit's parking space is usually assigned to the unit. These spaces are generally considered to be limited common area that is assigned to a unit for its exclusive use. Limited common area is not owned by the unit. Attached garages or individual basement garages are typically owned by the subject unit and their square footage is usually listed in the Declaration as part of the unit. Whether a parking space is assigned or owned should be specifically stated in the Declaration and shown on the plans that are filed with the Declaration.

BUDGET ANALYSIS

7. Ground rent would only apply to a Leasehold unit where lease payments f or the site are actually being made. The complex would have a procedure for determining the lease amount for each unit in the complex. This procedure may be stated in the Declaration or it may be in a separate lease agreement. A Fee Simple unit would have a Ground Rent

8. In many cases water and sewer bills are paid for out of the monthly condominium dues as these utilities are metered to the entire complex. Sometimes other utilities, such as heat, gas and electricity, are also metered to the entire complex.

Exhibit E. Budget Analysis

This would typically be true of older conversions that have central heating systems and/or a central hot water tank. This information can usually be found out from a homeowner.

An appraiser should take extra care in an older conversion in examining and stating what condition a central hot water or central heating system is in. Some of these systems are very old and may be in need of a major overhaul. This could result in a considerable expense to the Homeowner's Association for repairing the systems and possibly require a special assessment.

9. An appraiser should not rate the adequacy of a Homeowner's Association operating budget without some of its financial status. It cannot simply be assumed that the operating budget is adequate. The appraiser needs to examine a current Homeowner's Association budget and/ or financial statement. It is common for a new complex to have an inadequate budget, sometimes due to inexperience in understanding budgets by the developer and sometimes due to a desire by the developer to hold maintenance fees down to make the complex more attractive to a purchaser. An operating budget or financial statement can usually be obtained from a homeowner, the treasurer of the Homeowner's Association, or from the management firm, if there is one.

A project that has been run by the Homeowner's Association for three or four years would have a budget more reflective of actual expenses, but these budgets still need to be examined to determine whether they have adequate replacement reserves. Replacement reserves consist of funds that are put into savings so that there is enough money to pay for deferred maintenance items when it is time for the deferred maintenance to be taken care of. Replacement reserves would be established along the lines of the following simple schedule:

Deferred Maintenance Item	Years of Estimated Remaining Life		Estimated Replacement Cost	Average Yearly Cost
Roof	15	Years	$60,000	$4,000
Painting	5	Years	$16,500	$3,300
Carpeting	9	Years	$27,450	$3,050
Office Equipment	10	Years	$ 3,000	$ 300
TOTAL ANNUAL REPLACEMENT RESERVES				$10,650

Based on this schedule, the Homeowner's Association should be setting aside $10,650 every year, or $887.50 each month, from its dues for replacement reserves. If the present roof is ten years old, then there should be $40,000 allocated in a reserve fund for replacing the roof in another five years. Some complexes also set up reserves for annual insurance premiums. Without adequate reserves a special assessment of upwards of $1,000 to $2,000 per unit could be levied to pay for possibly a new roof or painting of the exterior. A pending levy of this size could very well affect the value of a unit and its marketability.

10. Items such as not allowing people of a certain age or pets in a complex should be noted. These restrictions can obviously effect the marketability of a unit by eliminating a segment of the purchasing market. These restrictions would be stated in the Declaration or in the Rules and Regulations for the complex.

The Right of First Refusal is felt to be an item that should also be mentioned. Some condominium complexes allow any of the present owners the right to match any offer from someone outside the complex to buy or rent another unit within the project. This is a controversial item to some people as it is felt that the Right of First Refusal can be used as a means to discriminate against certain groups of people. In any case, if a purchaser knows that any offer that they make can be matched by anyone in the complex and that their sale will then not go through, there could be a reluctance by a purchaser to go through with all the trouble and paperwork. This could result in the subject complex having a reduced marketability in comparison to other complexes.

MARKET DATA ANALYSIS

11. It is not unusual for condominium complexes to have dropped in value over the last several years and determining value trends has become very important in appraising condominiums. However, these value trends can vary from location to location and from complex to complex. Two complexes that are across the street from each other can have different marketability levels because their architectural design and price range will appeal to totally different markets. Thus one complex may have dropped as much as ten to twenty percent in value over the last two or three years and the other may be holding its value. An appraiser should not generalize concerning the entire condominium market, but should address the value trends within the subject complex itself. This can usually be done by reporting on the recent sales history of the subject unit, on other units in the subject complex that have fairly recently sold and resold, and/or on the sales history of the comparable sales used. Providing this information to the lending institution will allow them to be better equipped on their decision whether they make a loan in the subject complex or not.

Another valuable source of information to be able to use is the listing prices of other similar units in the complex, both current listings and listings that have expired because the units have not sold. Sometimes there are no recent sales in a subject complex for an appraiser to base value trends on. However, if there are two units on the market for $60,000 that have not sold in the last six months, the subject unit is obviously not going to be worth $65,000 even if it was purchased

Exhibit F. Market Data Analysis

Unit Charge $ _____ /Mo x 12 = $ _____ /Yr ($ _____ /Sq. Ft /year of livable area) Ground Rent (if any) $ _____ /yr

Utilities included in unit charge: ☐ None ☐ Heat ☐ Air Cond ☐ Electricity ☐ Gas ☐ Water ☐ Sewer

Note any fees, other than regular Condo/PUD charges, for use of facilities _____

To properly maintain the project and provide the services anticipated, the budget appears   ☐ High ☐ Adequate ☐ Inadequate

Compared to other competitive projects of similar quality and design subject unit charge appears   ☐ High ☐ Reasonable ☐ Low

Management Group   ☐ Owners Association   ☐ Developer   ☐ Management Agent (identify) _____

Quality of Management and its enforcement of Rules and Regulations appears   ☐ Superior ☐ Good ☐ Adequate ☐ Inadequate

Special or unusual characteristics in the Condo/PUD Documents or otherwise known to the appraiser, that would affect marketability (if none, so state) _____

Comments _____

NOTE FHLMC does not require the cost approach in the appraisal of condominium or PUD units

Cost Approach (to be used only for detached, semi-detached, and town house units)

Reproduction Cost New _____ Sq. Ft @ $ _____ per Sq. Ft = _____ $ _____

Less Depreciation: Physical $ _____ Functional $ _____ Economic $ _____   (_____)

Depreciated Value of Improvements _____

Add Land Value (if leasehold, show only leasehold value—attach calculations) _____

Pro-rata Share of Value of Amenities _____

Total Indicated Value   ☐ FEE SIMPLE   ☐ LEASEHOLD $ _____

Comments regarding estimate of depreciation and value of land and amenity package _____

The appraiser, whenever possible, should analyze two comparable sales from within the subject project. However, when appraising a unit in a new or newly converted project, at least two comparables should be selected from outside the subject project. In the following analysis, the comparable should always be adjusted to the subject unit and not vice versa. If a significant feature of the comparable is superior to the subject unit, a minus (−) adjustment should be made to the comparable. If such a feature of the comparable is inferior to the subject, a plus (+) adjustment should be made to the comparable

LIST ONLY THOSE ITEMS THAT REQUIRE ADJUSTMENT

ITEM	Subject Property	COMPARABLE NO 1		COMPARABLE NO 2		COMPARABLE NO 3	
Address-Unit No							
Project Name							
Proximity to Subj							
Sales Price	$	$		$		$	
Price/Living Area	$	$		$		$	
Data Source							
	DESCRIPTION	DESCRIPTION	+ (−) $ Adjustment	DESCRIPTION	+ (−) $ Adjustment	DESCRIPTION	+ (−) $ Adjustment
Date of Sale and Time Adjustment							
Location							
Site/View							
Design and Appeal							
Quality of Constr							
Age							
Condition							
Living Area, Room Count & Total	Total : B-rms : Baths	Total : B-rms : Baths		Total : B-rms : Baths		Total : B-rms : Baths	
Gross Living Area	Sq Ft	Sq Ft		Sq Ft		Sq Ft	
Basement & Bsmt Finished Rooms							
Functional Utility							
Air Conditioning							
Storage							
Parking Facilities							
Common Elements and Recreation Facilities							
Mo. Assessment							
Leasehold/Fee							
Special Energy Efficient Items							
Other (e g fire-places, kitchen equip., remodeling)							
Sales or Financing Concessions							
Net Adj. (total)		☐ Plus ☐ Minus : $		☐ Plus ☐ Minus : $		☐ Plus ☐ Minus : $	
Indicated value of Subject		$		$		$	

Comments on Market Data Analysis _____

_____ (If applicable) Economic Market Rent $ _____ /Mo x Gross Rent Multiplier _____ = $ _____

This appraisal is made   ☐ as is   ☐ subject to repairs, alterations, or conditions listed below   ☐ subject to completion per plans and specifications

Comments and Conditions of Appraisal _____

Final Reconciliation _____

Construction Warranty   ☐ Yes ☐ No   Name of Warranty Program _____ Warranty Coverage Expires _____

This appraisal is based upon the above requirements, the certification, contingent and limiting conditions, and Market Value definition that are stated in

☐ FHLMC Form 439 (Rev. 10/78)/FNMA Form 1004B (Rev. 10/78) filed with client _____ 19 ____   ☐ attached

I ESTIMATE THE MARKET VALUE, AS DEFINED, OF SUBJECT PROPERTY AS OF _____ 19 ____ to be $ _____

Appraiser(s) _____

Date Report Signed _____ 19 ____   Review Appraiser (if applicable) _____   ☐ Did ☐ Did Not Physically Inspect Property

FHLMC Form 465 9/10   REVERSE   L   FNMA Form 1073 9/80

for that price three years ago and another similar unit sold for that price two years ago. If a value trend is clearly downward, then this factor has to be reflected in market value. Some appraisers are reluctant to use bank repossession sales as comparable sales because these transactions are questionable fair market value sales. In many cases the bank simply wants to get rid of these units and these sales would probably fall under the definition of distress sales. However, in some cases these types of sales are about the only sales that are taking place in a complex and these transactions have to be establishing a market, particularly if the units were on the market for an extended period of time.

If a bank is selling similar units for $50,000, the subject unit is not going to be able to be sold for its original purchase price of $65,000. It should probably be able to be sold for somewhat more than $50,000 since this price would be at the low end of the value range, but the appraiser still needs to have evidence to support this.

12. Site descriptions are usually listed by appraisers in general terms such as average or good. However, care should be taken that some credit be given for complexes that have substantially lower densities or for smaller complexes, which are usually more desirable than similarly designed larger complexes. One way of doing this is to look at site descriptions as a reflection of density. Smaller complexes tend to have lower densities than similarly designed larger complexes. A townhouse style complex with a density of eight units per acre should be worth more than a similar complex with a density of fourteen units per acre. An appraiser should generally not compare townhouse style complexes to flats in elevator buildings, but if this becomes necessary, an adjustment can be made for the elevator building and its density of sixty units per acre compared to the townhouse complex and its density of fourteen units per acre.

The proper adjustment for differences in views is of great

importance as these adjustments can be very large, particularly in mid and high rise complexes. The value 'of a view is a reflection of not only how high up in the building the unit is, but it is also a reflection of some of the following factors:

A. The type of view the unit has. A water view, especially one where there is boat traffic, seems to be worth more than a territorial or city lights view. A westerly sunset view seems to be worth more than an easterly sunrise view.

B. The value of the unit in relation to the view. A good view in a $200,000 unit may be worth twice as much as the same view in a $70,000 unit. This would be based on the premise that a less expensive unit may be an under improvement for this view, but the same view in a much more expensive unit is not an under improvement for the view.

C. Whether the view is seen from the living area, sleeping area, or deck. A view from the living room is considered more valuable than the same view from a bedroom or deck. This is because most people spend their waking and entertaining hours in the living areas of the condominium. If the view is not seen very often, such as from the bedroom, or is in an area that is not utilized much, such as a deck, then its value is limited.

Knowing what adjustment to make for a view obviously means that the appraiser needs to know where the comparable sales are located within the building. The appraiser needs to be able to state whether the unit is in the southwest corner of the building and has a view of the lake and sunset or whether it is in the northeast corner of the building and looks directly at the apartment building across the street.

The actual dollar adjustment to make for these differences in views is determined by going to the market and looking at what buyers will pay for one view as opposed to another view. This is sometimes fairly easy in condominiums as some units will be identical in virtually all respects expect for differences in view. Thus differences in sale prices can basically be attributed to a difference in view.

13. Factors such as whether a unit is a top floor unit, interior unit, or end unit within a building needs to be known by the appraiser and compensated for. A top floor unit has a greater value than a unit on a floor below it, even if there is no view, due to the added privacy of not having anyone making noise above you. This privacy factor also applies to an end unit, where there is only one unit next to you, as opposed to an interior unit, where this is a unit on both sides. An end unit can also have increased value if there are windows at that end of the building, providing that unit with additional sunlight. Other factors that can affect value would include whether a unit is a ground level unit that has direct access to the common grounds, which seems to increase value, and whether a unit is below grade on one side, which seems to decrease value. Adjustments for these factors can be taken into consideration under Design and Appeal, Functional Utility, or under another category that the appraiser chooses.

The actual dollar adjustments to make for these differences would again be determined by going to the market and seeing how buyers respond to these factors. The appraiser, however, needs to be careful that more than just the sale prices are looked at, especially when the prices are being set by the developer in a new complex. An example would be the sales history of the Greenhouse, a four story, 68 unit complex in Seattle that was marketed in the first half of 1979. All four floors were essentially identical to each other and there were no actual views involved. The average sale price for each floor during the first six months of marketing was as follows:

	1st Floor,	2nd Floor,	3rd Floor,	4th Floor
1 BR units	$39,625	$46,938	$49,594	$52,237
2 BR units	$56,429	$59,344	$64,286	$68,098

The price difference per floor was as follows:

	1st & 2nd Floor	**2nd & 3rd** Floor	**3rd & 4th** Floor
1 BR units	+$7,313	+$2,656	+$2.643
2 BR units	+$2,915	+$4,942	+$3,812

The price difference between the one bedroom units on the first and second floor is substantially higher than any of the others, but this is somewhat due to most of the first floor one bedroom units being partially below grade. Looking at the other price differences between floors, an appraiser could simply conclude that the market would pay an additional $2,500 to $4,000 per unit for each floor going up. However, an examination of the sales history based on when the units sold provides some additional information. Looking at how long it took to sell the units with the above price differences per floor reveals the following sales pattern:

	1st Floor	**2nd Floor**	**3rd Floor**	**4th Floor**
50% Sold	2-15-79	4-03-79	5-09-79	2-13-79
80% Sold	3-13-79	4-25-79	6-04-79	3-29-79

The dates indicate when 50 percent and 80 percent of the units that were being marketed on each floor had sold. Looking at this information indicates that units on the first and top floor sold first, followed by the second floor and then by the third floor. The market seemed willing to pay $2,500 to $4,000 extra for a top floor unit, but was much less willing to pay $2,500 to $4,000 extra to simply go up a floor if it was not a top floor unit. The fact that the first floor units, even the two bedroom units, sold before the second and third floor units would seem to indicate that in this particular complex buyers reacted more to price than to what floor the units were on, if it did not involve being on the top floor. A buyer was willing to pay $2,500 extra to live on the second or third floor only when most of the units on the lower floors were not available.

After examining this sales history, an appraiser might now conclude that rather than there being a $2,500 to $4,000 value difference between floors, a more realistic value difference between units on the first and second floor and between units on the second and third floor in this type of condominium complex would be between $1,000 and $2,000.

An appraiser does not need to document adjustments such as these if the adjustments made seem reasonable. However, since these are the types of adjustments that are not made on a single family home appraisal, a reviewer needs to make sure that the appraiser has at least taken these factors into consideration and has not just ignored them.

14. It is difficult to judge what the interior condition of a condominium unit is in from the outside. In a single family home the same individual usually maintains the exterior and the interior and the condition of the exterior typically reflects the condition of the interior. This does not totally apply to condominiums since the exterior of the building is maintained buy the Homeowner's Association and the individual homeowner only has direct control over maintenance of the interior of their unit.

Apartment conversions are a special problem as some older complexes have completely remodeled interiors and some were sold in an "as is'? condition. Yet, a 1930 brick veneer building sometimes looks the same from the outside whether the interior has been remodeled or not. What is particularly difficult is when one owner who has purchased a unit in an "as is" conversion will completely remodel the interior and the owner of the next door unit will do no remodeling. When the two units then resell for a $20,000 difference, the appraiser can be left guessing at the reason for this price difference.

The appraiser should give some explanation of differences, or of a lack of differences, in condition between the subject and the comparable sales, if there is an obvious need for it. It is also helpful on conversions to list under Age both the year the complex was built and the year that it was converted.

15. The room count listed in the Declaration can be misleading. The appraiser should mainly pay attention just to the bedroom and bath count. Developers at times will count closets as rooms and an 800 square foot unit will be listed as having ten rooms/two bedroom/one bath when the unit really has only four rooms/two bedrooms/one bath. In these types of situations the reviewer and appraiser need to use common sense as to whether an 800 square foot unit really can have ten rooms. A one bedroom unit should not be compared to a two bedroom unit, if at all possible, due to their substantial difference in functional utility. At the same time there is felt to be little difference between a one bedroom plus den unit and a two bedroom unit as most people tend to use their bedroom as a den/study anyway.

16. Depending on what part of the country a house is in, average quality single family homes are typically adjusted at around $15 to $20 per square foot for living area differences. This is felt to be the lowest adjustment that should be made in appraising a condominium. More of a condominium's value goes into its actual living area than in a single family home and less goes into the land and other improvements, such as its exterior walls, parking facilities, and landscaping. Typically, square footage adjustments for condominiums might start at $20 per square foot and go up to $100 and more per square foot for a high rise, view unit. The reviewer needs to make sure that the appraiser is not making adjustments based on single family home appraising, but in terms of appraising a condominium.

If an appraiser is using a different square footage for the subject unit than that which is listed in the Declaration and is using comparable sales from the subject complex, the appraiser needs to make sure that all of the square footage figures being

Exhibit G. Market Data Analysis (continued)

used are consistent with one another. Most appraisal resources will list the square footage for the comparable sales as they are listed in the Declaration. Therefore, if the Declaration lists the subject unit as having 900 square feet of living area, but the appraiser measures it to have only 800 square feet, then the comparable sales from within the subject complex that are listed as having 900 square feet in the Declaration need to be listed as having 800 square feet in the report.

If the comparable sales in the subject complex do not have identical Declaration square footage figures as the subject unit, then they need to be adjusted to be consistent with the subject, possibly on a percentage basis. If there is a five percent difference between the Declaration square footage and the measured square footage for the subject, then maybe all of the comparable sales used that are in the subject complex should have their Declaration square footage adjusted by five percent. If the appraiser knows that the measured square footage discrepancy for the subject is due to the Declaration including extras square footage for something like the deck, then the deck square footage needs to be subtracted from the Declaration square footage for the comparable sales. Whatever approach is used, it is important that the appraiser be consistent in the square footages that are listed on the report.

17. Most condominium units have a separate storage locker that is limited common area and is located outside of the unit; on the deck or in a storage room. This storage should not be listed as livable area square footage unless it is actually inside of the unit. Extra storage can be very important to condominium buyers as most condominiums have much less square footage than single family homes. If the subject unit or any of the comparable sales do not have any separate storage, and some complexes do not have any, an adjustment for this should be made by the appraiser. The amount of this adjustment might be based on what a storage locker has recently sold for in the complex or by finding out what a locker rents

for at a storage rental place in the area and then capitalizing this amount using a typical capitalization rate. Depending on the size of the storage space, this might result in maybe a $500 to $1,000 adjustment.

18. Adjustments for parking can be a rather difficult task as, depending on how thorough an appraiser's resources are, it is not always clear how many spaces and/or what type of a space a unit has. In a single family home the parking is what is on the site. A condominium complex can have all of its parking spaces grouped together with no clear indication as to what unit has what space unless the parking space is actually attached to the unit. Some condominium complexes will have a combination of open and covered parking spaces and in other complexes not all units even have a parking space. Some complexes will assign all of their parking spaces to unit owners and in other complexes spaces will be left unassigned and can be used as guest or second car parking. It is even possible for a complex with a limited number of spaces to lease out the spaces to unit owners on a first come, first served basis. It is quite important to know what space a unit has due to the value differences in parking spaces, particularly in the more urban areas. It is not uncommon for a basement, security parking space to be worth as much as 25 percent more than an open space. An appraiser cannot simply assume that because one unit in a complex has a covered space that all of the units in the complex have a covered space. The comparable sale listing in a multiple listing book may provide the appraiser with the necessary information or the appraiser may need to research the Declaration or the excise tax affidavit.

19. Exterior recreational facilities such as outdoor swimming pools, tennis courts, and recreational buildings are easy to see. Indoor facilities such as indoor swimming pools, exercise rooms, and guest rooms are more difficult to observe. An appraiser may need to do some extra research at times to discover exactly what recreational facilities a comparable sale

has. The condominium Declaration and plans will usually provide this information. At other times the appraiser will need to look at a multiple listing book or possibly contact the complex manager or a realtor.

Since the recreational facilities in a complex are shared by all of the units within the complex, it is not felt that large adjustments should be made in this category as the value of these facilities are also shared by all of the units. A complex that has extensive recreational facilities also has higher dues to pay for maintaining these facilities. Adjustments in the $500 to $2,500 range would seem reasonable depending on the extent of the differences in recreational facilities.

Elevators, or the lack of them, should also be considered in this category, or possibly under Functional Utility. A unit on the third floor of a three story building without an elevator has inferior marketability and should also be worth less than a third floor unit that is in a complex with an elevator. Walking up two flights of stairs is not appealing to most people, particularly when one is moving furniture or carrying up the groceries. The higher the price range, the greater the loss in value as people who purchase expensive units would clearly expect the complex to have an elevator. An appraiser should not overlook the impact of this factor on marketability and value.

20. It is usually difficult to justify making an adjustment for differences in monthly dues as these differences can usually be attributed to one complex having more recreational facilities or common areas to maintain than another complex, or to one complex having more utilities paid for out of their dues than another complex. However, an adjustment should possibly be considered if the appraiser knows that dues in a complex are substantially higher or lower as a direct result of a special assessment, a lack of replacement reserves, or having to pay for improvements that most complexes typically already have. If a unit is paying $75 more per month in dues over the next

two years to pay off a special assessment on replacing its roof than another complex that has built up sufficient reserves over the last ten years so that a special assessment is not needed, a buyer may pay less for the unit with the special assessment. A unit in a complex that has $150,000 in replacement reserves may settle for more than a unit in a complex with only $10,000 in replacement reserves as the complex with only minimal reserves may be looking at a possible special assessment in the next year or two. Complexes with a live-in manager will have one unit set aside for the manager. In most cases this unit was part of the common area when the complex was originally marketed. In other cases the unit was purchased by the Homeowner's Association after the Association began operating and mortgage payments for the unit are actually being made by the Homeowner's Association. A unit's dues in a complex such as this could be substantially higher than in another complex and this could result in a lower sales price.

While adjustments can probably be justified in these cases, it is difficult to make these adjustments for a couple of reasons. First, it is not realistic to expect an appraiser to know the financial status of the Homeowner's Association of the comparable sales so that an adjustment could be made. Even if the appraiser could obtain the information needed, the time and effort spent on obtaining and analyzing it would be excessive. Second, it is questionable if the market is sophisticated enough to actually make a decision to pay more or less for a unit based on the dues paid and the financial status of the Homeowner's Association. It is doubtful if many buyers even bother to thoroughly investigate the financial status of the Homeowner's Association. However, when there is an obvious difference in dues, the appraiser should at least consider the reasons for this difference and possibly explain what approach was taken to deal with this difference.

21. If the subject being appraised is a Fee Simple unit, then only Fee Simple comparable sales should be used. If the subject is

a Leasehold condominium, then only Leasehold comparable sales should be used. If it ever becomes necessary to use one type of comparable sale when the subject is another type of unit, then an adjustment needs to be made by the appraiser. If a Leasehold condominium unit pays $100 per month for its lease, in addition to its monthly dues, this unit would obviously sell for less than a similar Fee Simple unit that did not have to make these payments. Exactly how much less is open to question. The $1,200 annual lease payment could be capitalized at a typical capitalization rate, say 10 percent, and then an adjustment could be made based on this $12,000 amount. Another method might be to total up the amount of lease payments made over a five year time period, a typical holding period for a condominium, and then make an adjustment based on this $6,000 amount. One just has to bear in mind that cost does not always equal value as most buyers are not going to figure out the purchase price of a condominium based on a mathematical formula unless the unit is being bought by an investor as a rental.

22. Sales or Financing Concessions is an area that comes under increased scrutiny when market conditions are poor and/or when interest rates are high. This applies particularly to condominiums as it is not unusual for new developments to have interest rate buydowns or other sales concessions. An appraiser needs to be aware of what these concessions are and make the appropriate adjustments when needed.

CONCLUSION

Reviewing condominium appraisals is enough to give reviewers headaches. Unfortunately, there is little to indicate that this is going to change in the near future. The condominium market has been, is, and probably will continue to be a volatile and difficult market to read. In some parts of the country the condominium market has been declining and the single family home market has not been declining or has been declining at a slower rate. This has sometimes resulted in the percentage of foreclosures on condominiums being substantially higher than the percentage of condominiums that is in a lender's overall residential portfolio. This situation has caused many lenders to be reluctant to issue loans on any condominiums and when they do issue a loan, they are more demanding on the quality of the condominium appraisal. These demands do get filtered down to the reviewer. The best approach that a reviewer can take to ensure that a condominium appraisal is thoroughly done is to make sure that their lending institution only uses qualified appraisers who have a good grasp of condominiums and the condominium market. It usually is not difficult to determine which appraisers know how to appraise condominiums if the reviewer knows what to look for on the appraisal. If the appraiser is not familiar with condominiums, it is too easy to end up with faulty appraisals and that situation clearly benefits no one.

CHAPTER TWENTY-ONE

REVIEWING THE VACANT LAND APPRAISAL

INTRODUCTION:

Establishing the value of a vacant parcel of land can be one of the most difficult tasks that an appraiser may be asked to undertake. Most parcels being appraised are vacant and unleased. The appraiser valuing a vacant, non-income producing parcel has a limited number of guides to aid with valuation as there is no traditional cost or income approach. The most reliable opinion will be afforded via the market or comparable sales approach. The approach requires the appraiser to find and adjust sales of other parcels and after adjusting for a variety of factors use them to estimate value. The absence of meaningful comparable sales or offering data may cause the appraiser to use a very sophisticated approach known as the land residual technique. The technique derives land value by establishing the combined total value of the land and buildings. The value of the building is then estimated, often by the cost approach technique. The building value is then subtracted from the combined value with the "residual" being the ascribed land value. The method works best with existing buildings but a hypothecation can also be used if no buildings exist on the land. As this technique requires an inordinate number of assumptions and calculations, it is not deemed to be as reliable as the comparative approach. Accordingly, it has not been further addressed in this guide. In areas lacking appropriate sales data, it is noted that it can be an appraiser's only method of estimating land value. If confronted by this approach, logic and common sense appear to be the reviewer's best allies.

PURPOSE:

The purpose of this brochure is to aid the reviewer in determining if the appraisal being reviewed has been capably prepared resulting in a reliable option of the current fair market value of a parcel of vacant land. It is assumed that the reader is generally familiar with the basic aspects of reviewing a residential, commercial or tract development appraisal report as well as sections I, II, III and IV of the Commercial Appraisal Review Form (4002). Your attention is also drawn to the Land Review Appraisal Checklist included herein as a further guide.

FOUR BASIC SITE CLASSIFICATIONS:

All parcels of land, even farm land and unbuildable land can be classified into one of four general categories described below. As this will broadly define how the appraiser and reviewer envision the parcel and approach its valuation the reviewer should make an early determination. The four categories describe and relate to a site's potential for development as either:

1. Unzoned and unimproved (least valuable)
   a. With utilities available
   b. Without utilities available
2. Zoned, unimproved and unapproved (more valuable than)
   a. With utilities available
   b. Without utilities available
3. Zoned, unimproved and approved (more valuable than #1 and #2)
   a. With utilities available
   b. Without utilities available
4. Zoned, improved and approved (most valuable)

Each major classification has a greater value than the preceding as suggested by the parenthetical comments. If the subject is located within the first three, the potential for "upgrading" should also be reviewed. It is important to note that (public) utility available also has a major impact on value. Where available, proximity to the site and the cost of bringing utilities to the site is very significant. In development situations, the cost of providing these utilities can exceed the price paid or the unimproved value of a development parcel. Accordingly, subgroups addressing utility availability should be used as above for the first three as "improved" denotes immediate utility availability to or on the site.

Reviewer's of single family tract development parcel appraisal, particularly for financing purposes, are specifically alerted to the fact that the total improvement costs when added to the acquisition price may dramatically exceed the fair market value of the "improved lot" value of the initial lots especially in a staged development. Simply stated, the front end load may not be recaptured until a substantial number of the lots have been sold at the improved market value prices. Additional caution should be taken against inadvertent "over lending".

The definitions within the categories are reviewed below.

DEFINITIONS:

1. UNZONED: A parcel that is not properly zoned to permit it from being legally used for anything but agriculture or open space. Some areas of the United States, however, do not have formal zoning codes and other procedures would apply.

2. ZONED: A parcel subject to specific governmental designation and control over its permitted development or use. Some basic zoning classifications are:
   a. Residential - usually permits single family housing
   b. Commercial - usually permits office buildings and retail type structures
   c. Industrial - usually permits heavy and light industrial buildings, warehouses, flex-buildings and similar

d. Apartment - usually permits garden, mid and high rise style multifamily dwellings. Depending on state law or local ordinances, this generally includes condominiums (as a form of ownership)

e. Special Exemption - Covers all other uses by requiring specific approvals by specific exception

Comment: Zoning designations will vary by community and can include many more classifications and subclassifications. Many zoning ordinances also must permit "more desirable" uses in lower classifications, e.g., residential may be permitted in most other zoning classifications. The reviewer should be cognizant of that possibility. The real question is "does the subject site have the proper zoning for the use contemplated by the report?"

3. UNIMPROVED: A parcel with no significant buildings or more importantly - no streets, water lines, sewer lines or other public utilities.

4. IMPROVED: A parcel that has been improved with public . Case by case the utilities can be near, on, or at the site concerning residential subdivision the term can also imply that streets have been installed. Extreme care should be used communications when discussing the "improved or unimproved" status of a site. The phrases are often confused with reference to the status of buildings on the site. When a site is developed or improved with significant building structures, it is rarely the subject of an appraisal as vacant land.

5. UNAPPROVED: A parcel that may be appropriately zoned for use contemplated but the specific governmental approvals have not yet been secured.

6. APPROVED: A parcel that has been fully approved for a use. This generally means that the local municipality, state, environmental agencies, highway authority have been properly

petitioned and have granted all of the formal approvals needed to develop the property. An approved site is one that is "ready to go". This is not to be confused with an appraiser's statement that "the site is appropriately zoned to permit the contemplated use". A site can be appropriately zoned but for a variety of reasons an owner may not be able to secure the formal approvals necessary to use the site even for a conforming use.

An approved parcel has more value than an unapproved parcel. Time, money and effort lead to the procurement of approvals and that has value. The approval levels of the comparables may vary at the time of their sale. Be certain that you understand the status of each and that the appraiser has made the proper adjustments if they are different. The reviewer is also alerted to the fact that approvals are generally available for a specific time and that if the necessary building-utility permits are not purchased and/or the work not commenced within the approved time period, the approvals can expire. Where a zoning variance or similar was incorporated into the approval, failure to proceed in a timely fashion may lose the approvals forever.

MAJOR ITEMS AFFECTING VALUE:

Once the reviewer has studied the appraiser's narration, explanation and representations concerning all of the traditional or basic items that affect value such as, location, size and shape, topography, plantage, trends, demand or other similar items that must be properly considered, there are ten items that deserve particular emphasis and attention when reviewing a vacant land appraisal:

1. Development Potential: is the site physically capable of supporting improvements? If it isn't, can it be made to be on a cost effective basis? Enhancements such as fill, pilings, bulkheads, underground parking, stream or road relocations, un-

derground drainage basins, and regrading can make a difference. If appropriate, be certain that the appraiser has considered the impact of sophisticated engineering and design.

2. Zoning: Site specific/nearby changes

3. Approvals: Have the necessary approvals been secured from
   all of the appropriate agencies? Are said approvals final and
   incontestable? If they have not been secured, are they readily
   available? Are there any unusual approval conditions? What
   is the potential for a lawsuit challenging the approvals? Frequently appraisers will address these in the "Assumptions and
   Limiting Conditions" section by stating something to the effect that the "appraiser conditions the value on assumption
   that all necessary approvals can be readily obtained for development of the parcel as contemplated herein."

4. Availability of public utilities - water, sewer, gas, electric, telephone and similar with emphasis on public water and sewer

5. Environmental - If official permits are not required, the owner
   should have a professional environmental report prepared. The
   appraiser should cite or enclose the report. If no report is available the appraiser may have excluded any and all environmental concerns within the "Assumptions and Limiting Conditions" section of the report. Check carefully for this as an
   appraiser' s opinion of value assuming "no environment concerns" will be dramatically different and, in fact, invalid if
   environmental cleanup concerns exist, i.e., there may be no
   value.

6. Highest and Best Use statement - The doctoral dissertation
   implied by the professional definition of this analysis is seldom seen in a land appraisal yet it is the "essence" of a site'
   value. State simply, the appraiser is saying that all of the site'

s development possibilities have been reviewed (as restrained by zoning, physical and all other factors) and that the use contemplated by the appraiser and the report will produce the highest return or value to the land and is, therefore, its best use. While this may or may not be perfectly accurate in the report being reviewed (as there may truly be a better use) the important aspects to check are the validity of the appraiser's assumptions and assertions, the consistency of that option throughout the report and the feasibility of development under existing or available zoning, etc.

7. Moratorium potential - This is most often overlooked. Building, public water, sewer and similar approval delays can adversely affect value and may occur momentarily after a value opinion has been rendered making it invalid. Check with local even if approvals have been secured and permits acquired.

8. Access problems - The reviewer cannot assume that property with street frontage has legal ingress-egress from the street. Make sure the property has legal, enforceable access directly or via easement, license or similar agreement. In the latter circumstances, the length of time may be a factor. Check the appraiser's assumptions and representations.

9. Easement problems - Appraisers often do not review a preliminary title report to ascertain easements of record. Failing that they may state within the assumptions and limiting conditions portion of the report that "good and marketable title is assumed and that the property is not encumbered by any easements having an adverse impact on its title or use". Occasionally they will state that no adverse easements were physically observed during the site inspection. If easements? Rights of way or similar exist, their impact must be addressed the appraiser. The durability and assignability of this right can also affect value and may require a legal opinion.

10. Condemnation - Many land value appraisals are prepared for condemnation proceedings and divergent opinions about a site' value. Be sure to question the appraiser and local authorities about the possibility of imminent or future condemnation possibilities. A major highway may have been proposed and while it may never be built or not built for a long period of time, its announcement alone will have an impact on the value of the subject. Hospital or university expansions are some other good examples of possible condemners. Simple condemnations include road wideners, a-cell and d-cell lanes, dedicated open space and utility rights of way.

MARKET VALUE APPROACH:

Once the foregoing have been satisfactorily reviewed and the property's appropriate category understood, the market of sales data material used by the appraiser in arriving at the opinion of value should be examined.

Often referred to as the sales comparison approach, the appraiser arrives at an opinion of value through a method of comparing the subject site with similar properties that have sold or that arc currently being offered for sale in the open market place.

Each of the comparables should be physically viewed by the appraiser and, if possible, a photograph of each should be included in the report. As no two sites are exactly alike, the appraiser will need to make adjustments to the sales data gleaned from the market. Adjustments will be made to correlate the difference between the subject and each comparable for such items as: time, size and shape, frontage, zoning, approvals, location, visibility, building area or number of units permitted, sales terms and financing available. Where current offerings are being used as a guide to value, they should be discounted in some fashion to reflect the fact that they are not a sale and are subject to tremendous negotiation. Reasonable offerings generally reflect or slightly overvalue the current market. A comparable site being currently offered can be very meaningful as its presence in the market supports the theory of the principal of substitution. The theory behind the principal, applied to the market approach, is that a property's value is generally set by the cost of acquiring a similar, equally desirable parcel or substitute site assuming no duress or undue cost or delay in acquiring the substitute parcel.

Most reports include a written comparison of the comparable sales and offering data to the subject in a chart or grid form with adjustments indicated. This permits easy comparison by the reviewer. The adjustments are typically expressed as percentage or dollar adjustments. They are added (+) or subtracted (-) for the sales price or offering. A sample grid is included. The grid is usually accompanied by comments about each sale or offering. Footnotes are frequently included to explain the adjustment factors such as "used 4% annual inflation factor for time." A more thorough narrative form of written explanation should be included within the report and should logically lead the reviewer to the appraiser's conclusion of value. If the report does not include a grid, the reviewer is urged to make their own, using the appraiser's data, so that an easy comparison can be made. A map showing the location for the comparables should also be included. Similarly, if the report does not include a comparative map of the location of the comparables, the reader is urged to make their own. Think about the adjustments made by the appraiser. Are they logically supported and reasonable?

APPRAISER'S TYPICAL ADJUSTMENT FACTORS:

1. Time
2. Location
3. Size and Shape
4. Frontage
5. Stage of Approval
6. Cost of Bringing Utilities to Site

TYPICAL VALUE DENOMINATORS:

When comparing the sales data the most common denominators used are the price per acre or price per square foot of lot area method of comparison. While often most accurate, the reviewer should also consider using the per unit or per square foot area of permitted improvement methods.

As most land appraisals contemplate immediate or future development, their value is generally predicated on their development use. When the value is predicated upon development, the use of these other denominators may be more meaningful guides to a site's value. Properties subject IO zoning may demonstrate wide variations in the building area permitted from community to community. Major items such as lot coverage, building height, parking required, front, side and rear yard set backs, overall density, green areas and open space requirements can differ substantially. This could allow parcels with similar zoning, size and shape but in separate communities to vary greatly in terms of permitted building area or number of units permitted.

Shape, topographic and open space or green area variances also affect the square foot of building area or number of units permitted. A parcel with a large stream or pond will generally not be permitted the same building area as a "dry" site of the same size. Other considerations including rental rates, retail sales prices and similar economic differences usually exist between the subject and the comparables that will also cause variation. Accordingly, the reviewer should be certain that the appraiser has considered the foregoing as applied to the subject and all of the comparables and not just simply relied upon a per acre or per square foot of land area common denominator. The sample grid also demonstrates how relying solely upon that method can produce wide value differences and a less, if not totally inaccurate, value opinion.

On the next page are commonly used denominators by type of planned development:

PROPERTY TYPE	DENOMINATOR
Apartment	per unit, per square foot or GBA* or # of units per acre
Office	per square foot of GBA
Retail	per square foot of GBA
Hotel	per room or per square foot of GBA
Industrial	per square foot of GBA or % of site coverage
Garage	per space
Mobile Home	per pad (home)
Nursing Home	per bed or per square foot of GBA
Townhomes	per unit, per square foot of GBA or density of units per acre
Single Family	per unit or density of units per acre, such as 1, 2, 4 or 6 to the acre
*Gross Building Area	

OTHER ITEMS:

1. Tax incentives impact
2. Temporary or interim use zoning
3. Subsurface, mineral rights,, subways, etc.
4. Depth chart method of value
5. Mixed zoning sites (sum of parts can exceed the whole)
6. Financing - typical rules of thumb?

CONCLUSION:

The foregoing has been designed to aid your review and to stimulate your thoughts and attitudes about the report you are reviewing.

When you have completed the review ask yourself these questions;

1. Is the report credible?
2. Has the appraiser been consistent throughout?
3. Is the report well documented?
4. Do you any unanswered questions?
5. Are you satisfied with the site's history?
6. Do you feel comfortable or uncomfortable with the comparables used, the adjustments made or absorption and representation about the demand for the site?
7. Do you need clarifications or supplemental from the appraiser?
8. Do you feel comfortable with approving the report?

The answers to the above should lead you to the proper course of action.

CHAPTER TWENTY-TWO

A SYSTEMATIC AND UNIFORM APPROACH TO THE COMMERCIAL APPRAISAL REVIEW PROCESS INTRODUCTION

Today appraisal reviews are being accorded more attention, are assuming positions of greater importance in the formulation of investment decisions and the performance of due diligence. With the increased importance and attention goes the need to develop a systematic and uniform approach to the appraisal review process. The purpose of this chapter is to offer one way of developing a standardized appraisal review and underwriting tool for income or commercial real estate. The suggested tool is the Commercial Appraisal Review Form (4002) which has been adopted and approved by the National Association of Review Appraisers and Mortgage Underwriters. The Commercial Appraisal Review Form offers a standardized format which will create a disciplined, timely, consistent and equitable approach toward the review process. It can expedite the review process, and can document and communicate the results of the review function to the end user.

CURRENT USE Of FORM 4002

Many of the current forms in use are primarily "checklists" which focus only upon an accounting of the appraisal report content. Some of them do not rate the quality of and the analyses contained in the report, nor do they develop the discipline needed

COMMERCIAL APPRAISAL REVIEW FORM

The appraisal report which is the subject of this review is briefly identified and described as follows:

Name of Project/Property _____

Location/Legal _____

Type of Property _____ ☐ Existing ☐ Proposed Construction

Name of Appraiser _____ Telephone _____

Address _____

Report Addressed to: _____ Telephone _____

Address _____

Type of Appraisal Report: ☐ Narrative ☐ Printed Form ☐ Other (identify) _____

Section I – Purpose and Function of Appraisal

Value Sought: ☐ Market Value ☐ Other (identify) _____	Date of Value: ☐ Current ☐ Future ☐ Past	
	Definitions Given For: ☐ Value Sought ☐ Interest To Be Valued	
Interests Valued: ☐ Fee Simple ☐ Leased Interest	☐ Market Rent ☐ Other (identify) _____	
☐ Easements ☐ Other (identify) _____	Assumptions and ☐ Standard ☐ Consistent with	
Real Estate Valued ☐ Land ☐ Improvements	Limiting Conditions: Valuation Process	
☐ Ground Lease ☐ Personal Property	☐ Third Party ☐ Unreasonable or	
☐ Other (identify) _____	Report Excessive	

Comments: _____

Section II – Property Identification, Ownership and Assessment

Does the report adequately contain or identify:	Yes	No	N/A		Yes	No	N/A
Property Location/Address	☐	☐	☐	Owners of Record	☐	☐	☐
Legal Description	☐	☐	☐	History of Ownership	☐	☐	☐
Real Estate Tax Information	☐	☐	☐	If Applicable to Subject Property:			
Assessments, Bonds, etc.	☐	☐	☐	Amount of Purchase Price ☐	$_____		
Existence of:				Pending Sales Price ☐	$_____		
Deed Restrictions	☐	☐	☐	Asking Price ☐	$_____		
Covenants, Conditions, Restrictions	☐	☐	☐	Option Price ☐	$_____		
Moratoriums	☐	☐	☐	Other ☐	$_____		

Comments: _____

Section III – Location Analysis

Does report adequately describe or identify:		Does report:	
Region	☐ Yes ☐ No ☐ N/A	Sum up and rate the area	☐ Yes ☐ No ☐ N/A
City	☐ Yes ☐ No ☐ N/A	Identify and discuss important trends	☐ Yes ☐ No ☐ N/A
Neighborhood	☐ Yes ☐ No ☐ N/A	Identify nuisances or hazards	☐ Yes ☐ No ☐ N/A

Comments: _____

Section IV – Property Description

Comment upon the descriptions and analysis of the following:

SITE:		IMPROVEMENTS:	
		Adequate description of physical features	☐ Yes ☐ No
Adequate description of physical features	☐ Yes ☐ No	Attention given to:	
Identification of encumbrances	☐ Yes ☐ No	Quality	☐ Yes ☐ No
Does report state adequacy of site for existing or		Functional Utility and Appeal	☐ Yes ☐ No
proposed use	☐ Yes ☐ No	Age	☐ Yes ☐ No
Utilities available	☐ Yes ☐ No	Condition	☐ Yes ☐ No
Special Problems:		Hazardous Conditions	☐ Yes ☐ No
Flood	☐ Yes ☐ No	ZONING:	
Environmental Hazards, Siesmic, Toxic etc.	☐ Yes ☐ No	Statement	☐ Yes ☐ No
Other (identify) _____	☐ Yes ☐ No	Definition	☐ Yes ☐ No

Comments: _____

Section V – Highest and Best Use

Definition	☐ Yes ☐ No	Does property conform to zoning and neighborhood	☐ Yes ☐ No
Components	☐ Yes ☐ No	Is use legal and physically possible	☐ Yes ☐ No
Conclusion of Highest and Best Use _____		Has the report in this or other sections discussed:	
Current Zoning _____		Marketability (supply-demand, market trends,	☐ Yes ☐ No
Status zoning change _____		absorption occupancy levels)	☐ Yes ☐ No
Status of building permit (if proposed construction) _____		Other (identify) _____	
Does report discuss feasibility/profitability	☐ Yes ☐ No	Were other studies/reports considered	☐ Yes ☐ No

Comments: _____

Review Form No. 4002

SECTION VI – Property Valuation

Comment and rate the approaches to value:

COST APPROACH:

	Satisfactory	Unsatisfactory
Format	☐	☐
Adequacy of data	☐	☐
Source of costs	☐	☐
Land value estimate	☐	☐
Estimated cost new	☐	☐
Depreciation estimate	☐	☐

SALES COMPARISON APPROACH:

	Satisfactory	Unsatisfactory
Format	☐	☐
Adequacy of data	☐	☐
Sources of data	☐	☐
Summary of sales table	☐	☐
Use of adjustment grid table	☐	☐
Comparative analysis of sales	☐	☐

INCOME CAPITALIZATION APPROACH:

	Satisfactory	Unsatisfactory
Format	☐	☐
Selection of proper capitalization method	☐	☐
Adequacy of data and support for:		
Comparable Rentals	☐	☐
Vacancy and Loss Factor	☐	☐
Operating History	☐	☐
Rent Roll	☐	☐
Income Estimate	☐	☐
Expense Estimate	☐	☐
Net Operating Income	☐	☐
Capitalization Rate	☐	☐

DISCOUNTED CASH FLOW ANALYSIS (DCF)

	Satisfactory	Unsatisfactory
Format	☐	☐
Adequacy of data and support for:		
Holding Period	☐	☐
Growth Rates	☐	☐
Discount Rate	☐	☐
Development of Cash Flow Estimates	☐	☐
Reversionary Value	☐	☐
Other Methods of Processing		
Income Stream (Mortgage Equity, Band of Investments, etc.)	☐	☐

RECONCILIATION:

Indicated values are:

Cost Approach	$_____
Sales Comparison Approach	$_____
Income Approach	$_____
DCF Analysis	$_____
Other (Pending Sale, etc.)	
Value Conclusion	$_____

Allocation as Follows:

Land	$_____
Improvements	$_____
Personal Property	$_____
Other	$_____
Total Value	$_____

Comments: _____
_____
_____
_____

Section VII – Other Report Requirements

Does report contain a certification	☐ Yes	☐ No
Is the report co-signed	☐ Yes	☐ No
Did principal appraiser sign report	☐ Yes	☐ No
Did principal appraiser personally inspect subject property	☐ Yes	☐ No
Does principal appraiser make statement of concurrence with value conclusion	☐ Yes	☐ No
Does report contain appraiser(s) qualifications	☐ Yes	☐ No

Section VIII – Final Rating of Appraisal

Report Format	Acceptable	Unacceptable
Readability and neatness	☐	☐
Mathematical accuracy	☐	☐
Exhibits (Photos, Maps, etc.)	☐	☐
Appraiser's analytical ability	☐	☐
Purpose and function of appraisal	☐	☐
Property identification	☐	☐
Locational analysis	☐	☐
Property Description:		
Site	☐	☐
Improvements	☐	☐
Highest and Best Use	☐	☐

Property Valuation:	Acceptable	Unacceptable
Feasibility/Profitability	☐	☐
Market Trends	☐	☐
Cost Approach	☐	☐
Sales Comparison Approach	☐	☐
Income Approach	☐	☐
DCF	☐	☐
Reconciliation	☐	☐
Date of Appraisal	☐	☐
Overall Rating of Appraisal	☐	☐

Brief Comments on Unacceptable Ratings: _____
_____
_____

Section IX – Reviewer's Conclusions – Recommendations

Scope of Review:

Read report	☐ Yes	☐ No
Interviewed appraiser	☐ Yes	☐ No
Field Review	☐ Yes	☐ No
Does the Reviewer concur with the soundness of conclusion:	☐ Yes	☐ No

If reviewer does not concur with the soundness of conclusion, then what is the recommended action:
☐ Totally reject appraisal
☐ Have appraiser rework, revise, update the appraisal
☐ Have another appraisal prepared by someone else
☐ Other

Concluding Comments: _____
_____
_____
_____

Reviewer's Signature _____ Date _____

Name of Reviewer _____

Position _____ Department _____

Address _____ Telephone _____

City, State, Zip _____

Review Form No. 4002

to lead the reviewer to a decision. In supporting the use of the Commercial Appraisal Review Form the following reasons are presented:

1. A form will develop a disciplined and uniform approach to each appraisal review. There is no systematic appraisal report format; therefore, a form will allow some partial reorganization and explanations of portions of the report being reviewed. As a result, the end user (client) will be provided with what is required, and a better understanding of the content of the appraisal report.

2. Many transactions require a very rapid review turnaround and the use of a form will expedite the process. 3. The form becomes a method of communication, and a permanent record. The review function bears heavy fiduciary and organizational responsibility; therefore, it must effectively provide a system of communicating the decisions and conclusions of the reviewer, and a way of retaining them for record keeping purposes.

THE DESIGN CONCEPT OF THE REVIEW FORM

An early lesson in the education and development of an appraiser is devoted to learning and understanding the appraisal process. The Commercial Review Form in this chapter employs the same concept which is to lead the reviewer through the appraisal report on a step-by-step basis. It develops a process which will lead to a decision, a recommendation or some other appropriate action.

Additionally, its format will force the reviewer to not only identify sections of the appraisal report (the "Checklist" aspect of the review), but to rate them and note their strengths and weaknesses as well. In order to assist the reviewer in analyzing the quality, completeness, consistency and accuracy of the appraisal, the review appraiser or loan underwriter should focus on the following items when conducting an appraisal review.

Section I Purpose and Function of the Appraisal

This section relates primarily to the introductory portion of the appraisal report; the emphasis is upon the determination of what is to be appraised and why.

Purpose of the appraisal

This is a brief statement of the purpose of the appraisal, usually to estimate the market value of the property.

Function of the appraisal use

What is the appraisal designed to do? i.e. Help the client make a decision in regards to a loan, sale, etc.

Definition of Market Value

Define the value to be reported. The definition used should be stated clearly so it is easily understood. It is preferable to include the source of the definition.

Property Rights Appraised

A statement and definition of the various rights being appraised, e.g., fee simple, fractional interest, leasehold interest, easement, subsurface rights, and water rights. It is preferable to include the source of the definition.

Section II Property Identification, Ownership and Assessment

Items under this heading are customarily part of every appraisal report. Property identification is required as well as encumbrances and liens recognized.

Identification of the Property

This is a brief statement to acquaint the reader with the property. It should contain an accurate street address and complete legal description that includes the city and/or county and state along with the recording data. A lengthy legal description may be included as an exhibit in the addenda and simply referred to at this point.

Assessment and Taxes

In addition to recording the current assessed value, tax rate, and taxes, there should be a review of the past three to five years and probable future projection with reasons. (Compare taxes levied on subject property with taxes levied on properties in the neighborhood and competing areas.)

Statement of Ownership of the Appraised Property - History

A brief history of the property must be included to provide specific background data pertaining to the price paid, dates of original acquisition, construction or remodeling, occupancies, changes in occupancy or use, former and present ownership, reputation, prestige, lease terms, etc. If the property has sold during the past five years, the date of sale and consideration must be reported.

Exhibit A.

COMMERCIAL APPRAISAL REVIEW FORM

The appraisal report which is the subject of this review is briefly identified and described as follows

Name of Project/Property _____

Location/Legal _____

Type of Property _____ ☐ Existing ☐ Proposed Construction

Name of Appraiser _____ Telephone _____

Address _____

Report Addressed to _____ Telephone _____

Address _____

Type of Appraisal Report ☐ Narrative ☐ Printed Form ☐ Other (identify) _____

Exhibit B. Section I

Value Sought	☐ Market Value ☐ Other (identify)	Date of Value	☐ Current	☐ Future ☐ Past
		Definitions Given For	☐ Value Sought	☐ Interest To Be Valued
Interests Valued	☐ Fee Simple ☐ Leased Interest		☐ Market Rent	☐ Other (identify)
	☐ Easements ☐ Other (identify)	Assumptions and	☐ Standard	☐ Consistent with
Real Estate Valued	☐ Land ☐ Improvements	Limiting Conditions		Valuation Process
	☐ Ground Lease ☐ Personal Property		☐ Third Party	☐ Unreasonable or
	☐ Other (identify)		Report	Excessive
Comments				

Exhibit C. Section II

Section II   Property, Identification, Ownership and Assessment

	Yes	No	N/A		Yes	No	N/A
Does the report adequately contain or identify							
Property Location/Address	☐	☐	☐	Owners of Record	☐	☐	☐
Legal Description	☐	☐	☐	History of Ownership	☐	☐	☐
Real Estate Tax Information	☐	☐	☐	If Applicable to Subject Property			
Assessments, Bonds, etc	☐	☐	☐	Amount of Purchase Price	☐ $		
Existence of				Pending Sales Price	☐ $		
Deed Restrictions	☐	☐	☐	Asking Price	☐ $		
Covenants, Conditions, Restrictions	☐	☐	☐	Option Price	☐ $		
Moratoriums	☐	☐	☐	Other	☐ $		
Comments							

Exhibit D. Section III

Section III   Location Analysis

Does report adequately describe or identify		Does report
Region	☐ Yes ☐ No ☐ N/A	Sum up and rate the area ☐ Yes ☐ No ☐ N/A
City	☐ Yes ☐ No ☐ N/A	Identify and discuss important trends ☐ Yes ☐ No ☐ N/A
Neighborhood	☐ Yes ☐ No ☐ N/A	Identify nuisances or hazards ☐ Yes ☐ No ☐ N/A
Comments		

Section III Location Analysis

This can be a rather bulky area of a report, and sometimes its content is superfluous. However, it is important that the appraiser recognizes critical locational factors and accesses their impact on the subject properties value and marketability:

Region or City Data

Starting with a brief but specific description of the geographical location, this section should then consider the four basic factors that influence value. The material gathered should be germane to the property being appraised. Emphasize facts which you consider indicative of a trend affecting the area or which may be significant for the probable future marketability or economic life of the appraised property. If rural, include area location, climate, rainfall, type of farming, regional markets, etc.

Avoid public discourses. If statistical data of any length are considered desirable, include it in an exhibit and analyze it within the body of the report.

The section should terminate with a reasoned conclusion on the probable future of the city, general property values therein, and relationship of this future to the subject property.

Neighborhood Data

This section normally begins with a geographic delineation of the neighborhood. Identification of the boundaries of the neighborhood and the reasons for their selection are important.

Include a map relating the neighborhood to the adjoining areas and a separate occupancy (strip) map of the immediate vicinity. As in the City Data, the material selected for this section should help relate the present state of the neighborhood with the past and the future, particularly as it relates to the Principle of Change. If rural, distance and direction to principal markets available, size of farms, urban influences, general level of operators and their ability, labor supply, etc., should be considered. Depending on the type of property being appraised, any or all of the following items may be significant:

- Distance and direction from the central business district or employment centers
- Percent built up and history
- Reputation
- Population characteristics and income level
- Trends
- Class and variety of retail stores and merchandise offered
- Types of buildings and tenancies in properties immediately surrounding subject
- Vacancy rates
- Pedestrian traffic
- Competition, present and/or contemplated
- Inventory of available and proposed competing facilities
- Public transportation facilities
- Major traffic arteries
- Proximity to expressways, toll roads, and airports
- Availability of parking
- Community facilities, such as schools, places of worship, hospitals, recreation, etc.
- Labor supply and wage level
- Housing
- Availability, cost and adequacy of sewers, water, power, and other utilities.
- Transportation and shipping facilities.
- Conclusion about the life stage of the neighborhood and its probable future.
- External obsolescence, if any

All neighborhood factors that are considered in the three approaches to value should be explained and analyzed in this section. The concluding remarks of this section should indicate the probable future of the neighborhood, with reasons, and how this future will influence the value of similar properties and the subject in particular.

Section IV Property Description

The emphasis is on an adequate description of the subject property as well as a determination as to the acceptability of the site and improvements in the marketplace based upon their existing or proposed use.

Site Data:

The land should be accurately described to include both land-site description and land-site analysis.
- Dimensions and area
- Shape
- Easements
- Topography and drainage
- Soil and subsoil
- Availability and description of utilities
- Street improvements
- Location in block (corner or inside, etc.)
- Functional adequacy of the site
- Relationship of the subject site to its surrounding (is it typical)?
- Nuisances and hazards, including floodplain
- Railroad trackage, if available

If rural, describe soils, carrying capacities, uses and limitations.

A plot or sketch should be included or referred to at this point and included as an exhibit.

Description of Improvements

Improvements concerning character or type should be identified and described in some detail. An outline form is generally desirable. A plot plan or floor plan (or typical floor plan) should be included here or among the exhibits with a reference thereto at this point. Points to consider well include

- Current use or uses
- Age and condition
- Dimensions and area
- Design and layout, number of units, rooms, etc.
- Details of construction and finish, including quality and workmanship
- Equipment, fixtures, etc.
- Deferred maintenance or needed repairs
- Discussion of functional utility or inutility
- Conclusion of effective age, remaining economic life, and remaining physical life, and support thereof or reference to support in other sections of report
- Yard or site improvements (if not included under land or site data section)

All physical and functional factors of the improvements influencing value as indicated in the various approaches to value should be analyzed and discussed in this section.

Zoning

Official zoning code designation pertinent to the subject property and all market data should be set forth in the report together with permitted uses, parking requirements, and other pertinent factors specified in the ordinance. If the full text of a section of the ordinance is required, it should be placed in the exhibit section of the report, with an analysis in the body of the report. A statement should be included that improvements represent a conforming or nonconforming use (if this can be determined).

Private or public restriction, if any, should be explained.

Exhibit E. Section IV

Section IV — Property Description		
Comment upon the descriptions and analysis of the following:	IMPROVEMENTS:	
SITE:	Adequate description of physical features	☐ Yes ☐ No
Adequate description of physical features ☐ Yes ☐ No	Attention given to:	
Identification of encumbrances ☐ Yes ☐ No	Quality	☐ Yes ☐ No
Does report state adequacy of site for existing or	Functional Utility and Appeal	☐ Yes ☐ No
proposed use ☐ Yes ☐ No	Age	☐ Yes ☐ No
Utilities available ☐ Yes ☐ No	Condition	☐ Yes ☐ No
Special Problems:	Hazardous Conditions	☐ Yes ☐ No
Flood ☐ Yes ☐ No	ZONING:	
Environmental Hazards, Siesmic, Toxic etc. ☐ Yes ☐ No	Statement	☐ Yes ☐ No
Other (identify) _____ ☐ Yes ☐ No	Definition	☐ Yes ☐ No
Comments: _____		

Exhibit F. Section V

Section V — Highest and Best Use		
Definition ☐ Yes ☐ No	Does property conform to zoning and neighborhood	☐ Yes ☐ No
Components ☐ Yes ☐ No	Is use legal and physically possible	☐ Yes ☐ No
Conclusion of Highest and Best Use _____	Has the report in this or other sections discussed	
Current Zoning _____	Marketability (supply-demand, market trends,	☐ Yes ☐ No
Status zoning change _____	absorption occupancy levels)	☐ Yes ☐ No
Status of building permit (if proposed construction) _____	Other (identify)	
Does report discuss feasibility/profitability ☐ Yes ☐ No	Were other studies/reports considered	☐ Yes ☐ No
Comments _____		

Review Form No. 4002

Exhibit G. Section VI

SECTION VI — Property Valuation					
Comment and rate the approaches to value:					
COST APPROACH:	Satisfactory	Unsatisfactory	**DISCOUNTED CASH FLOW ANALYSIS (DCF)**	Satisfactory	Unsatisfactory
Format	☐	☐	Format	☐	☐
Adequacy of data	☐	☐	Adequacy of data and support for:		
Source of costs	☐	☐	Holding Period	☐	☐
Land value estimate	☐	☐	Growth Rates	☐	☐
Estimated cost new	☐	☐	Discount Rate	☐	☐
Depreciation estimate	☐	☐	Development of Cash Flow Estimates	☐	☐
SALES COMPARISON APPROACH:			Reversionary Value	☐	☐
Format	☐	☐	Other Methods of Processing		
Adequacy of data	☐	☐	Income Stream (Mortgage Equity,		
Sources of data	☐	☐	Band of Investments, etc.)	☐	☐
Summary of sales table	☐	☐	**RECONCILIATION:**		
Use of adjustment grid table	☐	☐	Indicated values are:		
Comparative analysis of sales	☐	☐	Cost Approach	$ _____	
INCOME CAPITALIZATION APPROACH:			Sales Comparison Approach	$ _____	
Format	☐	☐	Income Approach	$ _____	
Selection of proper capitalization			DCF Analysis	$ _____	
method	☐	☐	Other (Pending Sale, etc.)		
Adequacy of data and support for:			Value Conclusion		$ _____
Comparable Rentals	☐	☐	Allocation as Follows:		
Vacancy and Loss Factor	☐	☐	Land	$ _____	
Operating History	☐	☐	Improvements	$ _____	
Rent Roll	☐	☐	Personal Property	$ _____	
Income Estimate	☐	☐	Other	$ _____	
Expense Estimate	☐	☐	Total Value		$ _____
Net Operating Income	☐	☐			
Capitalization Rate	☐	☐			
Comments: _____					

Section V Highest and Best Use

A proper definition of the term highest and best use (and source of definition). The highest and best use of land as legally permitted, "as if vacant," should be demonstrated, including not only the kind of use but the size and quality of buildings as well, leading to a convincing conclusion on highest and best use. If the market recognizes that rezoning is a possibility, this fact should be discussed and evaluated. The highest and best use of the property "as improved" should be analyzed, along with any reasonably probable alternate uses. For highest and best use of both land as if vacant and property as improved, a use must meet four criteria. The criteria are that the highest and best use must be 1) physically possible, 2) legally permissible, 3) financially feasible, and 4) maximally productive. The variances of the existing improvements from this ideal should be pointed out and a conclusion reached whether such improvements add to or detract from the value of the land "as if vacant." Any and all of the applicable basic principles of real estate valuation should be considered. Where applicable, mathematical support of the conclusion is desirable. If rural, correlate to a community, climate, rainfall, markets, improvements and land use, and probability of change in use. Segregate use to specific types of farming e.g., dairy, cash grain, etc.

Section VI Property Valuation

The appraiser should select good comparable data and handle it well. Comparable data should adequately support the value and marketability of the subject property. The reviewer should briefly note the strengths and weaknesses of each approach to value and give special consideration to the following factors.

The Cost Approach

A.   Give a brief explanation of the approach.
B.   Estimated cost new:
Estimate and support cost new. Greater credence can be obtained by using two methods. If a cost service is used, the source material should be specifically identified. The unit price should be adequately analyzed and adjusted to the subject property, showing all calculations and specific sources thereof. If a cost estimator or contractor supplies cost figures, their expertise must be established. If reference is made to recently completed comparable structures, they must be identified and analyzed with appropriate adjustments made to the subject property.
C.   Show estimate of depreciated cost of improvements.
D.   Show recapitulation cost approach including breakdown of depreciation and summation.

Land Valuation

Land value is best indicated from sufficient, factual market data. Reduce data to pertinent unit(s) of comparison and justify the unit selected. Lead the reader logically to the conclusion of value. Explain and justify any adjustments based on careful market analysis including but not limited to time, conditions of sale, location, physical characteristics, and financing. The comparable sales and their adjustments to the subject property should be presented by an adequate narrative and a brief explanation of each adjustment and support thereof; an adjustment chart may be included. For the conclusion, the adjusted sale data should be reconciled into a final value estimate. The land residual approach should be used only in absence of comparative data and only when essential information is available to establish a sound base for a residual approach. Give legal recording data, method of verification of sales, and photographs of sales.

The Sales Comparison Approach

A. Explain the approach to value.
B. Comparable sales data:
1. It is not advisable to select for demonstration appraisal purpose a property for which market value can be supported by only one to two sales. If data is limited and not available in the immediate vicinity, data from similar areas may be used. If the market is not limited to a local market, sales in similar communities may be useful. A few well substantiated and comparable sales are preferable to many that are unreliable.
2. Comparable sales must be actual. They must be adequately described and analyzed in order to justify all adjustment factors. Suggested elements of comparison are conditions of sale, financing terms, market conditions (time), location, physical characteristics, and income characteristics. In addition, the legal source (book and page number, plus data of instrument) and the identity of the individual confirming the details of each comparable sale must be given.
3. All comparable sales involved in syndications should be analyzed to determine whether non-real estate items were included in the price.
C. Common Denominator:
1. At least one unit of comparison, or as many as are applicable within the scope of market data, must be described and used: square foot, front foot, per room, gross income multipliers, etc. The use of two or more such comparisons should result

in a reasonable bracket of value within which a reasoned conclusion on market value can be reached.

2. A comparison chart may be helpful for presenting the data and adjustments. It is not required, but used alone, without explanation of the reasoning and adjustments, it is inadequate.

The Income Capitalization Approach

A. Give a brief explanation of the approach.

B. Income

1. The actual income history of recent years and a current rent roll should be shown.

2. Using unit(s) of rental comparison (per square foot, apartment, room, etc.), estimate current market rental for the subject. The market analysis should present an in-depth study so that differences in rents between the subject and comparable properties are readily explainable and supportable by adjustments that are representative of factual data.

3. The section should conclude with a reasoned statement on the probable future of rental rates and occupancies.

4. All major existing leases must be reviewed. A synopsis of lengthy leases may be reported in the body of the report and a more complete statement outlining the details of the lease may be placed in the addenda.

5. With retail properties it may be desirable to consider the actual and potential retail sales volume and derive a reasonable income stream expectancy. The conclusions may be used to support an analysis relating gross sales income with current market and/or contract rent. This analysis may further be used as a means of relating income generated by percentage sales to current market rent.

C. Expense

1. The actual itemized statements of expenses for recent years should be shown. Usually these should be restated to reflect classifications to be used in the stabilized statement.

2. In narrative fashion, the individual expense items should be analyzed before developing a stabilized expense statement. In addition to a review of the past expense experience of the subject property, comparison is also recommended on an item-by-item basis with the expenses incurred by similar buildings in the immediate area; allowances may be made for anticpated increases in taxes or other items.
Care must be taken to exclude those items that may rightfully belong in the owner's statement but not in the appraiser's stabilized statement. The total expenses may be tested or supported by showing total expenses in a ratio to gross income to be similar to that of other comparable properties.

4. If any decision above is predicated on credit strength to tenancy, explain the basis for such consideration.

5. If there is surplus income due to excessive lease rental or lease percentage clause, explain your treatment of this income. If there is an income stream below market level, this should be explained and properly treated.

6. If a portion of the income stream is due to furniture or equipment (e.g., a furnished apartment house), explain and Justify your treatment of this income and allocate your final valuation as it may apply to real estate and chattels.

7. If income depends on capital expense, make appropriate adjustment.

8. The value contribution or negative aspects of non-market financing should be identified in terms of dollars.

Discounted Cash Flow Analysis (DCF)

DCF is not a new method, but is used more now due to computer technology available now. DCF is based on the principle of anticipation, i.e., value is created by the anticipation of future benefits. Discussed and supported should include:

A. Holding Period

B. Growth Rates

C. Discount Rate

D. Cash Flow Estimates

E. Reversionary Value etc.

Reconciliation

The purpose of reconciliation is to sum up the process of correlation that has taken place throughout the report and to develop the several value indications to a final value estimate. Reconciliation affords the appraiser an opportunity to consider the quantity and quality of the data available for examination under each approach, the inherent dangers and advantages of each approach, and the relevancy of each to the subject property and the appraisal problem. Explain any wide discrepancy but do not lead the reader to believe that complete agreement of the three approaches to value is mandatory. Demonstrate by sound reasoning the facts and interpretations which led to your final conclusion, bearing in mind the definition of value previously presented and the use of the report.

Addenda

Addenda are supplements to a report. Data directly pertinent to your narrative, such as comparable sales and other market data, and maps and sketches should be included in the body of the report unless they are too voluminous. The report should conclude with necessary supplementary exhibits, including all or selected appropriate items from the following list. All exhibits should present a professional appearance if the report is to be of professional caliber.

Exhibit H. Section VII

Section VII — Other Report Requirements					
Does report contain a certification	☐ Yes	☐ No	Does principal appraiser make state-		
Is the report co-signed	☐ Yes	☐ No	ment of concurrence with value		
Did principal appraiser sign report	☐ Yes	☐ No	conclusion	☐ Yes	☐ No
Did principal appraiser personally			Does report contain appraiser(s)		
inspect subject property	☐ Yes	☐ No	qualifications	☐ Yes	☐ No

Exhibit I. Section VIII

Section VIII — Final Rating of Appraisal					
	Acceptable	Unacceptable		Acceptable	Unacceptable
Report Format			Property Valuation		
Readability and neatness	☐	☐	Feasibility/Profitability	☐	☐
Mathematical accuracy	☐	☐	Market Trends	☐	☐
Exhibits (Photos, Maps, etc.)	☐	☐	Cost Approach	☐	☐
Appraiser's analytical ability	☐	☐	Sales Comparison Approach	☐	☐
Purpose and function of appraisal	☐	☐	Income Approach	☐	☐
Property identification	☐	☐	DCF	☐	☐
Locational analysis	☐	☐	Reconciliation	☐	☐
Property Description			Date of Appraisal	☐	☐
Site	☐	☐	Overall Rating of Appraisal	☐	☐
Improvements	☐	☐			
Highest and Best Use	☐	☐			
Brief Comments on Unacceptable Ratings					

Exhibit J. Section IX

Section IX — Reviewer's Conclusions / Recommendations			
Scope of Review			If reviewer does not concur with the soundness of conclusion,
Read report	☐ Yes	☐ No	then what is the recommended action:
Interviewed appraiser	☐ Yes	☐ No	☐ Totally reject appraisal
Field Review	☐ Yes	☐ No	☐ Have appraiser rework, revise, update the appraisal
Does the Reviewer concur with			☐ Have another appraisal prepared by someone else
the soundness of conclusion:	☐ Yes	☐ No	☐ Other
Concluding Comments			

Reviewer's Signature   Date
Name of Reviewer
Position   Department
Address   Telephone
City, State, Zip

           Review Form No. 4002

Section VII Other Report Requirements

This section covers other required items of an appraisal report, such as appraiser's certification, property inspection and the appraiser's qualifications. A very important decision must be made here ... does the reviewer accept or reject an appraisal when the principal appraiser has not inspected the subject or does not make a concurring statement concerning the value?

- Statement of the appraiser's qualification. - Appraiser's certification that:

• the appraiser has personally inspected the property,

• the appraiser has no represented or contemplated future interest in the property,

• the appraiser has no personal interest or bias with respect to the report, or the parties,

• the amount of the appraiser's fee is not contingent upon reporting a predetermined value or upon the amount of the value estimated, and the information contained in the report is true and accurate.

Section VIII Final Rating of Appraisal

This is a critical and important section which summarizes the entire review. The reviewer has completed the review form as well as an analysis of the appraisal report content. Now is the time for the final process which leads to a decision. The summation of acceptable or unacceptable ratings is intended to force the reviewer to rate the overall acceptability of the appraisal report.

Section IX Reviewer's Conclusions-Recommendations

This section is devoted to the scope of the reviewer's work, conclusions and recommended action. If the reviewer arrives at a different conclusion than the appraiser, the reviewer's data and analysis should support his or her opinion. If any material exceptions included in the appraisal review have not been resolved, these should be discussed with the loan committee. Material exceptions should be waived only with the specific written authorization of the loan committee. As a general rule, a loan should not be closed if the appraisal review includes any material exception. The loan committee may reject the loan application or accept it subject to amendment of the appraisal report.

CONCLUDING COMMENTS

The sections of the Commercial Appraisal Review Form are intended to flow, step-by-step, toward the final ratings in Section VII and the conclusions in Section IX. By adopting a systematic and uniform approach to the commercial appraisal review process - an institution can avoid costly appraisals that fail to comply with the policies and procedures set forth. More importantly, however, through rigorous appraisal review procedures, institutions can assure the soundness of their loan underwriting procedures and avoid significant losses that may occur when loan decisions are made based upon faulty appraisal information.

CHAPTER TWENTY-THREE

REVIEWING AN OFFICE BUILDING APPRAISAL REPORT

INTRODUCTION

An office building can be utilized solely by the owner in self-interest, or it can be owned as an investment, either single tenanted or multi-tenanted. This chapter deals primarily with the multi-tenanted office building that is held for investment purposes. Despite the numerous subsections of an appraisal report, there are really only two parts: Part One consists of all the pages preceding and including Highest and Best Use; Part Two consists of the pages of valuation techniques based on the conclusion of Highest and Best Use. The section titled HIGHEST AND BEST USE is the focal point of the appraisal. An error in judgment, a misinterpretation of data or insufficient data leads to a faulty conclusion of Highest and Best Use which in turn leads to a faulty value estimate. There should be no "boilerplate" narration within the appraisal report. At the end of each subsection, you should ask yourself "So what? How does this affect the property?" A well prepared subsection does not necessitate these questions.

Property Rights Identified
Value Defined
Assumptions & Limiting Conditions
City or Regional Description
Supply and Demand
Neighborhood Description
Site Description
Improvement Description

HIGHEST AND AND BEST USE

Cost Approach
Income Approach
Market Approach
Reconciliation

VALUE CONCLUSION

There is a specific reason for the order of sections in an appraisal report. The appraisal report begins with a macro view. With each section, the study becomes more specific and focused toward the property, as graphed in Exhibit 1 at left. In conjunction with the review of an office building appraisal,

The following pages are overviews of the seven steps in the review process:

1. Develop a clear mental picture of the property by examining the photographs of the subject and reading the Summary of Salient Facts.
2. Denote the type of value the appraiser purports to conclude.
3. Identify the ownership rights being appraised.
4. Review the assumptions and limiting conditions.
5. Check for inconsistency throughout the report of base data. A chart for comparison between sections works well. (See Exhibit 2 on page xxx)
6. Begin reading from the city description through highest and best use. To identify the factors that influence risk and affect values, five significant variables are studied and analyzed in these subsections: market conditions, investment climate, the legal environment, the sociological environment and quality and competitiveness of the subject.
7. Study the various approaches to value. To estimate the price that a rational, knowledgeable buyer would pay for the property, the constraints, restrictions and the risk and return are evaluated.

APPROPRIATE DEFINITION OF VALUE AND PROPERTY RIGHTS APPRAISED

Definition of Value: Most appraisals begin with a definition of market value which is synonymous with "value in exchange." There are four components which are crucial to determine if the value reported equates to market value. These components are:

1. Most probable price the property will bring if offered for sale on the open market;
2. Given a reasonable time exposed to the open market;
3. Buyer and seller are knowledgeable and neither being under undue duress; and
4. Price paid is in cash or its equivalent.

Has the appraiser been consistent in the definition of the purported value, the analysis, and the final value estimate? The reviewer should understand each component of market value.

Component 1: Most probable price the property will bring if offered for sale on the open market.

This phrase means that market value ASSUMES a sale of the property. Watch for add-on phrases that may indicate that the appraiser has not treated the property as though it would be placed on the market for sale. Some red flags may include:

- "market value as the company headquarters of ZYX Corp."
- "market value as currently occupied by the owner."

These phrases indicate the appraiser may have estimated "value in use" rather than "value in exchange." Both types of value are common and are appropriate for many purposes, including loan underwriting. But "value in use" does not presume a sale. For example, when an office building is owner-occupied, particularly as a company headquarters, the quality of the improvements may prove to be a super adequacy when the current occupant vacates the premises and the facility is offered for sale on the open market. Forms of super adequacies include open stairwells between office levels, commercial kitchens and executive elevators. Although costly to install and functionally useful to the occupant,

EXHIBIT 2
CONSISTENCY CHECKLIST

REPORT SUBSECTIONS

Checklist	Letter Transmittal	Summary of Salient Data	Reconciliation	Site Description	Highest and Best Use	Site Valuation	Improvement Description	Cost Approach	Income Approach	Market Approach
Date of Report:	x	x	x							
Date of Valuation:	x	x	x							
Site Size:				x		x	x	x	x	x
Zoning:				x	x	x				
Age of Buildings:							x	x	x	x
Number of Floors:							x	x	x	x
Gross Building Area							x	x	x	x
Net Rentable Area:							x	x	x	x
Parking Spaces: Garage:							x	x	x	x
Uncovered:							x	x	x	x

VALUE CONCLUSIONS

	Site Valuation	Cost Approach	Income Approach	Market Approach	Reconciliation
Land Value	x	x			x
Property Value	x	x	x	x	x

those items may have little or no contributory value when the building is sold (unless the occupant remains as a tenant paying adequate rent to reflect those features). Value in use would conclude contributory value of these special building features. Value in exchange would not.

Component 2: Given a reasonable time exposed to the open market.

What is a reasonable time? A "reasonable time" varies from city to city, neighborhood to neighborhood, and from year to year as the balance between supply and demand change or economic conditions change. The support for a "reasonable time" comes from the improved sales utilized. The length of time an office building was listed before it sold and the relationship of the actual price paid and the listing price provides an indication of market behavior and demand. Of paramount significance is whether the economic climate changed or is now about to change which would indicate a shortening or lengthening of the anticipated exposure on the open market to constitute a reasonable time. When the appraisal states "presuming a sale within 30 days,?' It may be an indication that liquidation value was concluded rather than market value. Check the improved sales and see how long they were listed for sale before the transaction occurred. Perhaps they all sold within 45 days. Check the listings. If properties have been listed for a short time, then the 30 day assumption is the appraiser's opinion of "a reasonable time" for this property to be on the open market due to its superior characteristics (physical, economic or locational) as compared to the comparables that took 45 days to accomplish a sale.

If the listings have been on the market for two to eight months, then there is the inference that the appraiser is presuming a forced sale and the value would be equivalent to liquidation value.

And what if the reverse were found? Say the sales utilized had been listed for six or eight months, and all of the current listings had been offered on the market for less than two months. Superficially at least, it would appear that the market has changed, sale activity is expected to accelerate and therefore the 30 day timeline is reasonable. The reviewer should check to see if this correlates with the trends discussed in the area, neighborhood description and the supply and demand analysis.

One of the special assumptions may have been that the appraiser was to assume a sale within 30 days. That may be a red flag implying a liquidation value. A call to the appraiser may be warranted to make certain that your understanding of the value reported is consistent with the value estimated by the appraiser.

Component 3: Buyer and seller are knowledgeable and neither are under undue duress.

How does one know if the buyer and seller are knowledgeable? Foreign investors have paid premium prices for office buildings that Americans contend do not represent market value. Are these transactions dismissed presuming the buyer is not knowledgeable? The difference in prices paid by one investment group versus another does not necessarily reflect ignorance, but rather different investment criteria. As long as there are enough buyers with the same investment parameters to constitute "a market", then the prices paid probably constitute market value to that investment group. Part of the appraiser's task is to identify the market for a given property. Is it a foreign or domestic pension fund, an individual, a corporation, and so forth? The criteria of establishing value and the risk-return preferences are different for an individual versus a pension fund or versus a corporation. Obvious factors would include the appreciation expectations, tax shelter benefits, and financial leverage. Has the appraiser evaluated investment grade properties based on the criteria of buyers of that property type? Investment criteria that would be appropriate for a $150 million high-rise office building been mistakenly applied to a 30 year old, 15,000 square foot office building? The problem of identifying buyers or sellers as being "knowledgeable" can not be a blanket assumption based solely on name recognition. The level of knowledge is measured on a transaction by transaction basis. For example, a major corporation purchased a suburban garden-office complex and assumed parking was adequate. It later turned out that the city had granted a temporary variance at the time of construction to give the developer time to buy additional land for parking or make other arrangements. The buyer was unaware and when the variance expired, the city notified the new owner that 16,000 square feet of the complex could not be occupied for office usage. Other examples of not being knowledgeable at the time of sale would include:

- The buyer saying, "I STOLE the property" only to find out that the buyer did not realize that the frontage street was scheduled to undergo major reconstruction in two months and, due to access problems, resulted in lost tenants and reduced income during the construction period. The buyer actually paid more for the property than he would have if he had taken this basic information into consideration.
- A seller sells a three-story, 40-year old brick office building and thinks he has 'SCALPED' the buyer. The buyer on the other hand recognized that the land was worth more than the building and proceeded to demolish the existing improvements and construct a 50-story office building. The sale price was less than the value of the land as though vacant because the seller based his asking price on the income generating ability of the existing building - unaware of the high land value.

Component 4: Price paid is in cash or its equivalent.

Has the appraiser properly computed the variance between cash and financing worth? Has the appraiser properly computed cash equivalences for the improved sales utilized as comparables?

Property Rights Appraised

The property rights appraised are the legal rights of an owner or a tenant. For a multi-tenanted office building, the rights most commonly valued are those constituting the owner's position, the "leased fee estate", which is the same as saying "the value of the fee simple estate, subject to the leases."

A tenant's rights may also have considerable value, particularly if the lease terms are significantly advantageous to the tenant. The tenant's position is referred to as the "leasehold estate".

The sum of the leasehold estate and the leased fee estate do not necessarily equate to the value of the fee simple estate. Sometimes an appraisal will state, "We have appraised the property for market value without consideration of the existing leases." The reviewer should recognize this as a red flag. Once an office is leased, the owner has given up some of his rights (temporarily, for the term of the lease) and the value of his ownership rights or interest is directly related to the leases in effect.

Has the appraiser identified all of the ownership rights? The owner of the building may not be the owner of the site. Does the income statement include a deduction for ground rent? What does the ground owner get? Some ground leases require not only a base rental on the land but also a percentage of the income generated by the leasing of the office building. What about the lender? Participating mortgages are common. Have the lender's rights to receive a portion of the cash flow and share of the proceeds at the time of reversion been considered?

ASSUMPTIONS AND LIMITING CONDITIONS

It is essential to read all of the assumptions and limiting conditions for clues of what was or was not taken into consideration. For example:

1. Does the appraiser know the facility is free of asbestos, or does the appraiser "assume" there is no asbestos and the value reported reflects this assumption? This is an important consideration for appraisals of office buildings constructed prior to 1971. In fact, there are cases of the problem occurring in buildings constructed as recently as 1978 due to leftovers of materials being used in the later years.
2. Does the reported value reflect "after" certain improvements are made? How long will renovation construction affect the income production? Will it require additional releasing time and expense? Will renovation take the building out of production for eight months plus releasing time?

There is a common catchall phrase used "...these assumptions and limiting conditions as well as any others set forth in the text of the report..." Therefore, be cognizant of and specifically look for special assumptions in the site description, highest and best use section, improvement description and the approaches to value.

CITY OR REGIONAL DESCRIPTION

A good overview can be brief but valuable in its insightfulness to catch the pulse of a city. What makes the city tick and how is the office market affected? Change is constant and sometimes nearly indiscernible. The appraiser's task is to identify and evaluate the sometimes subtle changes as they may affect the property. This section (based on past, present and future knowns and perceptions) should present the continued and anticipated economics of the city. At a minimum, look for:

- Balance between industries;
- Employment changes;
- Physical changes that will affect future growth;
- Change in sociological pressures; and
- Trends of office building development.

Furthermore, consider the following:

1. Is the economic vitality of the city dependent upon one or two particular industries? What changes are anticipated in the future? What is the sociopolitical environment concerning Is a no-growth policy advocated?

2. What is the economic health and what affects specific real estate sectors: hotels, shopping centers, apartments, office buildings and so forth.

3. Does the report reflect recitation without evaluative analysis of the secondary data sources? Does it relate in a useful manner to the subject and its analysis?

4. How current is the primary or secondary data reported? Is it relevant or do you find yourself asking "So what?" Does it reflect error of omission (intentional or otherwise)?

5. When employing secondary data or forecasts, has the appraiser provided commentary as to his/her evaluation of this secondary source? Can the review appraiser distinguish between the opinions from secondary sources (planning departments, etc.) and the author?

6. There are correlations between employment growth (specifically white collar) and the demand for office space. Is this addressed? Do the employment statistics indicate increasing or decreasing service industry domination?

7. Do transportation routes preclude commercial development in certain sectors? Are transportation routes under construction anticipated to provide the impetus for a shift of white

collar activities?

8. Does this city have the ability to compete with other cities for major office users?

SUPPLY AND DEMAND - OFFICE SECTOR

Appraisers place this in various sections of the report. I prefer that this section follow the City Description as it focuses on a particular type of real estate in the city and helps to provide a foundation on which to assess the competitive ranking of the neighborhood. This section should consist of two parts: a citywide analysis and an analysis of the market sector in which the property competes. The market sector boundaries do not necessarily correspond with the neighborhood boundaries. The basic information to be presented typically includes:

Citywide Supply: Number of market sectors and competitive profile of each; Current inventory of class A, B and C space; Under construction of class A, B and C space; and Proposed construction of class A, B and C space.

Citywide Demand:

Historical absorption of class A, B and C space;
Anticipated absorption of class A, B and C space;
Current and historical rental rates of class A, B and C space; and
Anticipated rental rates of class A, B and C space.

Analysis:

How much office space has this city absorbed in the last 10 years? How many years, from peak to peak, is the city's office market cycle? Where is the city, on the curve of the cycle, as of the writing of the report? In reviewing the projections, has the appraiser provided the basis for supporting those projections? Do they correspond and are they consistent with the economic data and conclusions in the City Description? For example: What effect does the increased or decreased employment base have on future absorption levels? Is there pent-up demand? Is there evidence of a shift in popularity between various office sectors?

The same basic outline should be presented for the specific market sector in which the property is located. Frequently overlooked is the amount of space available to sublease.

NEIGHBORHOOD DESCRIPTION

The neighborhood description should convey how the office tenants and office buyers perceive the locale.

1. How old is the neighborhood and what is the composition? Is this an area that peaked 15 years ago? Is this office building the first new building proposed in seven years? If so, why is the area reviving, or is it? Is this an underdeveloped area? What physical, social, governmental and sociopolitical pressures are influencing its development?
2. Where is the competition? How does the property rank in terms of its ability to compete? How will the property compete in five years? Is it in the path of growth?
3. Are there any adverse influences encroaching or infiltrating the neighborhood?
4. How accessible is the neighborhood to major thoroughfares, shopping facilities and restaurants? What is the proximity to complimentary service sectors (couriers, copy shops, travel agencies, restaurants)? For instance, medical office buildings are typically situated near hospitals.

SITE DESCRIPTION

Areas of concern for the reviewer include the physical, legal, and political constraints that affect the property. This is of crucial significance when reviewing a report for a proposed office building. Information derived in this section provides much of the basis for the highest and best use analysis. Some particular items that should not be overlooked during the review are:

1. Ratio of land to building. Is there excess land or an inappropriate use of the site? For example, is there an office building of 800,000 square feet on a parcel that is legally, appropriately and physically adequate to serve as a site for 1.5 million square feet of building?
2. Zoning. Is there confusion in the report about what to do with a property that has mixed zoning and is affected by a comprehensive plan that designates the property for uses different from those listed in the current zoning ordinance?
   Does the appraiser talk about the likelihood of developing the property with one use or a combination of uses under the guidelines of the zoning? The reviewer needs to be aware that "use" is one of the elements that CREATES value. The presumed usage of the site will affect the selection of land comparables and the ultimate value ascribed to the site.
3. Utilities. The fact that utility lines are readily available at the perimeter of the site does not mean that the capacity is sufficient for a new building. A city may have imposed a sewer moratorium until a new treatment plant is constructed. An appraiser will usually ask the developer for a letter of confirmation from the appropriate jurisdiction if the utility issue is questionable. If the appraisal does not address this or there are bold caveats in this section that ASSUME utility availability, then the reviewer should confirm the facts.
4. Topography. In certain areas of the country, this can be a major issue. Some regional problems may include: lava flows, granite (which may require extensive blasting), high water tables, fault zones in earthquake sensitive areas, erosion or mud slides, and flood zones.

5. Location. Access to a property, taking into consideration one way streets, left turning barriers, and traffic volume is important to an office building. Are there street improvements planned that will enhance or detract from the current location of the site? Will the property be subject to condemnation proceedings and a loss of land area when the improvements are made?

   How far, in terms of walking distance as well as driving time, are other office buildings, restaurants and shopping facilities?
6. Was a title report reviewed for easements and deed restrictions that may adversely affect the property?

DESCRIPTION OF IMPROVEMENTS

This section of the report should provide a good mental image of the property and address physical deterioration and functional obsolescence.

The reviewer has previously checked the square footages for consistency with other sections by using the check sheet (see Exhibit 2 on page xxx). Does the narrative description of the property correspond with the pictures? Do you have a different impression of the type and condition of the building? A common problem for the reviewer is knowing what square footage figures have actually been used by the appraiser. Has the appraiser been clear? There are local customs and phrasing utilized in the leasing of office buildings. BOMA (Building Owners Management Association) measurements may or may not be used in various sectors of the country. Whatever standard is reflected by the market should be utilized in the appraisal. The appraiser must apply a consistent method in calculating the floor-by-floor rentable area. Some common phrases encountered include the following. The definitions may or may not be used in general practice in a particular sector of the country. They are provided as a general guide for the reviewer.

Gross building area:

Total floor area excluding un-enclosed areas, measured from the exterior of the walls.

Gross leasable area:

Typically used for shopping centers, but is used in some sections of the country for office buildings. It comprises the total floor area designed for the occupancy and exclusive use of tenants, including basements and mezzanines. It is measured from the center of joint partitioning to outside wall surfaces.

Net usable (net rentable) area:

Area actually occupied by a tenant.

Rentable area:

Defined and measured differently from city to city. Generally, the net rentable area plus a pro rata share of the restroom areas, elevator lobbies and corridors (excluding elevator shafts, stairwells and air ducts).

BOMA defines this as the area measured from the inside finished surface of the dominant portion of the permanent outer building wall, excluding any major vertical penetrations. This includes restrooms, janitorial and equipment rooms, and excludes elevators, shafts and stairwells.

Load factor or add-on factor:

The percentage difference between gross square footage and rentable square footage. This figure is applied to the rentable square footage of a tenant that occupies a partial floor.

Common area core factor or loss factor:

The percentage difference between usable (net) rentable square footage and rentable square footage. This figure is applied to the usable (net) rentable square footage, usually applicable to all tenants.

Efficiency ratio:
Ratio between net rentable square footage and gross square footage.

Physical deterioration:
One of the most frequently overlooked items is deferred maintenance and the cost to cure. When was the last time the lobby and hallway carpeting was replaced, the wallpaper replaced, common areas painted? When was the last time the roof was resurfaced and the parking lot repaired or resurfaced? An appraiser seldom has structural engineering or architectural background, and it is not reasonable to expect him or her to technically analyze a building as though they did. But some effort to ascertain the condition of the facility is reasonable.

What are some of the questions that a potential buyer may ask during the initial stages of due diligence, and has the appraiser considered them? When analyzing old buildings, appraisers may be asked to hire engineers and architects for specific studies. This is also typical where topographical problems are known to exist, where asbestos is suspected, when renovation or restoration is considered and so forth. In connection with these studies, has the appraiser made some special assumptions? In a renovation or restoration project, the studies may only address the problems and costs of moving walls and adding stairwells. Has the appraiser also considered old and inefficient elevators? Would a buyer of the building account for the cost to replace them? Does a boiler need to be replaced or overhauled ? For a newer office building, the focus of the buyer is on the short-lived items. There comes a time with every building when capital expenditures are necessary. That point in time will be dependent on a variety of factors: weather conditions, the quality of the building components, HVAC design and quality, and ongoing maintenance program. Typically in buildings of seven years and older, comments will be included that address the observable condition of the roof surface, gutters, parking surface, exterior paint, common areas, and problems resulting from ground settlement. In some instances, the effects of ground settlement may be severe. For example, utility lines that extend from the street underneath the surface parking area to the building can be broken or become misaligned. If there is detailed historical information on the property, the history of the capital improvements that have been made in the last five years can be summarized. A well managed property will also have a schedule of major capital improvements to be implemented in the next year or two. This information helps to provide a better basis of deductions in the income approach and cost approach. Specifically in the income approach, the amount of reserves to apply, and the amount of annual maintenance cost can be supported as well as the deferred maintenance cost that may be deducted in year one or directly from the concluded value. In the cost approach, these figures are basic to calculating the amount of deferred maintenance and the incurable physical deterioration.

Functional Obsolescence:

The functional utility of a building and parking facilities is paramount to its saleability. In older buildings, the ratio of net rentable area to gross area is typically lower than in new buildings due to the columnar spacing, support area necessary for elevator shafts, and so forth.

In any building, regardless of age, floor plans illustrating where tenants are located should be reviewed. Problems with design and layout created by intrusive columns will be evident. Also the building may have been leased in such a way that there are irregular shaped spaces remaining that will be difficult to lease. This may affect the vacancy rate and the absorption rate estimated in the Income Approach. In the Cost Approach, it may constitute curable functional obsolescence. Parking ratios need to be considered. One cannot assume there is adequate parking by stating that the building exists and the zoning would have required adequate parking. Change is constant and no where is it more evident than in the continuous changes in zoning regulations. In years past, a 1.5:1 parking ratio was considered appropriate in some areas of the country. The ratio has increased to as much as 5:1 in the same areas. Inadequate parking may be classified as functional obsolescence, curable or incurable. Inadequate parking may require a line item in the income schedule to provide for the rental of additional parking spaces in adjacent buildings. It may be necessary for a potential purchaser to buy additional land in order to achieve adequate parking. The emphasis on parking will vary from city to city. In New York or Chicago where the majority of people walk or utilize public transportation to commute each day, on-site parking may not be as imperative as it is in Los Angeles, where automobiles comprise the primary form of transportation. Building security may be a problem due to design. Is this addressed?

HIGHEST AND BEST USE

Highest and best use is the most vital component of the appraisal. There is an ongoing debate that this section of an appraisal, for lending purposes, should not be a highest and best use study, but rather an economic analysis.

Example:

A developer wants to build a 200,000 square foot office building. The lender wants to finance the project, subject to obtaining an appraisal. Question: Does the lender really want to know that the highest and best use (most profitable use) of the site if for a shopping center? Or, does the lender want to know if the proposed office building is going to be economically viable? Regardless of your philosophy, this is the culmination of all the preceding sections. Particulars of relevance include:

Legal: The use(s) must be legally permissible. Environmental issues, easements and deed restrictions and zoning are addressed. : The site must be adaptable and capable of supporting the development of the legally permissible use(s).

Market: The use(s) must be appropriate for and consistent with the neighborhood. Supply and demand issues are addressed.

Economic: The use(s) must be financially feasible and most profitable based on normal investment criteria. Everything that the appraiser has learned about the property, the pressures and influences to which it is subjected, are applied in this analysis to provide the foundation for the valuation approaches. Having read the previous sections of the report, do you, the reviewer, concur with the appraiser's conclusion of highest and best use as vacant and as improved?

COST APPROACH

This approach to value should not be under estimated. Although it is most frequently applied at the inception of a project to ascertain feasibility, this method affirms that an investor would not pay more for a property than what the site can be acquired for and for the cost of constructing an equally desirable building.

Land Valuation

Value is created when there is scarcity, utility, demand and effective purchasing power. The land sales and listings used by the appraiser should convey the interaction of the four economic factors. Understanding the principle of change is also paramount. If sales are spread over a wide time period, is there an indication that the appraiser understood the pressures and influences that affected the market at the different points in time that the transactions occurred?

Use or utility is probably the most common problem. Has the appraiser gathered land sales with consideration of their proximity to the subject but failed to consider the respective differences in zoning or use potential?

Have the items discussed in the site description, such as the availability of utilities or lack thereof been considered in the adjustment process? Are the adjustments made in the proper sequence?

Reproduction or Replacement Cost:

Is the appraiser using these words interchangeably? Reproduction means an exact duplicate. Replacement means another building of comparable utility. When replacement cost is utilized, functional obsolescence is eliminated and no deduction is required. For new office buildings, has the appraiser compared the actual cost of the building with others constructed to check for reasonableness, or has he/she relied on the cost figures provided by the owner/developer? If the latter, how reliable are the estimates?

If comparisons to other building costs are utilized, has the appraiser identified and compared the different components such as indirect costs, direct costs, tenant improvements, and financing. A component that often skews construction cost comparisons is financing. In times when interest rates are fluctuating, the financing cost portion can vary dramatically, and if included in the cost per square foot figure, can result in a distorted indication.

If a source such as a reference text is utilized, has the appraiser identified it and conveyed his/her confidence in the reliability of the source?

Has profit been included and applied properly?

Depreciation:

The proper calculation of accrued depreciation is critical. Have the depreciation deductions been made in proper sequence? For example: physical curable deducted before physical incurable. External obsolescence is frequently overlooked or mishandled in appraisals. Was this form of depreciation appropriately considered?

Was the appraiser consistent in calculating the income loss?

There are three ways to compute the loss.

1. Capitalize the rent loss (difference between market rent without the negative influence and the rent that is anticipated due to the negative influence) into perpetuity,
2. Capitalize the rent loss using a present worth calculation which is appropriate when the rent loss is considered temporary.
3. Compare the property with sales of other office buildings, some of which are subject to the negative influence and some of which are not.

The final step in the calculation is often missing - allocation of the loss between land and building. Because a reviewer is often asked to critique a report that was prepared several months or several years earlier, the reviewer must keep in mind the changing perceptions of the market and actual events versus forecasts. Hindsight is always easier. At the time the appraisal was prepared, were expectations as presented in the report? What were the actions of the buyers and sellers at that time? What did they anticipate?

MARKET APPROACH

The underlying premise in the utilization of market data as evidence for market value is that the building may be reasonably perceived by the purchaser as an alternative to the comparable sale. Therefore, when large or numerous adjustments are seen in an appraisal, it arouses suspicion as to the "comparability" of the comparable sales. All items of variance between a sale and the property may not be recognized by the market. When the implementation of adjustments is required, it should be based only on market perceived differences. The evaluation of the appraiser's adjustments requires consideration of both technical and nontechnical issues.

1. Have the proper techniques of extracting adjustments been employed? Adjustments to sales should be market based, and reflect the market perceived contribution of the item requiring the adjustment. The reviewer's task is to evaluate the adjustments and the appraiser's support for the adjustments as being both plausible and applicable, and to insure that significant variances have not been omitted from the adjustment process. Is the percent or dollar adjustment appropriate for the item being adjusted? Are the adjustments made in the proper sequence? Do the adjustments appear reasonable in terms of contributory value? How does the implied contributory value compare with cost or other alternative? Is there an internal integrity to the appraiser's adjustments? That is, if the reviewer compares the comparables relative to one another, as well as to the property, employing the appraiser's adjustments to the subject, does a bias or pattern of inconsistency appear? Do the adjustments reflect the total market, or are "normative" assumptions accepted? Are specific paired sales accepted as providing the "proper" adjustment because it appears more reasonable when other pairs are discarded? Are the same sales employed in the derivation of the adjustments that were utilized for comparables in the appraisal?

2. Did the adjustments consider the motivations of the buyer, the cash flow variances, ability to debt service and effects of various debt structuring? Was cash equivalency employed?

3. Is there other, external, corroborating evidence to avoid circular reasoning in the analysis?

4. Is there evidence of the presence and motivation of a rational purchaser to support the reasonableness of the estimated marketing time? Has the appraiser examined the market data for support of the estimation of marketing time? How does the marketing time of the sales correlate with the market exposure time of the competitive offerings? Does the appraiser's analysis of the market period employ both sales and offerings? In the analysis of the historical market exposure of a

sale, does the appraiser recognize the environment that existed at the time of the sale? As marketing exposure is a function of the external environment, how does the appraiser's estimate of marketing time correlate with the description of the city and neighborhood? Similarly, in employing competitive listings as evidence of a marketing period, has the appraiser adequately evaluated the interrelationship of these competitive offerings?

5. Can variances of overall rates be explained? It is seldom possible for an appraiser to analyze the tenant mix and credit worthiness of the tenants in the comparable building sales. However, the perceptions of the buyer are crucial regarding the inherent risk of the investment based on the stability of the tenant mix, the credit worthiness of the tenants, the number of rollovers and the percentage of the building affected. This understanding helps explain overall rate variation.

INCOME APPROACH

In this approach to value, the focus is on the ability of the building to generate income and the ultimate sale price as of a certain date that can be generated based on the anticipated future earning power of the building. When a property is held as an investment rather than solely a shelter for an ongoing business, the locational aspects are different and in some respects more sensitive, and there may be a difference in the degree of impact on value due to changes in the economic climate.

Income Generation - Existing Building

It is essential that the tenant mix be studied to determine if it is balanced and to ascertain which tenants are credit risks. Other questions to be answered with regard to occupancy include:

1. What is the probability of the execution of lease options to

expand or renew?

2. If a tenant expands, what happens if another tenant is relocated? Does the expansion result in additional vacant space? Can it be easily marketed?
3. Is space being left vacant, not marketed or leased because of anticipated expansion by an existing tenant? How long will the space be non-producing of income?
4. Has the appraiser included all of the income potential? Income is generated from the following:

   a. Base contractual rent usually payable monthly in advance.
   b. Percentage of sales. This is applicable in office buildings that have retail uses on the lower floors.
   c. Expense categories or percentage of expenses passed through to tenants.
   d. Parking charges, monthly and hourly.
   e. Miscellaneous, such as nonrefundable security deposits, storage rental, rental of an auditorium, or note payments from tenants.

Contractual rent:

The reliability of receiving this income is dependent on the financial ability of the individual tenants to make the monthly payment. There is often no mention of the credit worthiness of the tenants or whether certain tenants are in arrears with their rental payments. By silence, hasn't the appraiser made an assumption that all is well? It is unrealistic to place the burden on real estate appraisers to evaluate the business viability of each tenant in a building. However, the income approach focuses not only on the quantity of the income but also the QUALITY and DURABILITY of the income stream. The risk associated with continuation of receiving the income is crucial to the value estimate.

1. Are there tenants 90 days in arrears? Are any of the leases being renegotiated to assist the tenant through a difficult pe-

riod of economic hardship? What line of business are these companies in? Is it possible to detect a pattern, i.e. architectural firms during a no-growth period; or is the problem more wide spread, reflective of a regional or national economic downturn?

Looking for consistency throughout the report is crucial. Is there information presented in earlier sections of the report that prepare the reader and help to explain *why* there may be credit problems among tenants?

2. Is there a master lease? Are all of the terms known? The appraiser may be ASSUMING that the previous owner has the financial capability to meet those obligations. The term of the master lease may infer the length of time necessary to lease the property to a certain point.

   Does the appraiser agree that the estimated time to lease this building corresponds with the term of the master lease?

3. Nearly every type of business is subject to economic cycles. Therefore, is this building occupied by a mix of businesses that are unrelated economically, or is the building predominantly occupied by businesses that are subject to the same downturns? If so, that could result in unexpected lease terminations, credit losses and higher risk associated with the continuing income generation.

   The preceding comments are not meant to imply that single-tenanted buildings or buildings with two or three tenants are necessarily a higher risk than multi-tenanted buildings. On the contrary, if the large tenants are good quality (able to withstand temporary economic aberrations) and the lease terms are long, the investor market may perceive the risk as much lower, sometimes taking on a risk level similar to a bond rating.

4. Another significant factor is the number of leases that will be expiring in any one year and the percentage of building area that is affected.

   In some instances, the space of a tenant who has vacated may be kept off the market in order to provide the expansion area for an existing tenant. Has the appraiser considered the time the space will be non-producing of income?

Floorplan Review:

It is not always possible or even practical for all designated leasable space on a floor to be occupied. Despite excellent property management, the suite sizes required by tenants may result in "leftovers" of unusually shaped space or areas too small to be readily marketable. First, can anything be done with the space and second, how much potential income is lost for how long? The landlord may finish the space and make it available to the tenants as a conference room or a snack bar. The income generation is accordingly lower than if the area were leased to a tenant for office usage.

In multi-tenanted buildings, there may be the potential of adding value in the future. Either due to configuration of spaces, poor space planning or lease negotiations, a building may have the potential for several thousand square feet to generate additional income. Has the appraiser addressed this? Does the landlord have the ability to relocate tenants within the building in order to recapture potential area and increase income? The figures sometimes become significant, particularly in high-rises. Knowledgeable buyers frequently analyze a building specifically looking for areas that have been ignored or forgotten with which value can be "created." Has the appraiser assumed that the space is maximally utilized?

Percentage Income from Sales:

In the case of retail establishments, such as restaurants or clothiers, as tenants in the office building, there is the added income potential from sales. Has the appraiser estimated when a tenant will produce percentage rent or does he/she ignore it? If the tenant is not anticipated to be able to reach percentage rental levels for the foreseeable future, is it possible that the tenant is generating insufficient sales volume to indefinitely continue to pay the base rental amount? If the tenant is producing significant percentage rent at the time of appraisal, how long is it anticipated to continue? Frequently, when the lease is renewed, the new base rent absorbs a large portion, if not all, of the income which had been received as a percentage of sales. Has the appraiser increased the base rent AND continued to expect percentage income at the same level as before the renewal?

Parking Charges:

In large buildings there is often an agreement with a parking company. The landlord eliminates the management burden and receives a portion of the income as set forth contractually. For buildings without the operation agreement, both monthly parking and transient or visitor parking fees should be included.

Income Generation Proposed and Newly Constructed

The same guides are applicable as set forth in the preceding section. The most significant element for the reviewer to focus on in a building with a low occupancy rate is the lease-up forecast.

The lease-up projections need to correspond with the supply and demand section of the report. For example, suppose the office building is under construction and the building is expected to be finished in twelve months.

1. How many buildings and how much square footage in the market area have been added in the past year?
2. How much square footage has been absorbed in these new ?

Is there a specific type of tenant or industry that has dominated new space usage?

3. How many buildings and how much square footage is under construction that will be competitive with the subject and will be completed 1) before the subject, 2) at the same time as the subject and 3) after the subject?

   In other words, is this property expected to have a leasing advantage due to its completion schedule, or will it just be one of several buildings that will glut the market, and be vulnerable to a bidding war amongst landlords to attract tenants?

4. How does the supply correlate with the trends in employment? Are significant increases in employment anticipated? Does this lessen or heighten the prospects for an oversaturated market?

   Pass-Through *of Expenses:* This is not a difficult task since the advent of the computer and sophisticated programs. Of significance to the reviewer is the understanding of what line items have been passed through and the limitations of the computer program. For example, are management charges passed through? Has the appraiser imputed the contractual pass through on a lease by lease basis, or has he/she assumed that all leases include the same pass through clauses? The assumptions stated by the appraiser should reflect specifically what items and how the items have been handled.

EXPENSE PROJECTIONS - EXISTING BUILDING

Has the appraiser considered the actual expense trend line experienced by the property? Has the appraiser tempered projections based on his/her knowledge of legislation or local politics that have affected the expense categories in recent years and which may affect line items in the future? Examples are utilities, insurance, and real estate taxes. Sometimes appraisers only think of the potential of reducing taxes rather than increasing taxes. A recent report I reviewed read:

"Property taxes for the subject equate to $1.75 per square foot. Other office buildings are paying $2.00 to $2.30 per square foot. Therefore, it is unlikely that the subject will benefit from the pursuit of a tax appeal."

In this instance, the appraiser failed to recognize the likelihood of the property being reassessed and taxes increased to be more compatible with the comparable buildings quoted in his cash flow forecast. Has the appraiser compared the expenses of the property with other office buildings? The important aspect in the comparison is to be assured that the appraiser has compared like with like. Specifically, the expenses may be net of pass through, or they may represent gross expense figures. The buildings may not have similar occupancy rates. They may be of dissimilar quality.

It is important to consider capital expenditures. At some point, it becomes necessary to resurface parking lots and roofs, repaint and re-carpet common areas, and so forth. Has the appraiser taken these costs into consideration? Have reserves for replacement been included?

EXPENSE PROJECTIONS - PROPOSED OR NEW BUILDINGS

For new buildings, expenses are phased in as occupancy increases. For example, when the property is only 15% leased, janitorial costs will only occur on that portion of the property leased. Property taxes are not likely to reflect a full assessment for a year or two after completion. If the appraiser is estimating Investment Value rather than Market Value, no deduction will be taken for the tenant improvement costs during the initial lease up of the space. The investor/ owner will capitalize those costs. However, if the report states that Market Value is being concluded, the initial tenant improvements do need to be deducted. Value presumes a sale of the property, and an informed buyer would take into consideration how much money would have to be expended for the tenant improvements during the lease-up of the building.

DISCOUNTED CASH FLOW

This is the most frequently employed technique and considered the most appropriate for multi-tenanted office buildings as it provides for uneven cash flows during the holding period. The potential purchaser is concerned with anticipated future benefits and present worth. In this regard, the appraiser estimates the quantity, quality and duration of these benefits and then derives an estimate of present worth. The technique employed to convert the future benefits into a present worth conclusion may be to capitalize or to discount.

Checking the expense-to-income ratios in Years 1, 5 and 11 (year of reversion) is a quick method of determining if expenses have been correspondingly increased with income. Expense ratios in a multi-tenant of office building of 45% in Year 1, declining to 28% by Year 5, should be a red flag indicating that the analysis may be faulty. If there is a significant variance, the appraiser should provide an explanation. For example, in a depressed market with low occupancies and depressed rental rates, it is obvious that the initial expense-to-income ratio will be higher than "typical." Do the expense-to-income ratios return to generally acceptable norms during the period of market recovery?

Between Line items on the Cash Flow: Basic relationships are always good to use as a check for consistency in the cash flow. An example of spotting a problem is given below. A narrative report gave the following assumptions:

- Brokerage fees applied for new leases are 5% of the rental amount.
- Brokerage fees applied for renewals are 2.5% of the rental .
- Tenant improvement allowance for new leases is imputed at $12 per square foot for new tenants and at $5 per square foot for renewing tenants.

Below are the corresponding lines extracted from the actual cash flow titled "Leasing Commissions" and "Total Deductions" for the first four years of the cash flow.
(numbers are rounded in 000's):

Brokerage Fees	$15	$ 6	$110	$ 20
Tenant Improvements	$41	$31	$240	$250
Total	$56	$36	$350	$270

There should be a relationship between these line items. If we calculate the contributory percentage of the brokerage fees to the total we check for consistency. Following are the corresponding percentages:

% of Brokerage fees to the Total: 27%   17%   31%   7%

These percentages should not fluctuate so dramatically. Because of the variance in the rates charged for renewals and new leases, the percentages cannot be expected to be the same. The 7% in year 1993 is a very large red flag. The tenant alterations in that year are $250,000, almost the same as the previous year, yet the brokerage fee is only $20,000. In the previous year it was $110,000. Why are the leasing commissions extremely low?

The reviewer may not be familiar with the software program utilized to identify the error in the input, but the review should be detailed enough to identify a problem. The answer in this case was: The appraiser inputted 5% for brokerage fees to be applied to new leases and 2.5% for brokerage fees to be applied to lease renewals. However, the program treated the 2.5% input as 2.5% *OF THE 5%* initial brokerage fee. The appraiser should have input 50% for the renewals in order to have the computer calculate what was intended.

Capitalization Rate for Reversion

Check the capitalization rate utilized at the end of the holding period. Does the rate adequately reflect the fact that the building will be 10 or 15 years older and the office building may be classified as a Class B facility rather than a Class A building as it is today?

Discount Rate: The rate employed should be derived from the appraiser's analysis of market data. The market data may provide direct evidence of the rate, evidence of the component parts for building up, or parameters of investment.

1. If a rate is derived directly from market sales, are the sales truly comparable? They should reflect similar economic lives. An evaluation needs to include anticipated future benefits. What are the expense-to-income ratios? What is the vacancy level? Is one property anticipated to produce positive cash flow in Year 1, another not until Year 3?
2. Have the other items of comparability been addressed? Do they include the financial components of the sale? Also, do the rates from the sales reflect only real estate?
3. What historical trends are apparent, and has the appraiser discussed their impact upon the buildup rate components?
4. Is the relationship between risk and return adequately evaluated?

In the derivation of the applicable rates, has the appraiser adequately identified the rational and knowledgeable purchaser?

Computer Model Limitations: There are limitations to the computer models and the appraiser should explain what they are. It is common today for purchasers to use computer software (often the same program the appraiser uses) and the limitations associated with the attainment of absolute accuracy are readily accepted.

Sometimes overlooked is whether the buyers and sellers are actually using cash flows in their analysis. This is particularly important if the property is a small property.

RECONCILIATION

Throughout the report the appraiser has reconciled differences. In this section, he/she communicates the final reconciliation between the value estimates derived from applying the various approaches to value. Is there convincing rationale for the selection of the point value figure concluded? Do you believe it represents the most probable price requisite to the definition of market value?

CONCLUSION

The proper review of any appraisal report begins with

- The reviewer's understanding of the economic principles such as "anticipation," "change" and "substitution" that underlie the appraisal; and
- Working knowledge of the various types of "value." The reviewer needs to be able to distinguish whether the value estimated by the appraiser does, in fact, correspond with the definition stated in the report. The mere fact that an appraiser says the value estimate is "market value" is not enough. The selection of market data and subsequent analysis must be consistent.

By knowing which economic principles provide the foundation of each section of the report, the reviewer has a base from which to judge consistence, adequacy of research and analytical competency. I recommend that the reviewer stay up to date with these and be able to apply them.

CHAPTER TWENTY-FOUR

REVIEWING THE SHOPPING CENTER APPRAISAL

The appraisal of retail properties is problematic because, on a very basic level, it requires some knowledge of the retailing business. The source of income to shopping centers, unlike that of most other property types, is dependent upon retail businesses attracting consumers in large numbers, on a frequent basis, to purchase goods and services. Predicting or analyzing the success of retail operations is a specialized function, and will be the major focus of this chapter. The increasing emphasis by investors on the revenue-producing capabilities of real estate has made the income approach the predominant valuation method. This, in turn, has necessitated sophisticated analysis of the quantity, quality and durability of the income stream. Nowhere is this more apparent that in the case of retail properties, which are regarded as investments with an inflation hedge because of their percentage leases.

FEASIBILITY

Revenue generation by retail properties is heavily dependent upon location, which can provide an advantage in what otherwise may be characterized as an environment of almost pure competition. Elements of location analysis go far beyond traffic counts on the streets abutting the property. They include analyses of the primary and secondary (and sometimes tertiary) retail trade areas, population and disposable income, growth projections, demographic factors such as age and family size and, not least, competition. Additional factors that cannot be ignored include the tenant mix, leasing strategy, physical configuration of the improvements and design factors that may contribute to obsolescence. The appraisal of an existing shopping center, and its review, are far less complicated than the same functions performed for a proposed center because the revenue-generating capabilities of the property have already been demonstrated. Notwithstanding that, the same types of analyses must be done, but with a better body of evidence from which to draw conclusions. In the of retail appraisals, it is of paramount importance that the reviewer be satisfied that the income projections have been reasonably derived - that the assumptions are minimal and reasonable, and that the evidence and analysis support the stabilized income or projected cash flow used in estimating value.

An appraisal of a proposed shopping center is based on a feasibility study that may be done by the appraiser, but which is often performed by specialists. Such a study is crucial to estimating the revenues that will be generated by the proposed facility. If the appraiser performs the feasibility study, it should be included within the appraisal report. If the appraiser has relied on a study done by others, sufficient information should be excerpted to allow the appraisal reviewer to judge its validity. Failing that, the reviewer should obtain a copy of the study and incorporate it into the review.

There are certain useful questions the reviewer should ask about the feasibility report:

- Is the trade area adequately defined? - Is it defined in terms of driving time rather than distance? - Are its size and shape influenced by transportation arteries, natural barriers and competition? - Is it defined in the context of the types of businesses that will be located in the center?
- Are the population data current and accurate? What is the census date? Have the figures been updated? - Are separate population figures given for primary, secondary and tertiary trade areas? Do the relevant populations live entirely within their respective trade areas? How closely do census tracts

correspond with trade area boundaries? - What is the source of population growth projections?

- Is there a socioeconomic profile of the trade area that includes income age distribution and household size?
- Has buying power been estimated? - Have income levels been obtained? - Have data on per capita consumption been appropriately employed?
- What is the competition? - What are the existing competitive shopping centers or retail districts? - How successful are they? - What additional competition is planned? - How does the tenant mix of each competing property compare with the subject?
- Does the study include a convincing analysis of how the buying power of the trade area will be divided among the subject property and its competitors? Are the conclusions about the competitive advantages and disadvantages (including location) of the subject reasonable?

In all likelihood, the reviewer will conclude that the feasibility study is adequate. By the time an appraisal is needed, the developer will probably have leases signed with the anchor tenants and certain other key tenants, a necessary ingredient in obtaining financing. This means that decision makers at certain sizable retail companies already will have been convinced that the trade area will support their operations. Analysis of income is not complete, however, without a lease analysis.

LEASE ANALYSIS

Retail leases are typically leases with overage clauses requiring payment of a specified percentage of gross revenue above a base amount. The major exceptions to the overage rent norm are service businesses such as financial institutions, because gross sales volume is not readily measurable. The appraiser should have reviewed the leases and provided a rent roll in the appraisal report which denotes any material changes from the standard form of lease used by the center.

Significant issues in lease analysis include the following:

- *The credit of the tenants.* How much of the total rental revenue will come from "credit" tenants (those who are financially strong enough to honor their lease obligations)?
- *The pattern of lease expirations.* The durability of income is in question if a significant number of leases will expire in the near future, and the tenants have not indicated their intentions to renew. In the case of anchor tenants, the "near future" may extend throughout the projection period.
- *Rent levels.* Are projected rent levels typical of those paid by similar tenants in competing centers? A secondary source of information on rent levels (in addition to comparables) is Dollars and Cents of Shopping Centers, published by the Urban Land Institute.
- *The standard form of lease.* Does the standard form of lease provide the landlord with a strong expectation of collecting revenue. Does it provide protection from expense increases? Is it in other respects a good "landlord's" lease? Are exceptions to the standard form adequately explained?
- *The anchor leases.* The anchor leases, if any, are usually on the tenant's standard lease form, rather than the landlord's. As such, they should be carefully reviewed by the appraiser and their important provisions included in the lease analysis section of the appraisal report. It is a common occurrence that the shopping center will lose money on an anchor lease during its early years, so that shortfall must be subsidized by the shop leases.

Often anchors will build their own buildings on leased land or will purchase the land outright. In the latter case, it is the operating agreement between the anchor and the center which must be reviewed to ensure that the anchor is required to operate its store for a specified period.

Other Revenue Issues

There are several other issues an appraiser should consider that are relevant to revenue generation. They include:

- *Location.* Is the center in a location that will support the appraiser's contentions about its competitive position? Is access easy? Are left turns required for ingress or egress?
- *Design and configuration.* Is the design attractive and up to date? Has any obsolescence been noted? Is it functional or economic? Curable or incurable? Has a budget for curing obsolescence been presented? If revenues are projected to increase after a remodeling, are those increases reasonable? How is leasable area calculated?
- *Parking.* Is parking adequate? Does it vary significantly from the norm of 5.5 spaces per thousand square feet of leasable area? Does traffic flow easily on site?
- *Tenant mix.* Is the tenant mix appropriate to the type of shopping center being appraised? Do the revenue projections take the tenant mix into account?
- *Revenue growth.* Are revenue projections based on the feasibility study (proposed center) or on historic performance existing center)? Are increases in overage rents based on increases in sales volume and calculated according to lease terms, or are they based on an index of some kind? The purpose of the appraisal is for loan underwriting purposes, the overage rents may be treated differently from base rents because they are considered riskier. They may be discounted at a higher rate or not fully considered in calculating debt service coverage.

EXPENSES

In most cases, shopping center expenses include only the cost of operating the common areas because maintenance and utility expenses of the shop space are the responsibility of the tenants. Common area expenses, including maintenance, utilities, taxes, insurance and management, are billed back to the tenants according to formulas in the leases. These are usually calculated according to the ratio of the area of a given store to gross leasable area. Expense billbacks are reflected in the income statement as revenue, offset by the actual expense.

The reviewer should make sure that:

- The expenses are similar to historic expenses or to the expense history of similar centers in the area;
- Expense billbacks are calculated according to lease terms;
- Revenue from billbacks is reduced to reflect vacancies within the subject property.

DISCOUNTING

Methods for converting income to value are covered at length elsewhere in this book. It should be noted, however, that, in today's investment environment, appraisals relying on the discounted cash flow method should have the greatest credibility. It is essential, however, that cash flow projections be derived through rigorous analysis and that the discount rate reflect the hurdle rate required by the most probable buyer.

OTHER VALUE COMPONENTS

Two additional sources of value that are commonly associated with shopping centers are "pads" and surplus land. Pads are small parcels of land, generally located in the parking lot or on the property's frontage, that are reserved for freestanding buildings for occupants like bank branches, service stations or restaurants. Pads are usually either sold or ground leased to users. Analysis of the value of pads is, therefore, a bit different from analysis of the rest of the center.

An occupied leased pad is a fairly simple analysis because the lease probably will not expire for many years, so income will be known or rather easily projected. Valuation of an unoccupied pad is somewhat more complicated and involves the following steps:

1. Determination of the most probable buyer or lessee;
2. Estimation by market comparison of the price or rent that user will pay;
3. Estimation of the most likely timing of the transaction; and
4. Discounting the future price or rent to a present value.

In the case of surplus land, often called "expansion area," the reviewer should be satisfied that valuation assumptions are reasonable. The land will probably be valued by market comparison to other retail parcels in the area. This is valid only if an expansion of the center is the most probable use of the property. It may be unclear that the market will support additional retail space in the foreseeable future, or the surplus land could be Located behind the existing center or configured so that it is inferior for retail purposes. The reviewer must be satisfied that the valuation of surplus land is appropriate, and that the future value is properly discounted to present value.

CHAPTER TWENTY-FIVE

REVIEWING A HOTEL APPRAISAL REPORT

REVIEWING A HOTEL APPRAISAL

Hotels, as both real estate investments and ongoing businesses, are tricky properties to appraise. The need to resell every room on a nightly basis makes hotel properties extremely vulnerable to numerous variables which impact a hotel's ability to generate income. The many ways in which these variables may be addressed and analyzed in an appraisal report can make the reviewer's job a difficult one. This article will discuss some of the more pertinent factors to consider when reviewing an appraisal of a hotel property.

An understanding of the hotel business or what is termed the "hospitality" industry is critical for the proper valuation of a lodging facility. The hospitality industry has matured in recent years, and due to more limited growth prospects the industry is responding with product segmentation and other marketing tactics similar to those found in other retail consumer industries. An awareness of the numerous products in the market and their success is very important in projecting the potential earning capability of a hotel property. This point will be borne out by the various comments presented in this article.

The valuation of those lodging facilities which are bought and sold on the basis of their ability to generate income will be the focus of this discussion. The majority of hotels and motels are most appropriately valued via the income approach because they are purchased as income producing investments. Some smaller motels and "bed and breakfasts" may be more appropriately valued via the sales comparison approach because, due to their size, they are relatively uneconomical operations and primarily serve to provide employment for the owner and his or her family.

The easiest way to address the salient points involved in a hotel appraisal review is to follow the steps through a typical appraisal report. The order may vary, but the important topics which should be covered in all hotel appraisals are presented in this article. A review of some of the key points to look for and be wary of as one reviews a hotel appraisal are examined here.

NATURE OF THE ASSIGNMENT

The interests in the subject property being valued should be clearly addressed in this section of the report. The most common interest appraised is the fee simple interest in the land, improvements and furniture, fixtures and equipment. The mention of a ground lease or operating lease should always be explored.

Hotels are often constructed on leased land, and the terms of the ground lease can have a profound impact on value and should be clearly stated. Rent in the majority of hotel ground leases is tied to a percentage of revenues. The number of years remaining in a ground lease as well as the lessee's ability to subordinate the leased fee interest to a first mortgage can have an impact on a hotel's market value and should be discussed. Ground leases with terms approaching 40 to 45 years or less tend to impact a hotel's ability to be sold and refinanced. A reviewer should look for an increase in the applied capitalization or discount rate in such instances.

Hotels, both land and improvements, used to be routinely leased to operating companies. The operator would generate an income stream, pay rent to the owner of the leased fee, and retain any income available after rental payments. This clearly demarcated the income attributable to the real estate or leased fee (the rental payments) and the income attributable to the business or leasehold (net income after rent). However, it is very rare to come upon a hotel operating lease anymore. The norm today is for the owner to retain a managing agent to operate the hotel and pay the agent a base management fee, generally calculated as a percentage of gross revenue, and in addition an incentive fee calculated as some percentage of net income either before or after debt service. The net income available after payment of the management fees is considered income attributable to the real and personal property, while the management fees are considered to be the net income attributable to the business.

A few hotels are still owned subject to an operating lease, and the capitalized net income available after rent on the land and improvements reflects the value of the business. Capitalization and discount rates applied to such leasehold interests should adequately reflect the higher risk associated with a business investment.

Most hotels have some leased equipment, generally telephone or computer systems, televisions, Xerox machines and vans utilized for transportation. The annual equipment lease expense must be deducted as an operating expense of the hotel.

In some rare cases a hotel's entire furniture, fixtures and equipment (FF & E), from elevators to carpeting and mattresses, may be leased. A hotel with leased FF & E often signals that the hotel's developer ran out of funds or had some financing difficulty. The terms of the FF & E lease should be carefully scrutinized to understand the interests of the parties involved. If the leasing company has the ability to remove the FF & E upon default, then the first mortgage could be left with an empty hotel unable to generate income. Often the lease expense is quite onerous and will have a relatively quick payoff, such as five years. The amount to be paid off at the end of the lease, typically the "then market value", must be deducted from the projected income stream, in addition to annual lease payments up until that time.

DESCRIPTION OF THE LAND

The subject land's suitability for the development and operation of a hotel should be addressed in this section. The land must be of adequate size to accommodate the hotel improvements and to provide for good circulation and parking. Adequate parking facilities are critical for a hotel operation, particularly one with extensive food, beverage and banquet business. The shape and topography of the hotel must also be conducive for the existing or proposed improvements.

Two other key factors relative to a hotel's land are access and visibility. While factors such as chain affiliation and management are playing an increasingly significant role in a hotel's success, the importance of a hotel's location cannot be overemphasized. Access and visibility are particularly important to roadside hotel operations that derive a significant amount of their patronage from passing motorists. The characteristics of a hotel property must be judged in relation to those of its competitors. Many hotels have an access problem, however this may not prove to be deleterious to the operation of the hotel if the other lodging facilities in the area are equally handicapped.

DESCRIPTION OF THE IMPROVEMENTS

The physical layout and condition of the subject property should fully described in this section of the appraisal. The characteristics of a hotel's physical plant have become an increasingly critical factor in the determination of market value and can impact a hotel's ability to generate and sustain a projected income stream. Hotel companies have certain design criteria for their managed or affiliated hotels. Thus, a hotel's physical characteristics may render the property unsuitable for certain investors and, by limiting the universe of potential buyers, will make a hotel more difficult to sell.

The massive amount of new hotel construction over the past

eight years has served to render many existing hotels obsolete. In some market areas hotels of only five to seven years in age are already considered outdated and as a result have lost their competitive edge. In many cases the functional obsolescence of outdated design is curable, and can be overcome with significant capital expenditures which must be delineated in an appraisal. However, in numerous instances the functional "design" obsolescence may be considered incurable because market occupancies and room rates are too low for the capital expenditures to be economically justified.

Examples of such design deficiencies include a two-pipe heating and air-conditioning system, exterior corridors, and a round shaped guest room tower with pie shaped rooms. The income of a hotel in such a predicament may be most appropriately forecast to decline or, at best, to remain stable and not increase with inflation. A good analysis of a property's highest and best use is particularly important to the valuation of obsolete hotels which are in the declining stage of their life cycle.

The single most common omission in hotel valuations is the appraiser's recognition and accounting for the need for capital expenditures. An income stream is forecast to be generated by a well maintained and competitive lodging facility, yet the actual physical condition of the hotel improvements and furnishing, fixtures and equipment is largely ignored.

A discussion of what is required in today's hotel marketplace to remain competitive is too vast to cover in this article, but a few of the salient points one should consider are set forth below:

Franchise Requirements

The majority of hotels and motels are affiliated with a hotel chain, generally in the form of a franchise. The ability of an independent property to survive is becoming increasingly difficult. A chain affiliation, and connection to the hotel company's reservation system, is often the very lifeblood of a hotel or motel. All hotel franchise companies have a list of physical requirements for member properties, though the exact specifications of the hotel companies vary widely. Companies such as Holiday Inn have become extremely strict in their requirements in recent years and have been using their specifications to de-franchise a number of older, obsolete properties upon sale or upon expiration of their original twenty year franchise agreements. A number of new hotel companies have emerged to provide a name, affiliation and reservation system for the older hotels that have lost their Holiday Inn, Ramada or similar affiliation. Obviously, the specifications required by these chains are less stringent and in turn, the benefits that are generated by the affiliation may be minimal. It takes years for a new hotel company to establish a loyal following among consumers. An appraisal of a chain affiliated hotel should always contain a synopsis of the hotel's license agreement, and the appraiser should always request the hotel company's franchise inspection reports and a deficiency report to determine whether any outstanding violations exist. Upon sale a hotel's franchiser may require the new owner to adhere to strict physical requirements. A hotel may be targeted for franchise removal and, without extensive capital expenditures, the hotel may loose its affiliation and reservation system, and the value of the hotel may plummet.

Life and Fire Safety Systems

Due to a number of tragic hotel fires in recent years, state and local legislators, as well as the consumer public, have become increasingly aware of life and fire safety systems in hotels. Minimum requirements generally include:

1. Fully sprinklered public areas, guest rooms and back-of-the house (service) areas.
2. Hard wired smoke detectors in all areas, tied into a central annunciator panel.

3. Dry type sprinkler system in kitchen.
4. Emergency generator and lighting systems.
5. Directional signage for emergency evacuation in all guest rooms and front and back-of-the-house areas.
6. Elevators with fireman's safety returns.

While a number of hotel chains and states are requiring hotels to meet these standards (for example, Sheraton is requiring the installation of sprinkler systems in all its franchised hotels and the state of Florida is requiring hotels to be sprinklered by 1991), in many instances hotels are grandfathered under old laws and may continue to operate in their existing condition. Generally a change in ownership or a major renovation will trigger the need to meet new fire and life safety codes. When appraising a hotel's market value the cost of installing such systems, which can be significant, must be considered and is often overlooked. If a hotel is oriented to conventions and large groups the lack of modern fire and life safety systems can cause the property to be rejected as a possible site by professional meeting planners, and certain corporations will not allow their executives to patronize a hotel that is considered unsafe.

Periodic Refurbishment

The physical condition and style of a hotel's furniture and fixtures must be maintained and kept up to date to remain competitive and generate the projected income stream. The need for refurbishment of a hotel's public areas (front-of-the-house) and guest rooms often depends upon the requirements of the hotel chain, the condition of the hotel's competitors, and the competitiveness of the market. One will often see older, tired properties schedule major refurbishment once a new, major competitor becomes proposed or is under construction. In markets where demand is strong and supply is limited (few such markets exist today!), hotels are able to extend the- time period before refurbishing. An annual deduction for the funding of a reserve for the periodic replacement of a hotel's FF & E (furnishings, fixtures and equipment) should always be deducted as an operating expense from a projected income stream. While a reserve is a capital expense, and is often not expended each year, the premise is that funds should be set aside to accumulate for eventual refurbishment. Many hotel management companies, and lenders as well, now require that a certain amount, generally tied to a percentage of total revenues, be set aside as a reserve for replacement each year. Reserves typically average 3% of total revenues, but for a new hotel may be specified on a graduated scale at 1% of revenues in the first year of operation, increasing to 4% or as much as 7% in later years. In the description of a hotel's improvements, a review appraiser should look for a discussion of when the hotel's various areas and furnishings were last refurbished and when future refurbishment is scheduled.

A tastefully and timelessly designed lobby in a moderate occupancy hotel may last for as long as ten years before requiring significant expenditures, while the decor of a lobby whose style has become rapidly outdated and is subject to extensive wear and tear from high occupancy groups, may require refurbishment after only three to four years. Refurbishment can range from just re-carpeting to an entire renovation, including re-configuration of a front desk and seating areas. In guest rooms, for example, soft goods (which include carpeting, drapes, lamp shades, and bedspreads) may need to be replaced every three years, while case or hard goods (bureaus, night tables, headboards, desk, chairs, etc.) can last as long as ten years if of a good style and well maintained. Often an appraiser may suggest that a hotel's guest rooms will require refurbishment in the near future but then neglects to consider the cost of such a project in his or her valuation.

AREA AND NEIGHBORHOOD ANALYSIS

The area and neighborhood analysis section of an appraisal

should set forth a discussion of the economic and demographic environment within which a hotel is operating. While one is looking for the health of the local economy to support the value of the appraised real estate, the underlying characteristics that will generate demand for lodging facilities is also an important factor of this section. Economic and demographic statistics, both historical and projected, should be analyzed in terms of annual compound percent growth or decline, so that they may be correlated with projections of future lodging demand in the appraisal's forecast of the hotel's occupancy.

For commercial hotels, and those hotels targeted to serve locally generated group meetings, the profile of the local economy is very important. Employment trends are one of the most important factors of this discussion. Certain employment sectors, such as FIRE (finance, insurance and real estate), business services and wholesale trade tend to generate strong demand for hotel rooms, and strong growth in these sectors will portend increases in lodging demand. What is generating the employment is also equally important. Increases in manufacturing employment may have little impact upon lodging demand if it is generated by a revitalized steel mill, but may generate significant lodging demand if it is generated by high technology and research and development firms. The construction and leasing of office and industrial space are also important components of an area discussion. The annual increase in total occupied space should be analyzed and some discussion of the types for firms leasing the space should be included to discern if they are generators of lodging demand.

Often the makeup of the local economy will have little impact upon a hotel's ability to generate income. This may be the case for a roadside motel that caters to passing motorists or a hotel in a destination resort area. The local economy may be poor and unemployment may be high, but both the motel and resort may operate quite successfully. A review of national or international economic and demographics statistics, as well as currency that drive both international and national travel patterns may be more appropriate in the appraisal of a resort or roadside motel. Traffic counts, road patterns, and air passenger statistics are important indicators for these types of properties as well. Median household and per capita income statistics should be analyzed in comparison with those of the hotel's state and the nation at large and can provide a good indication of a hotel's ability to attain certain room rates. The neighborhood of a hotel can vary widely in nature, from residential to commercial and industrial, and still be highly conducive to the operation of a transient lodging facility. An appraiser should be concerned with crime levels and whether a neighborhood is in a state of improvement, stability or decline. However, generally, if a hotel is proximate to its demand generators, or easily accessed by transient traffic, the character of its surrounding neighborhood is less critical than for other types of real estate. The type of hotel and its access, parking and street orientation must be taken into consideration when weighing the impact of the surrounding land uses.

SUPPLY AND DEMAND ANALYSIS

A hotel appraisal's supply and demand analysis may be broken down into a discussion of a hotel's competitors and an evaluation of the market for hotel accommodations. The total supply of hotel rooms in a market area should be defined, with an indication of the location of clustering of facilities, the overall age and affiliation of the competitive supply and the area wide occupancy level. Those hotels considered to be the primary competitors of the subject property should be isolated and described in depth, including such information as age constructed, physical condition, market mix, and historical average rate and occupancy. The subject property may have secondary and tertiary competitors that are only partially competitive with the subject for certain segments of demand. These facilities should also be listed with available operating statistics.

Occupancy and average rate statistics are the single most difficult information for a hotel appraiser to attain, but the accurate compilation of such data is critical for an accurate evaluation of a hotel's ability to generate income and its market value. At minimum, area wide occupancy levels should be attainable from such sources as the local convention and visitors bureau or chamber of commerce. Individual property statistics can often only be obtained through individual interviews or an appraiser's connections with a hotel owner, managing agent or affiliation. Occupancy and average rate statistics must be set forth on an annual basis for a specific time period. Be alert for the classic misuse of quoted rack room rates. Hotels with quoted rates of $120 to per night may only attain an average rate per occupied room on an annual basis of $85, or even less.

A complete discussion of proposed additions to supply should be presented in an appraisal report. The location, number of rooms, chain affiliation, anticipated date of opening, stage and probability of development should be set forth for each proposed facility. If no new competition is proposed than the availability of desirable hotel sites and the ease or difficulty of new hotel development should be discussed so that any future competition can be anticipated. In some cases the environment for new hotel development is so strong that the addition of new supply to the market should be prudently factored into an occupancy forecast even with no specific projects in mind.

The discussion of the market for transient lodging facilities should address the various segments in an area which generate lodging demand. The three market segments prevalent in most areas are the commercial, group meeting and leisure demand generators. The objective of this analysis is to isolate the number of room nights (number of area wide hotel rooms occupied per year) which are generated by each market segment so that growth rates specific to each individual segment may be applied in the forecasting of future demand. The number of room nights historically accommodated in a market area is quantified by multiplying the occupancy of each competitive hotel by its number of rooms by 365 days in a year. The percentage of demand generated by each market segment is calculated by applying the percentage market mix of each hotel by its total room night demand.

Any particulars that impact demand patterns should be noted in this discussion, such as seasonality (a strongly seasonal market, such as Palm Springs, may have a limit to attainable annual occupancy), or price sensitivity (a market heavily dependent upon government demand may have a limit to attainable average rate.) Any major changes expected to dramatically alter an area's market mix should also be noted, such as the construction of a convention center. The development of a convention center or major new hotels with previously unavailable meeting space or first-class accommodations can be expected to induce or attract new demand into the market and, if relevant, should also be considered.

FORECAST OF OCCUPANCY AND AVERAGE RATE

A hotel's projected occupancy and average rate form the basis for the forecast of all other income and expense items and ultimately the hotel's net income before debt service and appraised market value. The reviewer should look for a clear and supportable forecast of these two variables. The subject's historical occupancy and average should be presented and discussed. If a hotel has sustained a relatively stable occupancy over the past few years and no additions to supply are anticipated that would impact the subject then no computational analysis of the hotel's future occupancy may be warranted. At minimum, the appraisal should contain a clear rationale for a hotel's projected future occupancy and average rate.

A room night or occupancy analysis is the preferred method for forecasting a hotel's occupancy. As was previously mentioned in the discussion of supply and demand, a room night analysis quantifies the existing room night demand in a market area, and projects growth in demand based upon economic and demographic statistics, or historical demand growth rates. Growth rates are applied to each market segment based upon the annual rates of change indicated by relevant economic and demographic trends. Any unaccommodated demand (i.e. demand that is turned away to sold out conditions on certain nights of the week or year) should be accounted for. A forecast of total annual room night demand is derived by adding the demand projected for each individual market segment.

The future annual room night demand is then divided by annual room night supply (hotel rooms in the market area multiplied by 365 days per year) to attain an area wide occupancy level. The occupancy of the subject property is then forecast based upon its ability to capture the demand generated by each market segment. This procedure may be performed through the use of competitive indices, penetration factors or some other comparative factor. The preparation of a room night analysis is not a science and has some inherent flaws. For example, it presumes that increases in demand can be accommodated at any time throughout the year, while in reality demand has both weekly and seasonal fluctuations. For this reason, any room night analysis must be reviewed with a degree of caution. Certain markets have a limit

Chart1

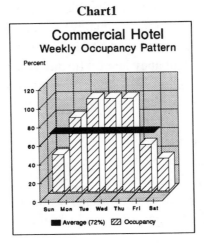

to attainable occupancy. Consider a strong commercial market, with the weekly occupancy levels indicated in Chart 1.

The maximum attainable occupancy is inherently 72%, unless the hotel under consideration has some special way of attracting weekend business.

Review appraisers should also be on the lookout for aggressive demand growth rates. Lodging demand in the United States has historically increased at a rate of 1 to 2% per year over the long term, and is currently estimated to be increasing at an annual rate of 3 to 4%. Certain market areas may be strong enough to sustain annual growth rates of up to 4%, but if growth rates are projected at 5% and greater for more than a year or two, a request should be made for support for such aggressive projections. Demand can increase by double digit rates in years of burgeoning growth, however compounded double digit increases are generally not sustainable, and a degree of conservatism must be factored into any projection as demand can decline significantly during recessionary periods.

Review appraisers should be on the lookout for an appraisal that either overstates or understates the size of a market area. It may appear that the appraiser is being conservative when including a large number of hotels and hotel rooms in the competitive supply. However, as new hotels enter the market, the larger the base supply of hotel rooms the smaller the impact the new rooms will have upon area wide occupancy. A realistic definition of the market and the impact of new competition is critical in the forecast of a hotel's occupancy level. The quickest way for a reviewer to assess the reasonableness of a room night analysis and occupancy projection is to calculate the subject hotel's overall market penetration.

Overall market penetration is calculated by dividing the hotel's forecasted occupancy by the area wide or competitive occupancy. A hotel may penetrate one certain market segment by more than 200%, but an overall penetration rate of greater than 112% to 115% is considered aggressive and should be questioned by the reviewer. For example, consider the occupancy levels and over-all penetration rates forecast in Chart 2. The hotel's occupancy is projected to stabilize at a strong 75% in the fourth year while the area wide occupancy is declining due to new additions to supply. Few hotels can attain such favorable operating results. Actual evidence of a hotel's chain affiliation or concept to attain above-average penetration in other market areas should be supplied if an aggressive market penetration is forecast. For example, Embassy Suite hotels have proven that in most market areas they are able to perform well above area wide occupancies and an overall penetration of greater than 1 115% may be justified. A room night analysis may not be appropriate for forecasting occupancy in certain market areas, such as evolving resort areas where a hotels occupancy is largely dependent upon the marketing efforts and abilities of its managing agent. A seasonality analysis by market segment may be appropriate for supplying support for occupancy projections.

The hotel's managing agent and reservation system are generally key factors in a property's ability to attain a profitable occupancy level and any review appraiser should ask for concrete evidence of a hotel's managing agent or affiliation to generate room night demand. Very few hotel companies in the United States today have the mass group marketing capability to book conventions and large group meetings. The assumption of "aggressive marketing" by an unproven management company will often translate into an unsuccessful hotel property. A hotel's forecasted average rate is a critical factor which must be considered in tandem with occupancy projections. An older, obsolete property may be sustaining penetration factors above 100% due to a pricing strategy that attracts low-rated business. As in any business, pricing is a factor in the inducement of demand. The United States hotel industry has been able to sustain occupancy levels in the sixty percent range over the past five years despite considerable overbuilding, but at the expense of average room rates which have remained stable or even declined in many market areas.

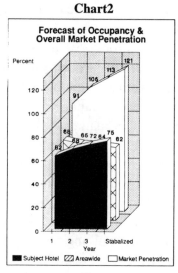

Chart2

Forecast of Occupancy &
Overall Market Penetration

■ Subject Hotel ▨ Areawide ☐ Market Penetration

A hotel's average room rate is calculated by dividing a hotel's rooms revenue by the number of hotel rooms occupied during a certain period. The average rate inherently reflects the discounting a hotel must normally do to sell its rooms. The average rate of an existing hotel can typically be tied to its historical average rate. Support for increases in average rate above the rate of inflation may be attainable due to the anticipated refurbishment of a hotel, or a change in market mix. For example, a hotel may have relied historically on low rate airline crews or military business due to its physical condition or even just a management decision. By upgrading the hotel or altering the amount of low-rated business a hotel accommodates, an increase in average rate can be justified if the market can support the anticipated change.

The average rate of a new or proposed hotel is more difficult to forecast. Room rates should typically be tied to the average rate of a close competitor, and may be forecast by market segment or as an overall composite average rate. Be on the lookout for a new hotel's first year average rate being tied to the stabilized average rate of an existing hotel. Hotels must typically discount their rates during the initial two to three years of operation in order to build occupancy. Even the largest hotel chains are known for initial discounting policies. Discounting during the initial years of operation must be taken into consideration in the average rate forecast. The lower rates generally charged for group or contract business should also be factored into a hotel's average rate forecast if the hotel will rely upon these market segments in filling its rooms. Room rates beyond the stabilized (generally the third or fourth year) should not increase at a rate greater than inflation, and may even increase at a rate less than inflation for an older, obsolete hotel. Only certain hotel chains have proven their ability to consistently increase their rates greater than inflation over a long period of time, through both up and down cycles, and support for such projections should be requested.

FORECAST OF INCOME AND EXPENSE

A hotel's occupancy and average rate serves as a basis for the forecast of income and expense. A several year forecast is generally appropriate for hotel properties to coincide with fluctuations in occupancy and average rate up through a stabilized year of operation. A new hotel or one recently repositioned or renovated typically requires two to four years to stabilize.

Historical operating statements provide the best basis for forecasting future net income and a minimum of two to three years of operating history should be included in the appraisal of any existing hotel. Poor management may reduce the relevance of historical statements, but any anticipated improvements in operating performance should be clearly discussed. An appraiser should perform a thorough investigation of the hotel's historical statements of income and expense statements and the supporting schedules for each operating department, looking for any unusual fluctuations in revenue and expense. Any expense items that are not applicable to the hotel operation, such as unusual legal expenses or salaries paid to the general partners of an ownership entity, should be noted.

The hotel's statements may or may not conform to the Uniform System of Accounts for Hotels but the appraiser should convert the statements to the Uniform System so that comparison can be made to industry averages. It may not be possible to convert historical statements to the Uniform System if payroll and related expenses are not allocated to the various operating departments.

Some appraisers will apply an overall expense ratio in forecasting a hotel's net income. The application of an overall expense ratio in a transient lodging facility is generally inappropriate and can widely under or overstate a hotel's value. The amount of food and beverage revenue can create a wide disparity in expense ratios and overall profitability. Operations without food and beverage revenues may generate a net income before debt service of anywhere from 30% to 60%, while the profitability of hotels with food and beverage revenues can range from 10% to 35%. The only way income and expense can be accurately forecast for a hotel is through a line-by-line analysis of revenue and expenses.

Hotels are very labor intensive businesses, with large amount of fixed operating expenses. Once fixed operating expenses have been covered, they can become very profitable as occupancy, average rate and overall revenues increase. Appraisers with experience in evaluating hotel properties will generally utilize computer software that considers the fixed and variable components of a hotel's revenue and expenses. As occupancy and average rate increases, a hotel's operating expense ratios should decline and the overall profitability of the property should increase.

The converse is true as well, as occupancy and average rate decline, so should a hotel's profitability. A net operating income ratio that remains fixed throughout a variable revenue projection indicates a lack of familiarity with hotel operations and should be questioned by the reviewer.

The projection of a hotel's income and expense will be discussed line item by line item, in the order established by the Uniform System of Accounts for Hotels. Rooms revenue is estimated by multiplying the number of hotel rooms by the projected occupancy and average rate for each forecast year.

For an existing hotel, food revenue is typically forecast as a ratio of rooms revenue and beverage revenue is forecast as a ratio of food revenue. The forecast of food and beverage revenue for a new or proposed hotel should be derived through a detailed average check and cover analysis by meal period for each operating outlet. Be on the lookout for the forecast of extensive beverage revenues generated in a discotheque or high energy lounge. While these facilities may generate extensive cash flow for a year or two, such volumes are rarely sustainable and can fall off dramatically. Telephone revenue is generally forecast as a percentage of rooms revenue, or as an amount per occupied room, and should be adequate to allow the telephone department to generate a profit. If a hotel is not generating a profit, the revenues may need to be increased by revising call markups or installing a call accounting system. Other income in a hotel is generated by vending machines, valet, parking, and gift shop or other rentals, and is typically forecast as an amount per occupied room or as a percentage of rooms revenues. This revenue category may be forecast either gross or net of operating expense. Support should be given for any substantial profit generated by this department. The operating expenses of a hotel are most appropriately analyzed and forecast on the basis of one or more of four indices: as a percentage of total revenue; as a percentage of departmental revenue, as an amount per available room or as an amount per occupied room. A knowledgeable hotel appraiser will be utilizing industry averages in combination with actual operating statements from comparable hotels as a basis for his or her forecast. If the hotel is being appraised subject to management by a particular management company then comparable statements from other hotels under the same management should be reviewed and utilized as a basis in forecasting.

Rooms departmental expense is generally forecast as a percentage of rooms revenue and is cross-checked against an amount per occupied room. Typically expense ratios for a well managed hotel range from 22% to 25% of rooms revenues, but can be as low as 18% or as high as 30% or more.

Food and beverage department expense is generally forecast as a percentage of food and beverage departmental revenue, after an independent analysis is made of food, beverage and labor cost percentages. Typical departmental expense ratios range from 75% to 85%, but can be as low as 65% for a hotel with a significant amount of profitable banquet revenue or a high energy lounge. Some hotels do not make any money in their food and beverage department and may have an expense ratio of over 100%.

Telephone expense is typically forecast as a percentage of departmental revenue cross-checked against an amount per occupied room. Other income expense will vary with the nature of other income generators.

Administrative and general expense is typically forecast as a ratio of total revenue, cross-checked against an amount per available and per occupied room. This expense generally ranges from 7% to 10% of total revenue, but can be as low as 6% for a hotel with an extensive amount of food and beverage revenue and as high as 14% for a hotel with extensive administrative staff and low revenue levels.

A hotel's income and expense forecast should always contain the cost of a base management fee, generally 3% to 5% of total revenues, for the compensation of a professional management company, even if the hotel is operated by its owner at no expense. This allows for a lender to foreclose on the property and retain a management company to competently manage the hotel and generate the projected income stream. Incentive management fees are generally not deducted as an expense for valuation purposes if they are subordinate to the payment of debt service.

Marketing expense is a budgeted amount and can vary widely, depending upon the competitiveness of the market. Franchise fees are included in this expense category and are typically charged as some percentage of rooms revenue, generally from to 7%. A franchise company's advertising assessment may also be included in

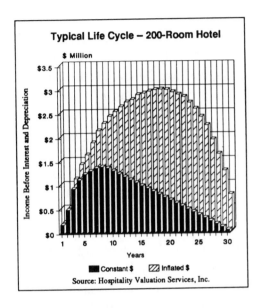

this expense category, while reservation costs may be allocated to marketing or room's departmental expense.

Other marketing expense is typically forecast as a percentage of total revenue or as an amount per available room. The total expense ratio can range from as low as 2.5% of total revenue to a high of 9% of total revenue, and is very property specific. A sharp decline or increase in this expense should be explained. A hotel may cut back on its marketing expense to increase short term profitability, while long term profitability will be eroded due to a lack of sales efforts for future bookings.

Property, operations and maintenance expense is generally forecast as an amount per available room, cross-checked against a percentage of total revenue. Also a budgeted expense which can vary widely, depending upon a hotel's size, age and condition, property, operations and maintenance can range from as low as $400 per available room for a budget motel to as high as $4,000 per available room for a full service, luxury hotel. Cutbacks in this expense category should also be explained, as short term profitability may be attained at the expense of the long term physical condition of the hotel.

Energy costs are typically forecast as an amount per available room and will vary widely depending upon the hotel's physical plant, its location, and local energy rates. The installation of an energy management system can often make a dramatic improvement in a hotel's energy expense. Newer hotels are now constructed with energy costs in mind, while many older hotels constructed before the energy crises of the 1970's have a very high energy expense that can only be reduced through the capital replacement of some building components, such as single pane windows.

Real and personal property taxes are specific to the laws of the state within which a hotel is located and the bias of the local tax assessor. For states such as California, where a property is automatically reassessed upon sale at the sales price, the tax rate can be loaded into the appraiser's capitalization or discount rate to build in the taxes at the appraised value. If a ten year discounted cash flow analysis is performed, then the reassessment upon sale to a new owner at the end of the tenth year must also be reflected. For proposed hotels, or property's that may be unfairly assessed, it is often worthwhile for a comparison to be made to the assessed value of the improvements of other comparable hotels within the assessor's jurisdiction. A case may be made for an appeal of a hotel's property taxes if they are significantly over assessed relative to other hotels or to the market value that has been estimated.

As has been previously discussed, an annual deduction for the funding of a reserve for the periodic replacement of furniture, fixtures and equipment must always be included in a hotel's forecast of income and expense. Reserves may be as low as 2% of total revenue for a motel, but typically range from 3% to of total revenues. Higher deductions may be warranted for a luxury hotel or an older property if no significant capital improvements are provided for in the valuation.

INCOME CAPITALIZATION

A single year forecast of net income may be capitalized into an estimate of value through the application of one overall rate, while a multi-year forecast will require some form of discounted cash flow analysis. While some appraisers prefer to apply market derived overall capitalization rates to a forecasted income stream, the accuracy of such rates is dependent upon the validity of the data used in the rate extraction. Sales prices and terms, as well as net income figures are very difficult to ascertain for a hotel property. Is the net income a past year historical figure, an estimate for the current year or a projection for the future? Have deductions been made for a management fee and reserve for replacement? As the purchasers of hotel properties will typically finance a majority of a hotel's purchase price and base their purchase decisions on the future earning potential of a hotel, some form of mortgage-equity capitalization technique is considered most appropriate for hotel properties.

Support for current interest rates of hotel mortgages should be presented in the report. The equity dividend or yield rate is more difficult to substantiate, but some form of support should be presented for a chosen equity return. Overall discount rates, without consideration to debt and equity components, are also utilized by some appraisers, but are more difficult to substantiate and provide a wider margin for error. A reviewer should look for discount rates or overall rates at one to two hundred basis points above comparable rates for other commercial real estate to reflect the risk associated with a hotel investment.

The reviewer should look for a reasonable relationship between the discount rate applied to the projected net income, the assumed underlying inflation rate, and the overall rate utilized to capitalize the last year's net income into a reversionary value. The application of a 13% overall rate in the calculation of a reversion may seem inappropriate in an analysis that utilizes a 13% overall discount rate and a 5% inflation rate; an overall rate of 8% may seem more appropriate to reflect the real rate of return indicated by the discount rate. However, increases in terminal capitalization rates for hotels are generally justified to reflect the large capital expenditures required to upgrade a hotel's physical plant every seven to ten years. Such expenditures are generally necessary in addition to the funds put aside in the reserve for replacement. Use of the extremely low capitalization rates being derived from the sale of recent "trophy" hotel properties can be justified in the appraisal of only certain types of lodging facilities, as will be discussed later in this article. Review appraisers should be on the lookout for an aggressive projection of the stabilized year's net income. The stabilized year's net income is supposed to reflect the average annual earning potential of the hotel over the assumed holding period or for its remaining economic life, and thus must inherently take into consideration the cyclical nature of supply and demand. An appraiser should not take the hotel's peak operating performance as the stabilized year's performance, but should moderate such a projection in anticipation of the inevitable downturns in profitability.

SALES COMPARISON APPROACH

Sales comparison approach, by bracketing a range of sales prices, is useful in providing support for the market value estimated via the income approach. The sales price per room of hotel properties is frequently discussed among participants in the hotel real estate market. However, the actual terms and motivations of such sales is rarely discovered. As the buyers and sellers of hotels do not base their investment decisions upon the sales price of comparable properties, but upon a hotels' ability to generate income, the sales comparison approach is considered inappropriate for deriving an estimate of a hotel's market value. Variations in hotel properties are so diverse that to even attempt to adjust the sales prices of comparable hotel sales is a futile exercise. Two identically sized hotels in similar locations may sell for widely disparate prices due to differences in each property's ability to generate income. The sales comparison approach may be appropriate for the valuation of some small, homogeneous motel properties, and should be given greater weight in the appraisal of motels of this nature.

The exorbitant sales prices which have been paid for a number of "trophy" properties over the past few years, generally by offshore and primarily Asian investors, has provided an opportunity for appraisers to present comparable sales and derived capitalization rates that can justify virtually any estimate of value. One common element to all of the "trophy" hotel sales is an irreplaceable site and improvements, and the inclusion of goodwill or business value that is tied to the identity of the hotel and/or its affiliation and managing agent. A number of recent sales include such hidden value components such as the right to the name of the hotel of other future development or the purchase of an established management company. Few hotels have the attributes to qualify as a trophy property and a review appraiser should be wary of an appraiser's attempt to classify a hotel as such.

COST APPROACH

The cost approach is a necessary component in determining the feasibility of new or proposed hotels. However, even in such a case the income approach is the ultimate determinate of market value. Many hotels today are over improvements, in that their construction costs cannot be supported by the income that they generate. It is very common for relatively new hotels costing $120,000 per room to be able to economically support only $80,000 per room in value. The difference between the cost of a new hotel and its value via the income approach is generally attributable to external obsolescence caused by overbuilding and the resultant depressed occupancies and average rates.

The cost approach is very difficult to utilize in the valuation of older hotels which suffer from both external and functional obsolescence, as well as physical depreciation. An appraiser can rightfully justify the omission of the cost approach due to its inapplicability to hotel properties. Some consideration should be given to the replacement costs of comparable hotels in certain depressed market areas. For instance, a well designed and well located hotel that would cost $150,000 per room to build new, but is only generating income to support $50,000 per room in value might be Justifiably appraised for $75,000 per room if it is the type of property that would attract certain investors, such as hotel companies desirous of a presence in the market.

CONCLUSION

A hotel appraisal presents a unique challenge to reviewers due to the numerous variables which must be considered in the valuation of a transient lodging facility. Minor aggressiveness in each variable can result in a greatly overstated value. A reviewer is charged with the task of considering the reasonableness of the final value estimate and will ultimately have to rely on his or her own good judgment in evaluating the appraiser's conclusions.

Hotel appraisers should be held accountable for all the data, judgment and analysis presented in the appraisal report. As it is impossible to include all the backup and support for a hotel's projected performance in a written appraisal it is the prerogative of the reviewer to ask the appraiser for additional support for any aspect of the valuation. An appraisal of a transient lodging facility should provide evidence of the appraiser's knowledge of both the business and real estate components which make a hotel investment so unique.

CHAPTER TWENTY-SIX

REVIEWING AN INDUSTRIAL APPRAISAL REPORT

INTRODUCTION

It is recommended that the periodical "Reviewing an Office Building Appraisal Report" be used as a base reference to this publication, as it contains many parameters of review applicable to any property type.

OVERVIEW OF THE REPORT:

The first step for the reviewer is to develop a clear mental picture of the property being appraised. Examine the photographs, read the summary of salient facts and then ask yourself three questions:

1. What type of industrial property is the subject of the report? There are five basic types, distinguished primarily by use and secondarily by building characteristics:

• Warehouse-distribution

Approximately 90% warehouse and 10% office. High ceilings maximizing pallet stacking are prevalent as are the combination of dock-high loading bays, ground level loading bays, and rail bays.

• Manufacturing

Approximately 60% manufacturing, 30% warehouse and 10%

office. The buildings are often considered specialized, particularly when the building serves primarily to protect equipment or was designed for a specific business, and the building is not conducive for other types of manufacturing.

• Research & Development

Approximately 85% to 100% of space in high quality finish characterized by specialized construction components such as "clean rooms" and laboratories.

• High Technology

Approximately 35% office and 65% finished open area. Usually distinguishable from R & D with the test question: Does this building serve for the manufacturing of the products that emerged from R & D? The line of distinction is a blurry one and in some regions, the terms are used interchangeably.

• Incubator

Generally 1,000 to 5,000 square foot units in buildings of less than 20,000 to 25,000 square feet. About 30% of the space is used for office and the balance for storage, shop or distribution. Ground level loading is utilized and clear ceiling heights typically do not exceed 12 feet.

2. What is the primary environment and locational influence?

Is it in an architecturally and use controlled industrial park? Is it in an area with a wide variety of uses from residential to commercial? The latter may indicate that the reviewer will pay special attention to the Neighborhood Section and Highest and Best Use Section of the report, as the property may be subject to future use change by encroachment, infiltration or the cyclical life of the neighborhood.

Is it oriented to a nearby airport, harbor or port district? If so, does it have the special overlay of a free-trade zone? Is it an inner city, freeway or suburban location?

3. Do you believe the appraiser clearly understands what type of industrial property he/she is evaluating?

This can be answered by checking the improved property sales and the rental comparables that are presented in the report. Do you find a mix of industrial types? Do you find homogeneity of the industrial type, but a broad mix of location orientation? In addition to having different physical characteristics, each industrial category caters to a different market profile of buyers, sellers and tenants.

The categories are often subject to independent and divergent economic constraints and considerations, as well as different supply and demand characteristics and different locational needs. All appraisal is predicated on the economic principal of substitution - comparing like with like. Therefore, for the to crossover between industrial categories is usually as beneficial as trying to find relevance in comparing the price paid per square foot of a high-rise office building to the price paid per square foot of an apartment building.

As the reviewer proceeds through the report, is there evidence of further refinement of these broad categories?

REVIEW ANALYSIS

Each type of industrial property could warrant its own article; therefore, the primary emphasis in the following sections will be to highlight areas that could be applied to the majority of industrial space. The review of the analysis of a facility requires understanding in three general categories:

Location

As stated in every publication and text, the primary consideration for real estate is *location, location, location.* It cannot be overly stressed. Whether the building is misplaced by one block or one mile, the result may place the investor in a nonrecoverable economic position. Good locations for an industrial property are as varied as there are types of businesses. The reviewer is looking for consistency and transferability between the economic analysis and the physical analysis. Does the identified user market fit with the location?

Ownership/Management

Frequently not addressed in a report but of major significance at any stage of the property's economic life is ownership and management. If not discussed in the report, the reviewer may wish to discuss this topic with the appraiser. Ownership philosophies differ from time to time and vary by owner type. For example, in the pre-leasing stage of a building, several business decisions are made. To compete, or not to compete, is the question. In soft markets, some owners with the financial ability to withstand economic adversity may elect to preserve their "image" and consciously decide to lease only at the original terms when the building was planned, or even to mothball the building until the market strengthens. Decisions will be made as to whether or not to give free rent or other incentives to attract tenants, and the lease terms will be set. Market value "assumes" competent management. Does the appraiser mention certain quirks or differences in management techniques that subtly indicate a red flag?

A decision to preclude three year lease terms could meet tenant resistance resulting in an extended lease-up. Will a strong pre-leasing program be implemented? The parameters set by the owner and management team will affect the rate of leasing activity.

Who has ownership selected to manage and lease the space?

Incompetent or apathetic leasing agents can cause higher than typical turnover, and delay the initial lease-up or releasing. Is the agent at the subject building also the agent at a competing building? Are the commissions paid to the agent the same, or is there a different commission structure? Variances could cause one building to be pushed more than the other by the leasing agent. Does the leasing agent like the building? Their own opinions will influence potential tenants.

Functionalism of the Building

This can be thought of from both a physical and economic perspective. An industrial building frequently becomes functionally obsolete before its physical life has ended. Functionalism ultimately effects the income generating ability of the property. How does the property compare with the state of the art? (See Building Description section).

AREA ECONOMIC OVERVIEW-MARKET ANALYSIS

The information should be tailored to the specific sets of criteria that ultimately affect demand for the particular industrial category being studied. For example, research and development is highly subject to the availability of federal funds and grants, and the supply of a highly specialized labor pool. However, these factors have little or no relevance to a warehouse-distribution center. Rather, accessibility to and from markets, shifts in market location and penetration are critical.

For the manufacturing property, the demand for the product should be addressed as well as identifying competitors (local and international) in order to assess the likelihood of continuation of the product line. If the appraiser has indicated that the product has an uncertain future, can the property be adapted to and is the location appropriate for the manufacturing of a different product? Incubator space absorption is commonly linked with an expanding economy and an influx of new entrepreneurs.

The reviewer should look for an indication that the appraiser has considered area and economic components that are pertinent to and will affect the viability of the type of industrial category being studied. Examples of general questions the reviewer will want answered are:

- Have inventories decreased or increased?
- Do transportation corridors and routes preclude industrial development?
- Is a particular mode of transportation phasing out?
- What does the labor pool consist of and what is the availability and convenience to the labor pool?
- What is the existing supply of vacant building space in the category being analyzed? How much additional space is proposed? Where is it? How will new development in these areas affect the subject?
- How much land with the proper zoning is in inventory for future growth in this segment? How much land is served with adequate utility capacity?
- How difficult is it to rezone in the jurisdiction?
- Do land prices and its general availability or lack thereof curtail or enhance future industrial growth?

SUPPLY AND DEMAND

All real estate markets are cyclical - some more pronounced than others. It is imperative for the appraiser to convey his/ her opinion as to where the market is in the cycle. This is critical for loan underwriting and for a supportable opinion of value, the conclusion of which is ultimately proven or dis-proven with the sale price.

For example, if an appraisal is prepared on a piece of real estate when the market is in the second stage of the upswing, it would be anticipated that the appraiser would make allowance in the cash flow for future anticipated softening of rental rates and potential for a lower percentage of leases being renewed. Despite the evidence of increasing vacancy levels and perhaps some concessions, does the appraiser increase rents by the same percentage as were historically achieved in the first half of the curve? Perhaps it is appropriate, but if so, then the appraiser should answer the question, "why?"

As vacancies increase, the competition for tenants increases, often blurring the lines of an identified user market. For example, when funds dry up for R & D, the unleased space in a building specifically designed for R & D often has to compete for general office use. How strong or weak is that market? With a weakening primary market, the strength of the secondary or alternate market becomes increasingly important.

BUILDING DESCRIPTION

Standards for an efficient building change with technology. Whatever the age and type of building, it competes with the state of art buildings. For either the tenant or the buyer, there is a breaking point between the rent paid for an older facility and the convenience and functionalism of a modern one.

Industrial Market

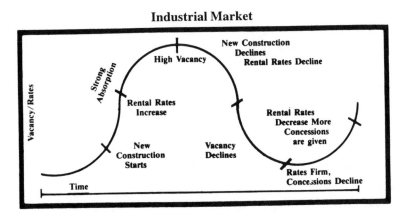

Probably the clearest example is to consider office space. In overbuilt saturated markets, tenants in Class B & C space find it economically viable for them to upgrade to Class A space. This occurs when the margin between the rental rates in Class A space and Class B & C space narrows significantly (or becomes equivalent). The same thing happens in the industrial sector. As discussed in the preceding section, if an R & D building has to compete with general office buildings, does it have the physical attributes to do so successfully? For many office space users there has been an increasing trend for more offices with windows. Many junior executives, as well as senior executives, now receive a window office. The change is seen in architectural design with buildings of irregular shape to specifically provide more window space. Depending on the market, it may be vital to look at the difference in the number of window offices that can be accommodated in one building versus another with the same area.

The point of this section of the report is to answer whether the building adequately serves the market, and for how long it can do so. A building may be on a rail line - but is service to end within the next year? Perhaps the spur has not been maintained and will require a large sum of money to be invested before it is usable and a benefit to the property. Building characteristics addressed in this section include the following:

- Bay Spaces,
- Clear Ceiling Height,
- Heat and Air Conditioning,
- Load Bearing Capacity of Floors,
- Lighting and Electrical Capacity,
- Loading Docks (number, type, width, and height),
- Flexibility for Multiple Tenants, and
- Building Shell (type and condition).

The appraiser should consider the following questions:

1. How does the subject compare to the state of the art?
2. Is it a new building with no more technical adaptations or operating efficiencies than a building constructed ten years ago?
3. Are there economic savings in operations?
4. Is the amount of parking adequate, convenient, and secure?
5. Is there adequate turning radius for trucks?
6. Is there adequate clear height for storage?
7. Are there adequate windows for an R & D operation?

HIGHEST AND BEST USE

This section is the focal point of the report. Particularly common with older industrial properties are legally nonconforming uses and uses that do not represent highest and best use.

Has the appraiser considered whether the land may produce more income, therefore more value, if it were vacant and available to be developed with a legally conforming use?

If legally nonconforming, has the remaining economic life of the improvements been carefully considered? Perhaps the industrial building is an under-improvement or situated in an area where change has occurred, greater density is permissible and more appropriate - i.e.; from industrial to suburban office or retail. Can this facility be converted?

For a variety of reasons, the existing buildings may not represent the highest and best use. Has the appraiser valued the improvements on a consistent basis with the *site's* highest and best use?

LAND VALUATION

Sites are as varied as the types of improvements that are constructed on them. When appraisers select land sales to use in a comparison analysis, it is imperative that they choose sites with similar or at the least, make careful analytical adjustments for the dissimilarities.

A frequent problem is comparing site sales located in one industrial park with those in other industrial parks without proper adjustments; or comparing site sales located in industrial parks with those outside a park environment without proper adjustments.

Not all industrial parks are created equal. The Specific restrictions and requirements are set to ensure that the overall appearance and homogeneity of uses within the park are preserved. Significant differences between parks can occur in a variety of categories including allowable uses, annual fees for maintenance, required building to land ratios, the amount of sidewalks a buyer is required to install, landscaping requirements, required screening of open areas, special assessments for flood control, sewer plants, etc.

Has the appraiser taken into account these factors to arrive at an *effective* price per square foot of each comparable in competing industrial parks?

When comparing sites in and out of an industrial park, the problem becomes more complex. Not only are there the aforementioned issues that can be empirically quantified, but what about the cost and time adjustment for getting raw land to an equal state of development as a park? Do the buyers of sites in industrial parks also match the market profile for buyers of raw land?

DIRECT SALES COMPARISON APPROACH

All items of variance between a sale and the property may not be recognized by the market. When the implementation of adjustments is required, it should be based only on market perceived differences. If the property is leased, has the appraiser considered the differences between the subject and the comparable in the quality of tenants and quantity of income generated? Has the appraiser taken into account the variances in the percentage of office space to warehouse space? Have variances in the remaining effective economic lives been considered? Are the physical characteristics carefully compared including, columnar spacing, clear ceiling height, load capacity of flooring, docks and leading facilities? Also, for this approach to value to be particularly viable, the buyers need to be similar. Gone are the days of appraisers gathering sales, shuffling well, looking for pairs and three of a kind that simply match physical characteristics. Many investors are sophisticated, site specific, and have specific investment criteria. In response, the analyst has become a site specific economist. For example, the expectations of the institutional investor may not be achieved by a targeted property, yet an owner-user would be an excellent match.

INCOME APPROACH

This approach addresses several issues independently of each other including Income Generation, Expenses, Capitalization, Equity, Dividend and Discount Rates.

Income Generation

Usually the rental rates are split: a rate for shell, unfinished space; and a rate applicable to finished and office space. If the project is new, has the blend of rates and percentage of use between finished high technology space, office space and warehouse usage been addressed? The financial capability of the tenants to continue to pay rent in the foreseeable future been considered?

Expenses

Is there clarity of which items are the landlord's responsibility? Is there an allocation for a reserve for capital improvements?

Direct Capitalization or Discounted Cash Flow

Has the appraiser selected an appropriate technique based on the characteristics of the income stream and investor actions? Are the rates supportable?

Cost Approach

This is particularly relevant for new properties and specialized properties. Has the appraiser considered all forms of depreciation? Has the appraiser calculated the deductions properly?

CONCLUSION

The reviewer must judge consistency, adequacy of research and analytical competency. The bases for a quality review are a comprehensive, working knowledge of the economic principles that underlie appraisal.

CHAPTER TWENTY-SEVEN

REVIEWING A GOLF COURSE APPRAISAL

In providing appraisal review guidelines for golf course valuation it is appropriate to consider the great changes which have happened and are continuing to happen in the golf world.

Up until just a few years ago, golf courses have been traditionally considered as "loss leaders" by the real estate and resort industries, i.e., necessary but costly amenities justified by the effectiveness of increasing the adjoining real estate value, the rate of lot and housing absorption, and increasing sales of food, beverage and room revenues.

A further incentive was that in golf oriented residential communities and country clubs, the golf course was written off, in whole or in part, as a cost of the real estate development; subsequently, the course could be sold to the membership for the capture of some of the operating losses sustained by the developer during the real estate marketing period, and occasionally provided some capital gain income.

In the past few years this financial situation has reversed itself. With the astronomically growing demand for golf tee times from currently over 23,000,000 golfers in the United States; the nearly universal use of golf carts and the increase in green fees (for club guests or for public courses) and monthly dues from club members, the golf course has now become, in most areas of the country, a profit center.

Golf courses are in short supply in the nation, and the USGA estimates that at least one golf course per day will be required in the United States to keep up with the expanding demand for golf.

Three (3) factors have been predominate in the increase in golfers. First, is the aging of the population. As the baby boomers move into the 35 to 50 year old group, the mild and attractive exercise of golf supplants jogging and those other sports which require superior physical conditioning. Second is the surge of women now taking up golf. Currently, nearly 40% of golfers are women and this trend is growing. Third is the intense TV reporting of golf. Due to these trends, the demand for golf appraisal is rapidly increasing and will continue to do so over the foreseeable future.

CLASSIFICATION BY TYPE

The appraisal review process begins with comments about the highest and best use of a site, the type and kind of golf courses, and the various approaches to value, all of which outline the range of circumstances encountered in golf course appraisal.

To select the proper approach to golf course value estimation, the first step is to classify the type of course; Golf courses fall into these general categories:

Non-Profit Courses:

- Proprietary Membership Clubs
- Municipal courses operated as non-profit

Profit Courses:

- Franchise country clubs or private franchise clubs
- Municipal courses operated under lease to professional course operators for profit
- Privately owned courses open to the public

Type of Course/Playing Quality:

Configurations for Regulation 18-hole courses include:
- returning nines
- single fairway continuous
- double fairway returning nines
- double fairway continuous
- core golf course

Length: 6,300 to 7,400 yards (average about 6,500 yards)

- Regulation 9-hole course: 3,200 to 3,500 yards
- Regulation 27 holes: combination of the above
- Executive Courses: may have any of the five configurations and averages from 4 ,000 to 5,000 yards
- Pitch and Putt, 18 holes: may have any of the five above configurations; about 2,000 yards average
- Pitch and Putt, 9 holes: average 1,000 yards.
- Miniature Golf Course - not covered by this data

Appraisal of Existing Golf Course—The appraisal process differs between an existing course and a proposed course, primarily in that the existing course provides operating history and financial statements which can be analyzed and adjusted to provide stabilized net effective annual income where the Income Approach is used. The existing course improvements and structures require that depreciation be applied based on age, condition and continued economic life expectancy.

Proposed Golf Course Appraisal— For a proposed course for which the Income Approach is to be used, all of the data which would be available on the existing course has to be synthesized by extraction from the market. This procedure requires investigation and analysis of existing competitive golf courses located within the established trading area. For clubs charging initiation fees, this must be reported with monthly dues, cart rental fees, and guest fees.

Gross income and operating expenses for food, beverage and Pro Shop are difficult to secure from current competitive operations, as such data is considered confidential by most competitive operators. The usual source for this information is derived from the data published by the major accounting firms and/or, if the appraiser has made a number of golf course appraisals over recent time, this information may be established from the appraiser's file data. For the reviewer, the source and verification of this data is important to assure that it realistically reflects the market conditions.

Under the highest and best use analysis, the time experienced by comparable golf courses in membership fill-up time for country clubs and/or the time required for public courses to reach stabilized patronage, will establish the absorption period for the respective types of courses and will become the basis for carrying costs over the absorption period. This period will also establish the rate of physical depreciation that would occur in the probable one to three year period of absorption in most areas.

HIGHEST AND BEST USE

Profit golf courses are approached on the basis of estimating the highest and best use of the underlying land as if vacant and available for use. In the absence of any limiting legal impediments such as covenants, conditions and restrictions which may determine or restrict the potential uses; easements; encroachments; or other impediments to a wide range of uses, all profit courses may have a potential for uses that can exceed the existing golf course use.

The constraint on other uses is the cost of conversion to a use or uses which may appear to provide a higher return on the land. The cost of the golf course improvements is substantial, and any use which promises to provide a higher return must cover the cost of removal of the existing improvements and still provide an economic return on the land and the alternate improvements. Although the existing use as a golf course may not represent the maximum creation of income, it may continue to be the best use of the site until income production falls below the level of economic yield, and thus is an interim use.

A thorough analysis of the existing use versus any potential higher use typically involves careful costing and income production, both of which must be thoroughly supported.

The potential of other uses rests among other considerations of the zoning and general plan for the area. If another use is to be considered the zoning must permit such alternates and/or reasonable assurance must be found and reported that the general plan can be changed.

Non-profit golf courses are generally country club courses or courses purchased or developed by private golf groups. Municipal courses also fall into the non-profit category - usually, not always - because the public outcry over more than nominal fees keeps them non-profit. Typically, the highest and best use of non-profit courses is for the existing golf course. Where such is apparent, the highest and best use analysis becomes relatively simple.

For proposed golf courses, an important element of the analysis is the inclusion of a market study of sufficient scope to provide enough market data that a reasonable conclusion may be made about the market demand. Unless the contributory or trading area has an unusual number of golf courses, the demand circumstance is generally a moot question. Under the present astronomical demand for golf playing capacity in most areas, it may be years before supply balances with demand. However, sufficient supporting data is required to establish the reasonable demand probability.

Market Data: Land

For profit oriented courses, the value of the underlying land should be based on the determination of the highest and best use decision. For non-profit courses for which there is no foreseeable future change of use, the market data search and the resulting value indication should be based on the assumption that the underlying land has a permanent use only as a golf course.

There may be alternate uses for golf courses without altering the basic use as a golf course. For example, in the Coachella Valley in California, many of the golf courses are developed in the valley's flood control channels and are designed to channel surface water in a manner least erosive to the course. These courses thus serve two uses: as both a golf course and, secondarily, as a flood control sheet spreading area during the rare and temporary occasions of extra-normal precipitation. In this case, despite its dual use, the approach to the value of the site is based on its primary use as a golf course.

Market Data: Golf Course Sales

Each golf course is a unique special use property which typically is designed to provide distinctive playing characteristics to entice golfers to challenge the course. Not only may courses vary widely in size and quality, the clubhouses and facilities they provide, the driving ranges, putting greens, practice sand traps and pitching greens also vary widely. Differences in locational influences, topography and soil types are common. The kinds of turf affect the quality of play, as does the presence or absence of lakes, streams, and quality and quantity of trees and shrubs.

Because of these wide variances, the traditional approach to value by direct comparison with other golf courses requires a myriad of compensating adjustments to equate such sales with the golf course being appraised. Units of comparison such as cost per hole, cost per acre or any other unit basis are generally NOT a meaningful measure of value for golf courses. Unless the comparable sales are closely equivalent in the major elements of comparison, numerous and significantly large dollar adjustments must be made; this tends to skew the value indications. This does not mean that the market data direct comparison approach should be ruled out, but unless there is close comparability, the adjustments must be carefully analyzed by the reviewer.

COST APPROACH

Under any circumstance, a golf course is a special use. For special use properties the primary indication of value has historically been the depreciated cost of reproduction of the improvements, plus the market indicated value of the underlying land. Although this approach traditionally tends to indicate the upper limit of value of a property, based on the principle of substitution, it also provides an anchor number to compare with the value evidence of the other methods of estimating value.

If the Income Approach results in a substantially higher or lower value indication, it may be an indication that some of the basic data used to develop the capitalization process may be in error. The same comparison applies to the value indicated by direct comparison of the subject golf course with recent sales of other golf courses. It is rare that all three approaches to value are within close range; however, substantially wide variances should alert the reviewer to a re-investigation of these processes.

The greatest area for error in the cost approach is the estimation of physical depreciation. When the building structures are newer than 10 years or so, the Marshall Valuation Service's Life Expectancy Tables and the Physical Depreciation Tables provide realistic guidelines. For any age facilities, however, the element of personal investigation and experience in structure depreciation is more important than any tables. For the reviewer, if the actual age is relatively short, reference to Marshall or other age/life tables should permit a realistic check.

For structures older than about 10 years, the reviewer has little foundation for assessing the rate of depreciation except by reference to the appraiser's supporting data and explanations and/ or by the reviewer's knowledge of the appraiser's experience and ability.

Depreciation of the golf course and the furniture, fixtures and equipment which are not part of the real estate, represents a more difficult area for the reviewer to check except by comparison with any file data available. If the reviewer believes that the depreciation factors are not realistic, he can resort to the appraiser's sources. Generally, unless the appraiser is also a machinery and equipment appraiser, the information about clubhouse FF&E, kitchen equipment and golf course maintenance equipment can be secured from venders of these items. If the property appraised is an existing course, the club manager and the golf course superintendent can be helpful in estimating depreciation.

INCOME APPROACH

This approach is generally used only for profit golf courses. For existing courses, careful analysis of the past 3 to 5 years' financial statements should result in a clear picture of the most probable net effective income, the basis for capitalization. The major area for careful review is the development of the capitalization rate.

For a proposed course, examination of the source and support of the capitalization rate, discount rate and sound support for the estimates of probable income and expenses can convince the reviewer that these factors are consistent with the market. Otherwise, further support may be needed.

SUMMARY AND CONCLUSIONS

This section provides (a) recapitulation of the value approach indications; (b) narrative support for the reasonableness of the approaches and a summary of the appraiser's reasoning for the final value conclusion; and (c) a statement containing the type of interest valued, the date of value, and the estimate of value.

In the summary reconciliation do the respective value indications widely differ? If so, is the range of value justified and reconciled with the final estimate of value? On which approach does the appraiser place most weight in reaching his final estimate of value, and why?

There are hardly any "perfect" appraisals. If there are any areas which are not clear or which leaves some doubt in the reviewer's mind, it is entirely proper and good practice for the reviewer to ask the appraiser to discuss the report with him. Items requiring clarification can probably be cleared up over the telephone or by letter from the appraiser.

In initially discussing the reviewer' s need for some supplementary information, it would be appropriate to make clear to the appraiser that the reviewer is looking at the report constructively, and is not intending to "pick the fly specks out". Many appraisers have had the experience of a reviewer picking out insignificant elements for criticism; unfortunately, this leaves the appraiser with the feeling that the reviewer was making a critique only to enhance the reviewer's ego or importance. Another common occurrence is the reviewer's request for information that is clearly set forth in the appraisal, indicating that the reviewer has not read all of the report.

REVIEWER'S CHECKLIST

The following constitutes a check list which generally conforms to the criteria of the Uniform Standards of Professional Appraisal Practice (assumed to be followed in the appraiser's report), to help the reviewer go through the appraisal without missing any significant data.

1. BRIEF PROPERTY DESCRIPTION

This should include at least the name and address of the course appraised, and the site should be located on an area map.

2. PURPOSE OF THE APPRAISAL

The interest to be appraised should be clearly stated: fee, leasehold, leased fee, or other estates in real property.

3. FUNCTION OF THE APPRAISAL

How the appraisal is to be used should be set forth, as the use of the appraisal determines the format: to determine offering price, for lending purposes, etc.

4. THE APPRAISAL PROCESS

This should be briefly described, e.g., in accordance with the Uniform Standards of Professional Appraisal Practice; in accordance with state certified appraisal requirements; in conformance with Eminent Domain Law, etc.

5. ASSUMPTIONS

All assumptions, special aspects or limiting conditions of the appraisal should be set forth.

6. DATE OF VALUE

If not a current date, an explanation of using a prior date: by Order of Court; by request of the client , etc.

7. DESCRIPTION OF THE PROPERTY

This should include all of the following categories:

General Description

This information should present a clear and comprehensive overall picture of the property, as this is the initial introduction to the property appraised. For example: "The Sands is a public course containing 18 holes being 7,100 yards in length. The holes are returning nines to a 42,000 s/f clubhouse with pro shop, men's and women's lockers bar, lounge and dining room, all on the upper level. The first level contains the cart storage area, cart maintenance area and the pro's office, with storage areas for miscellaneous clubhouse equipment. Adjoining the clubhouse on the North is a large 6,000 s/f practice green, sand trap and pitching green, and a 6-acre driving range with 30 tees."

"On the South side of the clubhouse is an Olympic size pool and health spa with large deck and gazebo. The club house parking lot lies opposite the club house entry and contains 150 asphalt surfaced vehicle parking spaces.

"The Sands golf course covers 170 total acres. The course is open to the public six days per week, being closed on Mondays. The property perimeter is enclosed with a 6' masonry wall, and the entry is characterized by masonry portals with intense landscaping.

"Refer to the attached Assessor's Plat Map, the overall Site Plan, Structure Plans (or appraiser's sketches), Aerial Photograph and ground level Site Photographs."

Outline Specifications

This data may be reported on a form or in narrative, but should include the following:

Land Area

In acres, designated as to fee, lease, etc. If any land portion is leased, the lease term should be reported.

Topography and Soils

And comments regarding affect on use/value.

Drainage

The contributory water shed area, if any; drainage structures; FEMA Flood Zone and description; and arroyos or active water courses which may transect the course should be discussed.

Climatic Conditions

Annual rainfall, seasonable times and playable days over the average year. Climatic conditions have a very substantial influence on the economics of the golf course.

Zoning

The golf course use should be related to both the Zoning and General Plan in effect for the area.

Golf Course Improvements

Each of the following should be provided, with adequate descriptions:

- age and condition of the course
- number of holes, showing par 3s, 4s and 5s
- length of the course: pro's, men's, women's tees
- type of cart paths and condition
- waterfalls, fountains, lakes (including depth, size, construction type such as earth shaped with no concreted walls, gunited, soil cemented, etc.)
- traps: number, type of sand, power rakeable or require hand raking
- water source: on site wells, public utility, etc.
- irrigation system: type, age, condition
- course rest rooms: type structures, age, condition, description, drinking water, etc.
- turf type and condition: for tees, greens and fairways; double seeding required? special conditions?
- practice green, trap and pitching green

- driving range size, number of tees, type of water system, covered tees, range office, special equipment or circumstances
- course maintenance building: size, type, age, condition
- course maintenance equipment: list of all mowers, tractors, trucks, cultivating equipment and other miscellaneous equipment (with ages and conditions)
- golf carts: number, type, gasoline or electric, age and condition
- golf cart storage maintenance and repair equipment: type of charging system and number of chargers for electric carts, age and condition; for gasoline carts, the fuel pumps and underground storage tanks (double walled? monitoring system?), used oil storage containers require description and method of disposal
- auxiliary structures such as snack bar, pools, gazebos, other outbuildings: type, size, age, condition

Clubhouse

Size, type of construction, age, condition; clubhouse kitchen equipment fixed and part of the real estate, and furniture, fixtures and equipment that are chattels; pro shop, bar, dining room, locker rooms, outdoor furniture, etc.

Landscaping

This should be shown on the site plan in sufficient detail to provide the measurement of the total landscaped area, the extent of the irrigation system, and the number of outdoor lighting facilities, including street lights and parking area lighting.

Property Perimeter Enclosure

Height, length, type and condition of fencing/walls, hedges or other property enclosures.

8. APPRAISAL FORMAT AND EXHIBITS

In packaging the appraisal, the usual method is to preface the report with a letter of transmittal which generally does no more than contain the estimated value and some brief introductory data.

It is also very typical that most readers of the report (including, unfortunately, some reviewers) look first at the "bottom line", being the estimate of value. If they read much further it is usually only particular excerpted sections. Consequently, the flow of the appraiser's reasoning from beginning to end is not fully comprehended, and often misunderstandings and erroneous conclusions are created. It is suggested that every appraisal of a golf course provide an "Executive Summary" at the beginning of the report.

Executive Summary

The executive summary should cover all of the most essential data leading up to the conclusion of value, and tends to assist the report "skimmer" and may prevent misunderstandings of the report. If the reviewer finds that the report does not contain an Executive Summary, inclusion of such a summary prepared by the reviewer would help understanding of the reviewer's report by those who will examine the written reviews of the appraisal. It is strongly recommended that the reviewer FIRST READ the appraisal report from beginning to end before any analysis begins.

Exhibits

Sufficient and clear exhibits are very important to provide the reader with an adequate visual concept of the property and as the basis from which the cost estimate of the improvements is generated. Most existing golf courses have no plans, or only incomplete plans, making it necessary for the appraiser to provide complete and accurate drawings. Some appraisers, probably in the interest of saving time, provide only sketches of the structures' floorplan exteriors for computation of structure site, with very little supplementary data. This is one area in which the appraiser should take the time to make the drawings as complete as possible, with full notations.

Where it is necessary to draw the structure(s), it is very helpful to show not only the floorplan perimeters, but also the interior partitions, the appurtenant walkways, planter areas, porches, steps, and enough detail so that in taking off quantities nothing is missed or glossed over.

Legal Description

Review of the legal aspects are very important. Often there are Covenants, Conditions, and Restrictions (CC&Rs) that may have substantial influence on use and therefore effect value. Encroachments are often missed and may be a source of value loss.

An instance of this kind is most likely in golf courses which are surrounded by residential lots: it is not unusual for portions of the fairways and sometimes even the tees or greens to encroach lot boundaries. Some public courses, particularly municipal courses, may lie on land which has been given to the city as a gift, with the donor having stipulated in the deed that failure to continue golf course use may result in reversion, or there may be a stipulation that the land can only be used in perpetuity as a golf course.

If any portions of the land are leased, a brief of the lease should be included under this section and a copy of the full lease should be attached to the Addenda of the report.

Vesting

The fee holder (property owner), and/or the leased fee and leasehold vestees in the case of a lease, require adequate identification. If the fee holder is a common interest such as a membership group, it should be identified as the legal entity, e.g., corporation profit, non-profit or other type of common ownership.

History of the Course

Membership and management history; history of greens and cart fees; recent sale of the course, if any, etc.

Assessor's Data

Plat maps, tax amounts, tax rates and assessed value.

Access to the Property

This should be identified as public street maintained by the City/County; private street maintained by a Home Owner's Association or by the golf course ownership, etc. Ease of identifying the access route should be described. Is the access to the golf course difficult or easy to find? Is the entry well defined?

Utility Availability

Typically, golf course irrigation water is provided by a private well and pumping system, as generally the cost of domestic water is excessive for golf course use. Many courses today are irrigated by reclaimed treated affluent from sanitary treatment plants, or the water source may be a local lake, river or other source. The source should be identified.

It is assumed that most golf courses have electricity, telephone, natural gas and TV cable service. The availability of each type of utility should be noted; the lack of any utility should be commented upon, and any alternate facility explained.

Special Hazards

Roofing problems, toxic contamination (e.g. underground fuel leaks), earthquake hazards, recurring heaving wind storms, dust or sand problems.

Covenants, Conditions and Restrictions

The former land owner or the developer, if a housing surrounded project may have recorded CC&Rs which may very significantly affect use and value. If CC&Rs are in effect for the golf course or any portion, the full content of the CC&Rs should be included in the Addenda of the appraisal report which gives the reviewer the opportunity to read them and ascertain that the appraiser's interpretation of the effect of the CC&Rs on the golf course is consistent with the reviewer s conclusions.

Encroachments

Existing encroachments often may not be ascertainable by casual visual inspection but, generally, by checking the perimeter of the course the appraiser can secure a reasonable identification of any apparent extension of fences, walls, paths and buildings that may encroach upon the golf course area. If the appraisers has not noted in the report that an encroachment does not exist and/or that neither the title report nor visual site inspection revealed any encroachments, the reviewer should query the appraiser about his investigation and knowledge of any encroachments.

Easements

Review of the title report should reveal any easements of record. Site inspection normally reveals what may be prescriptive easements by worn footpaths leading onto the golf course, or by vehicle tracks indicating regular passage onto the golf course area. The reviewer should be sure that the appraisal report covers the possibility of easements, stating there are no easements or, if there are any indications of prescriptive easements, describing the effect on use and value of the course.

Climatic Conditions

Annual rainfall, seasonal temperatures, estimated number of "playing days" per year based on the weather.

Environmental Influences

Neighborhood characteristics, contributory trading area population, general economic conditions for the area (this data, in addition to the market study information and the market study information and conclusions contained in the highest and Best Use section of the report).

Highest and Best Use Analysis

Determination of the highest and best use is the critical element on which the entire estimate of value rests. The respective elements and the narrative explanation providing the basis for the conclusion of highest and best use must be detailed and supported. The market study is an important portion of the analysis.

Is adequate economic and demographic data delineated? From this data are the conclusions of absorption properly extracted? In the market study is the status of any pending competitive golf courses) reported?

Is the trading area, the geographical area from which the sustaining club members and/or public patronage originates, clearly defined? Generally, the best source for securing data to establish the trading area is existing competing courses in the area of the subject golf course.

Are all existing competitive courses reported? Are initiation fees, monthly dues, guest fees and cart fees for private clubs and/ or greens fees and cart rentals for public courses reported? In some instances, although the income produced by a public course is sufficient to represent economic return on both land and improvements, there may be an alternate use that will provide a greater return, which will amortize the demolition and removal of the golf course improvements and still provide a higher return on the alternate improvements, thus representing the highest and best use of the land.

In the case of a proprietary country club, membership commitment is not likely to permit conversion to other uses, nor is it probable in a franchise club which has specific or implied commitment to the abutting property owners for the perpetuation of the golf course. Privately owned, and in some circumstances municipal courses, can be converted to higher uses.

Market Data: Land

The land sales must be consistent with the subject property's estimated highest and best use. If reasonably comparable sales fall within this criteria and the analysis of all the elements of comparison results in reasonable and minimum adjustments, the resulting value indication should be valid.

Market Data: Golf Course Sales

If direct comparison of the subject with recent sales of comparable golf courses is made, are the adjustments full and adequately explained? Do they appear to be logical and convincing? If the adjustments are numerous and substantial in degree, are they sufficiently persuasive to overcome the magnitude of adjustment and result in an accurate value indication?

Cost Approach to Improvement Value

As noted, the most probable area of error in this approach lies in the application of physical depreciation.

Income Approach

This method may provide a most significant indication of value. The most probable errors in this approach are (a) selection of a proper capitalization rate and (b) for a proposed course, the estimation of income and expenses.

SAMPLE

Executive Summary

Subject Property:

Whitewater Country Club, 2000 Green Street Anytown, California; a private country club

Improvements:

70 acres of fee land on which is an 18-hole, 6,900 yard golf course; 24,000 s/f clubhouse; driving range; practice putting green; pitching green; sand trap; and 120-vehicle clubhouse parking lot. The course is 11 years of age and is in excellent condition.

Type of Course:

Returning nines, single fairways, 2 course rest rooms, 3 lakes, Bermuda grass fairways overseeded with Rye grass in winter, greens of Seaside Bent

Membership/Fees:

410 golfing members; 40 social members; initiation fee of $20,000; $200 monthly dues; $40 guest green fees, $ 11 cart fees per player

Highest and Best Use:

The existing use as a country club; no foreseeable change in use

Value Indications:

Land	$4,080,000
Improvements	$6,720,000
FF&E	$1,200,000
by cost and Market Data	$12,000,000

by Direct Comparison
(2 country club sales) $13,000,000

by Income Approach $12,107,692

Conclusion of Value:

As of January 30, 1990, the estimated fee Market Value is:
TWELVE MILLION ($12,000,000) DOLLARS

CHAPTER TWENTY-EIGHT

REVIEWING AN APARTMENT APPRAISAL REPORT

INTRODUCTION

The appraisal of an apartment complex, and its subsequent review, can be one of the more complicated and demanding tasks in the field of real property analysis. While the vast majority of industrial, retail and office properties offer minimal amenities and require a relatively small number of adjustments, the income generated by a multi-family residential complex is more dependent on its amenities, such as recreational facilities, interior equipment and furnishings. In addition, each apartment unit is evaluated on the utility (bedrooms and bathrooms) it offers. These additional variables will have an affect on both sides of the net income equation, since they are reflected in both the income and the expenses generated by the property.

Therefore, because multi-family residences can be so diverse relative to other income producing properties, an apartment appraisal review must concentrate on the supportability and justification of the large number of potential adjustments, as well as supportability and defensibility of the appraisal report as a whole.

TITLE PAGE (Narrative Report) OR CLIENT INFORMATION (Form Report)

- Name and Address of for Whom the Report is to be Prepared
  — If Appraisal is for Loan Purposes, in Most Instances the Lender Should be the Client.
- Identify the Report as an Appraisal and the Type of Property being Valued
- Address of the Property Being Appraised
- Name and Address of Appraiser or Appraisal Company

LETTER OF TRANSMITTAL (Narrative Report)

- Name and Address of Client
  — If Appraisal is for Loan Purposes, in Most Instances the Lender Should be the Client.
- Address and Type of Property Being Appraised
- Type of Value Estimate (Example: Market Value)
- Nature of the Legal Interest (Example: Fee Simple Estate)
- Date of the Valuation Estimate
- Final Estimate or Estimates of Value
  1. If There is More Than One Value, it Should be Clear as to What Those Values Actually Mean or Represent.
  2. If There are any Contingencies to the Values, they Should be Mentioned or Referenced and be Easily Understood.

TABLE OF CONTENTS (Narrative Report)

Section Headings and Page Numbers Should Coincide.

PHOTOGRAPHS

Should be crisp, clear, and not out of focus. It is recommended that the photographs be placed close to the coinciding datum in order to make the report easy to visualize and understand accordingly. Remember the adage, "A picture is worth a thousand words."

Subject
1. Front
2. Rear
3. Street Scene or Scenes (two directions)
4. Amenities
5. Anything Unusual
6. Interior (optional)
    Improved Data
    — Front
    Rental Data
    — Front
    Land Data
    — Front
    Aerial

Reviewer's Note: Industry standards fluctuate considerably regarding photography and this should be clarified prior to starting an assignment.

MAPS, DRAWINGS AND SITE PLANS

Place the visual aids close to the coinciding datum for ease of reference (avoiding the reader having to flip back and forth from section to section).
Legibility

Reviewer's Note: Industry standards fluctuate considerably and it is recommended the requirements be clarified prior to starting an assignment.

EXECUTIVE SUMMARY OR SUMMARY OF SALIENT FACTS AND CONCLUSIONS

* Location
* Purpose of the Appraisal

- Nature of Legal Interest
- Owner of Record
- Land Area
- Improvement Description
- Highest and Best Use
- Estimated Value of the Land
- Estimated Value of the Improvements
- Estimate Value via the:
  1. Sales Comparison Approach
  2. Income Approach
  3. Cost Approach
- Value Indicators
  1. Per Unit
  2. Per Square Foot
  3. Per Room
- Income Multipliers (Gross Income or Gross Rent)
- Projected Income Data
  1. Gross Income
  2. Vacancy
  3. Effective Gross Income
  4. Expenses
      a. As a percent of gross income
      b. As a cost per square foot
      c. As a cost per unit
  5. Net Operating Income
  6. Overall Capitalization Rate
- Disclose any Contingencies
- Disclose anything Unusual
- Final Value Estimate or Estimates
- Date of Valuation

PURPOSE OF THE APPRAISAL

- The Type of Value—if anyone controls any figure within the report, whether it be over or under the market supported documentation, it should be disclosed, and the value cannot be market value. For example, investment criteria, underwriting policies, etc.

- A Current Definition of Market Value. Old definitions refer to "highest price" while recent definitions refer to "most probable price", and focus on central tendency instead of the upper limit of value.

FUNCTION OF THE APPRAISAL

What is it being used for?

PROPERTY RIGHTS OR INTEREST BEING APPRAISED

IDENTIFICATION OF THE PROPERTY

Type of Property
Complete Address
Legal Description

REAL ESTATE ASSESSMENT AND TAX RATE

Assessor's Parcel Number or Numbers
Assessed Value, Tax Rate and Total Tax
Address Exemptions, Special Assessments (Bonds) and their Effect on Value
Compare Assessments and Tax Rate with other Properties of Comparable Nature
Disclose Past Trends and Project to the Future

PROPERTY HISTORY

If the appraisal is prepared for lending purposes, in most instances, a three year history is required, including sales, contracts, options, listings, offers, foreclosures, etc.

EFFECTIVE DATE OF VALUATION

If the Value is Current it Should be Referred to as "Is."
If the Value is in Retrospect it Should be Referred to as "Was."
If the Value is in the Future it Should be Referred to as "Will Be."

AREA ANALYSIS

Physical Characteristics
Economics
    1. Trends
    2. General Make-up
        a. Diversity, etc.
Population Data and Supported Trends
Employment Data and Supported Trends
Governmental and Political Involvement and Attitudes
    1. Growth
    2. Anti-Growth
    3. Moratoriums
    4. Zoning and Zoning Changes
    5. Density
Availability of Livable Dwellings
    1. Attached and Detached Housing
    2. Apartments and Residential Income
Sociological Aspects
Environmental Aspects
    1. Noise
    2. Toxicologic Substances
    3. Water Pollution
    4. Air Pollution
    5. Hazardous Wastes
Financial - The Ability to Buy is Augmented by Purchasing Power.
    1. Lending Attitudes
    2. Government Programs, etc.
Availability of Natural Resources
    1. Water

2. Gas and Fuel
3. Energy/Electricity
Transportation
    1. Public
    2. Private
Tenant Mix and Turnover

NEIGHBORHOOD ANALYSIS

Neighborhood boundaries are defined by physical barriers such as railroads, traffic arteries, parks and a multitude of types of structures or land uses, or as is more often the case, by an invisible boundary that is reflected only by a change in the attitude of the inhabitants.

Consider the Neighborhood Life Cycle
    1. Growth Rate
        a. Rapid
        b. Stable
        c. Slow
    2. Property Values
        a. Increasing
        b. Stable
        c. Decreasing
Define and Explain Boundaries (Location)
Stability
    1. Zoning
    2. General Regulations
    3. Enforcement Policies
    4. Conformity and Compatibility
Accessibility
    1. Transportation
    2. Shopping
    3. Facilities
    4. Employment

Community Services—Churches, Schools, Libraries, Parks, Playgrounds, Theaters, etc.

Population

1. Family Income
2. Individual Income (has become increasingly important because of the increase in the singles market)
3. Area Density
4. Transiency
5. Family Size

Range of Sales Prices (by Complex or Unit) and Rental Rates

Availability of Lodging

1. Rental
2. Housing (could compete with the rental unit if the sales
price is less than 2 1/2 times the sales price per unit)

Vacancy and Occupancy Rates

Turnover in Ownership and Occupancy

Identify the Type of Apartment Market

1. Efficiency
2. Low-Income
3. Middle-Income
4. Luxury

Adequacy and Cost Trends of Utilities

Detrimental Influences, Nuisances and Hazards—External
(Locational or Economic) Obsolescence

1. Odors
2. Smog
3. Traffic
4. Noise

Community Services

1. Police and Fire Protection
a. Response and/or reaction time
2. Trash and Garbage Collection

General Appearance of Properties

— Curb Side Appeal (85% of all properties are still purchased
on emotion)

SITE ANALYSIS

Dimensions, Shape and Area of Site
Topography
Soil and Sub-Soil
Conditions
Drainage   .
Utilities, Services and Street Improvements
Easements
Encroachments
Accessibility
    1. Ingress
    2. Egress
Hazards, Nuisances and Insurance Requirements
Zoning, Restrictions, etc.
— Conformity or Non-Conformity
Functional Utility or Inutility
Parking Type and Ratios
Covenants, Conditions and Restrictions
Legal Aspects

IMPROVEMENTS ANALYSIS

Identify the Apartment Type
    1. Low-Rise (three levels or less)
    2. Mid-Rise (four to seven levels)
    3. High-Rise (eight levels or more)
Provide a Description of the Improvements
    1. Interior
    2. Exterior
    3. On-Site (garages, fencing, amenities, etc.)
Construction
    1. Type
    2. Quality
Condition
    1. Interior

2. Exterior

3. On-Site (garages, fencing, amenities, etc.)

Ages

1. Actual

2. Effective

Remaining Lives

1. Economic

2. Physical

Dimensions

1. Building

   a. Gross building area

   b. Gross rentable area

2. Unit

   a. Gross rentable area

Identify all Types of Physical Depreciation and Functional Obsolescence, and Check for any Interrelationship within the Three Approaches to Value.

Identify any Toxic Problems (Caution—never guess, if you do not know the type of insulation, etc., disclose as unknown).

Reviewer's Note: The most preferred amenities in an apartment complex are Swimming Pools, Spas, Tennis Courts and Recreation Rooms.

HIGHEST AND BEST USE

The determination of the Highest and Best Use Opinion requires two separate analyses: one as if the site were or is vacant; and the other as if the property were or is improved. It is to be recognized that in cases where a site has existing improvements, the Highest and Best Use may very well be determined to be different from the existing use. Although the existing improvements may not represent maximum productive use (not to be confused with greatest number of units) of the site, they will continue to be the Highest and Best Use of the improved property until the value of an alternative property exceeds the value of the land, the cost of demolition of the existing improvements, the contributory value of the existing improvements and the construction cost of a new structure or structures.

Site as Vacant

Property as Improved

It is Recommended that a Definition of Highest and Best Use be Included in the Appraisal for Reference.

If the Property is Not or Will Not be Appraised at its Highest and Best Use, then its Value in Use Should be Explained.

APPRAISAL PROCESS

Briefly Discuss the Reasoning Theory, and Applications of the Methods to Value Used
1. Sales Comparison Approach
2. Income Approach
3. Cost Approach

SALES COMPARISON APPROACH

Select data (sales and listings) that would be an alternative to a hypothetical buyer of the subject. A minimum of three comparable sales should be closed, and if adjusting by regression it is recommended that a minimum of four datums be used.

Analyze and Compare each Comparable Property with the subject as to:
1. Real Property Rights Conveyed
2. Financing Terms (cash equivalency)
3. Conditions of the Sale
4. Date of Sale
5. Location
6. Physical Characteristics

Adjust the Data for Dissimilarities between the Subject and the Datum. Adjustments must be SUPPORTABLE AND JUSTIFIABLE. Adjustment Grids themselves are not the solution to the justification of an adjustment. Typically, only one

EXHIBIT 1-C: EXAMPLE OF ADJUSTING BY INCOME

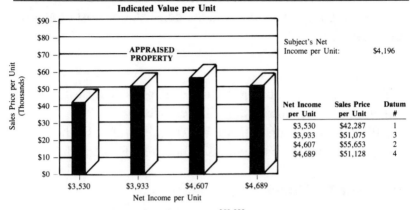

Indicated Value per Unit

Subject's Net
Income per Unit: $4,196

Net Income per Unit	Sales Price per Unit	Datum #
$3,530	$42,287	1
$3,933	$51,075	3
$4,607	$55,653	2
$4,689	$51,128	4

Value by Linear Regression: $50,090
Value by Logarithmic Regression: $50,327
Value by Exponential Regression: $49,846

Indicated Value for the Subject: $50,000 × 106 Units = $5,300,000.

Indicated Value per Room

Subject's Net
Income per Room: $1,222

Net Income per Room	Sales Price per Room	Datum #
$943	$11,293	1
$1,085	$14,095	3
$1,270	$15,341	2
$1,395	$15,213	4

Value by Linear Regression: $14,399
Value by Logarithmic Regression: $14,505
Value by Exponential Regression: $14,321

Indicated Value for the Subject: $14,500 × 364 rooms = $5,278,000 method of adjusting is employed, with adjusting by income differential (Regression), usually having the greater degree of accuracy.

1. Regression (usually a relationship between a component, such as Unit, Room, or Square Foot and a measurement of income). Optional methods of adjusting are by Gross Income, Effective Gross Income, or Net Operating Income, also referred to as Net Income.

    a. Value per unit
    b. Value per room
    c. Value per square foot

2. Physical Characteristics (if adjusting by Dollar Amount and Percentages, Dollar Adjustments come First. If adjusting by a component and the dollar amount is known, divide the amount by the number of components of the datum, or deduct the actual dollar amount from datum's sales price. If the adjustment is made on the proportional basis, divide the amount by the number of components of the subject).

    a. Value per unit
    b. Value per room
    c. Value per square foot

Reviewer's Note: Improper adjusting or not adjusting at all is the major cause of inaccurate values and the rejection of appraisals. In correlating into respective indicators of value, UNLESS THERE ARE MANY ADJUSTED DATUMS (certainly not less than five) and the appraiser can accept the assumption that each comparable has equal significance or validity, AVERAGING SHOULD NOT BE USED.

3. Income Multipliers

    a. Gross rent
    b. Gross income
    c. Effective gross income

d. Net income (net operating income)

Reviewer's Caution: In obtaining data, be sure to verify the type of income (Gross, Effective Gross, etc.), as there is much inconsistency in this area. For example, many Real Estate Personnel disclose the Effective Gross Income (income actually received) as the Gross Income, which correspondingly causes what was thought to be the Gross Income Multiplier to actually be the Effective Gross Income Multiplier. One way to overcome this problem, is to ask the question when verifying the data, "Is that Income before or after vacancy "? Gross Income or Rent Multipliers are used often when appraising apartments, but do not take into consideration the economic factors (vacancy, collection loss, and operating expenses) and for this reason should be carefully analyzed. Another frequent inconsistency is the use of the GROSS RENTABLE AREA OF THE COMPARABLES as a measure of comparability to the GROSS BUILDING AREA OF THE SUBJECT. (In essence, using the correlated adjusted Price per Gross Rentable Square Foot of the data and multiplying it by the subject's Gross Building Area). This can further be compounded in calculating unit and room sizes and their respective differentials between the subject and the data.

Reconcile (Do Not Average) the Respective Adjusted Indicators of Value with the Exception of the Multipliers which Should not be Adjusted, into an Indication of Value by the Sales Comparison Approach.

INCOME APPROACH

Potential Gross Rentable Income
— Rent Survey

      a. Proper adjusting of the data

      Reviewer's Note: The typical tenant is not so refined that they physically measure a unit. Therefore, using a dwelling unit and adjusting accordingly is preferred over the rent per square foot method, although it is recommended that both be employed.

      Reviewer's Caution: Economic Rents should not be confused with Market Rents; and since most appraisals are prepared for Market Value, Market Rents should be used. Economic Rent is defined as the amount necessary to produce a profit or to be economically viable (similar to the manner of economic life versus physical life). Market Rent is defined as rental income that a property would most probably command on the open market, as of the effective date of the appraisal (reference competitive rents backed by the principle of substitution).

Income from Other Sources

    1. Laundry

    2. Parking

    3. Commercial Income

    4. Miscellaneous

Vacancy

    1. Physical

    2. Economic (Collection Loss)

Effective Gross Income

Expenses

      Reviewer's Caution: Using current figures for future expenses or other estimates assumes no change in the future, regard less of the change in the past.

      Reviewer's Note: Total Expenses traditionally are compared and underwritten on the basis of a percentage of the Gross Income, or as an Expense relationship per Square Foot, or per Unit.

THE NUMBER ONE CAUSE OF OVER-VALUED APART-
MENTS IS THE UNDERESTIMATING OF EXPENSES.
1. Fixed
2. Variable or Operational
3. Replacement Reserves*

*Reviewer's Caution: If the expenses for the data do not in-
clude an allowance for this category then they should be omitted
from the expense statement for valuation purposes only, but are
still to be considered as an economic factor in maintaining the
property. A secondary method is to add an allowance for the Replacement Reserves to the data and readjust the capitalization
rate.*

Net Operating Income
Capitalization
1. Methods of Determining an Overall Capitalization Rate
   a. Net operating income/sale price
   b. Mortgage constant x debt service coverage ratio x loan-
   to-value ratio
   c. Band of investment—loan-to-value ratio x mortgage
   constant + equity position x cash on cash rate (equity
   dividend rate)
   d. NOI as a % of gross income/GIM
   e. NOI as a % of effective gross income/EGIM
   f. Ellwood formula (not accepted by FHA)
   g. Yield capitalization (yield rate + or—annualized change
   in value over the holding period)

Discounted Cash Flows—Market Value Discounted Cash Flows
should be supported by market-derived data and the assumptions should be both market and property specific. The spreadsheet should meet the challenge of "Who, Gets What, When
and How"?
1. Holding Period (sale and prior sale)
2. Discount Rate
   a. BAA bond rate plus allowance for illiquidity and management

  b. Capitalization rate plus the annualized change in value over the holding period
3. If using a terminal capitalization rate, reflect the uncertainty of the future, the increased age (depreciation), or lesser desirability of the property at the end of the period.
4. Sell-Out Costs
5. Projected Fluctuations in Income and Expenses

COST APPROACH

- Site Valuation—Sellers prefer to sell by the price per square foot or area, but buyers buy by the price per dwelling unit either permitted or developed. Since the latter more carefully addresses land use intensity measurements such as zoning, density, and other limitations, it is most preferred and commonly used. While the price per square foot or acre is used secondarily, it is recommended that the former and one of the other methods (selections two- four) be employed.
    1. Value per Unit (Permitted or Developed)
    2. Value per Square Foot
    3. Value per Acre
    4. For Proposed Construction or Vacant Land Appraisals, the Developmental Approach should be used. If the pur chase price is known, it can also serve as a solution to economic feasibility. The recommended secondary method would be the Value Indication Per Unit.
- Improvement Valuation (Provide Source of Cost Data)
- Depreciation
    1. Physical
        a. Curable
        b. Incurable
    2. Functional
        a. Curable
        b. Incurable

3. External
   a. Locational
   b. Economic*

*Reviewer's Caution: It is not uncommon for apartment properties in high density areas to have the land down-zoned. I n many instances this causes a Positive External (Economic) Obsolescence, as there is a greater number of units on the property than is currently allowed (legal non-conforming). The Site Valuation must consider the site as if vacant and not with the additional units currently in place. Therefore, this greater than allowable density must be adjusted for. (See Exhibit 3-C as an Illustrative Example)

EXHIBIT 3-C: POSITIVE EXTERNAL (Economic) OBSOLESCENCE

CAUSE: DOWN-ZONING

The subject has 44 units, but current zoning requirements will permit only 25 units; thereby causing a Positive External (Economic) Obsolescence because the property is legal non-conforming. The current land value was estimated at $16,000 per unit for 25 units at a density of 32 units per acre. With 44 units in place, the density factor is 54 units per acre. In essence, 19 additional units are on the properly that could not be built under current standards. Comparable sales indicate a land value of approximately $10,000 per unit, with a higher density, for a differential of $6,000 per unit. The following compares the values:

Value of Land with Current Zoning
25 Units at $16,000/Unit = $400,000

Value of Land "As Is"
44 Units at $10,000/Unit = $440,000

The increased value reduces as the improvements depreciate, since the obsolescence is dependent on the existing dwelling. The physical incurable depreciation was estimated at 12%. Consequently, 12% x $40,000 = $4,800, and is subtracted from $40,000 to equal $35,200 which is the amount of Positive External (Economic) Obsolescence attributed to the improvements.
- Depreciated Value of the Improvements
- Combine Site and Depreciated Improvement Values

ADDRESS SPECIAL ISSUES

(Example: Rent Loss for the absorption period).

RECONCILIATION AND FINAL VALUE ESTIMATE

Reconciliation is the procedure of coordinating and integrating related factors, evaluating and testing alternative conclusions, and selecting from the indications of value derived from each of the approaches utilized in the appraisal process, to arrive at a final estimate of market value. An orderly connection of interdependent elements is a prerequisite of proper reconciliation. This requires a re-examination of specific data, procedures and techniques within the framework of approaches used to derive preliminary estimates, and fits them into a cause-and-effect relationship, leading to a final conclusion. Each approach included in the preceding sections of the report is a recognized appraisal technique and was reviewed separately by comparing it to the alternative approaches in terms of adequacy, accuracy, completeness of reasoning and overall reliability. Under a given set of conditions, one solution or approach usually provides a higher degree of reliability than the others, and is thus weighted accordingly. Recapitulation
— Brief Review of Previously Presented Data
a. Logical analysis of strengths and weaknesses of the respective approaches to value (sales comparison, income and cost)
b. Consideration of quality, quantity and reliability of the data

c. Support and justify the selection of the final estimate of value (do not average)

d. Date of valuation

CERTIFICATIONS LIMITING CONDITIONS

- Specific
- General
- Assumptions

QUALIFICATIONS OF THE APPRAISER OR APPRAISERS ADDENDA

Anything unusual or unorthodox that does not blend in or cannot be integrated into the body of the appraisal.

FEASIBILITY

From the practical standpoint, that which may be done reasonably, and is broken down into three different levels. Namely, Highest and Best Use, Market (supply and demand) and Economic (generate enough income through sale or cash flow to support the initial investment plus an adequate return on the investment).

HIGHEST AND BEST USE

Greatest net return to the property through sale or cash flow.
Physically Possible
1. Shape of Site
2. Topography
3. Density
4. Ingress and Egress
5. Environmental Hazards, etc.
6. Availability of Utilities

Legally Permissible
1. Zoning

2. General Plan
3. Legal Restrictions
4. Deed Restrictions

Financially Feasible (Recommendations are Set Forth in the Economic Section)

Maximally Productive

— Address Improvements and Alternative Types of Unit Mix with Corresponding Support.

MARKET FEASIBILITY

Determine the Type of Apartment Complex (Low Rise, High Rise, etc.)

Avoid the Path of a Growth Location, as an Abundance of Land will Provide Substantial Competition for Future Apartments.

Determine Trends and Economic Diversification of the Economy.

Identify the Primary and Secondary Marketing Areas.

1. Identify the Various Types of Tenants

a. 25 % usually work close (within a few miles) of where they live and they should be professional or white collar workers).

b. 50% or less of the neighborhood should be rentals, have high visibility, good access to amenities, and show a scarcity of vacant land.

c. Not more than 50% of the population in a three mile radius should be blue collar tenants.

d. Check the apartment demographics for the predominate age of the tenants (the singles market has expanded proportionately).

Singles
Cohabitation market
Dinks (double income, no kids)
Empty nesters
Recently married, people living together, and roommates

Families
  e. Employment
     Types of vocations
     Distance
  f. Tenant preference
     Parking
     Density (privacy) 18-25 units per acre is
        most preferred
     Amenities
     Complimentary uses which should be in
     close proximity
        Neighborhood shopping
        Restaurants
        Services
  g. Transiency and stabilization of the tenants.
  h. Turnover ratio and how it affects cleaning costs.
3. Obtain Historical Data and Look for Past Trends to Make
Future Projections.
     a. Population Pattern—
Research and determine the pattern for the past years in relation to population
- The pattern for the past years in relation to population and the
  number of tenants (per capita).
- The number of tenants in relationship to the number of units.
- The number of unit types in relationship to the overall market
  (example: 20% of the units in the market place are bachelors,
  etc.).
- The household sizes and percent by category (example: 25%
  of the household have 2.5 to 3 people).
     b. Employment Pattern—
Show the relationship between job type or classification and
employment growth. Research and determine the family and individual income levels to determine the percentage of the market
that could qualify financially. Typically, 3½ to 4 times the monthly
rent should be the monthly gross household income.

Supply and Demand

1. Find Out the Existing Inventory.
2. Subtract the Older Period's Inventory from the Recent Inventory to Project Gross Demand.
3. Separate the Type of Units Occupied in Relation to the Overall Market and Establish Vacancy by Unit Category.
4. Research and Discover the Planned and/or Proposed Inventory.
5. Research and Discover the Existing Vacant Inventory and the Rate of Absorption on those Complexes which have Recently Attained Stabilized Occupancy, in Addition to those Currently in the Fill-up Stage.
6. Calculate the Potential Demand, Subtract the Vacancy Factor, and Establish if there is Demand for the Subject (adequate, and the proper mix of population to occupy the number and mix of the proposed units).

ECONOMIC FEASIBILITY

The Present Worth Should Equal or Exceed the Initial Investment Plus an Adequate Return on the Investment.

Reviewer's Caution: Assumptions, if any, should be supported and/or market extracted.

Important Factors Affecting Land Appreciation, Rent Raises and Property Values:

1. Inflation (typically good for real estate)
2. Recession (good for nothing)
3. Population and Employment Growth
4. Construction (recently completed and proposed)
5. Development of Infrastructure (utilities, sewer, transportation, etc.)
6. Availability and/or Scarcity of Developable Land
7. Legal Restrictions and Corresponding Costs (zoning, increasing and decreasing density, development fees, parking requirements, etc.)

8. Geographic Monopoly

Factors to Consider when Developing Apartments:

1. Ideally, Developers Would Like to Have the Minimum Family Income be Six Times the Average Apartment Rent, but in High Cost Areas the Ratio is as Low as Four to One.

2. Single Family Dwellings Should Sell for at Least 2 1/2 Times the Price per Unit of the Apartment, Otherwise, they are a Serious Competition.

REVIEWING IN A RENT-CONTROL AREA

In rent-control areas, there are three different types of rent which must be considered: actual rent, market rent and restricted rent, (which could also be referred to as "stabilized" rent). Actual (contract) rent is payment for use of a property as agreed upon by the tenant and landlord, and is equal to the rent being collected as of the date of appraisal. Market rent is payment for the use of a property, which is equal to the amount of income that the property would most likely command on the open market, based upon current rental rates being paid for comparable space. "Restricted" rent, which is sometimes referred to as legal or stabilized rent, is payment for use of a property with the amount of income regulated by law. Typically, under rent-control, both the amount and frequency of the rent increase is regulated.

When determining whether or not actual rent can be increased, the appraiser must consider legal restrictions and market limitations. Typically, a maximum annual-percentage rent increase is mandated by law under rent-control, and each tenant's rent can only be increased at the end of each year of occupancy. Therefore, when determining whether a rent increase is allowable, the anniversary date of each tenant's last rent increase must be considered. For example, if a 4% rent increase were the maximum allowable increase during that calendar year, then on each tenant's anniversary date, rent for that unit may be increased. When forecasting rents, if the rent has not been increased within the last year, an increase would be allowed, provided that market rents (as determined by a rental survey) support the increase. In the event that market rents do not support a maximum increase, then the rent should be forecasted at market rent. On the other hand, if market rents indicate a much higher rent for the subject's units, but there is restriction due to rent-control, the lesser amount would have to be forecast; that is, either the actual rent, or the actual rent plus the increase, if legally allowable. Additionally, income for the manager's unit and vacant units is forecasted at market rent.

RENT-CONTROL

To Summarize, the Procedural Steps for Forecasting Rents in a Rent-Control Area are as Follows:
1. Conduct a Rental Survey to Determine the Market Rent for Each Different Unit Type in the Subject Property.
2. Obtain a Schedule of the Actual Rents being Collected, including Anniversary Dates for Each Unit.
3. Obtain Information Outlining Applicable Rent-Control Restrictions.
4. Determine the Maximum Allowable Rent for Each Unit. In Other Words, "Stabilize" the Rent for Each Unit as Follows:

   a. If the tenant's rent has been increased within the past year (relative to the date of appraisal), rent is forecasted at actual rent, assuming that it is less than, or equal to, market rent. If it is more, market rent is forecasted.

   b. If the tenant's anniversary date is near the date of appraisal (perhaps, within two months), the actual rent plus the maximum allowable increase, is forecasted once again, assuming that the sum is less than, or equal to, market rent. If it is more, market rent is forecasted.

   c. For the manager's unit and vacant units, rent is forecasted at market rent, unless they are not exempt from rent-control.

If rental income has been forecasted properly, then no additional adjustment to the Income Approach to valuation is necessary. Furthermore, if the comparable sales presented in the Sales Comparison (Market Data) Approach to valuation have been adjusted based upon their ability to generate income relative to that of the subject, then no additional adjustment is necessary. Therefore, the following presents a method for determining the amount of external (economic) obsolescence resulting from rent-control, which should be used as an adjustment in the Cost Approach to valuation.

Exhibit I is an example of a format used to present actual, market and stabilized (forecasted) rent information, as well as to determine the rent-loss and to calculate the external (economic) obsolescence resulting from rent-control. In Exhibit I, the apartment number, or number of apartments, information on unit type and size, and rental data and forecasts are presented; also presented in a rent-loss column is the difference between the stabilized rent (which takes into consideration rent control), and the market rent, for each unit. The "stabilized" or "restricted" rent is subtracted from the market rent, and the difference placed in the rent-loss column. In the event that market rent is greater than stabilized rent, a loss in rent is represented. The stabilized rent can not be greater than the market rent, because market rent reflects the upper limit of rent. To determine the amount of external (economic) obsolescence due to rent-control, the amount of monthly rent-loss is totaled, multiplied by 12 to arrive at an annual rent-loss, and then multiplied by the annual gross rent or income multiplier (determined in the Sales Comparison [Market Data] Approach). The result of this calculation reflects the amount of external (economic) obsolescence due to rent-control, and is placed within the depreciation section of the Cost Approach to value.

Example:

Depreciation Section of the Cost Approach

Physical	Functional	External
-O-	-O-	$168,384

In the case presented, the total rent-loss is nor multiplied by the ratio of improvements to total value, as it would be in most cases of locational obsolescence, because properties built in the City of Los Angeles after 1978 are rent-control exempt. Thus, the rent-control restriction does not apply to vacant land but only to improved properties. In other words, rent-control restrictions in the City of Los Angeles do not run with the land, but apply only to existing improvements constructed before 1978. When those improvements cease to exist, rent-control no longer affects the subject site. Therefore, in this case, one hundred percent of the obsolescence is attributable to the improvements. However, depending upon the circumstances, rent-control may run with the land, even if the land is vacant, or the previous building has been demolished, and could apply to all future improvements on the site.

If rent-control runs with the land, the amount of obsolescence is proportional to the amount of value contributed by improvements relative to the overall value of the property, and this loss in value must be allocated between the land and improvements. The loss in value attributable to the land should be reflected in the prices paid by the developer for buildable sites (also under the same rent-control restrictions), and therefore, should have been taken into consideration in the estimating of land value.

To Summarize, External (Economic) Obsolescence Resulting from Rent-Control is Calculated as Follows:

1. After Market Rents have been Determined and Stabilized Rents Forecasted, Calculate the Rent-Loss for each Unit by Subtracting the Stabilized Rent from the Market Rent. The Total Monthly Rent-Loss for the Entire Project is calculated by Adding the Individual Losses.
2. Multiply the Monthly Rent-Loss by 12 (months) to Arrive at an Annual Rent-Loss.
3. Multiply the Annual Rent-Loss by the Annual Gross Rent or Income Multiplier to Determine the Amount of Obsolescence.
4. Multiply by the Ratio of Improvement Value to Overall Loss in Value if Applicable.
5. Insert this Figure in the Depreciation Section of the Cost Approach.
6. With Respect to the Income Approach, the Annual Stabilized Gross Rentable Income from the Units, plus

   any Additional Income from Other Sources (i.e., parking, laundry, etc.) Should be Used.
7. With Respect to the Sales Comparison (Market Data) Approach, if only the Gross Income from the Units is Available from the Comparables, Use Only the Gross Income from the Units for the Subject and Correspondingly a Gross Rent Multiplier. But if Available, (and this is the preferred method), Use the Total Gross Income (i.e., parking, laundry, etc.) from Both the Subject and Comparables and Correspondingly the Gross Income Multiplier. This Procedure Avoids Comparing Inconsistent Data which can Lead to an Incorrect Value Conclusion.

EXHIBIT 1: MONTHLY RENT SCHEDULE

APT #	UNIT RMS	# OF BDRMS	# OF BATHS	RENTABLE SQ. FT.	ACTUAL RENT	RENT SQ. FT.	MARKET RENT	RENT SQ. FT.	STABILIZED RENT	RENT SQ. FT.	RENT LOSS
1	4	2	1	794	0	MGR	825	1.04	825	1.04	0
2	4	2	1	794	521	0.66	825	1.04	521	0.66	304
3	5	2	1¾	1188	1300	1.09	1325	1.12	1300	1.09	25
4	4	2	1	918	521	0.57	935	1.02	521	0.57	414
5	4	2	1	880	750	0.85	905	1.03	750	0.85	155
6	5	2	1	988	832	0.84	1000	1.01	832	0.84	168
7	4	2	1	794	800	1.01	825	1.04	800	1.01	25
8	4	2	1	794	546	0.69	825	1.04	546	0.69	279
9	5	2	1¾	1188	1248	1.05	1325	1.12	1248	1.05	77
10	5	2	1¾	1198	1113	0.93	1325	1.11	1113	0.93	212
11	5	2	1¾	1184	1300	1.10	1325	1.12	1300	1.10	25
12	4	2	1	816	780	0.96	850	1.04	780	0.96	70
TOTALS:											
12					$9,711		$12,290		$10,536		$1,754

COMMENTS:
Total monthly rent loss of $1,754 × 12 (months) = $21,048 (Total annual Rent-Loss) × 8 (Annual Gross Rent or Income Multiplier) = $168,384, which is the amount of External (Economic) Obsolescence due to rent-control.

SUMMARY

In appraising apartments which are subject to rent-control, the review appraiser should verify that the loss in rental income and the corresponding loss in value, is taken into consideration in the appraisal report, and that the methodology used results in an appropriate adjustment to income and value.

CHAPTER TWENTY-NINE

REVIEWING A BUSINESS APPRAISAL REPORT

APPROACHES TO BUSINESS APPRAISAL

Beware of the appraiser who makes a blanket statement such as, "There are three approaches to valuing a business" or, "There are seven approaches to valuing a business." Trying to force the approaches to the appraisal of all businesses under all circumstances into a fixed number of labeled categories is vain. Business appraisal approaches tend to fit less neatly than real estate appraisal approaches into three narrow categories, such as "the income capitalization approach," "the cost approach," and "the sales comparison approach." One way or another, the financial benefits from owning an interest in a business enterprise must come from the following sources:

1. Earnings or cash flow:
   a. from operations
   b. from investments (e.g., interest and or/dividends received)

2. Liquidation of assets
3. Sale of the interest

Therefore, any valuation approach (at least from a financial point of view) must focus on measuring the ability of the business interest to provide benefits to its owner from one or some combination of the above sources. The most commonly used approaches to the valuation of a business are generally found under the following categories:

- Discounted future earnings or discounted cash flow
- Capitalization of current, normalized or historical earnings
- Capitalization of current, normalized or historical cash flow
- Capitalization of dividends or dividend-paying capacity
- Multiple of gross revenue or physical volume
- Excess earnings approach
- Adjusted net asset value
- Ratio of price to book value or to adjusted net asset value
- Prior transactions in, or offers for, the stock adjusted to current conditions

Most of the above categories of approaches can be focused on appraising either just the equity in the business (stock, partners' capital or sole proprietorship interest) or on appraising the total business as if it had no debt ("debt-free" approaches). It is, of course, critical that the approach or approaches selected are appropriate for the nature of the business or business interest being value and that the choice of approach or approaches is well justified in the report. In some cases, certain approaches may be either mandated or precluded by legal requirements applicable to the use to which the appraisal is to be put, such as estate taxes or dissenting stockholder actions. Finally, it is essential that the appraiser justify the relative emphasis or weight placed on different approaches in reaching the final estimate of value.

INTRODUCTION

Appraisals of businesses or business interests need to be reviewed by a wide variety of people for a wide variety of reasons, such as:

- An owner considering a sale
- A prospective buyer considering a purchase
- A fiduciary for an ESOP, estate, charitable trust or other entity for adequate due diligence relative to a transaction

- An attorney involved in litigation or potential litigation relating to a business valuation
- An owner or taxing entity determining value for various tax purposes, such as estate and gift taxes, inheritance taxes and state and local ad valorem taxes
- A commercial loan officer evaluating a credit
- An appraiser asked to review someone else's appraisal report
- A spouse for a marital property settlement
- A judge deciding a business valuation issue on the basis of appraisals submitted

In most cases, such persons will not have theoretical or technical training in the complex discipline of business valuation. Nevertheless, significant decisions, often involving substantial sums of money, must be made based on the acceptability of business appraisal reports. This booklet has been prepared to assist attorneys, fiduciaries, investors, and others who must rely on business appraisal reports in their efforts to critically assess the validity of such reports and the reliability of their conclusions.

APPRAISAL REVIEW CHECKLIST

STATEMENT OF INDEPENDENCE

Is there a statement that the appraiser has no present or contemplated interest in the subject property, or, if so, an explanation of the interest?

STATEMENT OF THE APPRAISAL ASSIGNMENT

Is the name of the party who retained the appraiser clearly disclosed? Is the name of the entity being appraised spelled out completely and accurately?

Is the form of organization indicated? (regular corporation, subchapter S corporation, general partnership, limited partnership, etc.) Is the state in which the entity is incorporated or registered indicated?

Reviewer's note: There may be companies with identical names in each of several states. More importantly, however, the statutory and case law of the state in which the company is registered or incorporated may have a bearing on acceptable appraisal practices in some situations.

Is the interest in the entity being appraised clearly indicated? (100% of the common stock; 5,000 shares of common stock out of 100,000 shares outstanding; a 40% general partnership interest; the value of certain assets for an asset sale; etc.)

Is the applicable standard of value specified? (fair market value, fair value, investment value, etc. See "Statement and Definition of Standard of Value" below for further elaboration.)

Is the effective date of the appraisal specified?

Is the purpose (function) of the appraisal specified? (for sale of interest, federal estate taxes, employee stock ownership plan, marital dissolution, etc.)

Reviewer's note: There can be wide variations in the appraised value of a business or business interest from one date to another, sometimes even within a fairly short time span. Also, acceptable appraisal procedures may vary for different purposes because of variations in applicable law and other factors. For this reason, business appraisal reports typically contain some statement in the "Assumptions and Limiting Conditions" such as, "This appraisal is valid only for the appraisal date or dates specified herein and only for the appraisal purpose or purposes specified herein."

STATEMENT AND DEFINITION OF THE STANDARD OF VALUE

Is the standard of value not only stated (as checked above) but also clearly defined?

For example, in an appraisal for estate or gift taxes:

Fair market value is considered to represent a value at which a willing seller and willing buyer, both informed of the relevant facts about the business, could reasonably conduct a transaction, neither person acting under compulsion to do so.

Among other factors, this appraisal considers all elements of appraisal listed in Internal Revenue Service Ruling 59-60, which generally outlines the valuation of closely held stocks and includes the following:

1. The nature of the business and history of the enterprise
2. The economic outlook in general and condition and out look of the specific industry in particular
3. The book value of the stock and the financial condition of the business
4. The company's earning capacity
5. The company's dividend-paying capacity
6. Whether or not the enterprise has goodwill or other intangible value
7. Sales of stock and size of the block to be valued
8. The market prices of stocks of corporations engaged in the same or similar lines of business whose stocks are actively traded in a free and open market, either on an exchange or over the counter.

If the appraisal is being done pursuant to a statute, regulation or documentary authority such as a buy/sell agreement, is the relevant language defining the standard of value quoted? For example, in an appraisal of dissenting stockholders' stock:

The standard of value was fair value, as set forth by Section 30-1-81 of the Idaho Code. According to the statute, 'fair value' of shares means their value immediately before the effectuation of the corporate action to which the dissenter objects, excluding any appreciation or depreciation in anticipation of such corporate action unless such exclusion would be inequitable."

If it is necessary to refer to case law to interpret the standard of value, some reference to that fact should be included.

Reviewer's Note: Definitions of standards of value such as ' fair market value" and ' fair value" vary somewhat from one legal context to another. Thus it is extremely important that the standard of value that the appraisal represents be clearly specified.

CAPITALIZATION AND OWNERSHIP

Is the amount outstanding and description of each class of stock or partnership interest clearly described?

Reviewer's Note: In a multi-class capitalization structure, the rights of one class of ownership may have an important bearing not only on the value of ownership interest in that class but on the value of other classes of ownership interests as well.

Is the distribution of ownership clearly described (list of major owners, usually those over 10%, number of other owners, broken down by class of ownership interest if more than one class of stock or other interest)?

Reviewer's Note: If less than 100% ownership position is being appraised, the distribution of the remaining ownership may have a bearing on the value of the interest. For example, a 49%

owner normally would have much more control over a company if there were many other small owners than if there were one 51% controlling owner.

COMPANY BACKGROUND AND OPERATIONS

- Brief history of company leading to where it stands today
- Location(s) of operations
- Product/services lines
- Markets served
- Customer base (type, degree of concentration/dispersion)
- Competition
- Position of subject company relative to its industry
- Competitive strengths and weaknesses (uniqueness of product, quality, service, price, location, etc.)
- Description of facilities (site, plants, equipment, etc.)
- Management and work force (size of work force, description and degree of dependence on key personnel, the latter especially if highly dependent on one or a few key people).
- If the company has subsidiaries, affiliates or significant interests in other entities, are the relationships (percentage ownerships, methods of accounting basis for transfer pricing, etc.) clearly spelled out?
- Overall, have the positive and negative aspects of the company's operations and resources been pointed out and/or summarized?

FINANCIAL STATEMENT ADJUSTMENTS

Have proper financial statement adjustments been made, or is there a statement that the financial statements have been analyzed and no adjustments are appropriate? Possible adjustments might include, for example:

1. Adjustments to recognize adequate reserves, such as allowance for doubtful accounts receivable or reserve for pension liabilities

2. An adjustment to inventory

   a.To write down or write off obsolete inventory or inventory in poor condition
   b.To adjust the basis of inventory accounting for com parison with other companies, such as an adjustment from the LIFO (last-in, first-out) method of inventory report ing to the FIFO (first-in, first-out) method of inventory reporting

3. An adjustment to remove nonrecurring items from the income statements for the purpose of estimating a "normalized" level of earnings. Such items could include, for example:
   a. Gains or losses from payment or settlement of lawsuits
   b. Losses from a strike
   c. Losses from a catastrophe
   d. Insurance recovery proceeds
   e. Gains or losses from discontinued operations
   f. Gains or losses from sale of major assets

Reviewer's Note: In order to be proper subjects of adjustment, nonrecurring items do not necessarily have to meet the strict defi- nition of "extraordinary" in an accounting sense. The point is whether or not the gains or losses would be expected to recur in the normal course of business.

4. Adjustments to depreciation, amortization or depletion
   a. To reflect a more realistic amount of depreciation in an economic sense
   b. To adjust the basis for depreciation accounting to make it comparable to other companies being used for comparative purposes

5. Have statements of companies used for comparative analyses been similarly analyzed and similar adjustments made if needed, so that financial comparisons are on an "apples to apples" basis?

6. Are there no improper adjustments to statements?

7. If a balance sheet has been adjusted to reflect unrealized appreciation on assets that might be liquidated, has the related tax on the gain also been reflected?

FINANCIAL STATEMENT ANALYSIS

Have relevant ratios been computed and strengths/weaknesses of subject company on its own and relative to peer companies and industry averages been adequately pointed out?

Are ratios computed clearly defined so that the reader could go to source documents and make the same computations?

If comparisons of financial information or ratios are made between the subject company and peer companies or industry averages:

Are the computations of the ratios defined in exactly the same way for the subject company as for the peer companies or industry averages with which the subject company is being compared?

Are the time periods for which the data are measured or estimated for the subject company the same as the time periods covered by the data for the peer companies or industry averages with which the subject company is being compared?

Are the results of the financial statement analysis summarized and conclusions drawn?

Does the financial statement analysis ultimately result in some statement or evaluation of implications for the degree of risk associated with the subject company, either on an absolute basis or relative to peer companies or industry averages?

Ratios. Exhibit 2 shows various operating and financial ratios for JMK and the comparative publicly traded companies. All ratios utilizing pretax and after-tax income have been adjusted to exclude nonrecurring items.

JMK's liquidity, as measured by the current and quick ratios, was close to the median of the comparative companies. As Exhibit I shows, all of JMK's activity ratios are below the comparative company medians, indicating that the company uses its assets less efficiently than the comparatives. However, as noted in the "Trend Analysis" section, JMK's activity ratios have improved steadily since 1984. Working capital turnover is on the low side, but is similar to that of three of the comparative companies.

JMK's coverage ratios, as measured by interest expense coverage and cash flow coverage of currently maturing long-term debt, are significantly below the median of the comparative companies. However, at 10.4 and 11.6, respectively, JMK's interest expense coverage and cash flow coverage of currently maturing long-term debt are more than adequate.

JMK has slightly more of its total capital in the form of long-term debt than the comparative companies, as is evidenced by JMK's long-term-debt-to-total-capital ratio of 0.17 versus 0.10 for the comparative company median. However, JMK's total debt-to-equity ratio of 0.75 is less than the comparative company median of 0.85.

The profitability ratios indicate that JMK's less efficient use of assets and slightly lower use of leverage have resulted in return-on-equity and return-on-asset ratios that are below the comparative company medians. JMK's return on equity was 9.9% versus a median of 18.9% for the comparative companies and its return on assets was 7.8% versus a median of 9.3%. JMK's net profit margin of 2.9% was slightly above the comparative company median of 2.7%.

JMK's sales and earnings growth at 30.0% and 28.8%, respectively, were also below the comparative company medians of 35.1% and 45.3%, respectively.

EXHIBIT 1

JMK, INC.
AND COMPARATIVE PUBLICLY TRADED COMPANIES
FINANCIAL AND OPERATING RATIOS

	Audio/ Video 1/87	Best Buy 3/87	Circuit City 2/87	Federated 2/87	Fretter 1/87	Good Guys 9/86	Highland 1/87	Luskins 1/87	Newmark & Lewis 1/87	Sound Advice 6/86	Tipton Centers 3/87	Average	Median	JMK 4/87
LIQUIDITY														
Current Ratio	2.7	2.9	2.0	2.7	1.8	1.9	2.7	2.0	1.5	2.0	2.6	2.3	2.0	2.2
Quick Ratio	0.4	0.4	0.5	0.3	0.3	0.5	0.8	0.6	0.3	1.0	0.4	0.5	0.4	0.6
Working Capital ($000)	48,156	48,750	97,320	77,596	30,758	13,310	105,172	18,603	13,857	5,297	14,505	43,029	30,758	22,584
ACTIVITY														
Days in Receivables (Avg.)	7	8	4	10	1	7	6	4	3	6	9	6	6	9
COGS/Inventory (Avg.)	3.2	4.2	5.5	3.7	4.7	7.5	3.8	4.1	5.7	4.2	3.6	4.6	4.2	3.3
Sales/Working Cap. (Avg.)	4.4	7.8	13.4	6.3	12.3	11.0	7.7	8.8	17.3	6.1	7.7	9.3	7.8	5.7
Sales/Net Fixed Assets (Avg.)	7.7	29.6	8.8	8.0	13.7	24.9	10.9	21.6	30.1	27.1	36.8	19.9	21.6	5.8
Sales/Total Assets (Avg.)	2.1	4.0	3.3	2.3	3.2	3.8	3.0	3.2	4.1	3.1	3.8	3.3	3.2	2.0
COVERAGE/LEVERAGE														
Int. Expense Coverage	23.9	NA	14.8	Df	5.0	NM	11.1	3.8	17.6[c]	23.8	27.0	15.9	16.2	10.4[d]
Cash Flow/Curr. Mat. LTD	31.6	29.3	28.6	0.3[a]	18.2	NM	34.8	44.5	NM	5.3	5.3	21.5	28.6	11.6[d]
Fixed Assets/Equity	0.5	0.2	1.0	0.9	0.4	—	0.7	0.2	0.3	0.02	0.2	0.4	0.3	0.6
LTD/LTD+Equity	0.06	0.10	0.40	0.56	0.16		0.36	0.18	0.08	0.02	—	0.17	0.10	0.17
Total Debt/Equity	0.44	0.57	1.42	2.22	0.80	0.91	1.15	0.62	1.32	0.65	0.52	1.0	0.85	0.75
PROFITABILITY														
% Net Income/Sales	3.3	3.2	3.5	(1.4)[a]	1.5	1.6	3.1	0.7	2.5[c]	4.0	2.7	2.2	2.7	2.9[d]
% Net Income/Equity (Avg.)	10.0	22.1	27.1	(9.5)[a]	9.7	12.1	19.4	2.1	24.5[c]	25.6	18.9	14.7	18.9	9.9[d]
% Net Income/Assets (Avg.)	6.9	13.0	11.7	(3.2)[a]	4.7	5.9	9.3	2.1	10.3[c]	12.2	10.1	7.5	9.3	7.8[d]
ANNUAL AVERAGE COMPOUND GROWTH														
% Growth in Sales	32.3	103.3	42.4	48.2	32.6	30.2	39.0	27.4	35.1	31.7	36.8	41.7	35.1	30.0
% Growth in Earnings	27.5	201.0	59.1	—[b]	13.9	24.4	45.3	1.1	93.2[c]	45.3	87.9	59.9	45.3	28.8[d]
OTHER														
Sales per Store ($000)	2,159	9,979	11,617	6,717	5,799	7,456	12,386	2,642	5,344	2,129	3,484	6,337	5,799	4,165
Sales per Sq. Ft. Sell. Space($)	965	1,053	1,489	NA	NA	1,427	909	NA	800	NA	456	1,014	965	403

[a] Before nonrecurring income from cumulative effect of change in accounting principle.
[b] Company had a deficit; therefore, growth calculation was not meaningful.
[c] Before nonrecurring gain on sale of securities.
[d] Before nonrecurring litigation settlement income.

COGS=Cost of goods sold
LTD=Long-term debt
NA=Not available
Df=Deficit
NM=Not meaningful

1 This exhibit is taken from Chapter 14, "A Sample Report," of *Valuing a Business: The Analysis and Appraisal of Closely Held Companies*, 2nd edition, by Shannon P. Pratt (Homewood, Ill: Dow Jones-Irwin), 1989.

In the consumer electronics industry, the sales per store and sales per square foot of selling space are analyzed to determine potential profitability on a per-store basis. JMK's sales per store, at $4.165 million, was below the median of $5.799 million but higher than Audio/Video's, Luskins', Sound Advice's and Tipton Centers'. Also, many of these stores sell appliances, which greatly increases sales per store. JMK's sales per square foot of selling space was $403,000, well below the median of $965,000, but this information was unavailable for four companies, three of which had below average sales per store. Tipton Centers, with $456,000 of sales per square foot of selling space, was the most comparable to JMK.

The preceding ratio analysis indicates that JMK's liquidity is about average when compared to the comparative companies, its coverage is below average but adequate, and its overall capitalization is about average. However, JMK's less efficient use of assets has resulted in below-average return on equity, return on assets and growth.

ECONOMIC AND INDUSTRY DATA AND ANALYSIS

Are the economic data and analysis adequate and relevant to the appraisal?   Are the industry data and analysis adequate and relevant to the appraisal?

PAST TRANSACTIONS

Is there a listing of past transactions in the stock or partnership interests and/or offers to buy (with dates, amounts, price, whether or not arm's length) or a statement that there have not been any?

COMPARATIVE COMPANY SELECTION

Are the criteria for comparative company selection (percent of sales in subject company's industry, size, capital, structure, location, etc.) clearly set forth?

Is the population of possible companies from which the comparative set is drawn clearly defined?

Is the population from which the comparative companies are drawn of adequate size and relevance to the subject company that it is likely that all or most of the best comparative companies are included? (For example, if appraising a closely held c o m p a n y with $15 million sales, it generally would be inadequate to draw comparatives from sources that contained only very large public companies, such as Value Line or the Standard & Poor's 500, rather than from broader sources that include many smaller companies, some of which might trade over the counter or on the American Stock Exchange.)

Are the sources and procedures for selecting the comparative companies clearly spelled out so that the reader could go to the sources, follow the procedures, and generate a similar list?

Is enough description of the comparative companies included in the report so that the reader can get a sense of their degree of comparability?

Does it appear that the comparative companies used constitute the best available list?

SELECTION AND JUSTIFICATION OF VALUATION APPROACHES

Is the selection of valuation approaches used adequately justified?

If seemingly obvious alternative approaches were not used, is there a satisfactorily convincing explanation of why not?

Are the valuation approaches used consistent with the statement of the appraisal assignment and the statement and definition of the applicable standard of value, including any applicable legal requirements or interpretations?

VALUATION METHODOLOGY AND PRESENTATION

Are the data and steps used in each valuation approach clearly presented, so that the reviewer could replicate the work done and reach the same conclusion?

Valuation measures or parameters may include such variables as capitalization or discount rates, or multiples of some fundamental data such as revenues, earnings, cash flow, book value and so forth. It is essential that these measures be clearly defined and used consistently between the subject and comparative companies if comparative analysis is used in the valuation procedures.

Is each valuation measure or parameter clearly defined so the reviewer can have an exact understanding of its meaning? For example, if price/earnings ratios are used:

1. The date of the price should be specified. This normally is the date of or a date very near the effective date of the appraisal, as indicated in the statement of the appraisal assignment.
2. The exact definition and time period for the earnings should be specified.

For example, the report may state that the earnings base used is net income after taxes for the fiscal year ended September 30, 1988, as adjusted in the financial statement adjustments of the report.

Reviewer's Note: There are many acceptable ways to define commonly used financial variables, such as earnings, cash flow, operating income, net asset value and so forth. The definition of each financial variable used should be adequate so that the reviewer can consult the financial statements and/or other data provided and determine exactly how the financial variable relied on in the appraisal was derived.

If valuation measures such as price/earnings ratios are derived from analysis of comparative companies, are the definitions of the variables derived from the comparative companies identical to the definitions of the variables for the subject company. (For example, if price/earnings ratios are used, is the definition of earnings for the comparative companies the same as the definition of earnings for the subject company, such as "net income after taxes, adjusted for extraordinary or nonrecurring items.")

If valuation measures such as price/earnings ratios are derived from analysis of comparative companies, are the time periods over which the variables were derived for the comparative companies the same as the time periods for which the subject company variables are measured or estimated?

Reviewer's Caution: A common error is to derive valuation parameters such as a price/earnings ratio based on comparative companies ' earnings for a certain time period and then apply that ratio to the subject company's earnings for a different time period, resulting in an invalid indication of value for the subject company.

Has appropriate recognition been accorded to the size of the block and its voting rights with respect to the degree of control or lack of it?

Has appropriate recognition been given to the degree of ready marketability (liquidity), or lack of it?

Were all data used known or susceptible of being known as of the effective date of the valuation (except to the limited extent of permissible ex post data)?

Are all discount rates, capitalization rates and multipliers used adequately justified? (Normally, discount rates, capitalization rates and multipliers will be based on empirical market data, which should be clearly explained as to definition and source, so that the reader can go to the source and verify its accuracy. The analyst may use the mean or median of such data, or may make adjustments above or below such market averages. The report should explain why the average of data from whatever market source is used is appropriate for the subject company or why some upward or downward adjustment from the comparative data is appropriate for the subject company.)

Where weightings of various factors and/or approaches are used, are the weightings used adequately justified?

Have all capital requirements needed to support continued or expected future operations been taken into consideration?

If there are significant differences in financial leverage (e.g., significantly different debt/equity ratios) between the subject company and the comparative companies, have these differences been adequately reflected in the valuation methodology?

Reviewer's Note: There are many ways to reflect differences in financial leverage. One is to require higher rates of expected return on equity for more leveraged companies to reflect the higher risk. Another is to analyze the subject and comparative companies on a "debt-free" basis, deriving a value for total invested capital, and then deduct the amount of debt to determine the value of the equity.

If there are potential obligations to issue additional equity, such as through exercise of warrants or conversion of convertible securities, has the potential dilution been reflected in the value of the common stock?

Is the degree of risk of the investment adequately addressed and reflected in the valuation?

Reviewer's Note: The higher the risk, the higher the expected rate of return the market requires. One of the most essential aspects of any business appraisal is the assessment of the risk of the subject company, usually relative to comparative companies, and reflection of the degree of risk in valuation parameters selected (discount rates, multiples, and so forth).

IF THE "EXCESS EARNINGS METHOD" (OR SOME VARIATION) IS USED:

In general, is the procedure used consistent with the steps and example shown in Exhibit 2?

Does the amount used for the asset base represent the value of net tangible assets (exclusive of intangibles)?

Is the earnings base used representative of ongoing earning power of the entity?

Is the earnings base net of reasonable compensation to any owner(s) involved in managing the business?

If a corporation, is the earnings base used net income after taxes?

Is the required rate of return applicable to net tangible assets adequately justified?

Reviewer's Note: This normally should be at least the company's cost of borrowing. A common error is to use some "safe" rate, such as the current rate on risk-free U.S. Treasury bills, or a rate of 8%-10% as used in an illustrative example in Revenue Ruling 68-609, reflecting economic and market conditions prevalent in 1968.

Is the rate at which the "excess earnings" (earnings over and above the amount required to support the tangible asset base) adequately justified?

Reviewer's Note: This normally should be a considerably higher rate than the rate of return applicable to tangible assets because of the considerably higher risk. As with the rate applicable to tangible assets, a common error is to use a rate of 15%-20% because that was the range of rates used in the illustrative example in Revenue Ruling 68-609, reflecting economic and market conditions in 1968.

Reviewer's Note: In many businesses, there are no "excess earnings," because the total earnings are not even enough to justify the investment in the net tangible assets. In some such cases, the business may even be worth less than the net tangible asset value (unless the asset values could actually be realized by net proceeds from liquidation).

EXHIBIT 2

THE EXCESS EARNINGS METHOD

BACKGROUND

Variations of an appraisal procedure referred to by different names, most commonly the "excess earnings method," often are encountered. The method was originated by the U.S. Treasury Department in 1920 for the purpose of computing the value of goodwill that breweries and distilleries lost because of prohibition. Referring to the method, Revenue Ruling 68-609 states "The 'formula' approach may be used in determining the fair market value of intangible assets only if there is no better basis available for making the determination " (emphasis supplied) .3 Nevertheless, perhaps partly because of its wide publicity and partly because its apparently simplistic nature is appealing, it is encountered frequently in appraisals of small businesses and professional practices. It is important that the appraisal reviewer be able to recognize this procedure (by whatever name it is presented), and evaluate whether or not it is applied correctly.

A STEP-BY STEP EXPLANATION

The steps in the excess earnings method can be summarized as follows:

1. Determine a net tangible asset value. (Note that this value is for net tangible assets only and would not include intangible items such as leaseholds, patents, copyrights, and so on.)
2. Determine a normalized level of earnings. This must be after all expenses, including reasonable compensation to any owner(s) involved in management and after taxes if the entity is a corporation.
3. Determine an appropriate percentage of rate of return, or, in the parlance of finance, a capitalization rate on the net tangible asset value. Multiply the net tangible asset value from Step I by that rate to determine the amount of earnings attributable to the tangible assets. Subtract that amount from the normalized earnings developed in Step 2. The result of this step is called the excess earnings, that is, the amount of earnings above a fair return on the net tangible asset value.
4. Determine an appropriate capitalization rate to apply to the excess earnings, which are presumably the earnings attributable to goodwill or other intangible assets, as opposed to tangible assets. Capitalize the excess earnings at that rate.
5. Add the values from Steps 1 and 4*.

*As an alternative to using the present net tangible asset value and normalized earnings, some appraisers base the computations of the value of excess earnings on average net tangible assets and average earnings for some period of time, usually five years. This procedure is satisfactory if the period used is representative of reasonable future expectations. If this procedure is used, the value of excess earnings still is added to the present net tangible asset value to arrive at the value for the total entity.

AN EXAMPLE :

Let's suppose that Flora's Flower Shop has a net tangible asset value of $20,000. Let's also suppose that, after allowance for a reasonable salary for Flora, the shop earns about $8,000 per year. For the purpose of this example, we will use a rate of return of 15% on the tangible assets, and will capitalize the excess earnings at 33 1/3%. (The matter of determining applicable rates must be discussed and supported in the appraisal report in light of economic and capital market conditions as of the appraisal date.) In this scenario, the value of Flora's Flower Shop would be computed as follows:

Net Tangible Asset Value		$20,000
Normalized Earnings	$8,000	
Earnings Attributable to		
Tangible Assets ($20,000 x 0.15)=	$3,000	
"Excess" Earnings	<u>$5,000</u>	
Value of Excess Earnings		
($5,000 divided by 0.333)=		<u>$15,000</u>
Total Value		$35,000

SOURCES OF INFORMATION

In general, the sources of information should be complete, and should be identified well enough that the reader of the report can locate the source and verify the information if so desired.

Company Financial Statements

Is there a complete list of the statements (and tax returns, if any) consulted by year, including the designation of the fiscal year-end?

Does the report indicate for each year whether the statements are internally compiled, compiled by a CPA firm, reviewed by a CPA firm, or audited by a CPA firm?

Did the appraiser use an adequate set of financial statements and schedules for an adequate number of years for the purpose of the appraisal?

Site Inspection and Interviews

Did the appraiser visit the operation(s)?
Did the appraiser interview appropriate management personnel?

Publications

Are publications used cited adequately, including issue date for periodicals, so that the reader can locate the publication and verify the information?

Coherence

- Does the report have a logical organization that is followed consistently?.
- Does all content under a heading pertain to the topic of that heading?
- Does each paragraph contain a sentence or group of sentences that pertain to a single topic?
- Does each sentence convey a single or closely related set of information or ideas?
- If a question logically is raised in the mind of the reader, is it addressed?
- If esoteric or potentially ambiguous terms are used, are they defined?
- Do the data and analysis presented clearly support the conclusion reached?
- Are the steps taken clearly spelled out so that the reviewer could independently replicate the steps and reach the same conclusion?
- If there are data or facts that would appear to contradict the conclusion, are they reconciled with the conclusion?
- Is all the material presented relevant to the valuation report?
- Is the degree of attention accorded to various factors in the report adequate relative to the degree of impact each of such

factors has on the ultimate conclusion of the report?

Internal Consistency

- Are all statements made in any part of the report consistent with statements made in any other part of the report?
- If statements are made concerning approaches to be used, factors to be considered, etc., were all such approaches and factors used or considered as stated?
- Is the conclusion consistent with all statements made and procedures used to lead up to that conclusion?
- Do the approaches and procedures used conform to the definition of the standard of value, including relevant case law, if applicable?
- Are all numbers, spellings, etc., referred to more than once in the report the same in all places?
- Do all headings in the Table of Contents and Lists of Tables, Exhibits, Appendixes, etc. conform exactly to headings in the body of the report?
- Are the calculations accurate (multiplications, divisions, additions, etc.)?

Qualifications of the Appraisers

An important aspect of evaluating an appraisal is evaluating its source—i.e., how well qualified are the people that prepared it to do this type of appraisal? Although the following factors are presented in list form with boxes to check (consistent with the format of other portions of this checklist), each category is really a matter of degree, which could be rated from strong to very weak.

- Academic and professional credentials
- Experience (related appraisal work, etc.)
- Professional involvement (membership and activities in professional organizations, committee service, offices held, speeches, courses taught, publications, etc.)

- Expert testimony on business valuation matters

Contingent and Limiting Conditions

Does the report contain a statement of contingent and limiting conditions?

Reviewer's Note: Since appraisal procedures and relevant factors can vary considerably from one appraisal purpose to another, one of the important limiting conditions is that the appraisal is only applicable to the purpose or function stated in the description of the assignment.

SPECIAL CHECKLIST FOR EMPLOYEE STOCK OWNERSHIP PLAN STOCK APPRAISALS

MARKETABILITY

Has each of the following factors been adequately addressed and reflected?

a. Repurchase liability arising from employee departures
b. Repurchase liability arising from the diversification requirement imposed in the 1986 Tax Act
c. Terms of the put option
d. Past record of stock redemptions
e. Financial condition of the company

OTHER ESOP VALUATION ISSUES

Is the date as of which the appraisal is done close enough to the date of the transaction?

If stock will be issued to the ESOP, has the resulting dilution been adequately accounted for in the valuation?

If a capitalization of earnings and/or cash flow approach is used, are the adjustments (or lack of them) to the earnings or cash flow to be capitalized appropriate?

If the ESOP is leveraged, is the risk arising from the leverage properly reflected in the discount or capitalization rates or multiples used?

COMMON ERRORS AND SHORTCOMINGS IN BUSINESS APPRAISAL REPORTS

- Inadequate Documentation of Sources (leaving reviewer unable to locate and verify the source material)
- Lack of Replicability (leaving the reviewer unable to follow through the steps purportedly taken and verify the conclusion)
- Failure to Clearly Define and/or Conform to Applicable Standard of Value

Amazingly, one of the most common errors is failure to identify and conform to the applicable standard of value. In some cases, this is merely an omission from the written report. In other cases, it may become apparent, from either reading the report or questioning the appraiser, that the appraiser has gone off heedlessly to do an "appraisal" without ever determining the applicable standard of value.

In some cases, the applicable standard of value is identified but apparently not understood, because the analysis and conclusion do not conform to the standard of value identified. The standard of value may be misconstrued, or the report may simply fail to address some of the factors implied in the standard of value or mandated for consideration as a matter of law or regulation.

- Internal Inconsistencies
- Extensive and Irrelevant Information
- Undefined Jargon

Many terms used in finance are ambiguous. That is, there may be two or more acceptable definitions, but no way to know exactly which is intended unless the writer makes it clear. A good example is cash flow, which has many definitions but can be very precise once the author has specified which definition applies. Some authors also use terms which simply lack any clear-cut definition.

- Inadequate Comparative Data (inadequate search for comparative data and/or lack of clear exposition of criteria for selection and exact method of using data)
- Comparisons of Non-Comparable Data (e.g., data developed for comparative companies for some certain time period and applied to the subject company for a different time period, or data defined or measured one way for comparative companies and a different way for the subject company)
- Leaps of Faith (the presentation of a fact or conclusion with no accompanying documentation of source or supporting analysis or data)

This is especially critical, of course, if the unsupported fact or conclusion is part of an integral link in the valuation process, such as a capitalization rate, so that the valuation conclusion depends on it. The variety of leaps of faith to which readers of business valuation reports may be subjected is almost boundless. The reader should evaluate whether all critical assertions are supported and consider that evaluation in determining the extent to which he or she is willing or able to rely on the report.

- Emphasis of Items Not in Proportion to their Relative Importance

The most common example of this error is probably the emphasis often accorded to developing the earnings base and the capitalization rates in a capitalization of earnings approach. The two variables are more or less equally critical to a value conclusion using that approach. Yet many reports devote 20 pages to painstakingly developing the earnings base to be capitalized and then cavalierly capitalize that earnings base at a capitalization rate supported only by one or two flimsy sentences. The reader should evaluate the report in light of whether the factors that really matter in reaching the final conclusion are indeed given their due consideration.

• Overemphasis on Past Data

As widely noted in regulations and in the literature of finance, a business valuation represents a prophesy of the future. The purpose of gathering and analyzing past data is only to provide guidance of reasonable expectations for the subject business. An appraisal is deficient to the extent that it relies on data without convincing support that the historical data is indeed relevant as a guide to reasonable future expectations.

• Reliance on Rules of Thumb

While rules of thumb bandied around for businesses in certain industries should not be ignored, they rarely can be relied on in and of themselves to produce an accurate valuation.

CHAPTER THIRTY

REVIEWING APPRAISALS OF PROPOSED DEVELOPMENTS AND THE ROLE OF RISK ASSESSMENT

INTRODUCTION

When reviewing appraisals of properties yet to be completed or occupied, the appraiser is often forced into projecting changes in value during the construction and absorption periods. Most appraisers realize that the accuracy of such forecasts is critically dependent on assumptions made about future market conditions. However, the astute appraiser also understands that a proper analysis of such projects includes reviewing the dynamic role that varying levels of risk play in the assignment of future values. This chapter addresses at what stages during the development process should separate values be rendered, and the varying levels of risk that affect the value of the property during development and fill up.

The necessity of correctly identifying the value changes projected to occur during development was clearly mandated in the Federal Home Loan Bank Board's R-41c requirements for appraisals used by lending institutions. The memorandum required that "when an analysis, opinion or conclusion of a proposed project, improvement or change in use is involved, all value

EXHIBIT 1. Value changes during the development process

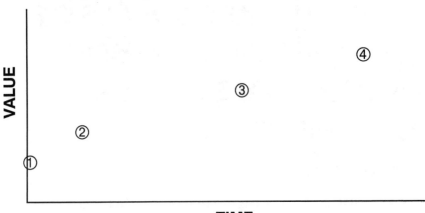

1. Raw land value with no intangible improvements
2. Raw land with intangible improvements (i.e. zoning, cond. use)
3. Point of Greatest Risk (PGR), built but unoccupied
4. Completed and fully occupied changes projected to occur from the conception of a project to its completion and/or stabilized occupancy should be set forth in sufficient detail so that the continuum of present value estimates over the life of the credit arrangement or investment can be reconciled with the values reported in the appraisal.

This requirement, however, was ambiguous as to when these changes occur and did not address how the changing level of risk affects value. For instance, the memorandum uses the term "completion and/or stabilized occupancy" and implies that the difference in property value between those stages is no more than income and expenses generated during the absorption period. However, the difference between these two levels of development is often as great as the difference between solvency and insolvency.

ASSESSING RISKS

In a perfect world, the review appraiser could precisely predict the conditions surrounding the construction, fill-up and disposition of a property. This would enable the reviewer to assign values at the various stages of development and ownership based on calculating the present value of all future income and expenses at a particular stage, and then making the appropriate adjustments. However, the analyst living in the real world must recognize the value impact of uncertainty. Risks associated with development occur throughout the development process in varying degrees and have a significant affect on the ever-changing value of the property.

It has been said that development is a creation of value process. When a project attains a higher degree of completion, many risks no longer pose a threat thereby increasing the property's value. When viewed as a time continuum (see Exhibit #1) the development process typically begins with raw land.

Before a shovel breaks ground, the dynamic role of risk may have already changed the value of the property. If the property has had a zoning variance granted, or a conditional use permit issued, its value may double or even triple. Likewise, a moratorium on development or an upzoning of the parcel can ruin its chances for development. Hence, when the appraiser is ascertaining land value, adjustments for intangible improvements are crucial. If land residual techniques are employed with comparables, they should be adjusted to reflect both the physical and legal condition of the subject property.

The first valuation in an appraisal of a proposed development, then, should be at the point in time immediately before the first physical improvements are made. A proper narrative report will include a discussion on the status of the unimproved land, along with the market value of raw land with and without the necessary intangible improvements. Paired sales analysis is usually the most reliable way for obtaining this.

POINT OF GREATEST RISK

The rationale behind rendering values at different points in time during development is to provide the owner, lender or investor with a decision making tool. This tool assists the reviewer in calculating how much should be invested and at what rate. It also can provide the financier a worse case scenario—should the property development go into default, how hard can I be hit?

As a development successfully reaches each stage of completion, the developer typically draws an additional amount of interim funding to continue construction. With each draw, the lending institution has extended more capital thereby increasing the potential damage wrought by default. The level of risk, however, is somewhat abated during construction as most developers are required to take out completion or performance bonds.

From the perspective of the lender, the worst point in time for a property to go into default is often just after completion but prior to any occupancy. This point in time is referred to in study as the Point of Greatest Risk (PGR) and reflects that stage in the creation of value process when the property has received the highest level capital outlay, with the least amount of assured income. Because of the level of risks associated with the PGR, a separate rendering of value should be made for that stage of development to give the reviewer an indication of the property's potential liquidation value.

FACTORS TO CONSIDER IN ASSIGNING THE "PGR" VALUE

The difference between values at the Point of Greatest Risk (i.e. completed but unoccupied) and completed with full and stabilized occupancy includes the present values of income and expenditures generated during the absorption period. To obtain the PGR value, the value estimated for the property as though it was completed and occupied should be adjusted downward to reflect such costs as promotion, advertising, leasing commissions, free rent and other concessions given to expedite fill up. Additionally, it should be adjusted to reflect holding or carrying costs incurred.

However, although Memorandum R 41c alluded to the contrary, making these adjustments alone may not result in an accurate PGR valuation. When the appraiser relies solely on these cash flow adjustments, an unrealistic scenario of the development process is portrayed that does not reflect the dynamic role of risk and how this role affects market value.

The lender or investor interested in the PGR value needs to know how much the property is worth at that point in time should there be a foreclosure. The reasons for a possible foreclosure are numerous. Absorption may have been too slow, there may have been poor management, or a combination of reasons might have led to default. In any case, the result usually is a distressed piece of real estate. Heuristic analysis tells the seasoned appraiser that when an unoccupied property is absorbed by a lender or investor because of default, an immediate loss of value occurs because of the property's status.

This loss in value can be significant if the completed property was unable to withstand market competition or was poorly conceived or constructed. The entity that took title after foreclosure must then consider its disposition. Undoubtedly, the original appraisal will be reviewed, and if the appraiser did not consider the entire scenario surrounding the possible distressed status of the property, the value rendered may be unrealistic.

THE ROLE OF ENTREPRENEURIAL PROFIT

When an unoccupied property is placed on the market block, it has an unproven track record that creates fear and uncertainty with potential buyers. If the property is partially filled with a poor absorption track record, it may actually be worth less than if it had a lower occupancy with a stronger record of absorption. Thus, the risk a buyer bears when he purchases property at the PGR stage must be compensated through additional profit.

Buyers who specifically target such properties usually have greater knowledge about maximizing returns in workout situations. These individuals are analogous to the corporate raider who makes a run at undervalued concerns. Also, they are typically in a much better bartering position than the owner, who is more concerned about disposing the property to get the red ink off the books. Consequently, the actual price is lower than that which would be indicated by only making adjustments for marketing and holding costs incurred during fill-up.

The needed downward adjustment in value will vary by both property type and regional submarkets. If the property to be built has already received lease commitments from large tenants with good credit, there may be no need for any adjustment. However, if the development is speculative, some adjustment for entrepreneurial profit should be made.

The best source for estimating the difference between the fully occupied value and the PGR value is through the collection of comparable real estate owned (R.E.O.) and trustee sales data. If enough comparable R.E.O. sales can be found, a separate PGR valuation can be included as part of the sales comparison section of the appraisal.

The PGR value would then be drawn directly from sales of properties with like occupancies, thereby reducing the number of adjustments needed. This methodology is most reflective of the market, and it eliminates potential errors from estimating absorption period income and expenses. However, the review appraiser should pay close attention to the conditions surrounding each sale. In a seller's market, the incremental difference in value between an unoccupied property and one with full occupancy is much less than the difference found in a soft market. When comparable sales are unavailable, the appraiser must rely on other alternatives. One such alternative is to review the amount of developer's profit used in the cost approach and apply a similar amount as a deduction.

The rationale for this is that when a development is in default, the developer has often retained no profit. The individual picking up the ball and running with it will do so in order to receive an entrepreneurial profit similar to what the developer left behind. However, when making the downward adjustment, it is necessary to include all income and expenses expected to be generated during the absorption period.

ABSORPTION PERIOD ANALYSIS

The final value rendered should reflect full occupancy with a concomitant discussion on the expected completion date. This discussion should also include a definitive absorption period analysis which estimates all income and expenses expected to occur during fill up. The analysis can be included in the highest and best use section or the income analysis section of the report, depending on how germane it is to either section. One methodology used in constructing the absorption period analysis involves reviewing the amount of space absorbed per period, (usually on a monthly schedule). A computer spreadsheet facilitates this analysis (see Exhibit #2). The objective of the model is to estimate two value adjustments:

1. The present value of all net income generated during the absorption period
2. The present value of all costs occurring during fill up that are atypical to stabilized operating conditions.

In the model above, the net income generated for a given period was calculated by multiplying the amount of space (or units) absorbed up to that period by the expected rental rate, net of any free rent or concessions. All other incomes, which were adjusted proportionately to reflect the level of occupancy, were also added.

EXHIBIT 2
ABSORPTION PERIOD ANALYSIS

Assumptions:

Total Rentable Units	48
Unit Absorption per Period	4
Absorption Rate per Period (% of total)	8.3%
Rent Income per Unit per Period	$139
Discount Rate (Simple)	11.5%

Period	Total	Units	Units	Gross Income	Operating	Net Income	Present Val.	Marketing	Present Val.
0	0	0	0	0	0	0	0	0	0
1	48	4	44	556	485	71	70	1,540	1,525
2	48	8	40	1,111	485	626	614	1,540	1,511
3	48	12	36	1,667	584	1,083	1,043	1,540	1,497
4	48	16	32	2,222	778	1,444	1,403	1,540	1,483
5	48	20	28	2,778	972	1,806	1,756	1,540	1,470
6	48	24	24	3,333	1,116	2,217	2,096	1,540	1,456
7	48	28	20	3,889	1,361	2,528	2,369	1,540	1,443
8	48	32	16	4,444	1,555	2,889	2,683	1,540	1,430
9	48	36	12	5,000	1,750	3,250	2,992	1,540	1,418
10	48	40	8	5,556	1,945	3,611	3,295	1,540	1,405
11	48	44	4	6,111	2,134	3,977	3,598	1,540	1,393
12	48	48	0	6,667	2,333	4,334	3,887	1,540	1,382
TOTALS:							25,806		17,413

From this amount, the estimated operating expenses were deducted to derive the net income received during absorption. In estimating operating expenses during the absorption period, the appraiser should indicate how expenses would differ from normal operating conditions. For example, insurance, utilities, payroll or maintenance may be less during fill up. Additionally, some expenses are typically higher during this period; immature landscaping, for instance, often requires much more care and maintenance than when it is mature.

Once the net income is calculated on a period-by-period basis, it is necessary to discount each income flow to the present value at the beginning of the absorption period. In certain situations, this may become too onerous a task and the review appraiser may elect to take the entire amount of net income received over the absorption period, and then make only one present value calculation with the income flow occurring in the middle of the absorption period.

It is not unusual to see in some appraisals an adjustment made to the final value to reflect the income lost during the absorption period. This adjustment is usually derived by estimating the average vacancy during the fill up stage and multiplying this amount by the gross income. Although the use of such an adjustment may be prudent in certain instances, it should never be included as part of the discounted cash flow model as presented in this chapter. This is because the "income lost" adjustment represents an opportunity cost rather than an actual cash flow. It is an intangible benefit perceived by the marketplace, and does reflect a physical exchange of cash or its equivalent.

The second adjustment, which we arbitrarily refer to as marketing costs, includes all costs incurred to expedite fill up in a competitive and timely manner. These costs typically include leasing or brokerage commissions, advertisement and promotion. They can also include other costs such as the reimbursement of moving expenses for prospective tenants or special tenant improvements. As with the net income adjustment, the present value for marketing costs should also be calculated.

Also, in constructing the absorption period model, it is a good idea to display all assumptions used in the model on the same spread sheet. This allows the analyst a quick review of all model inputs, and if the calculations are directly tied to these numbers it also allows the review appraiser an easy avenue for conducting sensitivity analysis.

APPLICATION OF ADJUSTMENTS

Before making the above adjustments to obtain the PGR value, the analyst must remember that the purchaser of the subject property will not realize the full value of the property until the end of the absorption period. Therefore, the completed and fully occupied value of the property must also be adjusted to reflect the cost of funds to hold the asset over this period. One way to approach this problem is to discount the value of the asset to reflect its present value at the beginning of the absorption period. To be conservative, the discount rate selected should be higher than the interest rate for both first and second deeds of trust for comparable properties. It should also reflect current yield expectations in the marketplace.

Currently, there is debate in academic circles over whether the discount rate should also include property-specific risks, which would eliminate the need to make a separate entrepreneurial profit adjustment. Whether entrepreneurial profit is handled through a higher discount rate or included as a separate front end adjustment becomes a question of practicality rather than an issue of technical correctness. Assessing the risk of a specific property in terms of a discount rate percentage is difficult if there is not enough precedence found in the marketplace to justify the rate selected. Therefore, without proper historical support, the selection of a discount rate that includes property specific risks may be too subjective and arbitrary.

EXHIBIT 3
FIVE YEAR DISCOUNTED CASH FLOW ANALYSIS
(Beginning with Stabilized Year 1)

	Year 1	Year 2	Year 3	Year 4	Year 5
Gross Potential Inc.	80,000	83,200	86,528	89,989	93,588
Less Vacancy	-4,000	-4,160	-4,326	-4,499	-4,679
Effective Gross Inc.	76,000	79,040	82,202	85,490	88,909
Less Operating Exp.	-29,600	-27,664	-28,771	-29,922	-31,118
Net Operating Inc.	49,400	51,376	53,431	55,568	57,791
Less Debt Service	-41,070	-41,070	-41,070	-41,070	-41,070
Debt Coverage Ratio	1.20	1.25	1.30	1.35	1.41
Equity Cash Flow	8,330	10,306	12,361	14,498	16,721
Present Value of Equity Cash Flow	7,504	8,363	9,038	9,550	9,923
Total Value Equity Cash Begin. of Stabilized Year 1					44,378

Reversionary Value Calculations:

Reversion Value: Year 5 N.O.I. Capitalized					$608,328
Less Sales Costs: (5% of value)					-30,416
Less Loan Balance: End of Year 5					-376,640
Reversion to Equity					$201,272
Value of Equity Reversion Discounted 5 Years to Beginning of Year (B.O.Y.) 1					$116,791

Summary:

B.O.Y. 1 Value of Equity Cash Flow	$ 44,378
Plus B.O.Y. 1 Reversionary Value	116,791
B.O.Y. Value of Equity Position	$161,169
Plus B.O.Y. 1 Value of Mortgage	390,000
Cash Flow Analysis Value with Full Occupancy (Beginning of Stabilized Year 1)	$551,169

Point of Greatest Risk Value:

Full Occupancy Value at B.O.Y. 1 Discounted to Beginning of Absorption Period (e.g. 1 year)	$494,322
Plus Estimated Net Operating Income Received During Absorption Period - present value	25,806
Less Marketing Costs - present value	-17,413
Less Entrepreneurial Profit (Sale Price Reduction)	-52,000
Indicated PGR Value - Built but Unoccupied	$450,715

PGR VALUATION THROUGH DISCOUNTED CASH FLOW ANALYSIS

In the income analysis section, it is possible to calculate both the completed and occupied value and the PGR value in one discounted cash flow model (see Exhibit #3). This author typically uses a five year investment horizon whereby Year 1 in the model represents the first year of full and stabilized occupancy. The model also reviews the ability of the property's income to service the debt, and examines the reversionary proceeds.

CONCLUSION

The success of a project is dependent on numerous factors, each of which carries some level of risk. It is incumbent upon the appraiser to include a risk analysis in all appraisals or feasibility studies of property yet to be developed. The discussion of associated risks in the highest and best use section of the report should serve as a fundamental part of the criteria in the selection of the most appropriate use for the property.

However, although the selected highest and best use may be appropriate, even the best conceived projects contain some level of risk associated with the development and fill up process. This chapter suggests a methodology whereby the qualitative assessment of risk can be turned into a quantitative analysis. In understanding the dynamic role of risk and how it affects value, the review appraiser can better serve his client with a more accurate and meaningful analysis.

SUMMARY

When reviewing appraisals of properties yet to be completed or occupied, the appraiser is often forced into projecting changes in value during the construction and absorption periods. Most appraisers realize that the accuracy of such forecasts is critically dependent on assumptions made about future market conditions. However, the astute appraiser also understands that a proper analysis of such projects includes reviewing the dynamic role that varying levels of risk play in the assignment of future values. This report addresses at what stages during the development process should separate values be rendered, and the varying levels of risk that affect these values during development and fill up. Within the discussion of these various stages of development, the chapter proposes that at a specific point in time, development risks are at their highest level. This stage of development, which is referred to as "The Point of Greatest Risk)PGR)", requires a separate rendering of value and the author suggests ways for obtaining this value.

Also included within this chapter are suggested procedures for conducting an absorption period analysis and a discounted cash flow model, which integrate concepts set forth within the report.

CHAPTER THIRTY-ONE

FEDERAL REAL PROPERTY APPRAISAL STANDARDS

I. Preface

The Federal Real Property Appraisal Standards represents an effort to establish basic appraisal standards applicable to all real estate related transactions involving Federal agencies. Federal agencies are a major consumer of appraisal services. It is estimated that approximately 80% of all appraisal reports are in response to Federal programs involving direct loans, insured and guaranteed loans, direct acquisitions or guaranteed loans by a Federal agency to satisfy a default or other guarantee claim, and sale, exchange or acquisition of property, including eminent domain. Consequently, Federal agencies are a major user of appraisal services, and have a responsibility for establishing and assuring implementation of appraisal standards which are cost effective and protect the Government's financial interest. Depending on specific agency needs, additional requirements may be included in agency policy, manuals or handbooks.

These standards were developed by the Federal Interagency Real Property Appraisal Committee. This Committee was convened to encourage the development of uniform real property appraisal standards applicable to Federal agencies. In addition, the Committee seeks to assure the protection of the Federal Government's interest in the development and implementation of Title XI, Financial Institutions Reform, Recovery and Enforcement Act of 1989 (FIRREA).

It is intended that individuals involved in appraising real property comply with applicable state laws. Private appraisers performing assignments directly for an agency or under policies of a regulatory agency must meet applicable state regulatory requirements.

Federal agency appraisers may be exempt under state laws, and therefore not required to be licensed or certified. However, it may be in the agency ' s interest to encourage staff appraisers to meet state qualification standards. Furthermore, staff appraisers may want to be regulated under state law in order to enhance their credibility as appraisers. Each agency will have flexibility in deciding the appropriate level of staff qualifications necessary to maintain public confidence in their appraisal program.

A. Federal Standards

The Federal Real Property Appraisal Standards considers current Federal standards incorporated into law or referenced by various agencies in their regulations or manuals. These included:

"Uniform Appraisal Standards for Federal Land Acquisitions" (1973) prepared by the Interagency Land Acquisition Conference and Government-wide appraisal standards contained in 49 CFR Part 24, published March 2, 1989 by the Department of Transportation, implementing appraisal provisions of the Uniform Relocation and Real Property Acquisition Policies Act of 1970, as amended. Both documents are applicable to the acquisition of real property.

The Department of Transportation standards apply to 18 executive branch departments and agencies administering federal or federally assisted projects. Other agencies having Federal credit programs have regulations and administrative procedures covering appraisal activity.

The Federal Real Property Appraisal also takes into consideration those standards being developed by regulatory financial agencies in response to Title XI, Financial Institutions Reform, Recovery and Enforcement Act of 1989. Standards developed by the financial regulatory agencies reference the USPAP and include additional appraisal requirements.

The Appraisal Subcommittee created by FIRREA, Title XI, has responsibility for monitoring requirements established by states for certification and licensing of appraisers, and appraisal standards developed by the Federal financial institutions regulatory agencies. The Subcommittee also has responsibility to monitor and review practices, procedures, activities and the organizational structure of the Appraisal Foundation.

B. Professional Standards

The "Uniform Standards of Professional Appraisal Practices" (USPAP) represent standards developed by professional appraisal organizations representing suppliers of appraisal services. The USPAP establish standards applicable to member organizations affiliated with the Appraisal Foundation These standards are applicable to activities involving the act or process of estimating value. Although broad in scope, they do provide specific guidance regarding appraiser competency, preparation and documentation of appraisal reports and performance of the appraisal review function. To maintain the highest level of professional appraisal practice, affiliated appraisers are required to observe these standards (Preamble USPAP). Appraisal standards adopted by the states will be in accordance with generally accepted standards issued by the Appraisal Standards Board (ASB) of the Appraisal Foundation. State regulated appraisers will be required to meet these standards.

Specifically, the ASB standards as they relate to real property and review are included in Standards 1-3 of the USPAP. Qualification standards for appraisers are established by the Appraisal Qualifications Board, a separate, independent board within the Appraisal Foundation.

The original USPAP prepared by an Ad Hoc Committee on Uniform Standards, and adopted by the ASB in January 1989, is currently being revised. The Ethics provision was approved December 4, 1989 and revisions to Standard 1-3 are pending final action by the ASB.

The Federal Real Property Appraisal Standards as they relate to preparation of unbiased, written appraisal reports estimating market value are consistent with provisions of the USPAP. These standards more directly relate to real estate related transactions involving Federal agencies.

II. Code of Practice

An appraiser involved in preparing appraisals for Federal or Federally assisted programs shall observe high standards of honesty, integrity and fairness in preparing written appraisal reports. Appraisers shall:

- Possess the knowledge and experience necessary to complete the appraisal assignment competently;
- Not accept an assignment in which payment for appraisal services is contingent on reaching a predetermined conclusion of value, or on the estimated value of the property interest;
- Not knowingly commit errors or withhold pertinent information that would affect the estimate of market value;
- Report conclusions of value in a manner that is meaningful, and does not mislead the client, parties to the transaction, or the public;
- Apply realistic assumptions an valuation methods consistent with market information;
- Disclose any instructions or extraordinary assumptions that may affect the estimate of market value; and
- Cooperate with investigators and authorities in providing factual information regarding an appraisal assignment.

III. DEFINITIONS

Applicable law, agency regulations and practice may require the use of definitions other than those set forth below.

(1) "Appraisal or Appraisal report" means a written statement independently and impartially prepared by qualified appraiser setting for an opinion or defined value of an adequately de-

scribed property as a specific date, supported by the presentation and analysis of relevant market information.

(2)"Appraiser" means an individual who is qualified under applicable state laws to prepare or review appraisals in conjunction with real estate related transactions.

(3) "Complex real estate related transaction" means any transaction identified by agencies requiring the services of a certified or equivalent level appraiser. Agencies should take into consideration the following:

(a) commercial or industrial improved properties;

(b) rural properties where the intended use is for the production of agricultural income or products;

(c) commercially valuable timber and mineral interests;

(d) acquisition or private property under eminent domain authority, or

(e) raw law with development potential and;

(f) requirements for a detailed appraisal (49 CFR Part 24, Subpart B).

(4) "Market value" means the most probable price in cash, or terms equivalent to cash, which a property should bring in a competitive and open market under all conditions requisite to a fair sale, and the buyer and seller, each acting prudently, and knowledgeably, and assuming the price is not affected by undue stimulus.

(5) "Qualified Appraiser" means an individual accepted, approved, or designated by the agency who meets applicable requirements.

(6) "Real estate related transaction" means any transaction involving: (1) the sale, lease, purchase, investment in or exchange of real property, including interests in property, or the financing thereof; (2) the refinancing of real property of interests in real property; and (3) the use of real property or interests in property as security for a loan or investment, including mortgage-backed securities.

(7) "Review appraiser" means a qualified appraiser or individual designated by a party to independently examine and evaluate an appraisal report for purposes of recommending, preparing or approving an estimate of value.

(8) "State certified appraiser" means any individual who has satisfied the requirements for state certification or equivalent requirements in a state or territory whose criteria for a real estate appraiser currently meet the minimum criteria for certification issued by the Appraiser Qualification Board of the Appraisal Foundation.

(9) "State licensed appraiser" means an individual who has satisfied the requirements for state licensing or equivalent requirements in a state or territory.

IV. Appraiser Qualifications

Appraisers involved in real estate related transactions shall comply with applicable state laws regarding appraiser qualifications. In those states not having state laws, or where state laws governing the activities of appraisers have been found to be inadequate, agencies may implement standards consistent with those developed by the Appraisal Qualifications Board of the Appraisal Foundation. In those states having state certification requirements, state certified appraisers shall be required for complex transactions as defined above.

V. Appraisal Report Guidelines

Agency appraisal criteria should be consistent with those set forth in 24.103 of 49 CFR Part 24. As necessary, agencies may establish appraisal standards in accordance with program specific objectives. Those standards may also include applicable provisions of the Uniform Standards of Professional Appraisal Practice.

VI. Appraisal Review

Agency appraisal review criteria should be consistent with 24.104 of 49 CFR Part 24. Agency standards may include review appraisal provisions of the Uniform Standard of Professional Appraisal Practice.

ISSUE: WHAT IS THE ROLE OF THE REVIEWING APPRAISER?

The Reviewing Appraiser performs a significant and important function in the overall appraisal process, and in some governmental programs appraisal review is considered to be equal to or even more important that of the appraisal. Often the reviewing appraiser may be the final control point before large sums of money are committed by a public agency. Errors made at this juncture may well be irreversible in many if not most cases.

Many agencies have, particularly in the last ten to fifteen years, recognize the vital role of the reviewing appraiser as the valuation process has become more complex, controversial and costly and there is greater competition for public funds for agency programs. The precise role of reviewing appraisers varies among the various agencies. The distinctions are related to differences in agency missions, size of appraisal program, organizational structure, centralization-decentralization, and general agency philosophy on the subject.

Generally speaking the appraisal review function can be subdivided into one of the three basic categories described below.

Category 1

This so-called review function consists primarily of checking factual data and information presented in the appraisal report. No authority exists to make judgmental decisions related to the valuation conclusion presented by the appraiser. "Approval" within the context of this type of review process extends primarily to a "box and blank" check requiring little, if any, appraisal type expertise. For the record, most agencies do not consider this type of evaluation within the commonly accepted definition of the term.

Category 2

The review function consists of an all inclusive evaluation of appraisals. Factually presented data as described in Category 1 above is verified (sometimes by a subordinate technician). Appraisal reports are critically evaluated in all respects with the validity and reasonableness of the final valuation conclusion being the principal focal point. Subject properties may be inspected by the reviewing appraiser along with comparable sales and other data presented in the appraisal report. The reviewing appraiser may have a variety of administrative considerations to check such as contractual performance, appraiser selection, assignment of appraisal work, developing a written appraisal problem, maintaining valuation consistency among parcels on a project, meeting with assigned appraisers, training of appraisers, determining if a particular appraiser should be maintained on an approved listing or restricted to specific types of property and other managerial responsibility.

With respect to the appraiser's valuation conclusion, the reviewing appraiser may have the responsibility of approving the appraisal or recommending an amount as representative thereof to higher authority for final approval consistent with valuation estimates provided by employed appraisers. A distinction may be made as to determining or recommending fair market value based upon dollar thresholds.

Under this operating structure the reviewing appraiser can approve or reject the conclusion set out in one of the submitted appraisal reports. The alternative is to solicit an additional appraisal. Authority does not exist for the reviewing appraiser to establish or recommend an independently developed value conclusion different from a submitted appraisal report.

Category 3

The fundamental role of the reviewing appraiser under this concept is nearly identical to that described in Category 2 above with one significant difference. Category 3 reviewing appraiser have the ultimate authority to establish their own independent valuation conclusion as representing fair market value-just compensation. They are not bound to an estimate provided by the appraiser(s). The reviewing appraiser may accept parts of one or more submitted appraisal reports or reject same depending upon his/or independent findings and conclusions. The reviewing appraiser may also reject the appraisal reports in total. This usually occurs in cases where only land is involved and there is a disagreement as to the unit value. At the same time the reviewing appraiser, under this process, could approve a submitted appraisal for a given parcel exactly as is the case under Category 2 above. In all probability this is precisely what occurs in 95% of the cases encountered.

When the reviewing appraiser establishes an independent value conclusion in lieu of approving a submitted appraisal report, he/she becomes the appraiser. In many, if not some instances the reviewing appraiser will meet with the appraiser prior to establishing an independent value estimate. Some agencies that employ this process take the position that the reviewing appraiser, where an independent value conclusion is developed, must have his "appraisal" formally approved by another reviewing appraiser since it is an appraisal estimate as opposed to a reviewing appraiser's determination. Other agencies do not have such a requirement though informal advice from a counterpart reviewing appraiser is normally solicited.

CHAPTER THIRTY-TWO

REVIEWING APPRAISALS FOR RELOCATION PURPOSES

A relocation appraisal may be completed for various reasons, one being a procedure where homes are being bought from "relocated" individuals whose homes are being eliminated due to eminent domain proceedings. The relocated individual will be compensated at the fair market value stated in the appraisal or appraisals. A relocation appraisal for a third party company is an entirely different concept. To define a "third party company", let's assume that the employer is the first party, the employee is the second party, and the home buying company is the third party.

The purpose of the third party appraisal is two fold. First, the property must be purchased from the employee at a price that he feels is fair. Second, the purchase price must also be a value that will allow the property to be resold quickly so that the entire process is cost effective to the employer.

The person reviewing a relocation appraisal must carefully scrutinize the appraisal for factors that would not apply in a mortgage or estate appraisal. A main concern is, "What will the property ultimately sell for and how long will it take?" The relocation appraisal is defined as "the most probable sale price of a residential housing unit, using the market approach to value".

The purpose of the relocation appraisal is to establish the most probable sale price for a relocated employee's primary residence, assuming an arms length transaction. The market data approach to value is defined as: The price at which a property would most probably sell, if exposed to the market for a reasonable amount of time, in an "as is" condition, where payment is made in cash or its equivalent. Implicit in this definition is the consummation of the sale with passing of title from seller to buyer under conditions whereby:

1. Both parties are well informed and acting in what they consider their best interests.
2. A reasonable amount of time is allowed for exposure in the local market. (This is usually up to 120 days unless market conditions indicate otherwise.)
3. Financing, if any, is on terms generally available in the community and typical for the property type in its locale, (if special financing is available, its specific effect on the appraised value should be stated separately).
4. Forecasting is applied in making an estimate of a future happening or condition, based on an analysis of trends in the recent past, tempered with analytical judgment concerning the probable extent to which these trends will continue into the future and reflecting an estimated impact, if any, upon value. The appraiser who is hired by a third party company or corporation is asked to follow some very specific guidelines. Some of these guidelines are:

1. Estimate the appraised value considering the property in an "as is" condition as of the date of the inspection. "As is" conditions should reflect the cost of those items (e.g. repairs, decorations, etc...) required to make the subject comparable with similar properties in that market area from a buyer's point of view. If the appraiser is unable to determine the "as is" condition, (e.g. in-process construction or improvements, suspected structural problems, water related problems, roof, etc...) they are instructed to notify the client immediately.
2. Stress what the property should sell for in the current marketplace. In this regard, give particular attention to the analysis of comparable sales (or homes under contract), competitive listings, supply and demand, and overall market conditions.

The appraiser should also consider other factors and make necessary adjustments such as the residence's exposure to the market, availability and terms of financing, over-improvements and location.

3. Reflect in their appraised value opinion as of the date of the appraisal:

    a. An adjustment for any value that may have been created by comparable sale prices (or homes under contract) that were influenced by discount points paid by the seller of FHA, VA, or conventional mortgages; or those comparables which were sold by loan assumption, installment contract, seller carry back, or any form of preferential financing. This also applies to situations where the seller pays certain buyer costs such as buy downs, fees, or credits. In these situations, adjustments should be noted and described for the specific comparable sale.

    b. The difference in discount points between those charged on the comparable sales (or homes under contract), and charged currently if it is the custom of lenders to charge discount points to sellers on conventional mortgages.

4. Develop the appraised value opinion, assuming the property is free and clear of all non-mortgage encumbrances with the owner responsible for discharging all liens and unpaid installments of special assessments for improvements completed. If the special assessments are still pending and the improvements are not yet completed, the appraiser should include any additional value which may attribute to the pending improvements. If paying off an assessment provides the subject property with an advantage over the comparable sales and competitive listings, this should be reflected in the appraised value.

In addition the appraiser must be aware of and follow these specific procedural guidelines.

1. Appraisers are frequently the sole visible representative of the client to the relocated homeowner. Therefore, a professional and courteous manner should be presented at all times.
2. When an appraiser's assignment is directed to a specific individual, that appraiser must personally inspect the property and complete the assignment unless approval for a substitution is obtained from the client.
3. On the day the appraiser is contacted with the appraisal request, contact should be made with the employee (or spouse) for an appointment. If the employee (or spouse) cannot be reached on the same day they must let the client know so they can assist in locating the homeowner.
4. Inspect the property within two working days and contact the client with the verbal figure within four working days of the original request (unless the transferring employee delays the process). If the appraisal cannot be completed in the required time frame, or if the appraiser will be unavailable to discuss the assignment after completion, the assignment should not be accepted.
5. If access to the property cannot be gained, if valuation problems arise, or if an inspection is required for clarification (such as a structural engineer's report, etc...), the client should be called immediately.
6. Completed copies of the typewritten appraisal report should be mailed within seven working days of the original request (providing there are not delays created by the homeowner).
7. Sufficient time should be taken when inspecting the subject property to impart confidence to the homeowner, even if the appraiser is familiar with the property.
8. Consider any information that the homeowner feels is important to the value of his/her home.
9. The appraiser should not discuss his/her appraisal opinions

or reveal sensitive information to anyone other than the client. If the homeowner (or spouse) asks general questions as it relates to the appraisal process, feel free to discuss generalities.

10. The appraiser who arrives at the homeowner's property while another appraiser or broker is present, should leave the property immediately and reschedule the appointment.

11. An appraiser will not accept an appraisal assignment if there is a conflict of interest such as: recently appraising the house for another party, an association with the listing agent/company, etc...

12. Appraisers will not solicit a listing or generate a referral as a result of an appraisal assignment.

13. Call the client to clarify the instructions if they are not completely understood.

14. Include the following exhibits:

   a. Photographs of the front and rear view of the residence, street scene of the property, factors in nearby vicinity which affect subject property, either favorably or adversely.

   b. Photos of all comparables, attached separately.

   c. Sketch of the floor plan of subject property (not necessarily to scale).

   d. Sketch of plot plan showing all improvements (not necessarily to scale).

   e. Map of the subdivision or area depicting locations of the subject, comparable sold properties and competitive listings.

In response to relocation management companies and the appraisal community's request for a standardized relocation appraisal report, the Employee Relocation Council (ERC), recently introduced an appraisal form developed by their Relocation Appraisal Practices Committee. The form, identified as the ERC Supplement to the FHLMC/FNMA Residential Appraisal Report, embodies two objectives that are of concern to the relocation appraiser: to establish definitions of the relocation appraisal and to develop appraisal performance and procedural guidelines. The qualitative and quantitative information provided for in ERC's supplement augments the "Fannie Mae" report, which is widely used by relocation appraisers but is designed primarily to support a mortgage value.

The supplement accomplishes a third objective: to develop an appraisal report to foster the standardization of the relocation appraisal process.

Each third party company has its own procedures regarding who reviews appraisals. Many companies have Relocation Coordinators who interface with the transferee and appraisers. We at the National Association of Review Appraisers and Mortgage Underwriters suggest that your company employ a specialist in relocation. We recommend this system which appears to work well for all concerned.

Overview of NARA/MU Appraisal Review Process

One unique aspect that we recommend is the presence of a full time Certified Review Appraiser (CRA) on staff. The review appraiser is familiar with all aspects of the appraisal process, especially as it pertains to the relocation appraisal. Having a review appraiser on staff who reviews all appraisals gives a quality of expertise that is not available through other methods. The coordinator's time is free to deal directly with the transferee's concerns and problems since all details of the appraisal review will be completed by the staff review appraiser.

The review appraiser uses only qualified appraisers who have maintained high professional standards. When obtaining an appraisal, the review appraiser may have to use non-designated appraisers but will only do so after ascertaining by interview that the person has the background to meet the performance standards, and is willing to comply with the requirements. If the appraisal assignment is in a remote area with no designated appraisers, a call to local lending institutions usually yields names of qualified appraisers who have done work for mortgage purposes.

When these names are obtained, the review appraiser places a call and interviews the appraiser, asking them the following :

1. Are you a member of an Appraisal Association?
2. Have you done any work for a third party company in the past?
3. Is appraising your full time occupation?
4. What percentage of appraisal business that you do is residential?
5. Are you willing to call the transferee within 24 hours of placement of the appraisal assignment and call the Review Appraiser with a verbal value figure within 48 hours of property visitation?
6. Can you have your written report in our hands within five working days?

In addition, the review appraiser keeps detailed performance statistics on each appraiser and if said appraiser does not consistently meet accuracy and time requirements, they will not be used. All data on appraisers is stored in a company computer. Performance statistics are tracked by the computer, and before using an appraiser, a check is made on their past performance. Accuracy is considered acceptable if the final sale price varies less than five percent (5%) plus or minus the particular appraiser's fair market value.

Time requirements include phoning the transferee to set up an appointment within 24 hours of notification, calling in a verbal figure within 48 hours of visitation of property and sending a written appraisal within 5 days of the verbal report. Appraisals are to be sent via an overnight mail service if necessary. The appraisers are not to accept an assignment if they will not be available to comply with the time constraints. They must also be available to answer questions from the review appraiser. They are requested by the review appraiser to use the official form devised by the Employee Relocation Council in order to facilitate easier review and continuity throughout the appraisal process. These forms are being used by most major third party relocation companies and appraisers who do business for them. After placing the appraisal assignment, the review appraiser instructs the administrative assistant to send a letter confirming the assignment and an appraisal form. The review appraiser then orders a Broker Price Opinion from a local broker who has met their standards of performance. The review appraiser meets with appraisers on a regular basis dependent on volume of business done with your company. High volume appraisers are reviewed in person twice yearly. Low volume appraisers will be evaluated and notified in writing, and periodic group appraisal seminars will be held. Your Senior review appraiser will have had experience in doing appraisals, in working for a third party company, completed college level appraisal courses, given appraisal seminars to appraisers throughout the country and is a Certified review appraiser. The Senior review appraiser is responsible for all Team review appraisers and all appraiser training.

It is important to stress the appraisal process and to have qualified people on staff to handle this aspect. The Fair Market Value is of highest importance to the transferee, since his home is usually the largest investment he will ever make. The employer must also be concerned about having the property acquired at a price that will permit resale in a cost effective manner. The ultimate goal is to have a Fair Market Value that is indeed fair both to the transferee and the transferee's employer. This goal can be met effectively by monitoring appraiser performance, using only persons who exhibit continued accuracy and professionalism, and by staffing the Review Appraiser position with highly qualified personnel.

Reviewing the Appraisal

The review appraiser, after receiving written copies of required number of appraisals and a Broker Price Opinion, compares figures to see if they fall within allowable guidelines. Each client company has different methods and requirements, however; the most typical system is to average the appraisals if they are within 5% of the highest.

The Broker Price Opinion is not used in the averaging of figures (in most cases). It is merely a guideline which we address in conjunction with the appraisals, and is used later by our Marketing Specialist in determining a list price and establishing marketing strategy. Naturally, if the Broker Price Opinion is remarkably higher or lower than the appraisals, we will question the appraisers and the broker very closely regarding the . Providing everything seems in order as far as the previous stipulations are concerned the review appraiser looks over the appraisals, comparing them for accuracy and consistency. Some areas addressed are:

1. Date of comparable sales. Are they no older than 6 months and if not, why were they used.
2. Proximity of comparables to subject property. Questions are asked if any discrepancies are noted.
3. Style of comparables used versus the subject. If subject property is a split level, why aren't split levels being used as comparables?
4. Size - Are comparables similar in size and if not have plus or minus adjustments been made to compensate?
5. Age - Are comparables similar in age to subject, and if not have adjustments been made?
6. Condition - Are all comparables similar in condition and if not, have adjustments been made for inferior or superior condition?
7. Financing - Were there any special financing concessions on the comparables such as points [paid by seller], or allowances,

and if so was an adjustment made?

8. Market conditions - Are there any influences that should be addressed, such as previous market better than today's, future market trends, such as devaluation due to plant closings and if so, have adjustments been made?

9. Design and appeal - Do the comparables have a greater or lesser appeal than subject and have adjustments been made accordingly?

10. Are there any unusual features or conditions that exist?

11. Are there any inspections necessary such as well and septic, structural, certificate of occupancy?

12. Has the appraiser discussed market conditions and probable that will be used when subject property sells?

When the preceding areas have been addressed, the review appraiser makes a list of questions and calls the appraisers with questions. After questions have been answered satisfactorily the review appraiser averages the figures.

Broker Price Opinion

In conjunction with every appraisal assignment, a Broker Price Opinion is ordered at the same time the appraisals are ordered. The broker is asked to phone the transferee within 24 hours. They are expected to phone with a verbal figure within 48 hours of visiting the property. The verbal report should include the following information:

1. The value they feel the home will actually sell for as well as a recommended list price.

2. Length of time it will take to sell the property.

3. Recommendations for any repairs or redecoration they feel will be necessary to put the home in top marketing condition.

4. Recommendations for any additional inspections.

5. The marketing strategy they would use to sell the property as

quickly as possible at their price should they receive the listing.

Their Opinion of Value should be made on the basis of the property's value in its "as is" condition, based on a sale in today's market conditions in the subject area within the average marketing time. If they feel the home needs any repairs or redecoration, they should give us an estimate of the cost to do the work and an estimate of the effect this work will have on the value of the home or its marketing time.

We may have asked them to order inspections of the property, such as termite, well, septic etc..., which we will need to have prior to acquiring the property. These inspections should be done immediately and invoices forwarded directly to us for payment. Require a verbal report on the results of any inspections requested, and if any repairs are required by those inspections we will also need firm bids on the cost of the repairs.

When completing their written report the following should be included:

a. Photos of front and rear of property.
b. Market Analysis
c. Property Inspection Report
d. Buyer Profile
e. Status Report
f. Market Action Plan

The Broker Price Opinion aids in reviewing the appraisals. If there are major discrepancies between the appraisers and broker, it is easily addressed up front before fair market value is extended to the transferee. The market analysis is carefully compared with the appraisals and is ultimately used as a guideline in setting the list price after it is acquired from the employee. We also will address any necessary inspections and alert the appraisers, who may adjust their value accordingly. In some cases, a BPO will address a deficiency that may have been overlooked by the appraisers. The buyer profile tells us who will most likely buy the property, what they can afford to pay. We then target that particular buyer in our marketing campaign after the property has been acquired. This information is also shared with the employee so he may adapt his efforts to the potential buyer, therefore possibly obtaining an assigned sale buyer. The status report that the broker fills out addresses recent sales activity, market strength, and availability of financing.

CHAPTER THIRTY-THREE

PROCEDURES IN REVIEWING EASEMENT APPRAISALS

There is no more difficult assignment in the appraisal field than to review an appraisal of an easement across a complex property consisting of a variety of land use categories involving numerous uses, land use capability classes and subclasses, an array of vegetation, all of which must be inventoried, classified, evaluated, then valued, with all of the land in transition from the present use (which may or may not be the highest and best use) to other higher and better uses. Before further uses can even be considered, the needs of the land must be fully considered for site protection, also all vegetation must be analyzed to determine what use(s) can be made for economical returns to the land and/or improvements thereon.

An easement across a property such as described will require the valuation of the different land use categories (forest land, range land, cultivated land, nonproductive lands, or urban-industrial lands)? And uses (grazing, crop land, etc.), and land classes (I, II, III, IV, V, VI, etc.) which will be called *horizontal* valuation. And in addition if the land is in transition (it is estimated that 50 percent of all land in the United States is in transition) the property must be valued for future uses *(second* valuation). This is called vertical valuation. Where both "horizontal valuation" and "vertical valuation" is accomplished, this is called *"cubic valuation"*.

Then the property must be valued (the third valuation) for the interests taken and left by the easement being appraised.

If the property is under lease, the review appraiser is faced with *the fourth* valuation, that of valuing the leased fee estate and the leasehold.

And in addition, crop damages will probably need to be reviewed (this will make *the fifth* valuation).

Along with crop damages will be *other damages,* such as damages to property, roads, non-usable areas resulting from sharp angles, surplus soil (and rocks uncovered) that must be hauled away, dust from the traffic during construction, etc. *(sixth* valuation).

Non-agricultural damages must be valued. The easement estate will usually take all future permanent construction rights on the easement area, therefore the review appraiser must check on the appraiser's handling of non-agricultural damages (or rights taken). This will be the seventh *valuation.*

One of the most accurate ways to determine the impact of an easement on land value is through "Land Economic Studies". This requires great skill on the part of the appraiser to eliminate all factors of value except for the existing easement. Some seven types of studies or analysis can be made to determine the economic impact. At least one of the seven types must be done, (previously and referred to, or at the current time when the appraisal is being done). The review appraiser must be certain that the appraiser is familiar with the mechanics of the study used and that all factors of value, except the easement area, have been eliminated. This is a form of valuation and must be done to provide a basis for easement valuation, and damages off the right of way. This will be the eighth valuation.

The proposed easement may be only one of many crossing the property. The existing easements must be evaluated to determine if subsurface, surface, or above surface rights have been taken. The proposed easement may enhance the property, have no apparent effect, or greatly reduce property uses and values.

Easements are of many types, but can generally be classified as: (a) subsurface (for pipeline, tunnels, etc.), (b) surface (highways, canals, railroads, etc., and (c) above surface or overhead (pole lines, electric transmissions lines, navigational, etc.). Many easements may be a combination of these, such as a pipeline and an access road over the pipeline, or an electric transmission line and a surface access road.

Easements create two distinct estates: The fee owner's remaining property rights, known as the underlying fee, which are permissive in nature. The second estate is the acquiring agency's property rights, or easement holder's property rights, known as the overlying fee. As to which has the dominant rights depends upon the wording of the easement.

A review of literature on easements reveal that, although there have been numerous articles written on various types of easements, there have been only a few articles on the specifics of writing the appraisal report. Consequently, this writer has cited the specific author that discusses a pertinent topic that must be considered by an appraiser and a review appraiser.

A total of ten authors have been cited as providing some guidance on pertinent topics. The author's full name, article published, publication date, and pages involved is shown in the bibliography.

A. Introduction and Definitions:

1. Classification of easements
2. Distinct estates
3. Interests and rights conveyed or retained
4. Attitudes of appraisers, right-of-way personnel, attorneys, and the courts concerning the current method of computation of the value of easement rights.
   Carll covers topics 1 through 4 on pages *333-4, 338-9,* and *348.*

B. Inventory and Classify Data

1. Inventory and classify agriculture land and value each use or class.

Carll—page *343*, Pilmer—page *43*, Dunlap—page .
2. Classify land for non-agricultural uses
    Carll—page *343*, Everhart—pages *32-36*
3. Land in Transition
    Carll—page *343*
4. Agricultural value compared using rural sales
    Carll—page 338
5. Agricultural value computed based on growth rings and re-
    maining agricultural life.
    Carll—page 342, Campbell—page 436
6. Speculative value (non agricultural value)
    Carll—page 333, Campbell—page 45

C. Valuation and Damages

1. Land Economic Studies
    Carll—pages 345-6, Campbell—pages 45-47, Derbes—
    page 375, Pilmer—page 33, Young—page 41, Patt—page
    334
2. Paired sales (controls and encumbered)
    Carll—page 346, Campbell—pages 47-8, Derbes—page
    377
3. Damages are outside of right-of-way. How to compute.
    Carll—page 348, Campbell—page 48, Derbes—page 376
4. Builders—Developers recognize full fee value as actual dam-
    ages to right-of-way.
    Kinnard—page 277
5. Studies divides sales into 4 categories
    Kinnard—page 272
6. Yields are reduced on agricultural lands. Examples cited.
    Carll—pages 342-4, Campbell—page 46, Pilmer—page
    300
7. Uses that can be made of the right-of-way
    Carll—page 343, Young—pages 41-2, Crawford—page
    372

8. Agricultural value or right-of-way after the taking, how to compare using present worth factors, capitalization rates and reduced income.

    Carll—page 344, Campbell—page 46
9. Using percent of fee for value of easement not proper method.

    Carll—page 348, Clark—page 16
10. Salvage value sales used to determine non-agricultural value remaining in the right-of-way.

    Carll—page 344, Campbell—page 46

Appraisers and review appraisers should be familiar with the latest accepted procedures in appraisal literature and include a bibliography of such literature in each report as proof of the type of research. Easements have been a field of controversy for the past 30 years. It is hoped that the consensus of the cited authorities will provide the needed guidance.

The following is a step by step procedure in reviewing easement appraisals. This is needed by all review appraisers and by all appraisers to guide them because a systematic approach must be followed to avoid omissions. Just like the appraisal process, review appraisers must follow a format or guide to insure that everything is presented that is needed and in the proper order. Since most easements involve lands that are not subdivided, the definition of the appraisal of rural lands is applicable. As stated on page 7 of "Everhart On Easements," the appraisal of rural lands is the systematic process of compilation (inventorying), classification, and evaluation of the natural resources involved in order to make a well-reasoned judgment of its value. The key words are "systematic *process,*" for without this, many items will be overlooked. The following is a suggested format for all land categories and uses where lands are in transition.

1. Inventory: This inventory includes a description of the natural resources such as soils, plants, animals, topography, climate, water supply and crops grown. Inventory those resources that should be considered for present uses and future higher and better uses. Give consideration to the multiple use concept wherein secondary (ancillary) economic returns play a part, as well as primary economic returns. (For example grazing use and wildlife use on range land). This inventory starts out with Land use categories (forest land, range land, cultivated land, nonproductive lands, and urban - industrial lands. If range land, Range sites and condition classes are used. If forest land, Timber Suitability Groups are used. If cultivated land, Land use capability classes and subclasses are used, if Nonproductive lands Urban Development Suitability classes are used, and if Urban-Industrial lands, also use Urban Development suitability classes.

2. *Classification:* Classify appropriate resources into categories, productivity groupings involving natural ecosystems, plant types, Range sites and condition classes, Timber suitability groups, (wildlife groups and recreation groups if applicable) soil capability classes, subclasses, and units, and others as needed. (See figure 1) Productivity represents the main purpose behind the inventory and classification because it brings together the various contributions of different resources to land value. Classify future anticipated uses, using Urban Development Suitability Classification (see page 21, "Land Classification For Land Uses, Management, and Valuation" by Everhart).

3. *Evaluation:* Evaluate all resources under the highest and best use concept, also consider all land needs such as erosion control, brush control, etc. Determine economic feasibility of all needs and maintenance. This will require a careful analysis of each resource and will require a knowledge of land and plants, therefore a consultant should be used where applicable, for instance in forest land a professional member of the Society of American Foresters should assist the review appraiser. On range land a certified Range Management Consultant should be used. On cultivated land, a Certified Professional

Agronomist should be considered. If the cultivated land is irrigated crop land, orchard, or vineyards are involved, specialists in those fields should be utilized by the Review Appraiser.

4. *Life in present use(s):* Determine the length of the interim use thereby establishing life in the present use(s). This can be done by studying trends toward subdivision or appropriate higher and better uses. Determine the appropriateness of extensive repairs or renovation of present use facilities. The determination of lives of various uses is known as "vertical" valuation. (See figure 2) If the present use is agricultural, the present life is known as "agricultural life."

5. *Ultimate Use(s):* Determine likely use based on comprehensive municipal projections, needs of the land, economic , water availability, erosion hazards, high water table, flooding, etc.

6. *Value All Lands:* Determine the value of all lands using appropriate valuation procedures and approaches. Value all uses, present, and future.

7. *Value Present Use:* Value present use by means of using the life in the present use determined under number 4 above.

8. *Value Ultimate Use:* Value ultimate use by subtracting the value of present use from the value of all uses as determined under number 6 above.

9. *Contributory Values:* Easements across property require the determination of contributory values of all portions of the property. Easements may involve only frontage or only backland, therefore contributory values are necessary for proper determination of easement value. Contributory values are referred to as *"horizontal"* valuation (see figure 23).

10. *Evaluate Easement:* The easement contract should be studied and all rights should be separated and rewritten for your report. All rights taken should be shown together under "Rights Taken," while rights remaining should be shown together under "Rights Remaining." Determine the highest and best use of the "Remainder Property," which includes all ease-

ment areas as well as other lands in the property. Determine the "before value" of the easement areas using contributory values determined in number 9 shown above.

11. *Non-subordinate Rights:* Non-subordinate rights also known as the "overlying fee" interest (rights taken) should be thoroughly understood and discussed in the report. How do these rights affect present and future uses?

12. *Subordinate Rights:* Subordinate rights (rights left to the land owner) also known as the "underlying fee" interest (rights remaining) are *servient rights* and should be thoroughly understood and discussed in the report. Can the land owner continue in the present use and if so what are the restrictions?

13. *Land Economic Studies:* Land economic studies of similar categories, types, and uses of land wherein studies have been made of similar kinds of easements (transmission, pipeline, , etc.) should be presented and show the conclusions of those studies. Studies of both (a) rural, and (b) urban areas should be discussed and analyzed. Discuss types of study analyses (encumbered and unencumbered, percent encumbered, proximity, etc.) (see Figure 3).

14. *Development Concepts:* Development concepts (corridor, back yard, side yard, etc.) should be discussed with respect to potential damages to the subject property. (See figure 4) If an navigational easement discuss noise pollution on various types of developments. If a transmission line easement discuss various types of damages (proximity, severance, biological, etc.).

15. *Value Easement:* After full consideration and analysis of "rights taken," land economic studies, and development concepts, the easement area is valued using the Sales Comparison Approach, the Income Approach, and the Anticipated Use of Developmental Approach. In most situations the Anticipated Use Approach will provide the best indication of value of the ultimate use of the easement area in the after condition.

16. *Present Use Damages:* Present use damages, usually called "agricultural damages" should be clearly understood and dis-

cussed in the report. Consideration should be given to noise, electric shock, weed problems, restrictions to airplanes, changes of soil texture, fertility, water absorption, etc. Value of all damages should be computed and shown on maps in the report.

17. *Future Use Damages:* Future use damages, usually through rights taken should be understood and discussed in the report. Sharp angles and narrow strips should be considered and all damages should be computed and shown on maps in the report. These may be referred to as "non-agricultural damages."

Appraisers should ask themselves if they have presented the entire problem that has been encountered in the valuation of restrictive easements. The only way this can be done is by following a systematic process.

INVENTORY AND CLASSIFICATION OF RESOURCES A BASIS FOR LAND VALUATION

SOILS
TOPOGRAPHY
LAND USE CAPABILITY CLASSES AND
SUBCLASSES
URBAN DEVELOPMENT SUITABILITY CLASSES
RANGE SITES AND CONDITION CLASSES
TIMBER SUITABILITY GROUPS
WOODLAND SITE INDEX
ORCHARD SUITABILITY GROUPS
PASTURE SUITABILITY GROUPS
HAYLAND SUITABILITY GROUPS
WILDLIFE HABITAT GROUPS
RECREATION GROUPS
WATER AVAILABILITY AREAS
MINERALS

FIGURE 1

HORIZONTAL AND VERTICAL VALUATION SCHEMATIC
(cubic valuation)
Shown before and after imposition of overhead transmission line easement

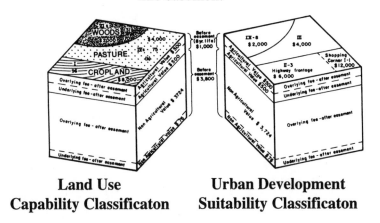

| Land Use | Urban Development |
| Capability Classificaton | Suitability Classificaton |

Suitability groups and productivity rating indexes shown for comparison purposes.

Horizontal Valuation is the use of contributory land values in the Cost Approach. Vertical Valuation is the use of economic lives of land uses in the Income Approach. Only the surface estate is shown. All dollar amounts are per acre values.

FIGURE 2

TYPES OF STUDIES APPLICABLE TO THE EVALUATION OF THE ECONOMIC IMPACT OF ELECTRIC TRANSMISSION LINES ON LAND VALUES
(a schematic representation)

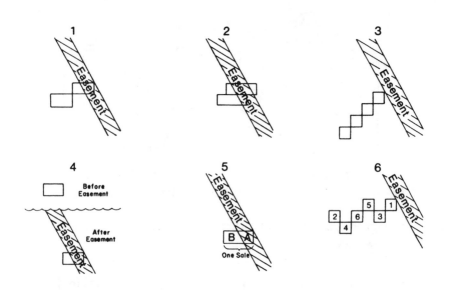

1. **Encumbered and Unencumbered**
2. **Percent Encumbered**
3. **Proximity**
4. **Before and After**
5. **Right of Way and Remainder Selling Separate**
6. **Marketablility**

LEGEND   □ = Real Estate Sale
                1,2,3,4,5,6 Under No. 6 = Order of Sale

CHAPTER THIRTY-FOUR

REVIEWING APPRAISALS FOR LEGAL PURPOSES A PRETRIAL CHECKLIST

This checklist was developed as an outline to assist the trial attorney in testing the adequacy of an appraisal presented by a real estate appraiser testifying as an expert witness. The issue of market value of real estate is presented in many legal proceedings. The trial attorney is often confronted with the issue of market value of real estate in probate, federal and state tax matters, estate planning, financial transactions, insurance losses, and other matters. The ultimate issues in a condemnation proceeding are dependent upon a proper determination and analysis of factors affecting market value of real estate.

A. *Subject Property:*

1. Survey plat of subject property showing:
   a. Location of improvements;
   b. Easements;
   c. Access roads or streets;
   d. Any restricted areas;
   e. Elevations, contours, and flood plains, etc.;
   f. Any other environs.
2. Ownership (Title Search or Abstract); List all owners and known addresses of:
   a. Fee owners and percent of ownership; parties in possession;
   b. Leasehold estates;
   c. Minerals;

     d. Reversions;

     e. Life estates;

     f. Easements and any apparent encroachments;

     g. Any restrictive covenants;

     h.   Statutory or agency restrictions or permits;

     i. Zoning or regulatory controls;

     j. Liens of any nature.

3. Legal Description:

     a. By metes and bounds;

     b. Area location if farm or rural;

     c. Street location if urban or city;

     d. Identify property right to be appraised.

4. Aerial Photos of subject property and surrounding area:

     a. These should be obtained as close as possible to date of valuation;

     b. Subject property and comparable sales should be identified and marked on aerial.

5. County or City Maps showing location of:

     a. Subject and comparable sales in relation to each other;

     b. Business districts;

     c. Schools;

     d. Major road and access;

     e. Economic impact areas, etc.

6. Comprehensive Narrative Description of Area:

     a. Area growth factors (population trends, social trends, etc.);

     b. Economic influences (employment opportunities, average purchasing power);

     c. Type of business community (farming, manufacturing, retail, etc.);

     d. Schools, recreational facilities and other civic factors;

     e. Narrative account of study of the flavor and the characteristics of area (changing land uses, utility patterns, population shifts, etc.).

7. Ground Photos of subject property (should be a comprehensive photographic description of property):

    a. Emphasis on utility of land use;

    b. Improvements;

    c. Any unique features.

8. Improvement Analysis (elements effecting admissibility of valuation to testimony):

    a. Locate all improvements and draw to scale on survey plat;

    b. Accurate floor plan of improvements;

    c. Narrative description of architectural design, general condition and age of improvements;

    d. Description of quality of construction (materials, equipment, workmanship, aesthetic features, functionality or balance of utility in use of improvements);

    e. Special purpose features and equipment;

    f. Where possible, attach architectural drawings and specifications; otherwise, list visible component specifications;

    g. Consideration of utility of land to improvements (landscaping, view, drainage, access, balance between land use and improvements of subject compared to that of the neighborhood and area);

    h. Depreciation factors (physical, economic and functional obsolescence).

9. Land Analysis (elements affecting admissibility of valuation testimony):

    a. Size of tract;

    b. Detailed narrative description of physical characteristics (soil, topography, water, vegetation, etc.);

    c. Location of tract in its economic environment (type of neighborhood, area uses, etc.);

    d. External access to tract and internal accessibilities;

    e. Relationship of subject tract to neighborhood and area land patterns;

    f. Type of ownerships, parties in possession and known claims;

    g. Encumbrances (liens, easements, restrictions by deed, re versions, and observed encroachments, etc.);

    h. Governmental regulation (zoning, building restrictions or requirements, etc.);

    i. Utilities.

10. Establishment of Highest and Best Use of subject tract:
    a. Present use;
    b. Transitional uses;
    c. Establishment of the highest and best use to which the property can be put in the reasonably foreseeable future by taking into consideration:
       (1) Neighborhood and area analysis;
       (2) Impact of the present social and economic atmosphere;
       (3) Anticipation of future markets, availability of capital, projected earnings, stability of national and local economy;
       (4) Property rights involved;
       (5) Trends in governmental controls and regulations;
       (6) Adaptability of land to uses and demand for the use;
       (7) Adaptability of improvements to land uses.

B. Definition of Market Value:

"Market value" the most probable price which a property should bring in a competitive and open market under all conditions requisite to a fair sale, the buyer and seller, each acting prudently, knowledgeably and assuming the price is not affected by undue stimulus.

C. Depreciation Factors and Terms:

1. Economic obsolescence: external causes (change in social patterns, economic trends, change in land patterns, changes in governmental controls, etc.).

2. Functional obsolescence: internal causes (inadequacy because of style, poor plan, size, age, etc.).

3. Physical deterioration (wear and tear, structural defects, rot, decay, etc.).

Note: "Accrued Depreciation" equals all past depreciation. "Accruals for Depreciation" is percentage of income set aside for "Future Depreciation;" return for invested capital over useful life.)

4. Depreciation rate includes:
   a. Recapture of invested capital;
   b. Percent of return (earned interest) on invested capital;
   c. Methods to establish depreciation rate;

   (1) Straight-line;
   (2) Sinking fund;
   (3) Annuity method;
   (4) Age-life tables;
   (5) Observed condition.

5. Important note: Depreciation factors must be considered in each approach to market value. Attention should be directed to curable and incurable items.

D. Market Data Approach to Valuation

(Use of prices paid for comparable or similar properties as the basis of a comparison to form an of the market value of the subject property); also referred to as substitution theory.

Factors pertaining to admissibility:

1. Similarity of type and uses of sales property (apartment site, single family dwelling, various kinds of commercial properties, various kinds of acreage, various kinds of farming units, leasehold estate, etc.) to the type or uses of the subject property.
2. Parties to transaction and type of conveyance (deed, contract, etc.).

3. Date of sale; proximity in time of sale date to valuation date.
4. Size of property.
5. Legal description and location of property.
6. Similarity of type and use of improvements.
7. Similarity of types and condition of land including access, topography, utility of uses, public utilities, etc.
8. Supply and demand of particular type of property (the number available in the market of the area or neighborhood, rates of turnover, vacancies, amount of similar construction, etc.).
9. Financial conditions of buyer or seller (hardship sale, purchase of necessity, etc.).
10. Length of time sale property on market.
11. Encumbrances on sale property.
12. Terms and financial conditions of sale.
13. Factors determining the degree of comparability of improvements:
    a. Square feet in improvements;
    b. Design;
    c. Physical condition;
    d. Age;
    e. Type of construction, materials, and equipment;
    f. Ratio of usable space to total space;
    g. Income produced;
    h. Tax structures;
    i. Number of rooms or office suites and relationships to each other;
    j. Relationship of improvements to neighborhood;
    k. Location of improvement on site;
    l. Utility of use of improvements to the highest and best use of the site, etc.;
    m. Depreciation factors (physical deterioration, functional obsolescence, and economic obsolescence);
    n. Kind or type of ownership.

14. Factors determining the degree of comparability of land:

    a. Kind or type of ownership;
    b. Shape, size, footage or acreage;
    c. Physical condition of tract, including topography, elevation, type of soil, etc.;
    d. External access and internal accessibilities;
    e. Encumbrances;
    f. Relationship to land patterns in the neighborhood and area;
    g. Availability of utilities;
    h. Governmental regulation;
    i. Growth trends in neighborhood or area;
    j. Economic and social stability of comparative areas or neighborhoods;
    k. Income data;
    l. Comparative highest and best uses.

15. Confirmation by buyer, seller or agent that the sale was an "arm's length transaction."
16. Tax renditions, contracts of sale, written options, leases, written offers and closing statements, when confirmed, are indications of market value in limited circumstances.

E. Gross Rent Multiple is a "rule of thumb" in the market data analysis process. Caution in its use is demanded and verification of the following is a must:

1. The similarities of the properties.
2. The comparative economic life of improvements.
3. The comparative highest and best uses of the properties.
4. Double check operating costs to gross incomes of comparables.
5. Verify comparative terms of lease or other income stream.

F. Definition of Reproduction Costs and Replacement Cost; Relation to Site Analysis:

1. Reproduction costs are the costs incurred in an exact reproduction; becomes particularly important in valuations of historical structures, special purpose improvements or unique properties.

2. Replacement costs are the costs incurred in replacing the structure or improvement with one having same utility of use. In most circumstances, the valuation will be reached by replacement costs less depreciation.

3. Changing uses brought about by population shifts, access changes, governmental regulation, deed restriction, etc., can cause a radical change in land (site) valuation. Thus, in many "valuation" court proceedings, the courts look with disfavor on replacement or reproduction cost methods as becoming the basis of opinions of market value.

G. Costs Analysis and Estimate Basis:

1. Character of construction determined by design, materials, equipment, workmanship, etc.

2. Availability of materials and their adaptability to local conditions (source, demand or desirability, soil conditions, climatic conditions, etc.).

3. Equipment necessary to provide the services and comfort required for the highest and best use; remaining useful life.

4. Quality and type of building materials.

5. Functionality and utility of design (size, shape and location of rooms, utility areas, garages, special purposes areas, etc.).

6. Any repairs and maintenance performed; any observed deferred repair or maintenance.

7. Indirect costs of improvements (financing costs, legal fees, design costs, supervision during construction, insurance, etc.).

8. Direct costs (labor, materials, etc.).
9. Depreciative factors and rates.
10. Market Value Conclusion based upon: land valuation plus direct costs of improvements plus indirect costs less accrued depreciation equals market value.

H. Income Approach; Appraisal Process:

There are several accepted "income approach" theories that are available to the expert appraisal witness on which the opinion of "market value" may be based. The opinion of market value based on one "income theory" may vary from the opinion of value based on another "income theory." The burden is on the trial attorney to assure the court and the client that the correct "income theory" and technique is used by the expert appraisal witness as the basis of an opinion of value.

The income approach to market value is admissible as the basis to support the appraiser's opinion of market value and not as direct evidence of market value. The income approach is the process of converting an income stream into an estimate of value. In applying income capitalization analysis to property value estimation, the appraiser must rely on and obtain market data at every step. This data must be verified and accurate. The nature of the problem and of the property, together with the availability of reliable and usable data, determine which processes, methods and techniques the appraiser must select and apply.

The judgment of the appraiser comes into play in analyzing the market, the property and the income stream to reach these conclusions. After the ownership or possessory rights to be appraised are identified, taking into consideration the highest and best use of the property, the next step is:

1. Identify Gross Annual Income to be Projected:
   a. Examine records of actual gross income from the property in past years and the current income schedule;

    b. Compare above factual data with known rentals for similar rental space in the same or comparable location. This comparison leads to an informed estimate of the probable prospective income from the property and the degree of risk involved in its realization;

    c. In the above analysis the appraiser is concerned with the quality, quantity and durability of the gross income estimates which can be summarized as follows:

        (1)   Quantity refers to the amount of gross income earned in a year. The projection of this quantity reflects the appraiser's consideration of:

    a. Past and present tenant occupancy and rental terms;

    b. Rentals being paid for comparable space;

    c. Analysis of the rental level that is economically warranted for the premises;

    d. Ability to pay;

    e. Analysis of lease agreements to determine abnormally high or low lease or rental agreements.

        (2)   Quality and durability of income refers to the probable period over which the property can be expected to produce the estimated income regarding the credit rating of the tenant.

2. Identify vacancy and rent loss allowance to deduct:

    a. The appraiser next determines an appropriate allowance for vacancy to deduct from the above determined estimate of gross annual income. This allowance, which is usually estimated as a percentage of gross annual income, varies with the type of property, the tenancy and general conditions. This vacancy allowance is determined by the market experience of competitive properties, general mar ket standards, and the actual experience of the subject property;

   b. This allowance for vacancy is then deducted from the gross annual income to determine effective gross income from rental sources.

3. Determine Any "Other Income:"

   a. Income from sources other than rental revenue are then determined and added to the effective gross income from rental sources to determine overall effective gross income. This "other" source of income can be from sources such as deposit forfeiture, laundry facility income, as well as other various miscellaneous sources.

4. Identify and stabilize amount and type of annual operating expenses to be projected:

   a. These expenses may fall into the separate category of fixed expenses, variable expenses and reverses for replacement;

   (1) Fixed expenses include primarily real estate taxes and building insurance. Although these expenses do not re main constant from year to year, they are not subject to the wide fluctuation of many other expenses. They do not vary in response to changing levels of occupancy, and they are expenses over which management has little control. This expense estimate is based on actual operating state ments with an allowance made for projected increases or decreases in the tax and insurance expense:

   (2) Variable expenses include all out-of-pocket costs involved in providing services for tenants and maintaining the in come stream. Variable expenses generally include:

   (a) Management;

   (b) Utilities;

   (c) Payroll;

   (d) Maintenance and repair of land and building;

   (e) Miscellaneous:

      1. Security;

      2. Supplies;

3. Janitorial.

(3) Reserves for replacements provide adequate allow
ances for the replacement of short lived equipment items
that wear out more rapidly than the structure itself and are
not covered by any other repair and maintenance charges
in the expense statement. The fixed and variable expense
totals and the allowance for reserves for replacement are
then deducted from the effective gross income estimate
in order to arrive at the net operating income estimate.

Capitalization Rates:

a. The net operating income estimate is then "capitalized" or
divided by a rate in order to produce an estimate of value for
the subject: Net Operating Income Divided by the Rate equals
Value estimate;

b. The capitalization rate is in turn determined and influenced
by the following:

    (1)   Risk inherent in the project;

    (2)   Type of investor;

    (3)   Financing patterns and terms;

    (4)   Equity—yield requirements;

Appreciation or depreciation anticipated over the holding period. The capitalization rate is simply the ratio between income
produced and the value. Again, proper selection of the rate is
based on the nature of the problem and judgment of the appraiser;

c. The resulting value estimate is then correlated with the value
estimate produced by the market data and cost approaches in
order to estimate an accurate market value for the subject property.

I. Income Approach; Analysis and Basis:

1. Definitions:

a. Gross Income equals total possible at 100 percent occupancy;

b. Effective gross equals gross total less any losses of income;

c. Net income equals gross less loss of income equals effective gross less general operating expenses less miscellaneous expense less repairs and maintenance less fixed changes less replacement reserve equals net income before depreciation.

2. Ownership and possessory rights of properties.

3. Gross income stream basis:

a. Highest and best use of property (strip commercial, commercial center, dwelling, agricultural, recreational, etc.);

b. Sources of income; quantity:

(1) Leases: actual and comparative rentals of similar type properties including primary term and renewal options, restrictive condition, legal obligations incurred, etc.;

(2) Concessions (snack bars, newsstands, etc.);

Miscellaneous sources (Beverage, studios, etc.);

c. Quality of income:

(1) Financial responsibility of occupants; add or detract based on stability;

(2) Payment terms (fixed, cost of living increase, percentage, etc.);

d. Durability (governed by economic analysis):

(1) Area and neighborhood trends;

(2) Location of property in relation to growth or decline areas;

(3) Economy (trend of income and job opportunities, purchasing power of dollar, etc.);

(4) Social trends;

(5) Age of properties, demand for particular uses, size, accessibility, etc.;

(6) External forces (governmental action such as rent control, farm land use on crop allocation, soil conservation, environmental controls, etc.);

e. Collection of vacancy problems:

(1) Economy generally;

(2) Competition, demand and supply of like property;

(3) Type of tenant;

(4) Managerial abilities;

(5) Correlation of present vacancy and probable future vacancies equals rate of vacancy.
4. Operating expenses; basis and analysis:
   a. Expense of land maintenance (flood and water controls, environmental controls, landscaping, soil treatment, recurring and/or nonrecurring problems and expenses);
   b. Building maintenance and replacement expenses (upkeep, rehabilitation or modernization);
   c. Equipment up-keeps; replacement and life expectancy (replacement reserve);
   d. Labor (employees, etc.);
   e. Managerial expenses;
   f. Utilities (electrical, water, gas, etc.);
   g. Supplies and miscellaneous expenses;
   h. Fixed charges (insurance, taxes, special fees or licenses, permits, etc.).
5. Capitalization Rates (determination of proper rates to represent the relationship between capital and net income):
   a. Factors: income, rate, value;
      (1) Known net income less value equals capitalization rate;
      (2) Known net income less rate equals value;
      (3) Rate times value equals income;
   b. Investment behavior or risk factor;
      (1) Assurance of yield and amount;
      (2) Demand or marketability (collateral);
      (3) Freedom from attention;
      (4) Duration of production;
      (5) Safety and stability;
      (6) Potential appreciation (hedge value);
   c. Selection method of capitalization rate;
      (1) Going rate (rate that investors require as a condition to purchase);
      (2) Summation method: Safe rate or interest rate plus:
         (a) Risk rate (compensation for hazard to the principal capital) plus:

(b) Rate for management (the portion of capitalization rate assignable to compensate for managing the capital investment) plus:

(c) Adjustment rate (depends on freedom from obsolescence, continuity of operation and management ability) can be a plus or a minus; Total of these equals capitalization rate.

(3) Comparison of other sales (net income less selling price equals capitalization rate (note: comparison depends on following factors):

(a) Quantity of income;

(b) Quality of income; factors to consider:

    1.   Certainty of income;

    2.   Reliability of expense projection;

    3.   Ratio of expense to income;

    4.   Marketability of property and stability of value;

    5.   Competitive future construction;

    6.   Location. The above factors regarding the sales properties are compared to the subject property to determine comparative ratio regarding quality of income.

(4) Band of investment; the weighted average between mortgage (or mortgages) and equity;

(a) Determine percent of interest on mortgage;

(b) Determine percent of interest on equity the buyer requires.

Example:

80% loan at 9% equals product of 7.2; equity at 9.5% equals product of 1.9; 100% value equals product of 9.1; Indicated capitalization rate of 9.1%.

6. Capitalization Procedure and Methods (income approach is admissible as the basis to support the appraiser's opinion and

not as direct evidence of market value).

a. Capitalization is defined as the procedure in the valuation process in which the capital value of the property or property interest is determined from the expected net income taking into consideration the quality, quantity and duration of that income.

b. Straight-line depreciation plus capitalization rate:

(1) Number of years of economic life of property converted to annual percentage necessary to recover capital investment;

(2) Add capitalization rate for interest on investment;

(3) Net income less amortization rate plus interest on invested capital equals capitalized value of net income before depreciation;

(4) When straight capitalization plus straight-line depreciation is used, make sure the rate of decline in net income is determined;

Formula:

R equals Capitalization rate;

D equals Straight-line depreciation rate;

R times D divided by R plus D equals Rate of annual decline of the net income imputable to the improvements.

NOTES

NOTES

NOTES

NOTES